American
Politics and Society

American Politics and Society

DAVID McKAY

Martin Robertson · Oxford

First published in 1983 by Martin Robertson & Company Ltd.,
108 Cowley Road, Oxford OX4 1JF

British Library Cataloguing in Publication Data

McKay, David
    American politics and society.
    1. United States—Politics and government—1981
    I. Title
    320.973   JK261

    ISBN 0—85520—636—5
    ISBN 0—85520—660—8 pbk

Typeset by System 4 Associates Limited, Gerrards Cross
Printed and bound in Great Britain by
The Pitman Press Ltd., Bath

Contents

Preface

No one disputes that American politics is an important and fascinating subject. Unfortunately, it is also a highly complex and sometimes confusing one — a fact which present and past generations of students would readily confirm. Outside of the United States, the task of learning about the system is made even more burdensome by the dearth of good up-to-date texts written specifically to appeal both to a non-American and an American audience. This book hopes to fill this gap by combining an outsider's perspective with sensitivity to what Americans themselves have written about their politics and government.

I must admit that although I have been teaching American politics for some years and am a regular visitor to the United States, at no time can I or any other student of the subject, afford to sit back and proclaim a true understanding of the system. American politics changes too rapidly to permit this luxury. Not only do events change quickly; so do the normative criteria by which governments and public policy are judged. Even since 1960, the dominating political theme (among many) has shifted from a concern with equality to public order to honesty in government to, most recently, questions of economic performance. When examining the main political institutions and processes, this book will show how and why the policy agenda apparently shifts so rapidly — although we will also be concerned to show why certain themes persist through time.

I could not possibly have written this book without the help and assistance of a number of institutions and individuals. Over the years I have been fortunate to receive grants for various projects from the British Social Science Research Council, the Nuffield Foundation and the American Council of Learned Societies which have enabled me to visit the United States for extended periods. As a 'foreigner' I never cease to be impressed by the hospitality and collegiality provided by American scholars. I owe a debt to the many individuals who have not only made me feel welcome, but also whose sheer professionalism has jolted me on more than one occasion. In the United Kingdom, the American Politics Group of the Political Studies Association of which I am a past chairman, is a constant source of stimulation. Even in the present hostile economic climate, British PhD students and lecturers continue to do good research and the American Politics Group has become a major forum for the exchange of research findings. With all its American contacts, my base at the Department of Government, University of Essex, has proved invaluable. Special thanks to Anthony King — possibly the ultimate US/UK link man.

Of those who have read parts or the whole of the draft manuscript, I am particularly indebted to the publisher's readers and to Larry Berman, Richard Hodder-Williams, Virginia Sapiro, Jonathon Tucker and Graham Wilson. As is customary, I must take full blame for the faults and errors that remain. Finally, thank you Lynne McKay, for putting up at close quarters with my sometimes neurotic desire to get this book finished.

David McKay
University of Essex, January 1983

CHAPTER 1

Introduction

'What do you think of our institutions?' is the question addressed to the European traveller in the United States by every chance acquaintance. The traveller finds the question natural, for if he be an observant man his own mind is full of these institutions. But he asks himself why it should be in America only that he is so interrogated. In England one does not inquire from foreigners, nor even from Americans, their views on the English laws and government; nor does the Englishman on the Continent find Frenchmen or Germans or Italians anxious to have his judgment on their politics.

James Bryce, The American Commonwealth, 1888

THE STUDY OF AMERICAN POLITICS

Although Bryce's observation on the relative interest shown by different nationalities in their political institutions is no longer entirely true — the British, for example, are now deeply immersed in self analysis and self criticism — it remains the case that Americans are truly obsessed with the functioning and even viability of their political system. To the student of American politics this is a problem, for literally thousands of books on American politics exist, many of which have something important or interesting to say about the United States. Even at the level of undergraduate textbooks the choice is formidable, and almost every teacher of American politics begins his or her course with an apology for having to recommend books which provide only a particular perspective or cover only some of the ground.

Non-Americans suffer from the additional problem that the vast majority of books have been written by Americans for Americans.

They therefore tend to assume a certain prior knowledge or they are tailored to the specific needs of the US educational system. The present volume was written for a non-American audience, although its particular perspective should also be of interest to Americans. Its approach is traditional in the sense that it covers all the main political institutions and processes of American national government. But no text on American politics can claim to be truly comprehensive, the subject is simply too vast to be covered by a single volume. This book narrows the area by concentrating on national as opposed to state and local politics (although intergovernmental relations are given special attention) and by providing extensive references to the major research findings in individual subject areas.

Perhaps the most difficult decisions facing authors of textbooks concern the relationship between factual presentation and more general comment and criticism. A book which confined itself simply to describing institutional and political processes would be dull in the extreme, while a book devoted to comment would more resemble a reflective essay than a text. The compromise reached in this volume will not please everyone, but it will, I hope, make each chapter more than mere descriptive account. Most chapters have, in fact, a central argument or arguments around which basic facts and figures are organized. Most of these arguments relate to current controversies in the literature or currently debated in the broader society and polity. Naturally these controversies change as both the political agenda and the central concerns of academics change. Moreover, no book could cover all of current debate; to be both coherent and effective it has to select a particular approach based on certain normative judgments. Whether wittingly or not, all texts on American government do just this — notwithstanding that most also aim to present the reader with factual information. A good way to justify the present book's stance is to review the main objectives and orientations which other texts have taken over the last 30 years.

Three main approaches can be identified: the self-congratulatory, critical and functional. Let us deal with each of these in turn. Perhaps predictably, self-congratulatory texts were most influential during the 1950s and early 1960s. At that time America's dominant position in world economic and military affairs, together with relative domestic tranquility encouraged optimistic interpretations of American politics. Some political scientists, worried about continuing inequality in American society and the apparent failure of the political parties to provide coherent platforms for social change were less sanguine,[1] but the general tone of the literature was optimistic. The system appeared to work, albeit imperfectly. Most Americans were prosperous as never before, recent Presidents were of an acceptably high quality and, the problem of Southern racial segregation apart, few issues divided the country.

By the late 1960s all had changed. Poverty was 're-discovered' and the often serious inequalities in wealth and income in American society became increasingly obvious. The 'revolution' in civil rights was followed by racial unrest in America's cities; crime and social pathology generally were rising rapidly, and between 1963 and 1968 three of the nation's most prominent public figures were assassinated (President John Kennedy, Presidential candidate Robert Kennedy and civil rights leader Martin Luther King). Above all, the war in Vietnam had inspired fierce domestic opposition and had helped to alienate large sections of American youth from political authority. The institutional response to these events was widely perceived as inadequate. · Presidents could apparently wield power in foreign affairs with relative impunity. Congressional control of the executive was hampered by fragmented decision making. The political parties, and particularly the Democrats, were internally divided, organizationally weak and often corrupt.

The subsequent events of Watergate and the Nixon Presidencies generally seemed to confirm the worst fears of many observers.[2] If Presidents could break the law so easily and only be discovered by the chance apprehension of paid criminals in the act of breaking in to the opposition party's headquarters, then how could citizens expect to hold political authority in high regard? In response to these events and to the traumas of the 1960s, American textbooks on politics began to take on a quite different look. During the 1950s titles referring to 'American democracy' or 'government by the people' were considered adequate. By the early 1970s the emphasis had shifted to 'democracy under pressure', or 'a critical introduction.' Even those books which had established themselves as standard texts felt obliged to add chapters on race, foreign policy, or political protest. This re-appraisal was not only motivated by the functional question of how the system could be improved and institutions reformed. Many of the new texts made fundamental criticisms of American government. Some employed perspectives informed by

---

1 The most eloquent of the dissenting voices in this period was that of E. E. Schattsneider in his book *The Semi Sovereign People*, New York, Holt, Rinehart and Winston, 1960.
2 The best history of the Nixon era is Jonathan Schell, *The Time of Illusion*, New York, Vintage, 1975.

radically different value positions. In particular, the late 1960s and early 1970s saw a new concern with the distribution of power in the United States and the consequences of this for patterns of wealth, income and racial equality. So, one of the most influential of these new books was entitled *American Politics: Policies, Power, and Change*,[3] and contained chapters on the 'power structure' and the role of ideology in moulding the political behaviour of elites and non-elites. Interest in power was not, of course, new. More than ten years earlier pluralist political scientists had joined battle with power elite sociologists in academic debate on 'who rules America?' or in many instances 'who rules particular cities or communities?'[4] The debate was never resolved because the two schools were asking similar questions inspired by quite different value perspectives on the very concept of power. What this and the later debates provoked by the troubled 1960s and '70s did produce, however, was a much greater sensitivity to questions of equality and the distribution of power. Scholars still disagreed, but they generally became more careful in their use of language when referring to the consequences for different social groups of America's particular political and institutional arrangements. And of course no-one now disputes the facts of unequal power resources, the existence of elites and masses, leaders and followers, the wealthy and the poor. Where controversy continues to rage is over the responsiveness of existing institutions to these inequalities, and over the *trade-offs* which exist between the pursuit of greater equality and other values, notably economic efficiency and individual freedom.

This brings us to the third and current emphasis of texts on American politics. During the 1970s and early 1980s the political agenda changed again, the new focus being on economic issues and the apparently intractable problem of how to achieve low rates of inflation and unemployment and high rates of growth all at the same time. Blame for poor economic performance was, at first, placed on OPEC and the fourfold increase in oil prices during 1973–4. Later, however, economists and politicians began to question whether the system of public benefits which the welfare state and Keynesian economics had brought was compatible with an efficient economy. Government had, so the argument ran, become too big; too many social groups depended on public largesse;

3 Kenneth M. Dolbeare and Murray J. Edelman, New York, D. C. Heath, 1st edn, 1971.
4 For an extensive summary and discussion of this debate, see Kenneth Prewitt and Alan Stone, *The Ruling Elites: Elite Theory Power, and American Democracy*, New York, Harper and Row, 1973.

inflation was encouraged by excessive government borrowing. At the same time, all those social problems which the programmes and policies of the 1960s and '70s had sought to solve, were still very much there. Small wonder then that public and politicians began to question a system which had encouraged high spending but had produced few results. Of course, antipathy to an intrusive state role is nothing new in American history, it has been a recurrent theme as later chapters will show. The difference in the 1980s is that government expenditure has reached a high level, and, although many observers are concerned at the economic consequences of this, few can provide realistic suggestions on how, exactly, the state *can* disengage from society. Through access to Congress and political institutions at all levels, industry receives aid, old people pensions, the poor welfare benefits, farmers subsidies, the military weapons systems, and so it goes on.

Texts on American politics now reflect these problems. They have, in other words, become more concerned with the *functioning* of government and the policy process and how institutions might be reformed to reconcile as well as possible the conflict between efficiency and equality or between effectiveness and accountability. As a result, they are both less optimistic and less passionate than earlier generations of texts. Neither the enthusiasm for democracy prevalent in the 1950s nor the moral fervour of the 1960s is appropriate today. Instead, students are advised to counsel caution when assessing plans for institutional reform or social change.[5]

The present volume is written in much the same spirit. It emphasizes the limitations of political institutions and of recent attempts to reform them. An essentially functionalist perspective is adopted, therefore — although other values are not ignored — and a particular effort is made to explain the persistence of political and social inequalities in a society so infused with an ideology of egalitarianism and opportunity. In one quite fundamental respect, however, this book does differ from its American counterparts: it puts the American experience in comparative perspective. In other words, the criteria by which US political institutions and processes are assessed are not derived exclusively from American history or peculiarly American values. How the United States looks in terms of British and European values and perspectives is also involved. Naturally, this entails making judgments and drawing conclusions

5   In spite of this new sober mood, almost all books on the current crisis end on a constructive if not optimistic note. This is, perhaps, related to the general tendency in American culture to stress the positive effects of social and political change.

which can differ from those which American scholars might make. Hopefully, the result will be an analysis which adds new insights into the workings of American politics to add to those already provided by the vast and often impressive output of American political science.

Finally, when discussing institutions and processes, the book adopts at least a partly inter-disciplinary approach. It is not unique for this, of course. Almost all of the more influential American texts recognize that in order to understand the budgetary process or urban politics it is necessary to have some grasp of economics, sociology and history. However, non-American texts on US politics have tended to take a rather narrow institutional approach to the subject, which this book consciously avoids.

THE CHAPTERS TO COME

As earlier suggested, the book follows a conventional format, although the balance between different subjects and areas reflects recent developments in American society and politics. Chapter 2 is very much a background introduction which presents basic statistical information on demography, society and economy. The chapter also includes a discussion of the role of beliefs and values in American politics, and places a special emphasis on the question of whether a 'dominant ideology' prevails in the United States. Chapters 3 to 12 cover the main institutions and processes of American government with each designed to present basic information and to discuss the significance of historical trends as well as the relevance of recent research findings in political science. Special attention is paid to the role of bureaucracy and organized interests – two areas often neglected at least by non-American students of the subject. Chapter 13 has two main purposes: first, to add substance and perspective to earlier chapters by looking at the policy process in three currently crucial areas – urban, economic and foreign policy; second, to discuss some of the more influential critiques of American political arrangements which recent economic and social difficulties have inspired. The general orientation of this and earlier chapters reflects my conviction that the study of political institutions can only be productive when placed in the broader social, political and economic environment. Such an approach can have costs – references to recent developments and events may lead to hasty judgments which can render a book painfully obsolete very quickly. But the cost of failing to put institutional relationships in broader context is even higher. For then the reader is condemned to an uninspired descriptive account, which is a fate I would not impose on any student of what should be one of the most interesting subjects in social science.

CHAPTER 2

Society, Economy and Political Beliefs

It has been our fate as a nation, not to have ideologies but to be one.

Richard Hofstadter, 1956

So powerful is the dominant ideology in this country that existing economic and political arrangements frequently appear not merely as the best possible arrangements, but as the only possible ones.

Ira Katznelson and Mark Kesselman, 1979

THE GROWTH OF THE USA: IMMIGRATION AND DEMOGRAPHIC CHANGE

Until the mid-19th century the United States was an 'imperialist' continental power, constantly expanding its territory by treaty, annexation and conquest. It was expansionist both in the sense that it dominated the other continental powers — Mexico, Britain, France and Spain — and in the sense that numerous native American tribes were overwhelmed by a technologically more advanced and populous society. It was, above all, America's economic might which enabled it to swallow up huge tracts of territory during this period (Map 2.1). Population increases were also very considerable and did not fall below 20 per cent per decade until 1920 (Table 2.1). Ever since then, the population has continued to grow rapidly and remains at over 10 per cent increase a decade — a remarkably high figure for an advanced industrial country with a small agrarian population. Both high natural increases and immigration account for this population

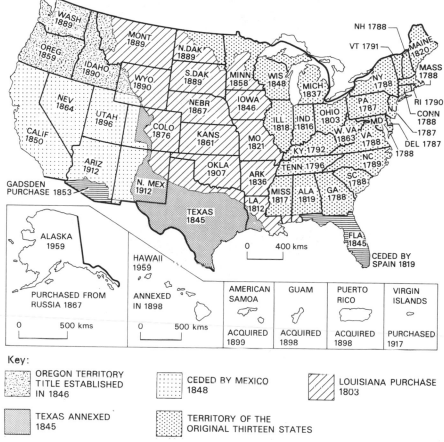

MAP 2.1   *The Territorial Expansion of the USA*

Source: *Statistical Abstract of the USA, 1980*, Figure 7.2, p. 208
Note: Dates under state names denote year of statehood.

growth although since 1971 there has been a natural *decrease* for the White population.[1] The United States was virtually built on an ideology of immigration, with successive generations of Americans promoting the country as a land of freedom and opportunity. The appeal was simple. Free from the corruption and oppression of Europe and rich in land and natural resources, the United States could and did absorb vast numbers of immigrants first mainly from Britain, then from Germany, Ireland, Southern and Eastern Europe,

1   Deaths and abortions have exceeded live births, see *Statistical Abstract of the USA, 1980*, US Department of Commerce, Bureau of the Census, 1980, Table 86.

TABLE 2.1 *Population and Area, 1790–1980*

| Census date | Resident population | | Increase over preceding census | | Area (square miles) | | |
	Number	Per square mile of land area	Number	Per cent	Gross	Land	Water
Conterminous US[1]							
1790 (Aug. 2)	3,929,214	4.5	n.a.	n.a.	888,811	864,746	24,065
1800 (Aug. 4)	5,308,483	6.1	1,379,269	35.1	888,822	864,746	24,065
1810 (Aug. 6)	7,239,881	4.3	1,931,398	36.4	1,716,003	1,681,828	34,175
1820 (Aug. 7)	9,638,453	5.5	2,398,572	33.1	1,788,006	1,749,462	38,544
1830 (June 1)	12,866,020	7.4	3,227,567	32.5	1,788,006	1,749,462	38,544
1840 (June 1)	17,069,453	9.8	4,203,433	32.7	1,788,006	1,749,462	38,544
1850 (June 1)	23,191,876	7.9	6,122,423	35.9	2,992,747	2,940,042	52,705
1860 (June 1)	31,443,321	10.6	8,251,445	35.6	3,022,387	2,969,640	52,747
1870 (June 1)	39,818,449	13.4	8,375,128	26.6	3,022,387	2,969,640	52,747
1880 (June 1)	50,155,783	16.9	10,337,334	26.0	3,022,387	2,969,640	52,747
1890 (June 1)	62,947,714	21.2	12,791,931	25.5	3,022,387	2,969,640	52,747
1900 (June 1)	75,994,575	25.6	13,046,861	20.7	3,022,387	2,969,834	52,553
1910 (Apr. 15)	91,972,266	31.0	15,977,691	21.0	3,022,387	2,969,565	52,822
1920 (Jan. 1)	105,710,620	35.6	13,738,354	14.9	3,022,387	2,969,451	52,936
1930 (Apr. 1)	122,755,046	41.2	17,064,426	16.1	3,022,387	2,977,128	45,259
1940 (Apr. 1)	131,669,275	44.2	8,894,229	7.2	3,022,387	2,977,128	45,259
1950 (Apr. 1)	150,697,361	50.7	19,028,066	14.5	3,022,387	2,974,726	47,661
1960 (Apr. 1)	178,464,236	60.1	27,766,875	18.4	3,022,261	2,966,054	54,207
United States							
1950 (Apr. 1)	151,325,796	42.6	19,161,229	14.5	3,615,211	3,552,206	63,005
1960 (Apr. 1)	179,323,175	50.6	27,997,377	18.5	3,615,123	3,540,911	74,212
1970 (Apr. 1)	203,211,926[2]	57.4	23,888,751	13.3	3,618,467	3,540,023	78,444
1980 (estimate)	226,505,000[2]	n.a.	23,293,000[2]	11.4	n.a.	n.a.	n.a.

Source: *Statistical Abstract of the USA, 1980*, Table 1, and *The National Journal*, 14 November 1981, p. 2019.
Notes: 1 Excludes Alaska and Hawaii   2 Rounded to nearest 1000

and most recently from Asia and, especially, Mexico, Cuba, Canada and other American countries. As Table 2.2 shows, a high level of immigration continues even today with more than 3.5 million new Americans arriving in the 1971–8 period.

TABLE 2.2   *Immigration, 1820–1978*

Period	Total Number	Rate[1]	Period or year	Total Number	Rate[1]	Year	Total Number	Rate[1]
1820–1978	48,664	3.5	1911–1920	5,736	5.7	1969	359	1.8
			1921–1930	4,107	3.5	1970	373	1.8
1820–1830[2]	152	1.2	1931–1940	528	4			
1831–1840[3]	599	3.9	1941–1950	1,035	7	1971	370	1.8
1841–1850[4]	1,713	8.4	1951–1960	2,515	1.5	1972	385	1.8
1851–1860[4]	2,598	9.3	1961–1970	3,322	1.7	1973	400	1.9
						1974	395	1.9
1861–1870[5]	2,315	6.4	1971 1978	3,502	2.0			
1871–1880	2,812	6.2	1965	297	1.5	1975	386	1.8
1881–1890	5,247	9.2	1966	323	1.6	1976	399	1.9
1891–1900	3,688	5.3	1967	362	1.8	1977	462	2.1
1901–1910	8,795	10.4	1968	454	2.3	1978	601	2.8

Source: Statistical Abstract of the USA, 1980, Table 131.
Notes:
1   Annual rate per 1,000 US population, 10-year rate computed by dividing sum of annual immigration totals by sum of annual US population totals for same 10 years.
2   1 October 1819–30 September 1830.
3   1 October 1830–31 December 1840.
4   Calendar years.
5   1 January 1861–30 June 1870.

In comparative context this is a high figure; for no other industrial country allows such an influx. During periods of labour shortage, many European countries have encouraged some (often temporary) immigration, but none permits a continuing high level of immigration which persists even during periods of high unemployment and low rates of economic growth.[2] Not that mass immigration has gone unopposed. During and following the truly massive waves of immigration from Southern and Eastern Europe which occurred in the 1880–1910 period, opposition to what for many Americans represented an 'invasion' by alien cultures was fierce and finally culminated in the 1924 Immigration Act. This law specifically discriminated against Southern and Eastern Europe by fixing national immigration

2   Other immigrant societies – Canada, Australia, New Zealand – have also encouraged immigration, but have generally been more selective in their policies towards newcomers, especially in recent years.

quotas favouring immigrants from Britain and Canada. Immigration fell dramatically during the 1940s and 1950s as depression and war took their toll both on economic opportunity and freedom of movement. With immigration increasing once more after 1950, criticism of the patent biases in immigration law intensified, and in 1965 a new law was adopted with fairer, more balanced quotas. Nonetheless, following amendments in 1965 and 1980, a total annual maximum of 270,000 was set which, together with a permitted total of up to 50,000 refugees, is still a relatively high figure.

Since about 1970 the immigration controversy has been fuelled anew by substantial illegal immigration, mainly from Mexico, and by the social tensions which large numbers of Cuban newcomers have brought, particularly to Florida. Illegal immigration has accelerated as poorer Mexicans have sought employment across a long and poorly policed border. Estimates of the numbers involved vary widely, but are at least in the low millions. In spite of these difficulties America's comparatively liberal attitude to immigration and the continuing belief that, at least for some, the USA should be a land of opportunity and freedom, still strikes many non-Americans as remarkable.

As the country and economy have grown, so both the composition and spatial distribution of the population have changed. Obviously with mass immigration during the 19th and early 20th centuries the country became more ethnically diverse, and although these earlier immigrants are now generally assimilated into American society, many retain some national, ethnic or religious identity which has its origins in Europe. More recently, immigration and high relative birth rates have led to substantial increases in the Black and Hispanic populations. By 1980 some 14.6 millions (6.4 per cent) of Americans were Hispanic (mainly Mexican, Puerto Rican and Cuban) and 26.5 million (11.7 per cent) were Black. In the case of the Hispanic population, a linguistic as well as ethnic dimension is involved, for Spanish is the mother tongue for many, and in some areas, notably California and the South West, demands for an official bilingualism grow stronger from year to year.

America today is a highly urban society, with some 73.5 per cent of the population living in cities over 2,500 in 1970. A more meaningful measure of urbanism is, perhaps, the number of people living in metropolitan areas, and in 1978 no less than 73.1 per cent of the population were classified thus.[3] One interesting post-1970 trend

3   According to the census category Standard Metropolitan Statistical Area (SMSA). Such areas do contain some 'small' communities because jurisdictional fragmentation ensures that large conurbations contain numerous governmental units.

has been an increase in rural living. Between 1970 and 1980 non-metropolitan areas grew by 17.1 per cent while metropolitan areas grew by just 10 per cent. These new rural dwellers are not, in the main, farmers, but people seeking a new lifestyle away from the crowded cities and suburbs. Indeed the growth of smaller towns and rural areas is a general phenomenon in advanced industrial societies.

Nonetheless, urban areas are still growing, although not in a uniform or even manner. The inner or central areas of the older industrial cities continue to decline, with every large city in the North East and Mid-west (except Columbus Ohio) losing population in the 1970–80 period (Table 2.3). Note also the very rapid growth

TABLE 2.3   *Population Change in the Nation's 20 Largest Cities,[a] 1970–80*

	1970 population	1970 rank	1980 population	1980 rank	Per cent change
New York	7,895,563	1	7,071,030	1	−10.4
Chicago	3,369,357	2	3,005,072	2	−10.8
Los Angeles	2,811,801	3	2,966,763	3	+ 5.5
Philadelphia	1,949,996	4	1,688,210	4	−13.4
Houston	1,233,535	6	1,594,086	5	+29.2
Detroit	1,514,063	5	1,203,339	6	−20.5
Dallas	844,401	8	904,078	7	+ 7.1
San Diego	697,471	14	875,504	8	+25.5
Phoenix	584,303	20	789,704	9	+35.2
Baltimore	905,787	7	786,775	10	−13.1
San Antonio	654,153	15	785,410	11	+20.1
Indianapolis	736,856	11	700,807	12	− 4.9
San Francisco	715,674	13	678,974	13	− 5.1
Memphis	623,988	17	646,356	14	+ 3.6
Washington	756,668	9	637,651	15	−15.7
San Jose	459,913	29	636,550	16	+38.4
Milwaukee	717,372	12	636,212	17	−11.3
Cleveland	750,879	10	573,822	18	−23.6
Columbus	540,025	21	564,871	19	+ 4.6
Boston	641,071	16	562,994	20	−12.2

Source: US Census Bureau, 1980 Census.
Note:

a   These data refer to *central* cities, not to metropolitan areas, so Los Angeles is ranked 3 as a city but its metropolitan area is second only to that of New York.

of the Southern and Western cities which is part of a general growth in the 'sunbelt'. While the sunbelt has expanded rapidly in recent years with the economy of the South and West booming, it would be misleading to characterize this as a permanent trend. During the recession of the early 1980s a number of Southern and Western states experienced serious economic difficulties, and some Southern states (notably Arkansas, Alabama and Mississippi) never really benefited from the earlier boom (see Appendix 1). What we can conclude is that many of the older industrial states have experienced serious population loss and economic decline, while the fortunes of the South and West have generally been better.

Americans are also getting older. The percentage of over 65-year olds in the population has increased dramatically over the last 60 years as medical care has improved and the birth rate has fallen. In 1920 only 4.7 per cent of the population were over 65, but by 1980 this figure had risen to 11.3 per cent. Both the size of the sunbelt and the 'aging of America' have important political consequences which later chapters will catalogue.

THE AMERICAN ECONOMY IN TRANSITION

From very humble beginnings the American economy had grown to the world's largest by the end of the 19th century and by 1945 the United States had established an effective global hegemony in economic affairs. America's *per capita* income was easily the highest in the world for a large country, and the economy had achieved a remarkable degree of self sufficiency. By the early 1980s the economy had grown to a staggering 2.5 trillion dollars and *per capita* reached $10,739 (in 1979). As the economy has grown so there has been a shift, first out of agricultural employment to manufacturing and, most recently, out of manufacturing into service industries. By 1979 only 3 per cent of the labour force were employed in agriculture — even though the USA is the world's largest food producer. Of the non-agricultural labour force those employed in goods-related jobs (mining, construction and manufacturing) fell from 37.7 per cent in 1960 to 29.2 per cent in 1980, while service sector jobs increased to over 70 per cent of the total. With most Americans working in the service sector talk of a post-industrial society is not entirely misplaced[4] — although it is only through great productivity

4 See Daniel Bell, *The Coming of Post Industrial Society*, London, Heinemann, 1974, for a discussion of this theme.

advances in agriculture and manufacturing that the economy is able to sustain such a diversity of service sector jobs.

In spite of these advances, it is now broadly accepted that the US economy is experiencing serious difficulties. Some of these derive from world economic recession, but others are a result of peculiarly American problems. The US labour force is growing more rapidly than those of most comparable countries, but the economy is expanding only slowly. Moreover, technological changes are making almost all sectors more capital- and less labour-intensive, so the potential for ever increasing numbers of unemployed and unemployable people is considerable. Worse still, American productivity increases have generally been lower than those of comparable countries (Table 2.4) so the relative economic position of the USA must

TABLE 2.4   *Productivity (Output per Employee),*
1974—81 Percentage Change and 1980, Selected Countries

	1974—81 percentage change	1980
Denmark	4.0	1.0
France	3.8	2.4
Ireland, Republic of	2.6	−4.5
Italy	2.5	4.7
Japan	5.6	6.3
United Kingdom	1.2	−4.2
United States	1.4	−0.1
West Germany	2.6	−0.6

Source: European Economy, EEC, 1981.

be expected to decline further. Indeed, both unemployment and inflation have risen during the 1970s, until by 1982 10.8 per cent of the workforce were without a job — the highest figure since the Great Depression of the 1930s (Table 2.5) and the lower levels of inflation in 1981 and 1982 were achievable only at the expense of this very high level of jobless. As we will discover in later chapters, governments have become increasingly involved in the economy both by attempting to pull broad levers of macro-economic management and through more detailed micro-intervention into the activities of individual sectors, regions and corporations. By 1978, 31 per cent of GNP was accounted for by public spending — a very high figure in historical perspective, although, as can be seen from Table 2.6, a lower figure than for any comparable country, except Japan. So, although government now plays a more intrusive role, the United States remains a country where, in comparative terms, the market and large corporations continue to play a major part in the distribution of resources. Note, however, that US defence spending takes a high percentage of GNP (and an increasing one since 1980). We will return to these themes in later chapters.

TABLE 2.5   *US Unemployment and Inflation, 1960–82*

	Annual Percentage Change in the Consumer Price Index	Unemployment (Percentage of Total Civilian Workforce)
1960	1.6	5.5
1965	1.7	4.5
1970	5.9	4.9
1975	9.1	8.5
1980	12.6	7.1
1981	9.0	8.9[a]
1982	4.5	10.8[a]

Source: Economic Report of the President, 1981, 1982, and *The Economist*, 15 January 1983, p. 67.
Note: a December.

TABLE 2.6   *Government Outlays as a Percentage of GNP Selected Countries 1978*

Country	Total Expenditure	Defence	Non-Defence
Sweden	60.8	4.0	56.8
Netherlands	54.5	3.0	51.4
West Germany	45.4	3.2	42.2
Italy	44.1	1.9	42.2
France	43.5	3.4	40.1
UK	40.0	4.7	35.3
USA	31.0	4.7	26.3
Japan	28.8	0.8	28.0

Source: OECD, *Economic Outlook*, various months and years.

One final point on the economy is that, with the decline of American hegemony, the United States has become more interdependent with the economies of other countries. Over 20 per cent of GNP is now accounted for by exports and imports, up from only 10 per cent in 1960. No administration can afford, therefore, to ignore the rest of the world. American governments and corporations have a direct interest in maintaining a stable and prosperous international trading environment. As later chapters will show, the relationship between this simple fact and American domestic institutional arrangements is complex.

SOCIAL STRUCTURE

One of the most fundamental questions in social science is the relationship between social structure and political activity. In most countries social class, religion, language or region are important determinants of how people think and behave in relation to political authority. The purpose of this section is, therefore, to provide some background on American society as a prelude to our later analysis of political attitudes and behaviour.

The study of social class in the USA is often influenced by the absence of a coherent working-class or socialist political movement. Americans are supposed to be essentially middle-class eschewing both the working-class and aristocratic values associated with many European countries. By many objective indicators the United States should, indeed, have a predominantly middle-class culture. In 1979 51 per cent of all workers were in white-collar jobs of whom over 50 per cent were classified as professional, technical, managerial or administrative. Only 33 per cent of all workers were in blue-collar jobs with a further 16 per cent in service[5] and farm employment (Table 2.7). Americans are also highly educated and enjoy a very high level of home-ownership, two indicators commonly employed to measure social class. In 1978 75 per cent of all 18-year olds had achieved a high school certificate and of these approximately 30 per cent went on to complete a 4-year undergraduate degree, a very high percentage in cross-national context. As notable are the housing figures, 65 per cent of all housing units being owner-occupied. Another measure of the middle-class nature of American society is the high level of stock (share) ownership in corporations. No less than 1 in 6 American families owns stock, dramatically more than in a country like Britain, although most stockholders own less than $10,000's worth of equity.

5 This is a narrower category than that implied by service *sector*, and includes workers in catering and domestic service.

TABLE 2.7   *Employment by Major Occupation Group*
1960—79, Percentage Distribution

Occupation Group	1960	1970	1979
White-Collar Workers	43.4	48.3	50.9
Professional and technical	11.4	14.2	15.5
Managers and administrators	10.7	10.5	10.8
Salesworkers	6.4	6.2	6.4
Clerical workers	14.8	17.4	18.2
Blue-Collar Workers	36.6	35.3	33.1
Craft and kindred	13.0	12.9	13.3
Operatives and	18.2	17.7	11.3
transport operatives			3.7
Non-farm labourers	5.4	4.7	4.8
Service Workers	12.2	12.4	13.3
Farm Workers	7.9	4.0	2.8
Total	100.0	100.0	100.0

Source: Adapted from the *Statistical Abstract of the USA 1980, op. cit* Table 696.

Yet some sociologists have questioned these 'objective' indicators, arguing that the relationship between employed and employer is little different for white- and blue-collar workers.[6] Moreover, these figures tell us nothing about the distribution of wealth and income, or about the continuing existence of many truly poor Americans. In fact most measures place the United States at or near the bottom end of income and wealth inequalities, when comparisons across countries are made (Figures 2.1 and 2.2). Moreover, calculations by the Urban Institute and the Institute for Research on Poverty have shown that recent tax cuts for the better-off combined with cuts in some of the federal welfare programmes will have the effect of increasing inequality further.[7] Estimating the number of poor people in the USA is difficult. Poverty is a relative concept and it is extraordinarily hard to measure accurately. The *official* measure in 1981 was an annual income of less than $9,287 for a family of four, and the federal government acknowledges that 14 per cent of the total population (about 30 million people) could be classified

6 For a discussion of this point see Ira Katznelson and Mark Kesselman, *The Politics of Power*, New York, Harcourt Brace Jovanovich, 2nd edn, 1979.
7 As reported in Joel Havemann, 'Sharing the wealth: the gap between rich and poor grows wider', in *The National Journal*, Vol. 43, 23 October, 1982.

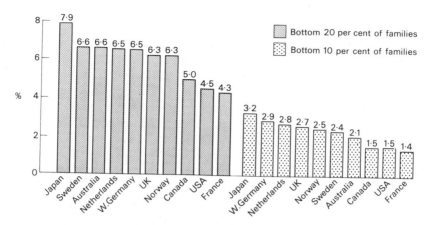

FIGURE 2.1 *Distribution of Income: After-Tax Income Shares, Selected Countries, early and mid-1970s**

Source: OECD. Reprinted by permission from *Minding America's Business* by Ira C. Magaziner and Robert B. Reich. © 1982 Law & Business, Inc./Harcourt Brace Jovanovich, Publishers, 757 Third Avenue, New York, NY 10017. All rights reserved.

Note: *Recent policy shifts in France and the USA will cause the USA to move into last place.

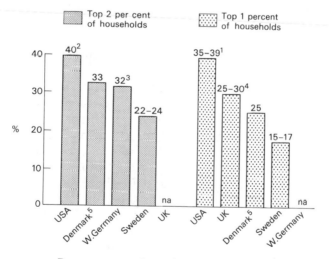

FIGURE 2.2 *Percentage of Wealth Held by Top 1—2 per cent of Total Householders, Selected Countries*

Source: Wealth Development in Sweden: Roland Spant, Stockholm, 1980, reproduced from Magaziner and Reich, p. 25.

Notes: 1 Derived from estate inventories, 1972.   4 Derived from 1972 data.
        2 Derived from income, 1969.   5 Derived from 1975 data.
        3 Derived from 1965 data.

as 'poor' by this measure. This represents more than a 2 per cent increase on 1979 reflecting both the impact of recession and some cuts in federal programmes. If, however, the definition of income is expanded to include in-kind benefits from local, state and federal governments (medical care, food stamps, subsidized housing and school lunches) then the figure falls to 9 or 10 per cent. Whatever the definition, one thing is certain: America does have a large population of poor people, not perhaps poor in the sense of living below subsistence level, but certainly poor in the sense of having little hope of full-time, secure employment and access to good housing and an acceptable living environment.

Of course poverty is not randomly scattered throughout the country. Its incidence is highest in the Southern states and in rural and inner-city areas. Blacks, Hispanics and one-parent families headed by women are also greatly over-represented among the poor. Indeed, the Black population is particularly badly off in spite of the enactment and often rigorous enforcement of civil rights laws. As Table 2.8 shows, the Black/White differential in income, education, infant mortality, and according to other important measures, has changed very little over the last 30 years. In fact since 1978 the differential has deteriorated somewhat as the effects of the recession have hit the Black population particularly hard.

In spite of these inequalities, most of which have been characteristics of American society for many generations, class and, to some extent even race have not emerged as major social cleavages in American politics. True, there have been occasions when at least the embryo of a national working-class or populist movement could be identified. And in particular geographical areas, class-based parties have achieved some considerable success. But their impact has been limited. Compared with the effects of radical movements on the national politics of other countries, it has been slight. Scholars have pondered long and hard as to why this should be so. As later chapters will show, institutional arrangements, particularly federalism and the electoral system mitigate against minority and radical political parties. Probably more important is the absence of a feudal and aristocratic past with all the deeply rooted social cleavages which such arrangements imply. Related is what has been called a dominant ideology of equality and liberty with its promise of unlimited opportunity and social mobility.[8] Certainly the United States has in the main been a

8 The classic statement of this position is Louis Hartz, *The Liberal Tradition in America*, New York, Harcourt Brace Jovanovich 1955. See also Seymour Martin Lipset, *The First New Nation*, London, Heinemann, 1964.

remarkably successful country economically. Even by the mid-19th century the American standard of living exceeded that of Britain, then one of the most affluent of the old European powers. Combined with bountiful and cheap land, this must constitute at least part of the explanation for the failure of socialism.

TABLE 2.8   *White—Black Comparisons, 1960—78*

	1960	1965	1970	1975	1977	1978
Median family income (thousands of dollars)						
Whites	5.8	7.3	10.2	14.3	16.7	n.a.
Blacks and others	3.2	4.0	6.5	9.3	10.1	n.a.
Median school year completed by adults						
All persons	10.6	11.8	12.2	12.3	12.4	12.4
Blacks	8.0	9.0	9.9	10.9	11.4	11.7
Pupils enrolled in higher education (in millions)						
Whites	3.3	5.3	6.8	8.5	8.8	8.5
Blacks and others	0.2	0.4	0.7	1.2	1.4	1.3
Infant deaths per 100 live births						
Whites	22.9	21.5	17.8	14.2	12.3	n.a.
Blacks and others	43.2	40.3	30.9	24.2	21.7	n.a.
Birthrate						
Whites	22.7	18.3	17.4	13.8	14.4	n.a.
Blacks and others	32.1	27.6	25.1	21.2	21.9	n.a.
Percentage of families headed by females						
Whites	8.7	9.0	9.1	10.5	10.9	11.5
Blacks and others	22.4	23.7	26.7	32.4	33.9	36.0

Source: Statistical Abstract of the United States, 1979, From The United States Revisited: A Study of a Still Developing Country by Ira Sharkansky, Table 3.5. ©1975 and 1982 by Longman Inc. Reprinted by permission of Longman Inc. New York.

Nonetheless, rapid urbanization and industrialization had their social costs, just as they did in other countries,[9] and the economy

9   For a graphic account of conditions in Chicago at the turn of the century see Upton Sinclair, *The Jungle* New York, New American Library, 1964.

has by no means always performed well. During the Great Depression, for example, the level of social distress among both working- and middle-class people was very high, as it is for some social groups in the early 1980s. Given this, many historians and social scientists are obliged to fall back on the explanations based on beliefs, values and ideology, when accounting for the absence of a powerful socialist party, which is a subject we will return to later.

Some scholars have argued that a repressive state (mainly at the state and local levels) in cooperation with repressive private (corporate) power prevented the emergence of a radical trade union and socialist movement during the late 19th and early 20th centuries. But comparisons with equivalent events in Europe appear seriously to weaken this argument. There certainly was repression in the USA but its character was essentially fragmented, erratic and uncoordinated, compared with what were often quite Draconian and highly centralized measures employed by European governments. The repression argument is convincing as far as the Black population is concerned, however. Until the 1960s, American Blacks suffered from what was effectively an apartheid system in the Southern states, and as already established, even today their socio-economic status remains low. However, although the political behaviour of the Black population is distinctive (as Chapter 6 will show), Black separatist or nationalist movements have never achieved any significant success. Along with other ethnic minorities, Blacks have tended to mobilize politically within the context of established institutions and political parties. This is not to deny the importance of an ethnic dimension to politics; within the Democratic party, for example, and at the level of local politics, ethnicity has been and continues to be a significant voting and organizational cue. But the United States has never nurtured an ethnic politics based on separatism or a complete rejection of the dominant 'American' values and political institutions.

Americans are a highly religious people – more so indeed than the populations of most comparable countries (Table 2.9). There is also a multiplicity of religions, sects and denominations, and some commentators have argued that religion has been a prime source of the 'creedal passion' associated with various reform movements in American history.[10] Yet in spite of this and the clear links between religion and politics, religion has not constituted a major social division in American society equivalent to the role played by

---

10   For a good discussion, see Samuel P. Huntington, *American Politics: The Promise of Disharmony*, Cambridge Massachusetts, Harvard University Press, 1981, Chapters 1, 2, 5 and 6.

denomination in Ireland, Holland, Belgium or even Germany. Like ethnicity, religious differences are important in the United States but they have, more often than not, been subsumed under a dominant set of peculiarly *American* beliefs, values and institutions.

TABLE 2.9   *Religious Commitments in the 1970s*
Selected Countries (per cent)

	Religious beliefs very important[a]	Believe in God[b]	Believe in life after death[c]
United States	58	94	71
Canada	36	89	54
Italy	36	88	46
Benelux	26	78	48
Australia	25	80	48
United Kingdom	23	76	43
France	22	72	39
West Germany	17	72	33
Scandinavia	17	65	35
Japan	14	44	18

Source: Surveys in 1974—5 by Gallup International Research Institute for non-US countries and in 1978 by the American Institute of Public Opinion (Gallup), Princeton Religion Research Center, and the Gallup Organization, Inc., for the United States. Reported in *Public Opinion* 2 (March/May 1979), pp. 38—39.
Reproduced from Huntington, *American Politics: The Promise of Disharmony*, Cambridge Mass. Harvard University Press, 1981, p. 156. Reprinted by permission.
Notes:
a   Question asked: 'How important are your religious beliefs — very important, fairly important, not too important, or not at all important?'
b   Question asked: 'Do you believe in God or a universal spirit?'
c   Question asked: 'Do you believe in life after death? Do you believe that there is life after death?'

Region has played a somewhat different role in American history. From the very beginning the South was culturally and economically separate from the rest of the United States, and although a rising sense of national identity strengthened North—South linkages during the 1820—50 period, this was shattered by the Civil War and its aftermath. Only very slowly between 1865 and 1960 was the South reincorporated into the mainstream of American society. The South's distinctiveness was, of course, based on its slave and later segregationist economy which produced a system of social stratification with no parallel in the rest of the country.[11] It was also a one-party region

11   The best characterization of Southern Society remains W. J. Cash, *The Mind of the South*, Harmondsworth, Middlesex, Penguin, 1973 p. 19.

dominated by racist and often corrupt local and state Democratic parties. But the South was different in other ways. Until the post-1945 period it was predominantly rural and poor. Immigrants avoided the region; industrial and infrastructure investment was sparse; change came only slowly. Not until what had effectively become an economic and social backwater was jolted by the rapid economic growth of the 1950s and '60s and by an increasingly strident civil rights movement, did Southern society begin to change. Since 1960, in fact, many Southern states have been transformed by migration, urbanization and economic growth. To the casual visitor many parts of the South are today indistinguishable from the rest of the country. Democratic party hegemony has in part broken down, although the region remains essentially conservative. But old style Southern society has by no means disappeared, especially in the poorer, less developed states (notably Arkansas, Mississippi and Alabama). Racism still exists as does a peculiarly 'unamerican' resistance to change. But the South can no longer lay claim to the very special and separate status which for so long distinguished it from the rest of the country.

BELIEFS AND VALUES:
DOMINANT IDEOLOGY OR POLITICAL CULTURE?

One of the most enduring debates in social science concerns the relationship between the public's beliefs and values and political authority. Liberal scholars label these beliefs 'political culture', or 'a historical system of widespread, fundamental, behavioural, political values actually held by system members (the public).'[12] Political culture therefore embraces the dominant pattern of beliefs and values, which are acquired and modify and change as a result of a complex process of socialization and feedback from the political system. In other words, individual citizens acquire attitudes towards politics through learning from parents and their environments (socialization) and these adapt and change as political authorities produce particular responses or policies over time (feedback). Political culture is made up of the sum of individual beliefs and values and, crucially, it is essentially *independent* of political authority. In some systems it may be incompatible with prevailing political institutions — as in pre-revolutionary Mexico or Weimar Germany — in

12   Donald J. Devine, *The Political Culture of the United States*, Boston, Little Brown, 1972, p. 17.

which case regime change occurs. In other systems, the political culture supports and succours the political system. Liberal scholars invariably label the American system thus. Politics and political culture may change in the USA, but they tend to be mutually supportive. Regime change is extremely unlikely in such a situation.

Advocates of the 'dominant ideology' position take a quite different stance. To them public beliefs and values are imposed from above by those in positions of power. Beliefs constitute an *ideology*, therefore, whose function is to legitimate the prevailing system of political authority and economic organization. This radical, usually Marxist perspective, identifies the United States as a country where the dominant ideology is particularly powerful:

> The dominant ideology is more powerful in the United States than in any other capitalist democracy. Most political debates in the United States take place within the framework of this ideology, a situation related to the absence of a broadly based working class movement pressing for fundamental change. So powerful is the dominant ideology in this country that existing economic and political arrangements frequently appear not merely as the best possible arrangements but as the only possible ones.[13]

These two apparently incompatible positions are not as far apart as they may seem, for when American beliefs are examined, both liberals and radicals accept the importance of similar public attitudes and values. Samuel Huntington has summed these up as 'liberty, equality, individualism, democracy and the rule of law under a constitution'.[14] Unfortunately we do not have the space in this chapter to do complete justice to what exactly these values mean in the American context, but we can summarize what is a very large body of research as follows:

Liberty

Survey research from the 1950s and early 1960s found a high level of support among Americans in favour of *general* statements of free speech and opinion (for example, 'people who hate our way of life should still have a chance to talk and be heard'), but much lower support for *specific* statements (for example, 'a book that contains wrong political views cannot be a good book and does not deserve

13 Katznelson and Kesselman, *op. cit*, p. 29.
14 Samuel P. Huntington, *American Politics: The Promise of Disharmony, op. cit*, p. 14.

to be published').[15] Moreover, the level of support for specific freedoms was much higher among elites (political influentials) than among the mass public. This disjunction between general and specific support is not exclusively American, citizens of many countries would answer positively to general statements advocating freedom. Clearly freedom of expression is not an absolute value and there have been times in American history when public tolerance of 'unamerican' values has been very low. The red-baiting periods following the First and Second World Wars demonstrated just how limited freedom could be in the United States.[16] And until the mid-1960s the attitude of Southern Americans towards the Black population was the very antithesis of libertarian.

Since the 1960s, however, there is evidence of some important changes. Racial tolerance has generally improved, and attitudes towards 'unamerican' beliefs (communism, atheism) have become more liberal (Table 1.20).

TABLE 2.10   *Changing American Attitudes Towards Conformity*

Percentage who say	Attitudes Towards (%)			
	Communists		Atheists	
	1954	1972–3	1954	1972–3
Should be allowed to speak in our community	28	57	38	66
Book should not be removed from public library	29	58	37	71
Should be allowed to teach in college or university	6	38	12	42

Source: James A. Davis, 'Communism, conformity, cohorts and categories: American tolerance in 1954 and 1972–3', *American Journal of Sociology*, Vol. 81 November 1975, p. 506.

In spite of these changes, antipathy to 'non-American' values clearly remains, so it would be quite misleading to characterize the United States as a country where 'freedom of expression' or 'liberty' is assigned an inviolate status.

15   More than 80 per cent of respondents to a 1962 survey agreed with the first question, and just 50 per cent with the second, Herbert McCloskey, 'Consensus and ideology in American politics'. *American Political Science Review*, Vol. 8 (1964), Tables 2 and 3. This article also contains a good summary of the literature on this subject.
16   See Seymour Martin Lipset and Earl Raab, *The Politics of Unreason: Right Wing Extremism in America, 1790–1970*, Chicago, University of Chicago Press, 1978.

Three final qualifications need to be added to this conclusion, which should serve as a warning against simple over-generalizations in this area. First, as later chapters will show, there have been quite dramatic advances in the legal protection of all individual rights, and especially freedom of expression over the last 30 years. Not all these advances have been simply procedural; objectively American citizens, newspapers, and other media enjoy much more freedom than they used to. As this development can often cause governments and officials serious difficulty and embarrassment, it seems to contradict the more reductionist of the 'dominant ideology' positions. Second, the American political system is uncommonly fragmented and devolved. Some of the worst examples of the infringement of individual freedom have occurred within *local* jurisdictions with the open acquiescence of local populations. This applies particularly to racial questions and criminal procedural rights. As society has become nationalized, so such activity has become more difficult to get away with. Although this development could be interpreted as part of the advance of a 'dominant ideology', it is difficult to make the connection between less repressive local polities and the particular interests of national political authorities or corporations. Third, if we expand liberty or freedom to include economic individualism or the freedom to accumulate wealth, then there is no doubting that the United States is a free country. We will return to this theme later.

Equality

Early foreign observers of the American scene, from de Tocqueville to Dickens and Bryce, noted the remarkable absence of deference to position or status in the United States. 'Equality of estimation' is what Bryce called it, or the tendency of Americans to treat each other as equals, whatever their education, occupation or social class. This remains broadly true — although, of course, European countries have been moving in the same direction. 'Equality' was one of the earliest rallying cries of Revolutionary America, but from the very beginning it implied an equality of opportunity rather than equality of condition. The argument ran something like this: provide equal status for all citizens (except slaves, of course) under the law and every individual would be capable of achieving self fulfilment. As the country developed, so it became accepted that the pre-condition for equality of opportunity was a certain standard of education. Consequently, education achieved

— and retains — a very special status in American social policy. Almost alone among the major social services, there is a broad consensus that education should be provided out of public rather than private funds.

Supporters of the dominant ideology position claim that the constant stress on equality of opportunity helps legitimize what is a very unequal society. Originally the emphasis was on the frontier and unlimited land. More recently the appeal has shifted to education and all the benefits this can bring. By constantly reassuring the population that everyone can succeed given personal effort and a good educational base, the citizenry are, so the argument runs, being duped into accepting the system. No doubt there is something to this — certainly Americans continue to believe that their economic position (or the position of their children) will improve[17] — but such a perspective fails to distinguish between equality before the law and the material or economic benefits which equality of opportunity can bring. The former, which is close to equality of dignity or esteem, is highly developed in the United States and recognized as an important element in citizenship. Legislation designed to prevent unfair or unequal treatment by private and public authorities is far-reaching and, in comparative perspective, is quite rigidly enforced. In recent years discrimination against women and racial minorities has been the main focus of these laws, but the idea that all citizens, irrespective of background, should be treated equally is deeply entrenched.

Individualism

Nothing more accurately seems to represent Americanism than a stress on individual rather than collective action. Trade union membership is low in the USA, collectivist political parties of the left (and also of the right) have failed to win mass support, and the society is infused with a degree of self reliance which is rarely found in other countries. This spirit of self reliance has its roots in the puritanism which flourished in both colonial and post-colonial America, and it remains a potent force as public antipathy to 'welfare scroungers' and a surprisingly wide acceptance of job insecurity shows. So, as far as distribution of resources is concerned, Americans prefer private

17   For example, in a 1982 poll 51 per cent believed their children would be better off than themselves, only 36 per cent thought they would be worse off. 70 per cent of the respondents considered themselves better off than their parents. If anything Blacks were more optimistic than Whites, *Public Opinion*, Vol. 5, No. 3, June/July 1982, pp. 24—5.

to public institutions. Indeed, the 'state' as such is held in quite low esteem compared with its status in other countries (Table 2.11).

TABLE 2.11   *Individual Freedom v. Duty to the State*

The individual owes his first duty to the state and only secondary to his personal welfare. (1960) (per cent)

	USA	UK	West Germany	Italy	Mexico
Agree	25	38	41	48	92
Disagree	68	55	45	32	5
Don't know, etc.	7	7	14	20	3

Source: ICPR, reproduced from Donald J. Devine, *The Political Culture of the United States*, Boston, Little Brown, 1972. p. 93.

Unfortunately social surveys have tended not to ask more sophisticated questions in cross-national context, so one must be wary of inferring that Americans are always antipathetic to state provided goods and services. If anything, the evidence suggests that when couched in general terms, Americans show antipathy to government provision, but when asked about specific programmes such as social security, health care or education, they show a high level of support.[18] Perhaps this is not unsurprising given the much more visible role that governments, and especially the federal government, now plays in economy and society.

America's anti-statist tradition has a number of roots and there is no time for an extensive discussion here. We should note, however, that this liberal tradition has at least in part depended on the continuing success of capitalism. From beginnings where self reliance and economic individualism was the very essence of the new society (a point to be developed in Chapter 3), capitalism flourished as in no other country, and not until the 1930s did it need sustained support from government. Industrialization, infrastructure development and urbanization were predominantly market phenomena. Of course government played a role, but mainly in response to the needs of capitalism, not as a leader and director of investment and resources. Even today when government intrudes into almost every aspect of society, it is treated with suspicion by many Americans. Again, it is very difficult to separate out the extent to which economic individualism has been 'imposed' on the American people by

18   See the *General Social Surveys, 1972–80*, Cumulative Codebook, National Research Center, University of Chicago, 1980, Questions 62–65, and 213–215 for details.

the needs of capitalism, from broader historical/cultural forces such as the absence of a feudal tradition and the fact that many Americans have benefited from economic development.

One final point on individualism. Some observers make the mistake of inferring a general *cultural* individualism when noting the undoubted prevalence of *economic* individualism in the United States. Yet as our discussion of freedom and references to religion suggest, Americans are often influenced by collectivist thinking. Whether it be McCarthyism, fundamentalist Christianity or a sometimes violent rejection of outsiders from carefully protected local communities, there is no shortage of examples of Americans moving, sometimes blindly, in masses. By this measure the society is almost certainly less individualist than British or French society, although, to repeat the point, collectivist action of this sort usually embraces only a small section of American society at any one time, or occurs at the local rather than national level.

Democracy and the Rule of Law

If democracy is defined in terms of a simple devotion to *majoritarianism* then there is no doubting that Americans believe in it. Majority opinion carries a weight and independent value in the US which is unusual elsewhere. This translates not only into a broad acceptance of the legitimacy of elections and, at the state and local levels, referenda. It also means that on occasion ill-judged policies and programmes have been adopted following a surge of (often populist) moral fervour. Such was the case with prohibition and, arguably, some of the tax cutting measures of the 1978—81 period.[19]

As far as general political arrangements are concerned, American attitudes present us with something of a paradox, for they combine strong support for the Constitution and the system as such with considerable disillusionment with particular processes and institutions. One of the first and most impressive of the political culture studies discovered that Americans were overwhelmingly supportive of the political system and Constitution (Table 2.12) compared with other countries. True, this survey dates from the early 1960s when people were generally more optimistic about society, but there is still evidence that Americans believe their system to be basically sound (few want to emigrate, most greatly admire the Constitutional

---

19   Starting with California's Proposition 13, many states and localities passed laws limiting property, sales and income taxes during this period. By 1982, however, these same laws were considered by many to be contributing to state and local fiscal problems.

TABLE 2.12 *Pride in National Characteristics,*
Selected Countries, early 1960s

Per cent who say they are proud of:	*United States*	*United Kingdom*	*West Germany*	*Italy*	*Mexico*
Governmental, political institutions[a]	82	46	7	3	30
Social legislation	13	18	6	1	2
Economic system	23	10	33	3	24
Characteristics of people	7	18	36	11	15
Spiritual values and religion	3	1	3	6	8
Contributions to the arts	1	6	11	16	9
Contributions to science	3	7	12	3	1
Physical attributes of country	5	10	17	25	22
Nothing or don't know	4	10	15	27	16

Source: Gabriel A. Almond and Sidney Verba *The Civic Culture: Political Attitudes and Democracy in Five Nations.* © 1963 Princeton University Press; Little, Brown and Co. Inc. © 1965. Table 1, p. 102, reprinted by permission of Princeton University Press.
Note:
a   The actual survey question referred to pride in 'American government or political tradition — the Constitution, political freedom, democracy and the like'.

framework). However, since the mid-1960s, increasing numbers of people have become disillusioned with the party system, the Presidency, Congress and the federal bureaucracy. So much so, in fact, that a 1978 survey showed that less than 9 per cent of respondents rated the ability of any of these institutions 'to get things done' as 'good'. This compared with figures of over 25 per cent for the Supreme Court, the media and big business.[20] But too much can be read into these figures. Citizens may be disillusioned with particular institutions, governments or politicians, but they are not *alienated* from the system in a way which threatens the regime.[21] The institutions and processes which succour American democracy and the rule of law are highly respected. If anything, recent evidence of declining trust in government reflects an increasing sophistication among voters who are now making more conscious connections between what parties and politicians promise and how they perform. Chapter 6 will deal with this point in some detail.

Claims that the system is essentially stable appear to be supported by the relative absence of regime-challenging parties and protest

20   Quoted in '1978 study of American opinion', *US News and World Report*, 1978, p. 12.
21   See Jack Citrin, 'The political relevance of trust in government', *American Political Science Review*, Vol. 68, September 1974, for a discussion of this point.

movements in American history. The Civil War apart, most protest activity has been inspired by single issues (civil rights, the Vietnam War) or has been accommodated within existing parties and institutions.[22] Radical critics are quick to point out that this is because truly revolutionary movements have been nipped in the bud by an unholy alliance of corporations and government. But much more repressive tactics have been employed in other countries to no avail. Why should much less extensive measures have been so successful in America?

More convincing perhaps is the claim that, unable to mobilize politically against the dominant ideology, increasing numbers of Americans have turned to anomic violence and anti-social behaviour. There can be no doubting that America is a violent society (more than 20,000 people were murdered in 1978 alone) but it is extraordinarily difficult to make clear causal connections between this sort of pathology and political values and institutions. Violence and crime have always been a part of what was for many generations a frontier society. What we can conclude is that until the 1960s (and possibly beyond), violence and intimidation in the South were part of a Southern social structure built on racism and exploitation. Obviously this was as much a political as social or economic phenomenon. As significant is the increasing incidence of random violence and serious crime among the racial and ethnic minorities of America's inner cities. It seems absurd to argue that these people are not politically excluded, isolated and socially alienated. If the dominant ideology thesis carries any conviction, it does so with respect to the inner-city poor. For them, the optimism, materialism, and egalitarianism which continue to dominate political discourse and which are encouraged by a highly commercial media, must seem either an irrelevance or must serve as a diversion from their plight.

We can conclude that both the dominant ideology and political culture perspectives carry some conviction. But the dominant ideology view is, with the possible exception of its effects on the new poor of America's cities, difficult to demonstrate as valid, while the political culture approach tends to understate the extent to which those in positions of political power can manipulate the mass public. Few dispute, however, that there is such a thing as the 'American creed' or 'American ideology', and that it has been uniquely effective in overpowering other systems of beliefs and values. Samuel Huntington has made this point well:

22   See Alec Barbrook and Christine Bolt, *Power and Protest in American Life*, Oxford, Martin Robinson, 1980.

It is possible to speak of a body of political ideas that constitutes 'Americanism' in a sense which one can never speak of 'Britishism', 'Frenchism', 'Germanism' or 'Japanesism'. Americanism in this sense is comparable to other ideologies or religions. 'Americanism is to the American', Leon Samson has said, 'not a tradition or a territory, not what France is to a Frenchman or England to an Englishman, but a doctrine — what socialism is to a socialist'. To reject the central ideas of that doctrine is to be un-American. There is no British Creed or French Creed; the Académie Française worries about the purity of the French language, not about the purity of French political ideas. What indeed would be an 'un-French' political idea? But pre-occupation with 'un-American' political ideas and behavior has been a recurring theme in American life. 'It has been our fate as a nation', Richard Hofstadter succinctly observed, 'not to have ideologies but to be one'.[23]

FURTHER READING

For a truly comprehensive statistical background, see the annual *Statistical Abstract of the United States*, US Department of Commerce, Bureau of the Census. Some fascinating comparative data on the US standard of living, as well as economic performance, can be found in Ira C. Magaziner and Robert B. Reich, *Minding America's Business: The Decline and Rise of the American Economy*, New York, Harcourt Brace Jovanovich, 1982. A good summary of the dominant ideology position is presented in Ira Katznelson and Mark Kesselman, *The Politics of Power*, New York, Harcourt Brace Jovanovich, 2nd edition, 1979. For a political culture perspective see Donald J. Devine, *The Political Culture of the United States*, Boston, Little Brown, 1972. The classic statement of the liberal view is Louis Hartz, *The Liberal Tradition in America*, New York, Harcourt Brace, 1955. Two stimulating critiques of recent developments in American society and economy, one written from a radical and the other from a conservative perspective, are Frances Fox Piven and Richard A. Cloward, *The New Class War: Reagan's Attack on the Welfare State and its Consequences*, New York, Pantheon, 1982, and Samuel P. Huntington, *American Politics: The Promise of Disharmony*, Cambridge Massachusetts, Harvard University Press, 1981.

23 Samuel Huntington, *op. cit*, p. 25.

CHAPTER 3

Constitutional Government

The American Constitution is the most wonderful work ever struck off at a given time by the brain and purpose of man.

W. E. Gladstone, 1878

Good government should be sufficiently neutral between the different interests and factions to control one part of the society from invading the rights of another, and at the same time sufficiently controlled itself, from setting up an interest adverse to that of the whole society.

James Madison, 1787

Almost all governments pay formal allegiance to a written or (more rarely) unwritten constitution, but in few countries is the constitution a real and continuing constraint on the exercise of power. Even more rarely do constitutions survive political and social changes, invasions and wars. The American Constitution is unusual, both because it has remained almost unaltered since its ratification in 1789, and because it continues as a major source of authority in the political system. Indeed, even the most cursory examination of America's basic political institutions — Congress, Presidency, federalism, the electoral system — instantly shows the influence of the Constitution. To the foreign observer, the apparent resilience of the Constitution and constitutionalism is one of the most remarkable features of American politics, and one which requires some explanation. Among the most important questions raised by this phenomenon are: Why has the Constitution been amended so little through history? Has it been a major contributor to political and social stability? What real influence does it have today? In particular, Does it remain an independent source of political power, or has it simply been interpreted in a way which reflects a pattern of political and economic power which would in any case have prevailed? Before we tackle these questions it is necessary to approach the crucial issue of why the Constitution took the shape that it did.

Most dramatic regime changes following a revolution or war are quite easy to explain. France in 1789 was seething with discontent at a corrupt and insensitive monarchy. Russia in 1917 was long overdue for a revolution to sweep away an archaic, semi-feudal order. And the numerous colonial wars of independence in the post-1945 period were predictable, given the rapid political and economic changes which the Second World War had precipitated. The American Revolution fails to fit any of these neat stereotypes, however. In fact, by some definitions it was not a revolution at all. Many of the citizens of the 13 colonies considered themselves 'true born Englishmen' who, being increasingly denied the rights which they thought all free English deserved to enjoy, were entitled to challenge the 'illegitimate' exercise of power by George III. They saw their task, therefore, as one of asserting independence from a regime which had betrayed its own principles. Moreover, unlike most revolutionary wars, the War of Independence and the eventual emergence of a new constitutional system had few immediate consequences for the distribution of wealth, power and status. If anything, it reinforced trends already underway. It was essentially a conservative revolution which, in marked contrast to parallel events in France, did not lead to new class divisions in society. This is not to say that radical or revolutionary elements were absent. They were very much present, but the real power remained in the hands of a solid middle-class and professional property-owning elite.

The unique nature of these events stems from the unique characteristics of American colonial society. From the very beginning, the British Americans had displayed a marked degree of independence and self-sufficiency. In the 13 colonies, and especially in New England, the local community became virtually the only meaningful level of government — and even then government is far too strong and modern a label to attach to what were remarkably successful self-governing entities. Sam Bass Warner has captured the spirit of these 17th-century communities very well:

For a generation or two, medieval English village traditions fused with a religious ideology to create a consensus concerning the religious, social, economic and political framework for a good life. Each of several hundred villages repeated a basic pattern. No Royal statute, no masterplan, no strong legislative controls, no central administrative officers, no sheriffs or justices of the peace, no synods or prelates, none of the apparatus typical of government then or now.[1]

Although such communities were partly transformed by economic development and population increases during the 18th century, the essential independence of the colonies continued to be expressed through local governments and, later, colonial assemblies whose activities were largely tolerated by Crown appointed governors. Admittedly, considerable variation existed between different colonies — and particularly between the plantation and slave economy of the South, and the more diverse agrarian and mercantilist economy of the North — but each colony respected the independence of the other.

This description implies a colonial rule which was essentially distant and benign, and such indeed was the case until the 1760s when the English, acting under a monarch determined to assert his power over increasingly corrupt and strident Whig interests at home, decided to exercise much greater control over the colonists. All goods imported to the colonies had to pass through British ports, a tax (stamp duty) was imposed on all legal documents and newspapers, a revenue tax was levied, and colonial assemblies were prohibited from issuing their own paper currency. These economic restrictions were viewed by the colonial elites as an outrageous infringement of basic rights. During the 18th century the idea that men possessed certain inalienable rights spread rapidly under the influence of the social contract theorists (Locke, Rousseau) and pamphleteers (Thomas Paine), and became particularly popular in a colonial America infused with a spirit of liberty and independence. Life, liberty and property were rights which governments were obliged to protect through the representation of the people in parliaments and assemblies. And should those assemblies fail to fulfil their contractual obligations to the people, then elections would ensure the incumbency of new representatives charged with carrying out the people's wishes. A monarch exercising executive power outside any representative mechanism was clearly not legitimate.

While this rather sophisticated view of events was probably held

1   Sam Bass Warner, *The Urban Wilderness: A History of the American City*, New York, Harper and Row, 1972, p. 8.

only by educated elites, the smallholders and artisans who made up the bulk of the population did have some notion of individual rights and were, by any European standard, highly independent and assertive. Indeed, for more than 100 years up to the Revolution, acts of political (usually mob) violence were quite common, as they were in England. Most people with some stake in society — a farm or other property, or a valuable manual or intellectual skill — were quite used to resorting to extra-legal methods should their grievances be ignored by established political channels.[2] Given this tradition, a growing sense of being 'American' which economic growth and better communications had brought, and the sudden change in English policy, outbreaks of armed resistance were almost to be expected. In 1774 the colonial assemblies sent delegates to a national Continental Congress — the first real assertion of national independence by the colonists. By 1775 fighting had broken out in Massachusetts and in 1776 the Continental Congress adopted the Declaration of Independence which, with stirring rhetoric, marked the true beginnings of the United States:

We hold these truths to be self-evident, that all men are created equal, that they are endowed by their Creator with certain unalienable rights, that among these are life, liberty, and the pursuit of happiness; that to secure these rights, governments are instituted among men, deriving their just powers from the consent of the governed; that whenever any form of government becomes destructive of these ends, it is the right of the people to alter or to abolish it, and to institute new government, laying its foundation on such principles, and organizing its powers in such form, as to them shall seem most likely to effect their safety and happiness.

For the next five years, the colonists successfully fought their revolutionary war against the British, and in 1781 established a new system of government under the Articles of Confederation. In effect this — the first American Constitution — was little more than a formal recognition of the Continental Congress. A congress was created, but no executive or judiciary. The new government was very much a confederation: individual states retained considerable autonomy giving to the Congress only limited powers — namely to declare wars, establish treaties, regulate weights and measures, oversee Indian affairs, run a post office and establish an army and navy. Crucially, no mandatory power to raise taxes was established.

2 See John C. Wahlke (ed.) *The Causes of the American Revolution*, Lexington, Massachusetts, D. C. Heath, 1973.

Instead, Congress had to rely on voluntary subventions from the state legislatures. Also, each state could issue its own paper money and generally regulate commerce within its boundaries.

Such a weak, leaderless system of government could not last long, especially in the face of a number of very urgent problems confronting the new nation. Revenue needed to be raised nationally to provide a common defence. Some central control of the currency and the enforcement of contracts needed to be created, and a common external tariff was needed to protect American goods from cheap British imports. Moreover, the war had widened the gulf between the better-off who had lent money to finance the fighting and a growing debtor class who had mortgaged small farms and houses to raise incomes in the face of economic dislocation. In 1789 a small rebellion had broken out in Massachusetts, a state where the law on debtors was particularly harsh, when Daniel Shays led over 1000 men to block the proceedings of the state's high court.

Although quickly put down, Shays' rebellion served to remind the better-off that the new Congress was ill-equipped to provide some degree of national economic security and uniformity. Prior to the rebellion a number of attempts had been made to strengthen Congress, and a convention to discuss trade problems had met at Annapolis, Maryland, in 1786. Although only five states attended, a resolution to meet in Philadelphia with the more ambitious aim of constitutional revision, had been agreed at the convention. Shays made such a meeting that much more imperative, and during the summer of 1787, 55 delegates assembled in Philadelphia charged with the momentous task of producing new constitutional arrangements for the United States.

THE AMERICAN CONSTITUTION

While the 55 delegates — the Founding Fathers — were obviously not operating in the absence of political and economic constraints, they were able genuinely to combine normative judgments on what best would make for a good system, with provisions imposed on them by political necessity. They were not, in other words, engaged in the exercise of naked political power. Nor were they obsessed with retributive measures against past masters. And unlike many 20th century harbingers of regime change, their actions were not informed by a single, closed ideology. Instead, they could afford to compromise, to show pragmatism and to draw on a number of political theories and constitutional arrangements at that time commonly discussed by the educated and liberal-minded.

The Founding Fathers were certainly educated, about one half having college degrees — a very high proportion for that time. They were also established (and comparatively young) men of property and status — merchants, lawyers, planters, doctors, intellectuals. George Washington presided over the meetings, although he played virtually no role in the proceedings. Inviting Washington — who came only reluctantly — was a clever ploy, as he was the one figure almost universally respected in the new nation. The real driving forces behind the convention and its proceedings were James Madison of Virginia, a brilliant young politician who had helped to write Virginia's constitution, and Alexander Hamilton from New York, one-time aide to Washington during the war, who had helped set up the Annapolis convention.

As delegates from the state legislatures, the Founding Fathers were not directly elected by the people — indeed one state, Rhode Island, was not even represented dominated as it was by a disgruntled debtor class. In one curious respect, this lack of a universal popular mandate gave them some extra freedom, for meeting in secret, they could eventually produce a document as a *fait accompli* and then lobby hard for its acceptance by the states. As we will see, this in effect is precisely what they did.

What were the main influences on the Framers? Four main ideas stand out: social contract theory, representation, the separation of powers and federalism. We have already mentioned the idea of the social contract, with its provision of obligation on both governed and governors. Although central to the thinking of Hobbes and Rousseau, it was Locke's vision of the social contract which most influenced the Founders. To Hobbes, the contract was a very one-sided affair where the people traded their freedom for the security which a strong state would bring. Rousseau's contract was far more idealized and democratic, involving as it did the identification and implementation of the general will of the people. Locke, in contrast, made *representation* the central canon of his ideal society. Citizens, or those with a stake in society, men of property, were entitled to a government which would champion their natural rights. Through representative institutions — free elections and assemblies — the people could hold the rulers accountable for their actions. Obedience to the law (the people's side of the contract) was, therefore, conditional on the government fulfilling its side of the contract — the guarantee of life, liberty, and property.

Representative government carries with it other notions, notably majority rule and the implication that there are clear limits to democracy. Both were accepted by the Founding Fathers and their limits on democracy were, by modern standards, quite severe. Only the lower house of the legislature, the House of Representatives, was to be elected directly by the people (Article 1, Section 2).[3] Senators were to be nominated by the state legislature (Article 1, Section 3) and the President was to be elected by an electoral college, the members of which were to be appointed by the state legislatures (Article 2, Section 1). The Framers' very limited acceptance of democracy reflected their fear of unbridled majority rule. If the people could vote for all the main officers directly, it raised the spectre of an insensitive — and possibly tyrannical — permanent majority capable of riding roughshod over the minority. As Thomas Jefferson had noted some years before the convention, 'an elective despotism was not the government we fought for'.[4] Note also that the electoral qualifications of those who could vote for the House of Representatives were to be determined by the state legislatures (Article 1, Section 2). In most cases this meant a very limited suffrage consisting of property-owning males. None of this was incompatible with popular sovereignty or a republican form of government. Sovereignty resided in the people (albeit a minority of them) not in a monarch or emperor. And this, together with the majoritarian provisions in the Constitution, guaranteed a republican system.

The Framers were not only worried about the possibility of tyranny by the majority; they were also aware of the dangers of concentrating too much power in any one institution. A powerful executive suggested monarchial or despotic leadership. A powerful legislature carried with it the possibility of rule by an insensitive majority. A device existed to overcome these dangers — the separation of powers. Borrowing in part from the ideas of the French philosopher Baron de Montesquieu, who greatly admired what he thought was a division of powers in the English system, the Framers went about a deliberate separation of authority between legislature, executive and judiciary. Congress was accordingly given a separate power base (or constituency) from the Presidency, and although the judiciary was not given the quite awesome power of judicial review it was later to assume, Supreme Court and other federal judges were to be appointed by the President. However, the precise

---

3 The full text of the Constitution is given in Appendix 1, pp. 302—28.
4 Quoted in T. Mason (ed.) *Free Government in the Making*, New York, Oxford University Press, 3rd edn, 1965, p. 165.

jurisdiction of the courts, as well as the final say on the appointment of judges, were accorded to Congress (Article 3).

To ensure a division of power between the major institutions, a system of *checks and balances* was introduced. So both houses of the legislature had to approve a bill, but the President could exercise a veto over it. The Senate and House of Representatives could, in turn, override a veto if two thirds of the members of both houses voted for it (Article 1, Section 7). Congress was also given some control over executive appointments, which had to be filled with the 'advice and consent' of the Senate (Article 2, Section 2). These checks and balances should not imply an *equality* of power and authority between the institutions. There is no doubt that the Framers intended the Congress, and in particualr the House of Representatives to be the key *source* of policy. This is clear from Article 1, Section 8, which enumerates the powers of Congress. As these included fiscal, monetary and regulatory powers, as well as the authority to raise armies and declare war, they were, in contemporary terms, quite comprehensive. Significantly, the directly elected chamber, the House of Representatives, was given special responsibility for revenue bills (Article 1, Section 7) thus reflecting the popular demand ('no taxation without representation') that the 'people's branch' should be directly accountable to the voters on taxation matters.

Executive and judicial branches were, in contrast, given few specific powers, although the dictum that the 'executive power shall be vested in a President', (Article 2, Section 1) leaves open the question of where executive power begins and ends. Congress was, then, expected to be the source of most legislation, but its power would be checked both internally (via bicameralism) and by the President. These checks are essentially negative in nature, suggesting that the Framers had a greater fear of the abuse of power than an inability to exercise it. We have already mentioned the fear of democracy, majority rule, and a despotic executive. In addition some of the Framers were deeply suspicious of the machinations of groups, parties or 'factions'. James Madison, in particular, feared that government might become the creature of some class or special interest. He eloquently outlined his position in *The Federalist*[5] :

---

5 *The Federalist* papers written mainly by Madison and Hamilton were published after the convention as a tract to persuade some of the states to accept the Constitution. They are a remarkable collection of essays which reflect some of the most crucial debates of the convention.

Among the numerous advantages promised by a well constructed Union, none deserves to be more accurately developed than its tendency to break and control the violence of faction....By a faction, I understand a number of citizens, whether amounting to a majority or minority of the whole, who are united and actuated by some common impulse of passion, or of interest, adverse to the rights of other citizens, or to the permanent and aggregate interests of the community. There are two methods of curing the mischief of faction: The one, by removing its causes; the other by controlling its effects. There are again two methods of removing the causes of faction: the one, by destroying the liberty which is essential to its existence; the other by giving to every citizen the same opinions, the same passions and the same interests.[6]

Madison is in no doubt that the only solution is to control the effects of faction. Liberty is essential and where it exists factions will exist, and giving an equal voice to every citizen can only be achieved in a democracy. Democracy is impractical and dangerous except in very small communities. This leaves the control of faction to a republican form of government, or the sort of representative system with a limited suffrage, some indirect elections, a separation of powers and the operation of checks and balances, which was eventually adopted.

The convention was no means united on basic constitutional arrangements. Alexander Hamilton feared that without a strong executive, few of the nation's pressing problems would be solved. Madison, in contrast, feared both a strong executive and an over-bearing legislature. More generally, the larger states (Virginia, Massachusetts, Pennsylvania) favoured a strong central government (whether dominated by Congress or not) while the smaller states, fearing an encroachment by the more populous areas, favoured more decentralized arrangements. In fact, debates on federalism and the delineation of powers between centre and periphery were among the most acrimonious at the convention. For in addition to the small/large state dichotomy, there was the thorny problem of the very different interests represented by the Southern as opposed to the Northern states. Following intense debate between those wanting a strong federal government (the so-called Virginia Plan) and those demanding decentralized power (the New Jersey Plan), a compromise was reached by giving the Senate a representative base founded on territory rather than population (two Senators from each state, Article 1, Section 3). The House was to be elected on a population basis and (a further compromise) given special powers over federal revenues.

6 Federalist, No. 10, in *The Federalist Papers*, New York, Mentor Books, 1961, pp. 77–78.

The distinctive economy and culture of the South posed a potentially even greater problem and was enventually resolved only by the unsavoury expedient of counting slaves as three-fifths of a free person for the purpose of representation in the House and in distributing federal taxes. Of course this did not mean that slaves played any part in the political process. They did not. Many Northern delegates disliked this compromise, but accepted it knowing that the South would not tolerate any serious incursion into its slave-based economy. The South was also an exporter of cotton and other agricultural produce and had much less interest in the protectionist policies which Northern politicians favoured. To safeguard their position, Southerners demanded that a two-thirds majority be required to ratify treaties in the Senate. In this way, it was hoped that trade agreements favouring the North would be avoided.

These controversies over the status of the South and large versus small states should not obscure the fact that the Framers were obliged to create some sort of federal system. After all, the convention was made up of representatives of the states, and the war had been waged against a strong central government. A unitary system in the style of England was completely unacceptable to most delegates. What eventually transpired was a highly flexible federalism. Indeed, reading the Constitution it is not at all clear where federal power begins and ends, which gives at least great potential power to the centre.

The genius of the Constitution was that although it was the first written constitution ever to be adopted by a country, and although it propounded the virtues of a republican form of government — a radical idea, indeed in the late 18th century — it remained intrinsically *conservative* in content and implication. The Founders, and particularly the most influential and able of them, Madison and Hamilton, were hardly social visionaries. Instead their hopes for the New Country were tinged with caution and not a little pessimism about man's greed and selfishness. As Madison put it:

As there is a degree of depravity in mankind which requires a certain degree of circumspection and distrust, so there are other qualities in human nature which justify a certain portion of esteem and confidence.[7]

As with most educated 18th-century men, the essentially inegalitarian view that there are worthy and unworthy, talented and talentless, wise and stupid men in the populace, prevailed. The

7 *The Federalist*, No. 55, *op. cit*, p. 346.

President was to be elected by an electoral college made up, it was hoped, with wise, educated and established citizens, free from the rabble-rousing and instant judgments which democratic processes inspired. Senators too, were expected to be elder statesmen elected by their peers for a leisurely six years and able, therefore, to hold in line a potentially capricious and unruly lower house. What the Framers hoped for, therefore, was firm, cautious and responsible government. The Constitution was designed to provide the basic framework for such a system of stable and limited political power. It was also intended to stand the test of time — an objective which was greatly aided by a cumbersome amendment process. Amendments have to be proposed by a two-thirds vote in both houses of Congress and then ratified by three-quarters of the state legislatures or by a ratifying convention in two-thirds of the states. Alternatively a national convention at the behest of two-thirds of the state legislatures can propose an amendment which in turn can be ratified by Congress or by a ratifying convention (Article 5). The first method (Congress proposing, the state legislatures ratifying) has become the normal amending mechanism, and it is testimony both to the flexibility of the Constitution and to the difficulties inherent in the amending process that, between 1791 and 1982, there have only been 16 amendments.

Reflecting on the personal interest which the Framers had in a successful economy and on the pressing economic problems which the Articles of Confederation had patently failed to solve, some commentators have claimed that the whole exercise in Philadelphia was motivated by economic interest rather than the higher ideals of liberty, republicanism and civic virtue.[8] While there is certainly something to this, it seems odd that the fundamental disagreements on major questions which did occur involved delegates with an equal stake in economic success. Virtually *all* the delegates were men of property, so the more reductionist of the economic theories of the Constitution should predict no real disagreement on basic principles. Yet those who voted against the Constitution had just as much a stake in prosperity and stability as those who voted for it.[9] A more persuasive way to characterize the Framers' motivations is to accept that they were indeed troubled by economic dislocation and the ever present threat of uncontrolled democracy, but differed markedly

8   The classic statement of this view is Charles Beard's *Economic Interpretation of the Constitution of the United States*, New York, Macmillan, 1913 (paperback, 1961).
9   As established by Forrest McDonald, *We the People — The Economic Origins of the Constitution*, Chicago, University of Chicago Press, 1958.

on which system would best overcome these problems. Crucially these differences were not only instrumental and pragmatic. Delegates also differed *intellectually* and represented more than one political philosophy and conception of human nature.

RATIFICATION

Fearful of failure, the Framers wrote into the Constitution the requirement that ratification could be achieved by just 9 of the 13 states and then by special state conventions rather than the (often untrustworthy) state legislatures. The Framers also labelled themselves *Federalists*, thus imposing on opposition groups the unattractive sobriquet 'Anti-Federalist'. Opposition was, in fact, fragmented, coming as it did mainly from the more remote rural areas. There was a geographical split, but not a North/South one. Instead, it was the commercial interests of the coastal areas, the larger towns and cities and the big landowners of the South who supported ratification. The Anti-Federalists were concentrated in 'the part most remote from commercial centres, with interests consequently predominantly agricultural. It included fractious Rhode Island, the Shays regions of Massachusetts and the centre of a similar movement in New Hampshire'[10] (see Map 3.1).

Federalist lobbying in favour of the Constitution was intense and inspired the first truly national political debate in the United States Very generally, the Anti-Federalists complained that the Constitution was insufficiently democratic and that it implied a strong and domineering central government. Complaints that individual rights were not specifically guaranteed by the Constitution were also common, and in order to ensure ratification in some states, the Federalists accepted that a Bill of Rights would be added as soon as the first federal government was established. Between 1787 and 1789, state conventions, one after the other, voted for ratification. Success was assured when the New York convention eventually ratified by a margin of three votes. The Federalists won because they were better organized, had all the leading politicians and statesmen behind them, and because the Anti-Federalists were obliged to fight a negative campaign, a return to the Articles of Confederation being their only immediate alternative to the Constitution. In order

---

10   O. G. Libby, quoted in J. C. Clark Archer and Peter J. Taylor, *Section and Party*, Chichester, John Wiley, 1981, p. 49.

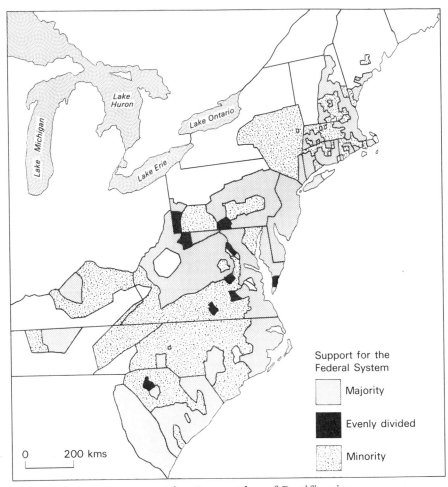

Lake Huron

Lake Ontario

Lake Michigan

Lake Erie

Support for the
Federal System

Majority

Evenly divided

Minority

0   200 kms

MAP 3.1   *The Geography of Ratification*

Source: O. G. Libby, as reproduced in J. C. Clark Archer and Peter J. Taylor *Section and Party*, Chichester, John Wiley, 1981. p. 50. Reprinted by permission of John Wiley & Sons Ltd.

to appease the remaining Anti-Federalists the first Congress quickly voted for 10 amendments, which, once ratified by the states in 1791, became the Bill of Rights. Interestingly, a number of additional amendments failed in Congress or during ratification, almost all of which would have made the system more democratic. One proposed that the electorate should issue binding instructions to their Congressmen thus turning them into delegates. Another suggested that there should never be less than one Congressman for every 50,000 inhabitants. The mind boggles at the consequences for American politics if either or both of these proposals had been adopted.

Change by Amendment

No constitution can elaborate the precise relationship between institutions and political forces. If it attempts to do so it runs the danger of being ignored. Successful constitutions must, therefore, be flexible and open to varying interpretations. In some ways, the shorter and vaguer the document the better. Completely unambiguous statements lead to rigidity and can render a constitution unworkable. The US Constitution is free of all these faults. It does, of course, lay down certain guidelines and rules, but it says remarkably little about the precise powers of the main institutions, or about how authority should be shared between federal and state governments. When a comparison is made between the United States of 1789 (3.5 million people, agrarian, confined to the East Coast) and the United States of the 1980s (220 million people, highly industrial, a continental and world power) the true success of the Constitution can be appreciated. For virtually the same document applies today as applied nearly 200 years ago. Moreover, if we examine the 16 Amendments[11] which have been accepted in this period, their significance is almost certainly not as great as the changes in interpretation to which the Constitution has been subjected.

Of the 16 Amendments, some are relatively trivial, two were devoted to the adoption and subsequent rejection of prohibition and the remainder are devoted either to electoral questions or to limiting and expanding the role of the federal government.

Amendments Affecting Elections

The first important amendment here was the 12th which was adopted in 1804 to provide for the popular election of the electoral college, which in turn elects the President. As mentioned earlier, the Founding Fathers hoped that a group of elder statesmen (the electoral college) would choose the President, but with the emergence of competing

11   Excluding the first 10 Amendments (The Bill of Rights).

political parties it soon became obvious that the college had become highly partisan. To ensure some democratic control, therefore, its members became subject to popular election. Surprisingly, this system persists. Americans still do not vote directly for a Presidential candidate, but for members of the college. Moreover, it is a *winner-take-all* mechanism, so that the candidate who gets a majority of votes in a particular state wins *all* that state's electoral college votes. What determines the number of electoral college votes in a state? Each state simply has one vote for each Representative and Senator which means that the votes are distributed roughly in proportion to population (the number of representatives in any state changes regularly in accordance with population shifts (see pp. 251 and 262), and as there are only two Senators per state this introduces a small bias in favour of low population states). The major criticism of this system is that it is possible for a candidate to win the electoral college vote, but receive fewer popular votes than another candidate. Just this happened in 1824, 1876 and 1888, although it has not occurred since. Another criticism focuses on the danger of electoral college members failing to vote for the candidate mandated by the electorate. Again, this has happened on rare occasions, but it has never been critical.

Clearly the electoral college system favours the larger states. If a candidate wins just seven states: New York, California, Texas, Pennsylvania, Illinois, Michigan and Ohio, he amasses 211 votes even if he wins by only a narrow margin in each of these states. And only 270 electoral college votes are needed for victory. Talk of reforming the system is never far from the surface in the United States, and the mechanism probably persists because there are only two main parties,[12] and some bias in favour of big population centres does compensate for other biases in the system in favour of smaller states and rural areas.

Almost all the other amendments affecting elections have been designed to expand the electorate or to hold elected officials more accountable or responsive to the public (Table 3.1). These changes, together with the abolition of property qualifications for voting at the state level during the first part of the 19th century have, in total, greatly increased the democratic element in the Constitution.

12   Should no candidate receive a majority in the college — a likelihood if the USA had a multi-party system — then the House of Representatives chooses the President on the basis of *one vote* per state delegation. This massive bias in favour of the small states would not be tolerated for long were the system put to the test (although it did occur twice in the 19th century). In recent years the USA has only rarely produced a serious third party candidate, and few have accumulated electoral college votes.

TABLE 3.1 *Constitutional Amendments Affecting Elections*

Amendment	Purpose	Proposed	Adopted
12	Direct election of electoral college	1803	1804
15	Voting rights extended to all races	1869	1870
17	Direct election of Senators	1912	1913
19	Voting rights extended to women	1919	1920
20	'Lame Duck' session of Congress abolished[a]	1932	1933
22	Presidents limited to two terms	1947	1951
23	Voting rights extended to residents of District of Columbia	1960	1961
24	Voting rights democratized — abolition of poll tax	1962	1964
25	Reform of Presidential succession in case of disability	1965	1967
26	Voting age lowered to 18	1971	1971

Note:
a This changed the date of new Congressional sessions from March to January to shorten the period during which the old Congress could act.

Amendments Affecting the Powers of the Federal Government

In one sense, changes in electoral qualifications were to be expected as the democratizing trends of the 19th and 20th centuries took hold. If this is so, it would also be unsurprising if the Constitution had been frequently amended to expand the powers of the federal government. Yet as Table 3.2 shows, only three amendments have had this purpose, the 13th to assert federal power over those states practising slavery, the 14th imposing the Bill of Rights on the states and the 16th establishing the power to introduce a national income tax. And of these three, the 14th Amendment was not, in fact, applied to the states until the 20th century.[13]

13 Proof of the problems involved in amending the Constitution is provided by the failure to adopt the Equal Rights Amendment (equal opportunity for women, see Appendix 1, p. 327). Originally proposed in 1972, the amendment was three states short of ratification by the end of the original deadline in 1979. Although extended by a further three years, the amendment remained three states short in 1982, in spite of broad popular support. The Reagan Administration is not sympathetic to the amendment and it is unlikely to be renewed.

TABLE 3.2 *Amendments Affecting the Powers
of the Federal Government*

Amendment	Purpose	Proposed	Adopted
11	Limited federal courts' jurisdiction over suits involving the states	1794	1798
13	Abolished slavery	1865	1865
14	Extended due process of Bill of Rights to the states	1866	1868
16	Established power to introduce a national income tax	1909	1913

Change by Interpretation

Much more important have been changes in Constitutional interpretation which owe more to the development of American society and economy than to the wording of the Constitution as such. We can identify four such changes:

(1) The assertion of federal over state power.
(2) The assertion of executive over legislative power.
(3) The emergence of the Supreme Court as the final arbiter of the Constitution.
(4) The growing protection of individual rights under the federal government.

Each of these four will be dealt with in detail in later chapters. For now it is enough to point out the first two were certainly not intended or envisaged by the Framers, the third probably was and the fourth has developed in a way which could not possibly have been predicted in 1787.

Although the Constitution is ambiguous on the question of federal/ state relations, there can be no doubt that the relationship which had developed by the 1970s was light years away from anything the Framers could have intended. Today the federal government intrudes into almost every facet of economic and social life, leaving to the states very little that *constitutionally* they can call their own except perhaps their territorial integrity. In 1791 it was broadly expected that the 10th amendment's dictum: 'The powers not delegated to the United States by the Constitution, nor prohibited by it to the States, are reserved to the States respectively, or to the people', would leave

the states unequivocally in charge of a number of governmental functions. As the next chapter will demonstrate, this was not to be.

Similarly, Congress was expected to be the major source of legislative initiative, while the President implemented laws with prudence and efficiency. The late 20th-century reality is very different. For while Congress does play a greater role in policy initiation than most national legislatures, and is indisputably a powerful and independent institution, it has forfeited the lion's share of the legislative function to the President and to an awesomely large and complex executive branch.

The reasons why government has become larger, more centralized and concentrated in executive rather than legislature will be addressed in detail in later chapters. But these trends have occurred in almost all countries with rapid economic and social development, the mobilization of populations by parties and groups and the corresponding increase in demands placed on all governments, particularly those with the greatest potential for resource distribution and regulation — central governments.

In 1803 the Supreme Court asserted the power of judicial review, or the right to declare any act of Congress or action by the executive branch as incompatible with the Constitution and therefore illegal. Actions by states can also be struck down by the Supreme Court. Although used sparingly at first, this power has been utilized with increasing frequency, and as we will see in Chapter 12, has had profound consequences for the working of the political system. Although some of the Founders may have envisaged the Court playing the role of final arbiter of the Constitution, none could have foreseen the intimate involvement of the nation's highest court in such questions as abortion, electronic bugging and political party campaign finance.

Finally, citizens' right to free speech, assembly, religion, and privacy, and to 'due process' and the equal protection of the laws have slowly been extended to apply to the states. This is crucial, for slavery was an institution protected by state governments and constitutions. Following the Civil War, the 13th and 14th amendments swept away slavery and, in theory, discrimination. However, the Supreme Court failed to enforce the 14th Amendment in the South until after the Second World War, so allowing the perpetuation of segregation and the worst sort of racial discrimination. Deference to states rights extended to other areas such as standards of occupational safety, employment conditions and criminal justice. So for many Americans, civil rights and liberties were anything but 'God given rights'. Only under federal legislation did they exist, and until

the 20th century the federal government played only a small role in the lives of individual citizens. Beginning in the 1930s and accelerating between 1945 and 1970 this anomalous situation was slowly corrected, with the Supreme Court insisting in case after case that the Bill of Rights and 14th Amendment apply to all American governments, whatever their status. So in cases involving national security, privacy, racial, religious and sex discrimination, and the administration of justice, the Supreme Court has insisted that all authorities have an obligation to heed constitutionally defined rights. Of course this does not mean to say that the Court has always favoured the individual rather than government — although in recent years more often than not it has. Changes in official attitudes to civil rights and liberties parallel the growth of government noted earlier. As governments at all levels have increasingly intruded into the lives of individuals, so the need for protection from arbitrary governmental authority has grown. As we will discover in Chapter 12, governments — and especially federal governments — have also been active in controlling the abuse of individual rights by *private* bodies, in particular corporations. It seems highly unlikely that the Framers could have foreseen that the question of individual rights would have become part of a complex web of interaction between myriad private and public institutions and individuals.

ASSESSING THE CONSTITUTION

Some of the most dramatic changes in American government and society over the last 200 years have involved institutions and political processes not even referred to in the Constitution. Parties emerged during the early years of the 19th century as the major agents of political mobilization. Interest groups have grown in number and influence until today some commentators seriously argue that they are the true sources of political power and influence. Similarly a nationally organized media equipped with formidable electronic resources can play a critical role in swaying political opinion. Does this mean that the Constitution is of relatively little importance? Not at all, for all these changes have had to be accommodated within certain institutional limits which the Constitution imposes. Political and economic changes have indisputably altered the relationships between institutions and the broader society but they have not been transformed in such a way that the document has ceased to have meaning. Congress remains separated from the

Presidency. Interest groups, Presidents, individual citizens, the media — even foreign governments — have to accept that the independent power of Congress can and frequently does thwart Presidents. The Courts are also independent and have shown, especially in the last 40 years, that President and Congress must sometimes tread warily when exercising their powers. States too, remain important political units — although, as we will discover in the next chapter, their relationship with the federal government is now more one of interdependence than autonomy.

Criticisms of the modern Constitution usually concentrate either on the continuing political hiatus between executive and legislature, or on the progressive weakening of the states in relation to the federal government. The first of these will become a constant theme in later chapters, and there is little doubt that American Presidents are, in comparison with most industrial countries, uncommonly constrained by the essentially negative power of Congress. But as we will see, American government is not only fragmented by the separation of powers. Getting policy efficiently formulated and implemented is also affected by the complexity of the executive branch and, simply, by the many competing interests in American society which have created and nurtured so many access points to those with political power. It seems reasonable to infer that this would have happened whatever the precise constitutional arrangements in force.

Arguments suggesting that the decline of the states is in part attributable to the Constitution's failure to define precisely where state sovereignty begins and ends are less persuasive. Such a strict delineation of powers would have been inflexible and ultimately unworkable, and in any case the states were admirably independent until this century. The gradual erosion of their powers is not, therefore, a matter so much of constitutional failure as it is a consequence of the states' inability to deal with the pressing social and economic problems which industrialization and other changes have brought. Any assessment of the Constitution has to recognize that, as with any constitution, its continuing influence is ultimately dependent on those in positions of political power accepting its legitimacy. Had its provisions proved a major threat to power-holders, it would have been ignored or radically amended. No doubt the Founding Fathers recognized this and, anticipating problems, deliberately opted for a short and rather vague document which would stand the test of time. But this would hardly have been enough had America been torn by fundamental divisions based on class, ethnicity, language or religion. The Framers knew that good government was all about the business of reconciling differences between competing groups and interests in society, and no doubt they were aware that the United States would experience social and political conflict of varying intensity. But the conflict between North and South apart — and this very nearly put paid to the Union — the United States has been remarkably unaffected by fundamental political divisions. Free from a feudal past and lacking deeply rooted religious, ethnic, linguistic and, after the Civil War, regional divides, the country was able to accommodate quite extraordinary economic and demographic changes within a single, almost unchanging, constitutional structure. Above all it is this relative consensus on political fundamentals amid rapid change that has allowed what is in any case a brilliantly adaptive Constitution to survive.

This does not mean to say that the Constitution will continue for ever, of course. And there are more than enough critics who claim that the basic division of power between legislature and executive is inappropriate for the sort of efficient policy making needed to run an economically powerful late 20th century world power. Whether this is true, later chapters will reveal. But whatever the charges, the Constitution is under no imminent threat either from domestic political conflict or from radical amendment. According to the simple measure of its ability to survive, therefore, it must be deemed a success.

FURTHER READING

Among recent interpretations of the origins and consequences of the pre- and post- revolutionary periods, two stand out: Bernard Bailyn, *The Ideological Origins of the American Revolution*, Cambridge, Massachusetts, Harvard University Press, 1967; Garry Wills, *Inventing America*, Garden City, New York, Doubleday, 1978. For a textbook account of the Constitution, see Edward S. Corwin, *The Constitution and What it Means Today*, Princeton, New Jersey, Princeton University Press, 14th edn, 1978. For a non-American history of the period, see M. J. Heale, *The Making of American Politics*, London, Longman, 1977.

CHAPTER 4

80,000 Governments: Federalism and Intergovernmental Relations

Over the past decade and a half, a new system of domestic government has emerged in the United States — one whose degree of complexity and interdependency, extent of inter-level contacts and constraints, and vastly expanded scope of intergovernmental financing and servicing arrangements are in marked contrast to the simpler, more separated features of its predecessor patterns of the nineteen fifties and certainly of the nineteen twenties.

David B. Walker, Assistant Director,
Advisory Commission on Intergovernmental Relations, 1981

This Nation has never fully debated the fact that over the past forty years, federalism — one of the most essential and under-lying principles of our Constitution — has nearly disappeared as a guiding force in American politics and government. My administration intends to initiate such a debate...

Ronald Reagan, 1981

To the European student of American government, the practice of federalism presents itself as something of a conundrum. On the one hand is the extraordinary variety of contrasting public policies displayed by the states. Most states levy an income tax, but six do not; most have capital punishment, but 12 do not; state mandated land-use planning is light years away from the policy agenda in Texas — a state which prides itself on its free market in land — but in Oregon and Hawaii state planning is a fact of life. In California the possession of marijuana is no longer a criminal offence; in Missouri it *is* a major offence carrying with it up to a 20-year prison sentence. On the other hand, American observers repeatedly tell us that federalism is dying — or is even dead; that the federal government has effectively usurped the powers of the states and now plays the dominant role in American government. Federalism, so we are told, has been transformed from a system of shared sovereignty with each level of government supreme in its own sphere and converted into a complex web of intergovernmental relations where political and economic forces, not constitutional imperatives, are the key variables.[1] A major purpose of this chapter is to explain the apparent paradox of continuing state variety and increasing federal power. To achieve this, special attention will be paid to what has been called 'fiscal federalism' or the financial relations between different levels of government. As will be shown, such an approach focuses attention not only on federal–state relationships, but also on *local*–state and *local*–federal links. Finally, some reference will be made to the Reagan administration's attempts to revive the institution of federalism.

FEDERALISM IN THEORY AND PRACTICE

It was not so long ago that Europeans viewed the federal arrangements of the United States with a combination of distanced interest and condescension. A constitutional division of powers between centre and periphery might, so the argument ran, suit such large and diverse countries as the United States, but they were clearly inappropriate for homogeneous countries like Britain and France, with their centralized metropolitan political cultures based on dominant capital cities. For social reformers, federalism was viewed with particular scepticism. How, after all, could resources be distributed from rich to poor areas and from the haves to have-nots of society in the absence of a powerful central government operating unhindered by 'regressive' state governments? Critics pointed to the stark inequalities of American society which seemed so often to correlate with state boundaries — abject poverty in Mississippi and Alabama, an easy affluence in Connecticut and Iowa.

In recent years, however, the institution of federalism has experienced something of a revival. Centralized governments have been criticized as spendthrift and insensitive, and federalism has

1   See Michael Reagan, *The New Federalism*, New York, Oxford University Press, 1972.

been cited as a compromise solution to the claims by increasing numbers of regions and ethnic minorities in a variety of countries for more autonomy. To the critic of the over-centralized state, federalism's advantages seem obvious. Local and regional cultural, political and economic characteristics can be preserved; government can be brought 'closer to the people'; and central power can be limited by ensuring that the administration of a whole range of domestic policies is conducted at the state and local level. Federalism is, of course, much more than the mere devolution of powers which, to a greater or lesser extent, exists in all states, unitary and federal. *Dual sovereignty* is the central theoretical condition for federalism. This involves not just the sharing of policy reponsibilities between different levels of government, it additionally *guarantees* constitutional integrity to state governments. No federal government can abolish its constituent states as a British government can, theoretically at least, abolish all its local governments. Naturally the crucial question is: Which powers should reside in the state governments and which in the federal government? Historically under 'classic' or 'dual' federalism,[2] defence and foreign affairs together with some aspects of financial management have been considered federal government responsibilities, while most domestic policies – education, roads, welfare, the administration of justice – have been allocated to state and local governments.

Few constitutions, however, specify precisely which policy areas should be the responsibility of different levels of government. Article 1, Section 8 of the US Constitution, for example, does enumerate the powers of Congress, but it does not do so in a way which unambiguously defines the federal role. Congress is given the power to regulate inter-state commerce, but what does this mean: The regulation of inter-state transport? The movement of manufactured goods across state boundaries? The regulation of banking across state lines? The regulation of those aspects of *intra*-state commerce which are affected by *inter*-state transactions? Or what? Clearly what Congress does here and what remains a state responsibility is left undefined by the Constitution.

In reality the delineation of the federal and state roles has been left to judicial interpretation and to the ways in which the courts have reacted to shifting political and economic environments. As was pointed out in Chapter 3, workable constitutions have to be flexible and open to new interpretation and any attempt to lay

2   For a discussion of the operation of dual federalism see Morton Grodzins, *The American System*, Chicago, Rand McNally, 1966.

down in a permanent fashion the limits to federal or state powers would be doomed to failure. As we shall see, for federalism the cost of flexibility has been the gradual and steady erosion of the states' powers by the federal government.

In strict constitutional terms, the states are guaranteed just four things: equal representation in the Senate (Article 1, Section 3); the right to jurisdictional integrity (Article 4, Section 3); the right to a republican form of government (Article 4, Section 4); and protection against invasion and domestic violence (Article 4, Section 4). What in reality they have retained in addition to this has varied with the historical period and a whole range of economic, social and political forces. They remain an important level of government, not just for constitutional reasons, but also because they are a convenient jurisdictional base for a range of powerful actors and interests in contemporary America. Political parties, for example, are organized on a state rather than a national basis — a fact which gives the states a key role in nominating Presidents and in electing Congressmen and Senators. We will elaborate on this point later, but for now it is important to stress that local as well as state governments are important power bases in the American system. Localism is as strong in the USA as in any country and this in spite of the weak constitutional position of local governments (in theory, they are constitutionally subordinate to state governments). The power of local governments is reflected in their resilience. In spite of the many pressures to consolidate into larger units — pressures which exist in all industrial countries — the number of local units in the USA remains high (Table 4.1). Note also the *variety* of local units which derives from variations in state law. 20 states, for example, have townships which generally have the powers of municipalities but which, unlike municipalities, cover areas irrespective of population concentrations. Special districts which continue to increase in number have been created to perform a specific local function such as fire protection, soil conservation, water supply or sewerage. They are legally separate from, although almost always linked politically to, municipal and county governments.

In recognition of the weakness of classic or dual federalism, and of the strength of local governments, some commentators have argued that, rather than become involved in arcane discussions on the constitutional status of federalism, it is now more appropriate to talk of *intergovernmental relations* (IGR).[3] Such a focus obliges the student

---

3   This abbreviation is taken from Deil S. Wright, *Understanding Intergovernmental Relations*, North Scituate, Massachusetts, Duxbury, 1978.

TABLE 4.1   *Types of Government, USA, 1967—77*

	1967	1972	1977
US Government	1	1	1
State governments	50	50	50
Local governments	79,862	78,218	81,248
Counties	3,042	3,044	3,049
Municipalities	18,862	18,517	18,048
Townships	16,822	16,991	17,105
School districts	15,174	15,781	21,782
Special districts	25,962	23,885	21,264
Total	79,913	78,269	81,299

Source: 1977 Census of Governments, Vol. 1, Governmental Organization, Bureau of the Census, 1978, Table A, p. 1.

to examine the political and economic relationships between different levels of government — a focus largely adopted by this chapter.

To understand why the federal role has increased so rapidly and why, as a constitutional concept, federalism has declined in importance, it is necessary to examine the historical evolution of IGR in the USA.

THE EVOLUTION OF AMERICAN FEDERALISM

Opting for a federal rather than a unitary or confederate system of government in 1787 was understandable. Government under the Articles of Confederation had been minimal. A weak Congress (there was no executive branch) was obliged to rely on the cooperation of 13 near independent states. In economic affairs this proved almost impossible and internal tariff barriers, together with the absence of a common currency rendered the new Republic almost impotent against the economic might of Britain. If a confederate system, relying on the cooperation of constituent states was unworkable, the other most tried alternative, unitary government, was inappropriate for historical and political reasons. It was, after all, the centralized and highly insensitive power of England which had prompted the revolt of the colonies. Each colony had in addition its own traditions and history which might have been threatened by a centralized system. Finally, unitary government was associated with a strong executive — not a feature likely to endear the system either to the artisans and smallholders who made up the bulk of the American population or to those sections of the elite who supported Madison's notion of limited government.

A federal system involving the sharing of authority between central authority and constituent states was a natural compromise. Hence the Constitution gave to the federal government authority to raise armies, to tax, and to regulate inter-state commerce — powers that were notably absent under the Articles of Confederation — while the individual traditions of the states were protected both by the checks and balances imposed on the central institutions of Congress and Presidency and by the 10th Amendment.[4] The fundamental problem which federalism attempts to solve — the tension between central authority and local autonomy — is still very much with us today. In the late 18th century, however, this tension took on a very different form from that presently at work in the United States. Then, a strong federal government was needed for two purposes: to defend the young republic against a hostile outside world and to provide an open and orderly market for the free exchange of goods and services within the borders of the new nation state. At all levels government's role was limited and, although some conflict between state and federal governments existed, it rarely reached the point where it intruded greatly into citizens' lives. In an agrarian and small town society characterized by poor communications and a strong tradition of localism, the federal government was a remote and, in terms of people's everyday dealings, a relatively minor authority. Today, in contrast, federal, state and local governments intrude into almost all areas of social life through a bewildering array of policies and programmes. It is not surprising, therefore, that federal–state–local relations today are very different from those of late 18th-century America. Initially, debate was concentrated on the *regulatory* powers of the federal government — and especially the extent to which federal law was *supreme* in the regulation and promotion of commerce. By the mid-19th century, with the emergence of slavery as a national issue, the role of the federal government in protecting the rights of citizens was added to the policy agenda. These issues remain an important part of current debate on federalism, but they have been overshadowed by the vastly enhanced spending power of the federal government. An examination of the more celebrated Supreme Court cases on federal–state relations confirms these shifts in emphasis. Prior to the Civil War, the most significant cases concerned

4 'The powers not delegated to the United States by the Constitution, nor prohibited by it to the States, are reserved to the States respectively, or to the people'.

such things as the right of the federal government to establish a national bank (*McCulloch* v. *Maryland*, 1819) and to run ferries between New York and New Jersey (*Gibbons* v. *Ogden*, 1824). Later the Taney Court resolutely defended the right of the states to permit slavery — a right promptly removed by the War and the subsequent 13th and 14th Amendments. Between 1870 and 1938, the Court resisted attempts by the federal government to regulate industrial and commercial life — although anti-monopoly laws were upheld and a federal income tax was eventually approved through constitutional amendment (16th Amendent, 1913). With the exception of the income tax question which did inspire a vociferous debate on the role of the federal government, the period up to 1933 was characterized by a general agreement that the states were the proper level of government for most domestic policy formulation and implementation. Federal government power was on the increase, but Presidents and Congresses generally accepted that *direct* intervention by the government in the economic and social life of the nation was undesirable.

All changed with the depression of the 1930s and the advent of the New Deal. From 1933 the federal government began to legislate in a variety of new areas from social security to public works. In reaction to what it saw as an unlawful interpretation of the Commerce Clause and Necessary and Proper Clause, the Court struck down much of this new legislation in the name of states' rights. Had the decisions in such cases as *Schechter Corporation* v. *the USA* (1935) and *USA* v. *Carter Coal Company* (1936) prevailed, Roosevelt's New Deal would have been in serious trouble, and only a last minute change in Court opinion prevented a constitutional crisis. (See Chapter 12, p. 259.)

Since this famous turnabout, the executive and judicial branches have been in approximate agreement over the economic role of the federal government in American society. Conflict has not disappeared from debate on federalism, however. The civil rights issue, in particular, inspired intense dispute between the states and all branches of the federal government during the 1950s and the 1960s. While state (and more recently local) resistance to federal civil rights laws and judicial decisions should not be underestimated, scholars have probably been right in emphasizing that conflict as such is not now the main characteristic of American federalism. Morton Grodzins was the first to recognize the cooperative nature of federalism in the 1940s and 1950s. Using the metaphors of layer cake and marble cake to characterize conflictual and cooperative federalism, Grodzins

identified the crucial transition of federalism from the intergovernmental antagonisms of the 19th century to the mutual interest and
collaboration typical of the late 1930s to the late 1950s period.[5]
Economic distress and external threat combined to transform the
role of the federal government during this period. Lower level
governments responded to national emergency not with antagonism
but in a spirit of cooperation and consensus. Since the late 1950s,
however, federalism has developed further, and cooperation is
certainly not the main characteristic of intergovernmental relations
today. Now, with the proliferation of programmes and policies at
all levels of government, a much more confused and fragmented
situation exists. Various scholars have attempted to describe this
in terms of a single metaphor or characteristic.[6] The task is not
easy, however, because of the sheer complexity of the IGR system.
What follows is an attempt to unravel this complexity by explaining why the number of programmes and policies has increased so
dramatically and by giving some specific examples of how governments interact today.

COMPETITIVE INTERDEPENDENCE: AMERICAN INTERGOVERNMENTAL
RELATIONS IN THE 1970s AND 1980s

The reasons why the federal role has increased over time are complex.
Most relate to the close connection between administrative and
political centralization and what has been called the nationalization
of economic and social life.[7] It is easy to be overdeterministic in
this area — certainly the causal lines run in many directions. The
evolution of mass-based political parties nominating Presidents
with national appeals was no doubt both an effect and a cause of
the increasingly nationalized nature of economic life during the
late 19th and early 20th centuries. As corporations began to organize
on national lines, so the need for national standards and regulations
grew. Demands for minimum standards of (say) food processing
or for fair competition required the sort of political mobilization
which could only come from mass-based political parties. As these

5 Morton Grodzins, *The American System, op cit.*
6 Deil Wright, for example, has described the period since 1960 in terms of 'picket fence'
federalism, but it seems doubtful that this produces the accurate image which the layer
and marble cake metaphor invoked. See Wright *Understanding Intergovernmental Relations,*
op cit, p. 41.
7 See the collection of essays edited by Theodore Lowi and Alan Stone, *Nationalizing
Government: Public Policies in America,* Beverly Hills, Sage, 1978.

strengthened, so the need for better and more centralized organization on the part of commerce and industry to combat (or cooperate with) the federal government emerged. The growth of news dissemination inevitably aided this process, especially after the introduction of radio and television.

While all these forces were important, the main impetus to the growth of federal power came from two rather different sources — economic depression and war. As we noted earlier, it was the programmes of the New Deal and the massive military spending on the Second World War which transformed the federal role. As can be seen from Table 4.2 public spending as a percentage of GNP increased from just 9.9 per cent in 1929 to 23 per cent in 1949, and the federal share of this expenditure increased from 2.5 per cent to 16 per cent — much of it, after 1939, as a result of increased defence spending. The other most startling trend shown in Table 4.2 is the dramatic relative decline in local government spending since 1929. Since that year local government's share of all spending has declined from 53.9 per cent to 13.9 per cent. Of course this is in effect the corollary of an increased federal role. The New Deal and the Second World War added new responsibilities to government which local and state governments were either unwilling or unable to take on. But Table 4.2 is misleading on the declining role of local government, for if we take into account *intergovernmental transfers* a rather different picture emerges. As Table 4.3 shows a good chunk of increased federal spending derives from transfers to state and local government. State governments in turn have transferred increasing amounts to local governments. Hence, after transfers, a full 8.2 per cent of GNP was accounted for by local government spending in 1980, a significantly higher figure than as recently as 1959. Table 4.3 also reveals the massive increase in real spending at all levels of government between 1929 and 1980. Again, while the federal share has generally increased, the absolute level of state and local spending has also increased. Perhaps most dramatically, apart from the 1929–1939 period, real federal domestic spending experienced its largest boost during the 1969–75 period, and this followed a considerable expansion of federal state and local spending between 1959 and 1969. Clearly, forces other than depression and war account for the increasingly important role of governments during the last 20 years. Earlier we mentioned how American federalism of the 1940s could be characterized as cooperative in nature, there being relatively little conflict between different levels of government. Governments and the public were generally agreed on the need for intervention to

American Politics and Society

TABLE 4.2 *Government Expenditure, From Own Funds, Selected Years 1929—80*

Calendar Year	Total Public Sector	Federal			State	Local
		Total	Defence	Domestic		
As Percentage of GNP						
1929	9.9	2.5	1.1	1.5	2.0	5.3
1939	19.2	9.8	1.7	8.1	4.1	5.3
1949	23.0	16.0	8.5	7.5	3.4	3.5
1959	26.9	18.7	11.0	7.7	3.8	4.4
1969	30.5	20.1	10.2	9.9	5.3	5.1
1974	32.4	21.2	7.5	13.8	6.1	5.1
1975	35.0	23.6	7.6	16.0	6.3	5.2
1977	32.9	22.4	6.9	15.5	5.9	4.7
1979	32.0	21.5	6.6	15.0	5.9	4.7
1980 est.	32.4	22.1	6.9	15.2	5.8	4.5
Percentage distribution						
1929	100.0	25.5	10.8	14.7	20.6	53.9
1939	100.0	51.1	8.6	42.5	21.3	27.6
1949	100.0	69.6	37.1	32.5	15.0	15.3
1959	100.0	69.5	40.9	28.5	14.3	16.3
1969	100.0	66.0	33.4	32.5	17.4	16.7
1974	100.0	65.6	23.1	42.5	18.7	15.7
1975	100.0	67.4	21.6	45.8	17.9	14.7
1977	100.0	68.0	21.0	47.1	17.9	14.3
1979	100.0	67.2	20.3	46.9	18.4	14.7
1980 est.	100.0	68.2	21.3	46.9	17.9	13.9

Source: Adapted from Advisory Commission on Intergovernmental Relationships (ACIR), *Significant Features of Fiscal Federalism 1978—9 and 1979—80*, Washington DC, 1979, 1980, Table 1. For full notes on these data, see originals.
Note:
est. = estimated.

solve pressing problems. The 1960s and 1970s have been quite different. Consensus on the nature and extent of government intervention has largely broken down; jurisdictions are now in competition with one another for federal or state aid; and, above all, governments are now economically and politically *interdependent*.

A major spur both to increased federal spending and to producing qualitative changes in intergovernmental relations has been the growth of federal grants in aid to state and local governments. There are two distinctions within any intergovernmental transfer system

TABLE 4.3   *Government Expenditure after Intergovernmental Transfers, 1929—80*

Calendar Year	Total Public Sector	Federal			State	Local
		Total	Defence	Domestic		
As Percentage of GNP						
1929	9.9	2.4	1.1	1.4	1.6	5.9
1939	19.2	8.7	1.7	7.0	3.3	7.3
1949	23.0	15.2	8.5	6.7	3.0	4.8
1959	26.9	17.3	11.0	6.3	3.6	6.0
1969	30.5	18.0	10.2	7.8	4.7	7.8
1974	32.4	18.1	7.4	10.7	5.5	8.9
1975	34.9	19.8	7.5	12.3	5.9	9.2
1977	32.9	18.8	6.9	11.9	5.3	8.2
Per capita on constant (1967) dollars						
1929	163	40	18	22	27	97
1939	320	145	28	118	55	121
1949	555	366	205	161	72	117
1959	844	542	344	198	113	189
1969	1,283	755	417	328	200	328
1974	1,464	816	335	481	247	401
1975	1,548	878	331	547	261	409
1977	1,555	884	326	558	271	401
1979	1,580	893	320	573	272	416
1980 est.	1,540	895	327	568	254	390

Source: ACIR, *op. cit*, adapted from Table 4.2.

which must be drawn if the system is to be understood. First, it is necessary to distinguish between grants and payments which are paid *directly* to the population by the federal government and those which are paid to lower level governments. The former — in the USA such things as social security,[8] Medicare,[9] agricultural subsidies — do constitute a major part of federal spending. Grants to states and localities include both aid which goes directly to individuals through state and local governments — welfare is the most important item

8   In the USA, social security applies specifically to *contributory* benefits such as unemployment, old age and disability allowance. *Welfare* applies to non-contributory maintenance benefits (the equivalent of British supplementary benefits).
9   Medicare is the national health allowance scheme for the old introduced in 1965. It is mainly contributory, whereas Medicaid, a similar scheme for the poor, is not.

here — and aid for programmes such as urban renewal and highways, where the state or local government constitutes the final stage in the transfer transaction. Table 4.4 makes these distinctions by breaking down federal budget outlays for the 1969—79 period.

TABLE 4.4   *Percentage Composition of Federal Budget Outlays 1969—79*

Outlays	1969	1977	1979[a]
Grants to states and localities			
Direct to individuals	4	5.7	5.4
Other	6.9	11.3	11.5
Subtotal	10.9	17.0	16.9
Direct federal payments to individuals	24.6	39.5	37.4
Net interest	6.9	7.5	8.0
Defence	43.5	24.0	23.5
Other	14.5	11.8	14.0
Total	100.0	100.0	100.0

Source: Budget of the US Government, Fiscal Year 1979, Washington DC, 1978, adapted from data on p. 38.
Note:
a estimated.

Note the rapid rise in the 'other' category of grants to states and localities between 1969 and 1979 and the concomitant relative fall in defence spending during these years. Federal payments direct to individuals also increased rapidly — largely because with an aging population and economic recession (between 1974 and 1977) the federal government had no choice but to pay out more in social security benefits. Since 1980, defence spending has increased, and in the context of a new recession so have transfers direct to individuals. As will be discussed later, grants to states and localities have declined slightly. A clue to the rapid rise in grants in aid to lower level governments during the period 1969—75 is the increase in general purpose block grants after 1972. Indeed, the second crucial distinction in IGR is between *block* grants which are general appropriations given to states and localities, and *categorical* grants which are given for specific programmes and policies and which often have strings attached. For example, the Urban Renewal Programme introduced in 1949 was categorical: it allocated monies to local governments specifically for the financing of downtown renewal. From 1954 until 1974, this money was available only if recipient governments abided by a 'workable programme' or general plan of how new development would fit in with existing housing and other facilities.[10] Since 1974, however, Urban Renewal, along with a number of related programmes have been replaced by Community Development Block Grants which carry considerably fewer restricting regulations. The Community Development Block Grant was just one of a series of block grants introduced by the Nixon and Ford administrations between 1970 and 1976. President Nixon was the architect of the main block grant scheme, General Revenue Sharing, introduced in 1972, the history of which tells us a great deal about American intergovernmental relations in the 1970s.

Table 4.3 confirms that the 1960s as well as the 1970s were a period of rapidly rising federal expenditure. Many of the programmes through which this money was spent were associated with Lyndon Johnson's Great Society: model cities (1966) to reinvigorate inner-city areas; mass transit (1966) to provide cities with more efficient public transport; subsidized housing for 'moderate' and lower income families (1968); Medicare and Medicaid (1965), and a whole host of smaller social welfare and other policies. In addition, the Great Society period witnessed an expansion of *existing* programmes[11] — Urban Renewal, public housing, welfare, social security. Many of these programmes — and especially the newer ones — had two features which, although not new, became much more pronounced during the 1960s. There was, first, the tendency for them to by-pass the states and transfer monies directly to local governments. The states had long been identified as 'regressive' or 'backward' participants in the social reform process.[12] Dominated by rural conservatives,

---

10   For a history of the Urban Renewal Programme see the collection of essays edited by Jewell Bellush and Murray Hausnecht, *Urban Renewal: People, Politics and Planning*, New York, Anchor, 1967.

11   The 1960s saw a particularly rapid increase in welfare spending. For a discussion of the causes of this, see Frances Fox Piven and Richard Cloward, *Regulating the Poor*, New York, Pantheon, 1971.

12   A reputation which was reinforced by the depression of the 1930s which exposed the inadequacy of existing state welfare provision. See Walter I. Trattner, *From Poor Law to Welfare State*, New York, Free Press, 2nd edn, 1979. Even after the passage of the 1936 Social Security Act, provisions in the law requiring that welfare funds to be distributed on a matching basis, with the federal government agreeing to match whatever states were willing to put up, resulted in massive discrepancies in welfare assistance. In 1977, for example, *per capita* expenditure on welfare in Arizona was $55, whereas in New York State it was $297.

state legislatures tended not to favour social reform measures. Given this, the Great Society's focus on aid to local governments was understandable. Second, it was within the jurisdictions of local, not state, governments that the social problems which inspired increased federal aid existed. Urban problems — racial conflict, inner city decay, crime, poor housing, poverty — began to dominate the policy agenda during these years.

Small wonder that these new emphases, together with burgeoning civil rights legislation bothered both fiscal conservatives and defenders of classic federalism. By-passing the states was bad enough, but when this was combined with huge increases in government expenditure, it appeared to many that not only federalism but America's free enterprise tradition was withering away. It was in this context that the Nixon administration came into office in 1969. The new administration was broadly sympathetic to the conservative position, and was also eager to respond to the growing sentiment that government — and especially the federal government — was getting too big; that federal bureaucrats were interfering in the everyday lives of people. Nixon's response was, first, to disband or reduce some of the more criticized Great Society programmes, and second to introduce General Revenue Sharing and other block grant programmes. We now know that the closure of such agencies as the Office of Economic Opportunity (OEO), a major instrument in Johnson's War on Poverty, was largely symbolic in nature. OEO was never a big spending agency, and its closure meant little, especially as many of its programmes were transferred to the Department of Health, Education and Welfare (HEW). Meanwhile, many other categorical programmes continued to expand.

Revenue Sharing was the major plank in Nixon's 'New Federalism'. Its rationale was simple. Instead of having a mass of categorical programmes with all their Washington and field bureaucrats, why not give a lump sum to the states and localities which they could then spend as they wished? This would cut out the bureaucrats and, given the right formula, remove what was perceived to be the bias in federal programmes in favour of the larger cities. It would also ensure that the states, who were to receive the lion's share of revenue sharing, would be re-established as a major level of government. In addition to revenue sharing, other block grant programmes would be introduced to consolidate confusing arrays of categorical grants. The spirit of what the President wanted was well reflected in a Presidential radio address on 21 October 1971:

Do we want to turn more power over to bureaucrats in Washington in the hope that they will do what is best for all the people? Or do we want to return more power to the people. It is time that good, decent people stopped letting themselves be bulldozed by anybody who presumes to be the self-rightous moral judge of our society. In the next four years, as in the past four, I will continue to direct the flow of power away from Washington and back to the people.

In his subsequent State of the Union Message, he added:

[Revenue Sharing] would reverse the flow of power resources from the states and communities to Washington, and start power and resources flowing back from Washington to the states and communities and more important to the people all across America.[13]

Although Revenue Sharing was enacted into law in 1972 and soon became a $6 billion a year programme, and although Community Development Block Grants and other block grants initiatives followed, Nixon's New Federalism achieved almost none of its objectives. As we noted, spending continued to increase rapidly. Categorical programmes continued to mushroom parallel to Revenue Sharing. And while federal civilian employment did not increase during these years, state and local employment increased very rapidly, largely as a result of increased federal aid.[14] Moreover, a mass of new regulatory federal programmes assured the continued rise in federal 'interference'. Finally, rather than the big cities and poorer localities declining in importance as recipients of federal aid, they actually received more and more money from the federal government. The Nixon and Ford administrations' failure to make the New Federalism work has three interlinked causes.

1. They seriously underestimated the political strength of the agency—client link characteristic of most categorical programmes. Federal bureaucracies have customers—local and state governments, private individuals and groups — and it is in the interest of all parti cipants in the transfer process to see programmes flourish. Murray Edelman's reference to the symbiotic relationship which exists

13   Quoted in Dennis R. Judd and Frances N. Kopel 'The search for national urban policy, from Kennedy to Carter', in T. Lowi and A. Stone (eds) *Nationalizing Government, op. cit*, pp. 173–4.
14   Between 1968 and 1978, federal executive branch employment decreased from 2.87 million to 2.82 million, while state and local government employment increased from 9.14 million to 12.82 million, *Special Analyses, Budget of the United States Government, Fiscal Year 1980*, Table 1.4, p. 258.

between these actors is apt.[15] Each needs the other and each 'feeds' off the other. Congressional subcommittees are also part of the transfer process and they too win kudos and power by maintaining and strengthening programmes. What happened after 1970, therefore, was that most categorical programmes continued to grow and many new ones — especially in the area of regulation — were added parallel to the rise of General Revenue Sharing and other general assistance programmes. Table 4.5 notes just some of the new programmes enacted between 1970 and 1976. It is a formidable list.

2. Nixon and Ford also underestimated the power resources of the intergovernmental lobby. In a 1978 article Samuel Beer referred to the rise of 'topocracy' during the 1960s and 1970s.[16] Topocracy is rule by intergovernmental officials — city managers, mayors, governors and their lobbyists. There can be little doubting the growing influence of such officials, mainly through their lobbying organizations such as the National League of Cities, US Conference of Mayors, the National Governor's Conference, the National Legislative Conference, the Council of State Governments, the National Association of Counties and the International City Management Association. Through carefully cultivated links with Congressmen, Senators, federal officials and the press,[17] these organizations and others have built up an intricate network of influence, any part of which can be mobilized should the need arise. When in 1974 and 1975 deep recession hit the US economy, it was the mayors and city managers who pleaded for anti-recession aid to help combat the serious fiscal difficulties being experienced by a range of localities. Their pleas were not for help for specific programmes or policies, but for general aid to meet municipal payrolls and debt interest. Such broad appeals, which carried with them the veiled threat that without help some cities would be forced into bankruptcy, proved too much for most Congressmen.[18] How, after all, can a Congressman, elected every two years in small constituencies often continguous with a particular city or part city, be seen to refuse aid under such circumstances? By 1977 some $4.6 billion had been appropriated for anti-recession aid of one sort or another.

15   Murray Edelman, *The Symbolic Uses of Politics*, Urbana, Illinois, University of Illinois Press, 1964.
16   Samuel Beer, 'Federalism, nationalism and democracy in America', *APSR*, March 1978, pp. 9–21.
17   For example state officials interested in urban affairs have close links with Rochelle Stanfield and Neil Peirce of the influential *National Journal*.
18   See D. Judd and F. Kopel, in Lowi and Stone, *op. cit*, and Theodore Lowi's first chapter, 'The Europeanisation of America?' in the same volume.

TABLE 4.5   *Federal Regulatory Laws and Programmes Enacted Since 1970*

1969–70	Child Protection and Toy Safety Act
	Clear Air Amendments
	Egg Products Inspection Act
	Fair Credit Reporting Act
	Occupational Safety and Health Act
	Poison Prevention Packaging Act
	Security Investor Protection Act
1971	Economic Stabilisation Act Amendments
	Federal Boat Safety Act
	Lead-Based Paint Elimination Act
	Wholesome Fish and Fisheries Act
1972	Consumer Product Safety Act
	Equal Employment Opportunity Act
	Federal Election Campaign Act
	Federal Environmental Pesticide Control Act
	Federal Water Pollution Control Act Amendments
	Motor Vehicle Information and Cost Savings Act
	Noise Control Act
	Ports and Waterways Safety Act
1973	Agriculture and Consumer Protection Act
	Economic Stabilisation Act Amendments
	Emergency Petroleum Allocation Act
	Flood Disaster Protection Act
1974	Atomic Energy Act
	Commodity Futures Trading Commission Act
	Consumer Product Warranties Act
	Council on Wage and Price Stability Act
	Employee Retirement Income Security Act
	Federal Energy Administration Act
	Hazardous Materials Transportation Act
	Housing and Community Development Act
	Pension Reform Act
	Privacy Act
	Safe Drinking Water Act
1975	Energy Policy and Conservation Act
	Equal Credit Opportunity Act
1976	Consumer Leasing Act
	Medical Device Safety Act
	Toxic Substances Control Act

Source: Reproduced from, T. Lowi and A. Stone (eds), *Nationalizing Government*, Beverly Hills, Sage, 1978, p. 19. This list also includes some new general revenue programmes.

The intergovernmental lobby's influence has been greatly helped by two other factors. First, for structural economic reasons, lower level governments have been experiencing increasing financial difficulties. New York City and Cleveland were extreme cases of a more general although not universal phenomenon — services are becoming increasingly expensive to provide while the resources available to pay for them are limited. At the local level, property taxes (the equivalent of the British rates) are unpopular and inflexible. At the state level, income and sales taxes are also unpopular. Reactions by citizens to constant attempts by governments to increase these taxes have been fierce. During 1978 and 1979 a variety of referenda to limit state and local taxes were successful. The most celebrated of these, Proposition 13, limited California property taxes to 1 per cent of its 1975—6 market value. At a stroke this almost halved many local governments' revenue. If local and state taxes are limited, then either services will be cut — not an easy alternative to pursue in most cases — or the federal government has to step in with aid. The intergovernmental lobby has been quick to recognize this fact and take advantage of it.

Second, the American system of government seriously inhibits any attempts by a central authority to plan or control spending on particular programmes. Fragmentation between programmes and agencies at the federal level and between federal, state and local governments ensures that at any one time literally thousands of different policies are being implemented, each with its own political, interest group and bureaucratic supporters. The structure of the party system where nomination to Congress is organized on a state and local basis aids this fragmentation by insisting that Congressmen and Senators are beholden to state and local not national interests. And it is not only federal and state authorities which are legislating. Local governments too often have discretionary powers to legislate for their own jurisdictions.[19] Combined with a long and resilient history of localism this gives local governments considerable independence. Mayors can go to Washington not as political subordinates but as *partners* with governors and federal politicians. Small wonder that in this context it is highly misleading to talk of dual federalism.

But resources are not infinite and some mechanism must exist for parcelling out federal monies to states and localities. As suggested

---

19   This power, first established in the 1930s, is known as Home Rule. It should, however, be emphasized that local governments make relatively few laws in comparison with state and federal governments. Their influence lies more in *political* rather than legal resources.

this mechanism is largely political, consisting of brokerage, bargaining, logrolling, compromise and, above all, *competition.* Large cities compete with small cities for federal funds; the North East with South; states with localities; Representative with Representative; Senator with Senator. This sort of highly complex bargaining world is a lobbyist's paradise, and again the intergovernmental lobby has been quick to exploit it.

3.   Faced with all the pressures described above, the Nixon and Ford administrations might have been able to hold down spending had they had the assistance of a sympathetic Republican Congress. They had the very opposite. President Nixon failed to make any significant inroads into the Democratic majorities in the House and Senate in 1972. In 1974 following the President's disgrace and resignation the House shifted dramatically towards the Democrats and the Senate Democratic majority was consolidated. As Demetrios Caraley has shown, Congressional voting on aid to cities is quite closely correlated with party with Northern Democrats generally supporting urban aid.[20] At a more general level, Congress was instrumental in voting in Counter-Cyclical Revenue Sharing (an anti-recession programme which survived a Ford veto) as well as a host of manpower-retraining and other big spending programmes which were of benefit to a wide range of states and localities. One final point on Congress: as we will discuss in Chapter 7, members of Congress are increasingly beholden not to party doctrine and platform but to their constituents. As such they are almost certainly more likely to be influenced by lobbyists acting on behalf of constituents (such as the intergovernmental lobby) than be party loyalists. If this is true, then the party complexion of Congress in the 1972–8 period may be rather less significant than has been suggested.

We can conclude, then, that the pattern of intergovernmental relations prevailing by the early 80s is very different from that of earlier eras. Governments of all types compete with one another for federal aid, and fragmentation within the system, combined with the power of the intergovernmental lobby, has assured a prominent federal role. This does not, however, mean that the federal government is always increasingly *dominant.* The ways in which federal aid is distributed are too political and complex to provide any one institution or political leader with complete control. Of course, the level and

20   Demetrios Caraley, 'Congressional politics and urban aid: a 1978 postscript', *Political Science Quarterly*, Vol. 93, No. 3, Fall 1978.

type of aid does vary with Congressional opinion, Presidential preference and political and economic climate.

In his campaign speeches and his inaugural address, Ronald Reagan made the revival of federalism a central part of his programme to rekindle traditional American values. The federal government had become inefficient, insensitive and cumbersome and, so the argument ran, should be reduced radically in size. One way to achieve this was to revive Richard Nixon's original idea and consolidate myriad categorical grants-in-aid programmes into a number of block grants. In this way, the states would be returned to their 'rightful' position as the main source of domestic policies and programmes. Accordingly, during 1981 the administration proposed consolidating 83 categorical programmes into 6 human services block grants (health services, preventive health services, social services, energy and emergency assistance, local education services and state education services). The total amount of federal money involved here was $11 billion. In addition, the President proposed that all of medicaid (medical services for the poor) should be taken over by the federal government while the states assumed responsibility for welfare.

While admirable in theory, these reforms have not been successful and are unlikely to be so in the future. For one thing the proposals were accompanied by a 25 per cent cut in funding. Naturally state and local governments were unhappy with what had become budget cuts. Moreover, Congress, perhaps predictably, amended the President's programme quite radically. The number of block grants was increased, and, crucially, many of the most important categorical programmes were exempted from cuts. State discretion over the block grants was also weakened. What in effect was happening was the familiar Congressional dynamic, whereby Congressmen were protecting pet programmes in deference to constituents, local and state governments and executive departments and bureaux.

In sum, while the Reagan administration achieved some success with these proposals, it has little hope of turning the clock back to the 1950s by massively reducing the federal role. Some consolidations will occur, but many categorical programmes will survive and there will be no clear rationale behind the cuts that are made. As is usual during periods of fiscal retrenchment, the politically weakest programmes will be the hardest hit (welfare and capital spending), but the final pattern of cuts will be the result of the usual mixture of political in-fighting, lobbying and bargaining in Congress. To repeat the point, *interdependence* between different level governments is now the main characteristic of the system. State and local governments are cemented in to federal programmes and policies; they cannot withdraw because federal monies are used as *general revenue* as well as for specific programmes. At the same time, a whole range of federal agencies (and the work of many Congressional committees) depends on the continuation of aid. Add to this the political interaction of mayors, governors, Congressmen and constituents described above and the interdependence of all parties becomes obvious.

Indeed, by early 1983, with economic recession deepening, Congress was already proposing new public works programmes which would be of direct benefit to hard pressed states and localities. Even the Administration itself was beginning to accept the need for such a programme, and in the meantime, in spite of its initial popularity,[21] Reagan's 'New Federalism' slowly moved away from the centre of the political stage.

IS FEDERALISM DEAD?

Classical federalism, with state and federal governments each sovereign and separate in their own designated area is very much dead — indeed, there is serious doubt that it ever applied in the United States. Cooperative federalism, which dominated intergovernmental relations from the 1930s to the 1950s, is also inappropriate as a description of the 1970s and 1980s. Competitive interdependence is a much more accurate label; but it describes federal, state and local relations not just federal–state interactions. If this is so, what is left of federalism? In strictly constitutional terms, not very much. Given the encroachment of federal powers and the relative independence of local governments, it is highly misleading to talk of shared sovereignty in the USA today. However, the states do remain important administrative and political units. As we noted at the beginning of the chapter, the states preserve variety — each continues to have

---

21   In 1936 56 per cent of a sample of voters said they preferred power to be concentrated in the federal rather than in state government. By 1981 the figure had fallen to 36 per cent. However a large majority, 76 per cent, still believed that the federal government had a responsibility for providing certain services for those who could not afford them. All figures from *Public Opinion*, Vol. 4, No. 6, December/January, 1982.

its own separate legal and political system and travelling from state to state the observer is aware of distinctive political cultures. Certainly, the states preserve a degree of local or regional political autonomy which is quite unfamiliar in unitary systems. The states are now also much more *efficient* and professional as policy makers than ever before. As state government has increased in size and status it has attracted more able personnel. Governors are of higher quality and corruption, although still very much a part of some states' political cultures, is almost certainly less prevalent than it used to be. Finally, as suggested earlier, states now do a great deal more than they used to, not only in administering federal programmes but in running their own,[22] but this resilience and growth derives not so much from constitutional imperatives as from traditions, custom and the fact that the states remain *convenient* jurisdiction for the representation of a variety of interests.

In an area like industrial relations, for example, state law remains vital. Some states prohibit the closed shop, others allow it; unions are often organized on a state basis so that bargaining and industrial action is focused on state rather than federal employers and governments. These arrangements fragment industrial conflict and, in sharp contrast to the UK, relieve the federal government of much of the mediating and controlling function in industrial relations. Few argue for more centralization in this area, and although the federal government (via the courts) could standardize industrial relations law, federal legislation has given the states a permissive role. *Local* bargaining in industrial relations is also important, and although working within a framework of state law, variations between localities can be considerable. Again, the significance of local power needs to be emphasized. The states may be a key level of government according to the Constitution, but in political terms local governments can almost equal them in importance. Political party organization reflects this fact. Parties are organized on a state basis which obliges any aspiring President, Representative or Senator to focus his or her campaign on individual states. But local parties are also important and can come to dominate the state party — witness Chicago's Cook County Democratic Party under Mayor Daley, or Mayor Coleman Young's Detroit party organization which has become so influential in Michigan Democratic politics. Both of these local parties have also wielded considerable influence at the national level.

22 See David H. McKay, 'Fiscal federalism, professionalism and the transformation of American state government', *Public Administration*, Vol. 60, Spring 1982.

Indeed, the most enduring feature of American IGR is the strength of state and localist traditions. Even as federal spending increases and federal programmes proliferate, state and local governments continue to play a major and by no means dependent role. Publics mistrust federal power but demand more federal aid for their state and local governments. And political parties, sometimes confused and fragmented at the national level, retain coherence at the state and local levels.

We can conclude, then, that although the constitutional position of the states has been eroded, they remain highly convenient political and administrative units for the implementation of a broad range of federal and state programmes.

While federalism has been utilized by localist and anti-statist interests to inhibit the coordinating and planning role of the federal government, social reformers should be wary of criticizing the institution of federalism as such. They would be better advised to study those political and economic forces which have used federalism so successfully. The great paradox of the 1980s is that the main critics of federal power often have strong links with states and localities which are now locked into an interdependent relationship with the federal government.

FURTHER READING

The best general introduction to US intergovernmental relations is Deil S. Wright's *Understanding Intergovernmental Relations*, North Scituate, Massachusetts, Duxbury, 2nd edn 1982. For the traditional view of the transition from conflictual to cooperative federalism, see Morton Grodzin's *The American System*, Chicago, Rand McNally, 1966. Michael Reagan's *The New Federalism*, New York, Oxford University Press, 1972, second edition with John G. Sanzone, 1981, is a well written account of changes in IGR during the 1960s and 1970s. For a critique of the state's role as social innovators, see Roscoe Martin, *The Cities in the Federal System*, New York, Atherton, 1965, and for a defence of the states see Ira Sharkansky, *The Maligned States*, New York, McGraw-Hill, 2nd edn, 1977. Donald Haider's *When Governments Come to Washington: Governors, Mayors and Inter-governmental Lobbying*, Free Press, 1974 is a good account of the rise of 'topocracy', and Theodore Lowi and Alan Stone's edited collection *Nationalizing Government*, Beverly Hills, Sage, 1978, is an up to date review of the nationalizing influences in the USA. For a defence of Ronald Reagan's 'New Federalism', see Claude E. Barfield, *Rethinking Federalism*, AEI, 1981. State politics and policy are comprehensively covered in Sarah McCally Morehouse, *State Politics, Parties and Policy*, Holt, Rinehart and Winston, 1981.

CHAPTER 5

American Political Parties in Transition

A democratic society has to provide a mode of consistent representation of relatively stable alignments or modes of compromise, in its polity. The mechanism of the American polity has been the two party system. If the party system, with its enforced mode of compromise, gives way, and 'issue politics' begin to polarize groups, then we have the classic recipe for what political scientists call 'a crisis of the regime', if not a crisis of disintegration and revolution.

Daniel Bell, The Public Interest, 1975

By the 1970s, enough had changed to usher in a basic transformation of the American party system. Let us, then, bid fond farewell to the old New Deal conditions. The system of which they were parts, along with the social era which nurtured it, having served us well, have slipped into history. And let us read well the new chapter that is opening, in the hope that by understanding it we can proceed intelligently in the quest for a full and secure democracy.

Everett Carll Ladd Jr and Charles D. Hadley,
Transformations of the American Party System, 1975

To the outside observer, the American party system conjures up almost a caricature picture of American politics. Parties appear non-ideological, organizationally weak and in a constant state of crisis. In contrast, most European political parties have quite vivid public images based on class, regional, religious, linguistic, ethnic or ideological divisions. And when new parties emerge claiming support based on social consensus rather than cleavage (as did the British

Social Democratic Party during the early 1980s) their 'pragmatism' or even 'opportunism' is viewed with distrust and suspicion.

While this is an oversimplified characterization of the two types of party system, it remains broadly true that American parties cover a much narrower band of the ideological spectrum than do their European counterparts. They are also much less *programmatic*, offering their supporters very general and diffuse policy options rather than the highly structured and specific policy programmes associated with European parties. What is true of almost all party systems is that they are constantly developing and adapting to rapid social and economic changes — a fact which leads so many commentators to attach the label 'crisis' to the most recent development or electoral event. The remarkable thing about the American system is that it has always had just two major parties — although not always the same two parties — competing for major offices at any one time. Moreover, these parties have been largely non-ideological in style and policy substance, and this in a country constantly being buffeted by the very major social changes which immigration, industrialization and urbanization have brought.

A large part of this chapter will be devoted to explaining why the American party system has taken this particular shape. As we shall see, however, although this system has retained its two-party, largely non-ideological status through history, it has by no means been static or unchanging. In organization and function the parties have changed quite dramatically over the last 200 years. To understand these changes it is first necessary to discuss the functions which political parties normally play in political systems.

THE FUNCTIONS OF PARTIES

Although often abused by politicians and publics alike, political parties do perform vital functions in every political system, and in countries with democratic traditions they are an indisputably necessary part of the democratic process. In the American context parties perform at least five major functions.[1]

1 This list of functions — although not the discussion of them — is taken from Gerald M. Pomper, 'Party functions and party failures', in Gerald Pomper *et al*, *The Performance of American Government: Checks and Minuses*, New York, Free Press, 1972, pp. 46–63.

Aggregation of demands

In any society, social groups with particular interests to promote or defend need some means whereby their demands can be aggregated and articulated in government. Traditionally, political parties have performed this function — hence the association of party with particular social groups, regions or religions. In the USA parties have acquired just such associations, although to a rather lesser extent than in some other countries. Hence, the Democrats became the party of Southern interests quite early in history, although by the 1930s the Democrats had also become the party of the Northern industrial working class. The Republicans emerged from the Civil War as the party of national unity and later became identified as the party most interested in defending free enterprise and corporate power, an identification which remains to today.

But generally, parties in the United States have not been exclusively identified with one social group or class or one geographical region. Instead they tend to be coalitions of interests, aggregating demands on behalf of a number of social groups and regional interests. Given the relatively low level of ideological division and conflict in the USA (see Chapter 2 pp. 20—4), this is, perhaps, unsurprising.

Conciliation of groups in society

Even in the most divided society some conciliation between competing or conflicting interests has to occur if government is to operate efficiently. Political parties often help this conciliation process by providing united platforms for the articulation of diverse interests. Indeed in the USA, there has hardly been a major political party which has not performed this function. In recent history, the Democrats have attempted (and until 1964 largely succeeded) in reconciling a segregationist South with the interests of Northern industrial workers. In specific elections, the particular coalition of support established is uniquely determined by contemporary issues and candidates. So in 1960 Democratic Presidential candidate John F. Kennedy managed to appeal both to the Catholic voters of the North (Kennedy was himself a Catholic) and Southern Protestants. In 1968 and 1972, the law and order issue cut across regions and classes and helped bring victory to Richard M. Nixon, the Republican candidate. By 1980 the Republicans had forged a new coalition consisting of a regional component (the West and South West), a religious component (the Fundamentalist Christian right) and an economic/ideological component (the affluent middle classes and supporters of a 'return' to free enterprise). By conciliating such diverse groups and offering a common programme, Republican candidate Ronald Reagan was assured victory.

Clearly, political parties have to appeal to a number of competing and potentially conflicting interests if they are to succeed in a country as diverse and complex as the United States. As a result, parties have tended to move towards the middle of the ideological spectrum avoiding those more extreme positions which are likely to alienate potential supporters. Noting this tendency towards moderation, political theorists have produced a more general model of party behaviour which assumes that if parties are rational and really want to win elections they will *always* move towards the centre. For only in this way can they ensure majority electoral support.[2] Whatever its merits in other countries, this theory seems particularly apt in the Unites States where with rather few exceptions (of which more later) parties have remained remarkably moderate.

Staffing the government

In a modern, complex society parties are a necessary link in the relationship between government and people. According to social contract theory, governments must be held accountable for their actions. If they are perceived to be failing, then the people can always replace them at election time. Unfortunately, accountability and responsiveness can never be continuous or complete except in very small societies or communities. Given this, parties provide the public with a focus for accountability. Once elected, a President appoints government officials to fill the major posts in the new administration. Not only departmental chiefs (members of the Cabinet) but also the top civil service positions are filled in the main through party linkages (see Chapter 10, p. 206). When judging the performance of the government, therefore, the public can look to the record of an administration united by a common party label and, presumably, a common set of policies. As the party is rooted in society via democratic party organization, staffing the government through party helps to ensure an intimate link between the implementation of policies and public preference. This at least is the

2   Anthony Downs, *An Economic Theory of Democracy*, New York, Harper and Row, 1957.

theory of how party should operate in government. As we will discover later the practice is rather different. One serious practical problem occurs when party organization, rather than reflecting the interests of social groups or regions, is instead merely the vehicle for the promotion and election of a particular *candidate*. Another problem, to which we will now turn, occurs when different branches of government have different constituencies and therefore distinct party organizations.

Coordination of government institutions

As has already been noted several times in this book, American government is uncommonly fragmented. National legislature is separated from executive. Federalism adds further fragmenting influence by giving state (and through the states, local) governments considerable independence from the federal authorities. In centralized systems with cabinet government, parties actually dominate institutions. In Britain for example, powerful political party organizations nominate candidates, fight elections, and, if successful form the government out of a majority in the House of Commons. By exercising control over the party organization, governments (or oppositions) can usually ensure the obedience of individual Members of Parliament. In this sense party is hardly needed as a coordinating influence, because a system of party government prevails. In marked contrast, America's separated powers and federal arrangements greatly aggravate problems of coordination, and as numerous American political scientists have pointed out, party is the main means whereby disparate institutions can coordinate the formulation and implementation of policy.[3]

So, even if state and local government, Congress and President have different constituencies, a common party label can provide a means of communication and coordination. In fact, Democratic mayors and Congressmen normally do have more in common with Democratic Presidents than with Republican Presidents — although we will discover later they often do not. Moreover, there have been periods in American history when relations between Congress and President have been greatly aided by political party ties. During the Jeffersonian period, for example, something approaching party

---

3   Hence the pleas for a system of 'responsible party government' in the USA. For a summary of this literature, see Austin Ranney *Curing the Mischiefs of Faction: Party Reform in America*, Berkeley, University of California Press, 1975.

government prevailed. More recently, Presidents Franklin Roosevelt and Lyndon Johnson (both Democrats) used party ties greatly to enhance their relations with Congress and thus erect major new social programmes.

At the state and local levels, the coordinating function of party has taken a rather different form. In the decades immediately following the Civil War, municipal and to a lesser extent state governments proved less than adequate in dealing with successive waves of immigrants from Europe. Hopelessly divided and fragmented institutionally and politically, local governments could do little to improve transport, housing and other urban facilities, or even to ensure a reasonable degree of public order. Political parties filled this void through the creation of the political machine — an informal 'government' based on patronage, bribery and corruption.[4] Machines depended on tightly knit grass-roots organization with the party providing ordinary citizens with direct access to the political authorities. Officials in the legitimate government gained through patronage and bribes and the party was given a guarantee of political power in return. Although hardly welfare organizations, the urban machines of the late 19th and early 20th centuries did at least keep government going in the great cities by providing an essential buffer between the immigrant masses and a hostile economic and political environment.

Promotion of Political Stability

Parties do not always promote political stability. In many countries parties mobilize movements against existing regimes and are a major force in bringing regime change. Moreover, if *governmental* (as opposed to regime) stability is the measure, it is clear that the multi-party systems of Western Europe do anything but promote stability as the Danish, Dutch and Italian systems testify. In 'mature' democracies, however, parties do help socialize citizens into an acceptance of the regime, if only by legitimizing national parliaments and assemblies and facilitating the peaceful transferral of power from one government to another.

For reasons which we will discuss later, America's two-party system has proved remarkably resilient, with the result that the country has never suffered the problems associated with a proliferation of organized parties. Although the causal lines are blurred it does seem reasonable to argue that American political parties have

4 The classic account of the machine is by Harold F. Gosnell, *Machine Politics: Chicago Model*, Chicago, University of Chicago Press, 1937.

helped promote political stability. Quite frequently, for example, political movements outside of the mainstream of American political life have had their policies pre-empted by one of the leading parties. This happened to the Populists during the 1890s when much of their programme was adopted by the Democrats, and to a number of left-wing parties and movements during the early New Deal period. Moreover, the two most significant third parties of the 20th century, the Progressives and the American Independence Party grew out of existing parties and were eventually re-incorporated into them. In both cases the breakaway was led by a single charismatic figure — Theodore Roosevelt in the case of the Progressives and George Wallace in the case of the American Independent Party. In fact George Wallace effectively *was* the party and without him it simply disappeared. But the crucial point is that the issues which inspired both movements — dispute over the federal governments role in economy and society and the racial integration of the South — and which the existing parties could not accommodate, did *not* lead to a permanent split in the party movement. Instead, either the Democrats and Republicans adapted to the new demands or the movements themselves were re-incorporated into the mainstream once the protest had been made.

The constantly impressive ability of American political parties to absorb potentially destabilizing social movements has no doubt contributed to the stability of the system, although the more enquiring mind could note that the two major parties have been able to perform this function only because there have been so few deep ideological divisions in American society. A more divided society could not possibly sustain such a monopoly of power shared by two such amorphous and adaptable parties.

CRISIS AND CHANGE IN THE AMERICAN PARTY SYSTEM

At least since the early 1950s political scientists have bemoaned the decline of American political parties. The 'crisis' has been identified mainly in terms of a constant erosion of the five functions listed above. In what is already a highly fragmented political system, the decline of these functions has, so the argument runs, led to highly inefficient government ridden with indecision and confusion.

In order to understand this critique it is necessary to be familiar with the development of American political parties. Table 5.1 provides a schematic outline of their history by identifying five

TABLE 5.1 *The Development of American Political Parties*

Period	Majority Party	Minority Party
1789–1800	*Federalist:* A coalition of Mercantile and Northern landowning interests led by Alexander Hamilton, George Washington and John Adams	*Republican* (the first Republican party): A coalition of farmers and planters based in the central and southern states and led by Thomas Jefferson.
1800–56	*Democratic–Republican:* The original Republican coalition was consolidated in this period under James Madison. Later under the leadership of Andrew Jackson and Martin van Buren, the party broadened its mass appeal and was renamed the Democratic Party.	*Federalist then Whig:* Federalists, whigs and a number of smaller parties failed to challenge the Democratic–Republican ascendancy. Victories by the conservative Whigs in 1840 and 1848 were temporary exceptions and led to the rather inauspicious presidencies of William Harrison and Zachary Taylor, both of whom died in office.
1856–1932	*Republican:* The Civil War produced a second Republican Party championing the Unionist cause under Abraham Lincoln. Following the War, a formidable coalition of industrialists, bankers, Northern and Western farmers and some industrial workers proved virtually unbeatable. Apart from Abraham Lincoln, only Theodore Roosevelt (1901–9) proved a memorable President. The era of strong local and state party organizations and machine politics.	*Democratic:* Democratic strength remained firmly rooted in the South where both poor Whites and larger land-owners supported the party (Those Blacks briefly enfranchised after the War supported the Republicans). The four Democratic victories of 1884, 1892, 1912 and 1916 were greatly aided by splits in the Republican ranks.
1932–68	*Democratic:* The era of the New Deal coalition with the South, the unions, the big cities, ethnic groups and intellectuals providing a near permanent majority in the House and the Senate. Franklin Roosevelt, Harry Truman, John Kennedy and Lyndon Johnson are all notable presidents.	*Republican:* Relegated to minority status, the Republican victories in 1952 and 1956 are attributable to the charismatic appeal of Dwight Eisenhower. Main Republican support comes from rural areas, big business, middle-class suburbanites, the West and New England.
1968–	Support for the two main political parties becomes much more volatile and unpredictable. The New Deal coalition partly breaks down with the South generally voting Republican in Presidential elections. Some claims by 1980 of an emerging Republican majority consisting of the West, the South, big business and middle-class suburbanites. Local and state party organization declines, but national party organization is strengthened during the 1970s and early 1980s.	

distinct stages of development. Such a brief summary of the parties' growth must oversimplify somewhat. In particular the outline implies that the parties have mobilized different regions and social groups in a coherent way throughout history. But this has never been the case. With the notable exception of the Civil War period, the parties have always represented broad coalitions, and they have almost always eschewed appeals to those class-based ideologies which exploit social divisions in society.

Until the early years of the 19th century, parties were considered useful only as temporary expedients, or as 'factions' necessary to mobilize political power in response to particular crises. As was emphasized in Chapter 3, the Constitution and the political culture generally in the New Republic was deeply suspicious of political parties and their implied threat of government by factions, tyrannical majorities and mass political action. Significantly when, under the guidance of Andrew Jackson and Martin Van Buren mass parties did develop, they did so in a way which largely avoided the dangers foreseen by the Founding Fathers. The new Democratic Party appealed to broad principles of political equality (at least for White males) rather than to narrow class and sectional interests. It also transformed the party into a highly *instrumental* organization. For the first time the idea that working for the party could bring specific rewards for the individual became influential. So party membership and loyalty brought with it rewards or political 'spoils' of which patronage was the most important. Clearly, delivering the vote and distributing patronage required organization, and it was during this period that local and state parties acquired permanent organizations, as Michael Wallace and others have documented.[5] What united these new party organizations was a simple belief in equal opportunity for white males (and a concomitant opposition to aristocratic political values) and in the party as a distributor of spoils. Beyond this the party represented little that was tangible. Great local and regional variety was encouraged rather than tolerated.

A party based on equality and democracy (achieved mainly through the extension of the franchise) and which adopted a new instrumentalism in organization was hardly likely to undermine the Republicanism and constitutionalism which the Founding Fathers so feared would be threatened by mass parties. From the very beginning, therefore, mass political parties in the United States built their electoral competition not on appeals to class, ethnic or religious

5　Michael L. Wallace, 'Changing concepts of party in the United States: New York, 1815–28', *American Historical Review* 74, 1968, pp. 453–91.

division, but rather by adapting their programmes to what was always a broad base of support for individualism and democracy. In this context the parties were also able to aid the Presidential nomination process by limiting competition and providing truly national constituencies.

As we know, this new party system was far from being completely successful. Southern Democrats were determined to champion their exclusive sectional interests, and the Civil War effectively destroyed the first mass party system. As Table 5.1 shows, what emerged after the War was a dominant Republican party, again depending on a broad coalition of support. It was also during the latter half of the 19th century that parties became associated with corruption and the growth of the large urban political machine. Much has been written about the machine, although nobody quite captured the spirit of the period as did George Washington Plunkitt, the notorious boss of New York's Tammany Hall. His comment that 'you can't keep an organization together without patronage. Men ain't in politics for nothin'. They want to get somethin' out of it'[6] gives some of the flavour of the time. Milton Rakove has characterized the machine in slightly more academic terms:

An effective political party needs five things: offices, jobs, money, workers, and votes. Offices beget jobs and money; jobs and money beget workers; workers beget votes; and votes beget offices.[7]

It follows that if one party controls all the offices it effectively controls the politics in that jurisdiction. Just such a pattern emerged in numerous 19th-century towns and cities (and in a modified form in some states). Scholars have cited a number of reasons for the spread of machine politics, the most important being the growing need for an institution capable of integrating a diverse and ever increasing number of urban immigrants into American society. With state and local authorities unwilling or unable to provide immigrants with good government, political machines stepped in to fill the gap. The new Americans, confused, intimidated or exploited by employers, landlords or the police could turn to party precinct captains or ward bosses for help. In return the machine demanded electoral loyalty.

6 William Riordan, *Plunkitt of Tammany Hall*, New York, E. P. Dutton, 1963, p. 63.
7 Milton Rakove, *Don't Make No Waves, Don't Back No Losers*, Bloomington, Indiana University Press, 1975, p. 42.

Machine politics permeated party systems from the lowest ward and precinct level up to city and in some cases state committees. Figure 5.1 shows the basic party organizational structure which emerged during this period and which still holds true in most states today. As will be developed later, this structure is very much a 'bottom up' affair with the committees at county level and below as the key organizational units.

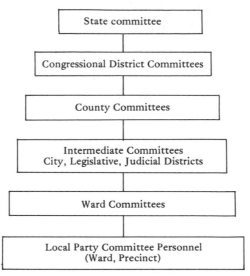

FIGURE 5.1 *Party Organizational Structure*

In spite of the emergence of a largely middle-class reform movement intent on cleansing the cities of machine politics, the machine remained an important part of the American scene until well after the Second World War. But some of the reforms introduced in the late 19th and early 20th centuries did have a significant and lasting effect on American politics. A major concern of the reformers was to remove the partisan element from the electoral process. Accordingly, most of the proposed changes involved weakening the link between parties and electors. Party labels were removed from voting lists; elected mayors were sometimes replaced by city managers appointed by the local assembly; candidates were elected 'at large' or from a list covering the whole city rather than on a ward-by-ward basis, and, most significant, *primaries* were introduced in order to deny the party machines control over nominations for office. Instead, voters were given a direct say in who was to be nominated through an intra-party primary election. These and other reforms hardly transformed the American party system. At best they had a limited effect in certain areas and regions, particularly in the more populist Mountain and Western states. *Local* party machines were, in any case, the main target of the reformers for it was in the burgeoning industrial cities that the most corrupt regimes had developed.

Primary elections, however, soon affected national parties as an increasing number of states adopted them for Presidential elections. By 1916 no less than 20 states required the parties to go direct to the voters to decide the selection of delegates to the national nominating convention[8] rather than rely on party machines with party bosses deciding among themselves who should go to the convention pledged to a particular candidate.

In fact, between the 1920s and the 1960s this democratizing trend in American political parties received little fresh impetus. On the contrary, this period witnessed something of a return to old fashioned party politics. Presidential primaries declined (to a mere 16 or 17 in 1968, see Table 5.2,) as the nominating power reverted to the state party caucuses. And at the local level parties often found ways of by-passing the institutional obstacles to party hegemony.[9] However, it would be misleading to characterize these trends simply as a return to the old model. In many ways they were profoundly different from the late 19th century. Above all, after 1932 the Democratic Party emerged as the 'majority' party constructed around a seemingly invincible coalition consisting of the South, Northern industrial workers, ethnic minorities and an increasingly insecure middle class. Local, state and even national Democratic party organizations were greatly strengthened by this enduring coalition which scored victory after victory at every level of politics. But unlike the 19th century, these party organizations did not primarily function as intermediaries between the authorities and urban masses. By the 1930s welfare and social security reforms reduced the dependence of the poor on party workers, and government officials themselves became increasingly professional and less susceptible to bribery and corruption. Instead, parties developed into modern organizations performing, albeit imperfectly, many of the functions described above. The parties also became markedly

8 Nominating conventions are the party conferences held during the summer preceding Presidential elections to choose Presidential and vice-Presidential candidates. For a fuller discussion, see Chapter 9.

9 Chicago, for example, was 'reformed', but the Mayor retained his position as 'boss' through control over the Cook County Democratic Party which contains the city of Chicago. See Mike Royko, *Boss. Mayor Richard J. Daley of Chicago*, New York, Dutton, 1971.

more ideological with the Democrats clearly emerging as the party
of the left and the Republicans as the party of the right. Indeed
almost all the major social and economic reforms of recent years
have been initiated by Democratic administrations. While hardly
socialist in conception or outcome, these have resulted in a much
enhanced role for the federal government in society.

But even by the 1940s there were signs that the New Deal coalition
was not completely secure. The South, in particular, found what
were very hesitant steps taken by the Truman administration on civil
rights unpalatable and by the 1968 election the Democratic led
integration of the South resulted in open revolt, with George Wallace
leading a breakaway Southern party intent on preserving racial
segregation. As important, the considerable − and very 'unamerican'
− ideological cohesion of the Democratic party began to crumble
as suburbanization, affluence and a changing occupational structure
slowly transformed the political agenda. We will discuss the relationship between these changes and voting in some detail in Chapter 6,
but for now it is important to explain their effects on political
parties.

It is obvious that if parties are to perform their functions competently they must have some internal cohesion. Within Congress a
party label must mean something more than mere nomenclature. If
a common party is the major means whereby Congress and President
can liaise, then President and legislators must have at least some
shared policies and perspectives. When a President staffs the executive branch, he must assume that his appointees broadly share his
philosophy of government. Such party cohesion must have roots
in the broader society; in effect some form of party organization
must exist to facilitate the exchange of ideas, and to mobilize electoral support and nominate candidates. It was the apparent erosion
of cohesion and party organization from the mid-1960s that worried
so many commentators. Three major questions are raised here: What
was the nature of party decline? What explains it; and, more contro-
versially, does it really matter − especially given recent evidence of
some revival in the national parties.

PARTY DECLINE

There are a number of ways of measuring party decline, the most
common of which are: membership, party identification, organization and control over candidate nominations, ideological cohesion

and, of course voting patterns. By all these measure parties have been in decline, although party membership is not a meaningful measure in the USA as it is equivalent to the simple act of registering (sometimes as a Democrat or Republican) to vote in most states. In other words, people do not *join* and pay dues in the European manner. Party identification, or the psychological attachment which individual voters have to particular parties has been weakening steadily over the last 30 years with the number of Independents[10] clearly on the rise. (See Figure 5.2.)

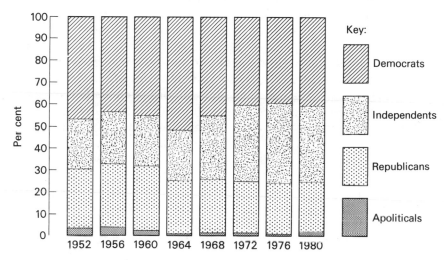

FIGURE 5.2   *Party Identification in the United States*
1952—80

Source: Center for Political Studies, University of Michican as reproduced by Martin P. Wattenberg and Arthur H. Miller, 'Decay in Regional Party Coalitions 1952–80', in S. M. Lipset (ed) *Party Coalitions in the 1980s*, San Francisco, Institute for Contemporary Affairs, 1981, Fig. 1, p. 344.

As we will discover in Chapter 6, weaker party identification produces a much more fickle electorate prone to sudden shifts in loyalty, to ticket splitting, and to voting for individual candidates or issues rather than according to traditional party ties. Measuring changes in party organization is rather more difficult. Certainly the party machine model no longer applies. Recent research has shown that even in an archetypal machine city, elected officials no longer

10   The concept of 'independent' voter, virtually unknown in most European countries, is well established in America. See Chapter 6, p. 110.

expect party loyalty and service in return for the patronage they dispense.[11] But the typical party organization described earlier still applies even if individual activists' motivations have changed.

Party organization has always been loose in the USA, and the higher the level of committee the looser it becomes. Local party committees have the greatest coherence, with state organizations effectively being coalitions of local committees. At the national level, links become even weaker. National committees do exist with most states holding conventions or primaries to choose their members. But the national committees do not really do very much. The national party platforms are adopted by the nominating conventions, and the actual business of campaigning is now more of a candidate-centred than party-run affair. In theory the national committee elects the national chairperson and runs the nominating conventions. In practice, the Presidential candidate selects the chairpersons whose role is very limited compared with equivalent positions in European parties. In essence, the formal party structure reflects the fragmentation and complexity which federalism and localism have imposed. The absence of coherent programmes and ideologies based on class, religion, language and other social divisions has reinforced this loose, decentralized structure.

What of the party activists themselves? Only about 2 per cent of the adult population are active members of party organizations almost all of which are locally based. Generally over the last few years these activists have become more candidate and issue oriented, one of their main motivations being to promote a particular candidate or to fight for just one special issue. Critics argue that these trends have weakened party organization and coherence even further.

One area where the role of party organization can be accurately measured is control over nominations. At the Presidential level, at least, the trend here is unequivocal. As Table 5.2 shows, primaries have spread to the point where, in 1980, 74.7 per cent of Democratic delegates to the national convention and 74.3 per cent of Republican were chosen or bound by primary elections. In quite dramatic fashion, therefore, the intra-party means of choosing delegates (party caucuses and conventions whose use actually increased between 1916 and 1968) have been rejected, leaving this key decision to the mass of voters themselves. As we will discuss later, this particular change has had particularly significant consequences for the state of the modern Presidency.

11   Rodney Forth, Maureen Moakley and Gerald Pomper, *The Withering of an Urban Machine*, forthcoming, 1983.

TABLE 5.2 *Proliferation of Presidential Primaries,*
1968—80

Party and Coverage	1968	1972	1976	1980
Democratic Party				
Number of states using a primary for selecting or binding national convention delegates	17	23	29[a]	31[a]
Number of votes cast by delegates chosen or bound by primaries	983	1,862	2,183	2,489
Percentage of all votes cast by delegates chosen or bound by primaries	37.5	60.5	72.6	74.7
Republican Party				
Number of states using a primary for selecting or binding national convention delegates	16	22	28[a]	35
Number of votes cast by delegates chosen or bound by primaries	458	710	1,533	1,482
Percentage of all votes cast by delegates chosen or bound by primaries	34.3	52.7	67.9	74.3

Source: Austin Ranney (ed.) *The American Elections of 1980*, Washington DC. American Enterprise Institute, 1981, Appendix E. © AEI.
Note:
a Does not include Vermont, which held a non-binding Presidential-preference poll but chose all delegates of both parties by caucuses and conventions.

The evidence on intra-party cohesion is also pretty unequivocal. A host of surveys have shown how, since the mid-1960s, the issues which bound the New Deal colaition together — and which provided a convenient target for the Republicans — have either receded in importance or have been diluted by the emergence of other, less class-based issues. Until the mid-1970s, the major change involved the decline of economic issues in relation to 'social' issues. In 1975 Walter Dean Burnham characterized this shift in the terms shown in Figure 5.3.

What Burnham was describing here was what social scientists call 'cross-cutting cleavages' or the fact that individuals and social groups often lack ideological coherence across all issues. Hence in the late 1960s many industrial workers and trade unionists remained left wing on economic or class issues, while finding themselves on the

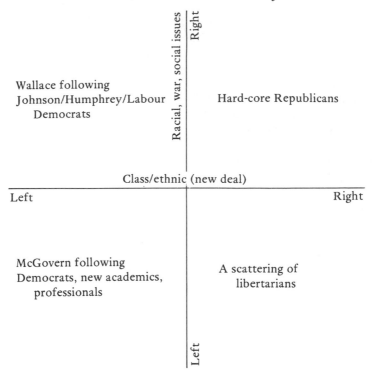

FIGURE 5.3   *Cross-Cutting Issues in the late 1960s*
and early 1970s

Source: adapted from *The American Party Systems: Stages of Political Development*, 2nd ed., edited by William Nisbet Chambers and Walter Dean Burnham. © 1975 Oxford University Press, Inc., p. 340. Reprinted by permission.

right of the political spectrum over racial questions and the Vietnam War. While Figure 5.3 is now out of date, the phenomenon of cross-cutting cleavages is still very much with us. Figure 5.4 attempts to characterize the divisions of the 1980s. Although not shown by these figures which give no indication of the *distribution* of support for these issues, the major shift from the earlier period is the emergence of a much more ideologically coherent right, organized around the Presidency of Ronald Reagan. In the early '70s, the majority party, the Democrats were in disarray, their support being split between the two left-hand segments of Figure 5.3. By the early 1980s this division continued to affect the Democrats, although the gradual elevation of the economic issue to a dominant position may provide a basis for a reorganized Democratic opposition. But we should be wary here; as the next chapter will emphasize, volatility has been the main characteristic of the American electorate since the mid-1960s and we should treat with caution any claim that a new majority party is emerging or that polarization between the two parties is just over the horizon.

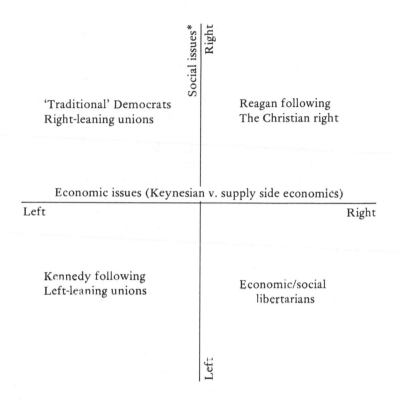

Social issues* — Right

'Traditional' Democrats
Right-leaning unions

Reagan following
The Christian right

Economic issues (Keynesian v. supply side economics)

Left — Right

Kennedy following
Left-leaning unions

Economic/social
libertarians

Left

FIGURE 5.4 *Cross-Cutting Issues in the Early 1980s*

Note: * Affirmative action, abortion, civil liberties, the environment.

So as far as the parties are concerned, cross-cutting issues continue to prevent the return of the relative ideological cohesion associated with the New Deal. As a result, there are often as many differences between Democrats or between Republicans as between the two. It is this confusion which inspires so much criticism from commentators eager to see the parties perform their 'traditional' functions competently and effectively.

EXPLAINING PARTY DECLINE

Reference has already been made to the social and economic changes usually invoked to explain decline. Affluence, increasing levels of education and suburbanization have produced less 'solidaristic' communities, as the sociologists put it. In other words, a political life based on an individual's place of work or neighbourhood has become increasingly irrelevant as the mobile service sector worker living in a sprawling suburb or, more recently, semi-rural area, replaces the blue-collar inner-city industrial worker as the 'norm' in American society. This new, essentially middle-class citizen has acquired a political life defined not just in terms of occupation or geographical location, but also in terms of his or her individual preferences, prejudices and particular interests. In response to this much more complex and less categorizable voter, the parties have themselves changed, becoming even less programmatic and ideological. But in trying to be all things to all citizens, parties have become progressively less appealing. It stands to reason that a class- (or region-, or religion-) based party can have instant attraction to voters whose lifestyles and occupational interests coincide closely with those represented by party policies. A more amorphous, non-ideological party is rarely as appealing and always runs the risk of alienating a particular section of society should it commit itself to a specific policy.

But we should counsel caution in accepting this sociological analysis. Many groups — and particularly ethnic and racial minorities — remain 'solidaristic', concentrated as they are in ghettoes and in lower paid manual jobs. More importantly, this analysis suggests some simple past when American political parties represented 'left' and 'right' in society with reasonable coherence. But as repeatedly pointed out in this chapter, this has never been the case. Parties have always been essentially non-ideological and even the New Deal Democratic Party was marked by a degree of internal dissension and compromise over policies which would be unusual in European class-based parties.

A related explanation for the decline of parties concentrates less on societal changes and more on the performance of government itself. Hence the 'overload' thesis argues that the increasing democratization of American society has placed an excessive load on what is in any case a complex decision-making system. Unable to cope with the array of competing demands placed on them, institutions have increasingly come under fire from a disenchanted public. Indeed, during the early 1970s a burgeoning literature on declining trust in government hinted that public disillusionment with political institutions posed a threat to democracy itself.[12] Although this particular argument is now largely discredited, it remains the case that parties continue to take much of the blame for public disenchantment with politics. For to repeat the point, it has been the failure of parties to provide coherent programmes, to staff the government, to help smooth relations between Congress and President which, so the criticism goes, accounts for the failure of successive administrations to solve America's problems.

Paradoxically, attempts within the parties to improve their performance may actually have aggravated the situation. By the mid-1960s activists in both parties, but particularly from within the ranks of the Democrats, became increasingly disillusioned with the undemocratic nature of intra-party decision making. Both parties were dominated by age cohorts recruited during the New Deal period — male, White, middle aged and middle-income (upper middle-income in the case of the Republicans). The new activists, most of whom were strongly committed to the 'new' issues of the 1960s — social reform in the case of the Democrats, economic liberalism with the Republicans — slowly but surely began to take over local and state party organizations. In doing so they insisted on more open decision-making structures and better access by under-represented groups — within the Democratic Party, Blacks, women, the poor and younger people. It was this quite virulent intra-party reform movement which paved the way for the spread of primary elections and for new rules at nominating conventions favouring delegates from under-represented groups (For further details, see Chapter 9. As we have mentioned, the spread of primaries actually weakened both parties as the crucial power of control over nominations passed directly to the voters. And more open conventions led, in the case of the Democrats, to party opinions and policies seriously out of tune with those supported by the 'typical' Democratic voter. Hence the now famous 1972 Democratic convention was dominated by new 'social issue' delegates (see bottom left quadrant of Figure 5.3) who nominated a candidate, George McGovern, with very little support from traditional 'economic

---

12 For a discussion of this literature, see David H. McKay, 'The United States in crisis: a review of the political literature', *Government and Opposition*, Vol. 14, No. 3, Summer 1979.

issue' Democrats.[13] Since 1972 the Democrats have modified the
party rules so as to permit a less rigid selection of delegates, but
in one important sense the change was permanent, for the events of
the late 1960s and early 1970s reduced the influence of regular
activists in myriad state and local parties. In their stead, a new breed
of party volunteers had taken over many party organizations. Paradoxically, this new type of activist was *more* middle-class than the
people they replaced, in spite of the fact that the changes were
themselves inspired by calls for equal opportunity and greater
representation of the poor and minorities. The explanation here
is simple: people who *volunteer* their services and who care about
issues are usually educated, competent and well informed. Many
of the old style party workers were recipients of party patronage
or had become active during the 1930s and 1940s when there was
a clearer relationship between party and class. As a result, the old
style Democratic activists, although White, male and middle-aged,
were decidedly less well educated and generally of lower socio-
economic status than the new style party workers who replaced
them.

Unravelling cause and effect when explaining party decline is
difficult. The rise of the social issue during the 1960s resulted
in large part from changes in American society, although also from
the way in which the Vietnam War was being conducted. Parties
and political institutions were profoundly affected by these changes
and, once affected, in turn influenced the public's perception of the
performance of government. This complex interaction of institutions
and society is, of course, a continual process and it may well be that,
not only in the USA but in other mature democracies, the age of
the highly organized and effective political party is over. A crucial
question is raised by this prospect: can liberal democracy function
properly without strong political parties?

DOES THE DECLINE OF PARTY MATTER?

To the more pessimistic observers, the fact of party decline is
incontrovertible. Pointing to the indicators discussed above, they
reluctantly accept the demise of the parties, warn of the deleterious
consequences and plead, somewhat forlornly, for party revival,

13   See Jeane Kirkpatrick, *The New Presidential Elite*, Russell Sage, Twentieth Century
Fund, 1976.

or more 'consensual' institutions.[14] In essence, weak parties erode the vital five functions discussed earlier. Presidential/Congressional liaison becomes difficult; Presidents have few cues to guide them when appointing officials; a Presidential nominating process outside the control of party boosts 'media created' candidates who may be skilful at winning primaries but rarely make good Presidents. Above all, political competition based on special interests or causes, rather than on broadly contrasting party programmes results in a politics of confusion and waste. Certainly, examples — and sometimes dramatic examples — of all these maladies can easily be found in recent American politics. The Carter Presidency alone appears to vindicate the critics.

Before we accept the critique in full, however, we should note the following. First, amid all the furore over disintegrating parties, not a single third party has emerged with even the semblance of electoral strength.[15] The institutional obstacles in the way of third parties in the USA are well known[16] and continue to apply. But a much more significant obstacle is the continuing distaste among the American electorate for parties based on class, region, religion, ethnicity or a single ideology. Second, it may be that the parties have *not* declined in the sense that they have ceased to be important in government or to be an indicator of electoral behaviour. Instead they have *changed*, and today perform rather different functions or perform traditional functions in a different manner. Indeed, recent research shows that state and national party organizations have in some respects been strengthened in recent years.[17]

For the very same forces which precipitated the reforms of the early 1970s also set in motion a period of soul searching which is

14   Two eloquent essays on this theme are Samuel P. Huntington, *American Politics: The Promise of Disharmony*, Cambridge, Massachusetts, Harvard University Press, 1981, and Austin Ranney, *Curing the Mischiefs of Faction: Party Reform in America*, Berkeley, University of California Press, 1975.

15   Excluding George Wallace and his American Independent Party which, as emphasized, was a single issue and ephemeral phenomenon. In 1980 independent candidate John B. Anderson managed to attract 7 per cent of the vote.

16   The US electoral system puts additional burdens on third parties, for all states require a minimum number of registered voters to sign a petition before a party can field a candidate. Also, acquiring strength in one state or region — the usual pattern for American third parties — is rarely enough to ensure national impact. Victory in a Presidential election is achievable only via mass national support, and without at least the prospect of winning at this level, third parties cannot hope to be taken seriously.

17   See Malcolm E. Jewell and David M. Olson *American State Political Parties and Elections*, Holmewood, Illinois, Holmewood Press, 1978; Cornelius P. Cotter and John F. Bibby, 'Institutional development of parties and the thesis of party decline', *Political Science Quarterly*, Vol. 95, 1980.

still very much with us. Within the Democratic Party, the National Committee has been strengthened and for the first time in 1974 a mid-term conference was held to discuss the Carter Presidency's progress and to plan ahead for the Presidential election. Although unlikely to assume a central position as far as party policy is concerned, the introduction of the mid-term conference does demonstrate the increasing awareness that in a more nationalized society, the parties too, however reluctantly, must become more national in nature. The Republicans have been just as aware of this need as the Democrats, and by 1980 their state and local organizations were more representative of the population, especially as far as women activists are concerned. The Republican National Committee was also strengthened under the Chairmanship of Bill Brock who, by 1980, had established good links both with the grass roots and with Ronald Reagan and his supporters. Indeed, the Republicans have, if anything been more successful at creating a more coherent national party organization than have the Democrats — although both parties are now in the business of national advertizing and direct-mail fund raising.

Recent party revival is not equivalent to the party strength associated with smoke-filled rooms and party machines, but more not fewer people are now actively involved in party organizations. Party activists may be motivated more by issues or candidates than by party loyalty — in any case nothing new in American politics — but the label 'Democrat' or 'Republican' continues to mean something to most Americans. That this is so is amply demonstrated by the continuing importance of party label in congressional elections — very few candidates dare to call themselves independent. Research has also revealed that the electorate, rather than being *alienated* from the parties, increasingly view them neutrally. They continue to see important differences between them but, crucially, find it difficult to link these differences to the policies of particular candidates.[18] So rather than the parties disintegrating into a 'shambles', they have become even looser coalitions of diverse interests. In some ways they have gained organizational strength, particularly at the national level. But their control over candidates and nominations has weakened.

All this implies that, should politics again crystallize around a few central issues, the parties are poised to resume the role they played during the New Deal period. They are not about to disappear. On

18   Martin P. Wattenberg, 'The decline of political partisanship in the United States: negativity or neutrality?', *American Political Science Review*, Vol. 75, 1981.

the contrary, they continue to function in the erratic, confusing and often inefficient manner which is the hallmark of the American system.

FURTHER READING

The best historical (but analytical) account of American parties is William Nisbet Chambers and Walter Dean Burnham (eds) *The American Party Systems: Stages of Political Development*, New York, Oxford University Press, 1975. For a well written discussion of recent changes in the parties, see Everett Carll Ladd Jr, and Charles D. Hadley, *Transformations of the American Party System*, New York, Norton, 1975. Critiques of the reforms of the early 1970s include Austin Ranney, *Curing the Mischiefs of Faction*, Berkeley, University of California Press, 1975. More optimistic views are presented by Gerald Pomper (ed.) *Party Renewal in America*, New York, Praeger, 1980. On the increasingly coalition-building nature of party dynamics in the United States, see S. M. Lipset (ed), *Party Coalitions in the 1980s*, San Francisco, Institute for Contemporary Affairs, 1981.

CHAPTER 6

Political Participation and Electoral Behaviour

Elections commit the people to a sense of responsibility for their own betterment...It seems clear that they are essential to us as props of the sentiment of legitimacy and the sentiment of participation.

W. J. M. Mackenzie, Political Studies, 1957

Most Americans don't think they have much to do with the way government operates. During the Carter–Ford campaign, almost three out of every five people contacted in a nationwide survey said they thought that the government is pretty much run by a few big interests looking out for themselves, rather than for the benefit of all the people. About two out of five felt that they had no say about what the government does.

Bruce Campbell, The American Electorate, 1979

America's claim to status as a democratic country depends almost entirely on the nature and extent of public participation in political life, and from the earliest years of the Republic there has been dispute and controversy over what, precisely, participation means. To the educated 18th-century man, 'democracy' was equivalent to a republican form of government which limited electoral participation to those with an established stake in society — men of property. Any further extension of participation raised the spectre of rule by the mob and the eventual breakdown of civil society. In contrast, many artisans and small farmers, especially in the North East, were imbued with a more egalitarian brand of democracy which implied participation by a much wider electorate. Slowly, during the 19th and 20th centuries, this egalitarian spirit gained ascendancy over the more elitist views of the Founding Fathers.

Today, the degree of electoral participation would truly shock 18th-century man. Measured in terms of the number of public offices open to electoral choice, the United States is the most democratic of countries. In total some 526,000 posts are elected, from the humblest local officials to local and state judges, mayors, councillors, governors and legislators to the Vice President, President, and members of the US Congress. In addition, many Americans vote in primary elections to nominate which party candidates will stand in the election proper. Many states and localities have also introduced a number of devices associated with populism or direct democracy. Hence, some citizens vote in referenda, or in initiative and recall elections all of which are designed to give the voter a direct say in policy making.[1] Further, there are no formal barriers to the participation of any particular social group. Property and taxpaying restrictions were abolished by the 1830s, effectively enfranchising all adult White males. Women won the right to vote in national elections through the passing of the 19th amendment in 1920. Formal restrictions on Southern Blacks' electoral participation were swept away by the 1965 Voting Rights Act and by a number of Supreme Court decisions. Finally, the 26th amendment, ratified in 1971, reduced the minimum voting age to 18.

By the simple measure of electoral access, therefore, there is no doubting the democratic nature of the American system. Yet as our discussion of political parties revealed, there is very much more to participation than mere access to elections. More important are questions of *choice* and *control* over government policy. Many people ask whether the United States can be 'truly' democratic when electoral turnout is so low and when the choice offered by elections is so narrow. Others probe further and claim that in modern complex societies elections must, by their very nature, be but limited means of control over governments and bureaucracies. The remainder of this chapter will be devoted to these and related questions. The first section will concentrate on electoral behaviour — why Americans vote as they do, what sort of choice they are offered by the electoral process, and how patterns of behaviour have changed over time. The second section will introduce a discussion of non-electoral participation which will be continued in later chapters.

1   Recalls enable the electorate on presentation of a minimum number of signatures to hold a special election to recall an official from office. Initiatives are similar devices enabling the electorate by petition to vote directly on a proposal (such as a tax change) rather than go through the local or state legislature. Initiatives are, in fact, a type of referendum and are often referred to as such.

PATTERNS OF AMERICAN ELECTORAL BEHAVIOUR

Basic Questions

Observers of voting behaviour usually first ask the simplest and most obvious question, 'who has voted for which party'? So we are used to reading opinion poll findings which indicate that support for a particular party has risen or fallen or that some region, ethnic or social group has shifted its allegiance away from or towards a party. Survey or poll data can be an invaluable aid when answering these questions, and have helped to establish some very general norms or expectations about people's voting behaviour. So, Table 6.1, showing the distribution of votes by social group over the 1976 and 1980 Presidential elections, confirms tendencies which apply in most democratic countries: older, higher socio-economic status, White voters tend to be more conservative than younger, lower status group ethnic minority voters. Table 6.1 also reveals patterns which may be peculiarly American: Jews and Roman Catholics are more liberal than Protestants; the West of the USA appears markedly more conservative than the East. But even these general trends provoke a number of deeper questions. What, precisely, is meant by conservative and liberal in the American context? To what extent does the *party* as opposed to candidates and issues determine voting behaviour? It must be that the balance of influence shifts quite markedly between the three for in 1980, of those considering themselves Democrats, only 69 per cent voted for Jimmy Carter, compared with 82 per cent in 1976 (Table 6.1). Other questions arise. Why are Blacks so overwhelmingly Democratic in their loyalties? What accounts for the regional variations in voting behaviour? We will return to these questions in detail later, but for now it should be noted that American voting behaviour seems considerably more complex than electoral participation in other countries. In many European countries, for example, class, regional, ethnic or religious divisions are quite clearly defined and can act as an accurate predictor of voting intentions.[2] In the USA, however, the political parties are loose coalitions and ideological and other social cleavages are relatively weak, so analysing who votes and why can be that much more difficult. We can broadly categorize the Democrats as

2   Although even in Europe, traditional voting patterns are breaking down in many countries. For a review see David Butler, Howard R. Penniman and Austin Ranney (eds), *Democracy at the Polls: A Comparative Study of Competitive National Elections*, Washington, American Enterprise Institute, 1981.

TABLE 6.1 *1976 and 1980 Presidential Votes, by Groups*

Group	1976 Vote (per cent)		1980 Vote (per cent)			Change (percentage points)	
	Carter	Ford	Carter	Reagan	Anderson	Dem.	Rep.
All	50	48	41	51	7	−9	3
Men	53	45	38	53	7	−15	8
Women	48	51	44	49	6	−4	−2
Whites	46	52	36	56	7	−10	4
Non-Whites	85	15	86	10	2	1	4
College	42	55	35	53	10	−7	−2
High school	54	46	43	51	5	−11	5
Grade school	58	41	54	42	3	−4	1
Professional/ business	42	56	33	55	10	−9	−1
White-collar workers	50	48	40	51	9	10	3
Manual workers	58	41	48	46	5	−10	5
18−29 years old	53	45	47	41	11	−6	−4
30−49 years old	48	49	38	52	8	−10	3
50 and older	52	48	41	54	4	−11	6
Protestants	46	53	39	54	6	−7	1
Catholics	57	42	46	47	6	−11	5
Jews	64	34	45	39	14	−19	5
Labour union families	63	36	50	43	5	−13	7
Democrats	82	18	69	26	4	−13	8
Independents	38	57	29	55	14	−9	−2
Republicans	9	91	8	86	5	−1	−5
East	51	47	43	47	8	−8	−
South	54	45	44	51	3	−10	6
Mid-west	48	58	41	51	6	−7	1
West	46	51	35	52	10	−11	1

Source: various polls, Reproduced from Austin Ranney (ed.) *The American Elections of 1980*, Washington DC, American Enterprise Institute, 1981, Table 7.10. © AEI.
Note: Post-election poll, November 1980, *N* = 2,393.

the liberal or even 'left' party and Republicans as the conservative or 'right' party, but when the whole range of candidates in each of these parties is examined, there are numerous exceptions even to this generalization. To complicate matters further, federalism and the separation of powers have spawned myriad elections and distinctive levels of government each with a different constituency. At the national level this shows itself most graphically in the relationship between Presidential and Congressional elections. Individual Congressmen are beholden to their own constituents whose interests may be quite separate from those of the national electorate responsible for electing the President. Admittedly, it is probable that a successful party at the Presidential election will also at least be partly successful at the Congressional level, but there is no guarantee that this will be so, especially in recent years. In 1972, for example, the near landslide victory of a Republican President, Richard Nixon, was not accompanied by any significant inroads by his party into the Democratic majorities in both Houses of Congress.

A second question raised in any simple description of voting behaviour is, who actually votes? A wealth of social science and professional opinion poll research enables us to make quite accurate assessments of electoral participation patterns.[3] Very generally people of higher socio-economic status (a combination of income, occupation and education) vote and participate in other political activities to a much greater extent than people of lower socio-economic status. The relationship between voting and age is a little more complex, with participation rising from a low at 18 to a peak during middle age and then declining gently in later middle and old age. Until the late 1960s one of the most dramatic differences in participation was between Black and White Americans. Until the civil rights legislation of the mid 1960s, very few Southern blacks were able to register to vote (for example in 1964 a mere 7 per cent in Mississippi) and among those registered, actual turnout was low. Since the 1965 Voting Rights Act, however, registration has steadily increased, and by 1980 the percentage of Blacks registered to vote was only 10 per cent below the figure for Whites. Black turnout remains generally lower than that of Whites, but mainly because a disproportionate number of Blacks are of low socio-economic status.

Finally, turnout among women is slightly lower than for men (in Presidential elections 51 per cent of men always vote and only 48 per cent of women). However, the gap has been closing and compared with differences based on socio-economic status and age, voter participation rates between men and women are comparatively close.

A third basic question is: How many of the people actually vote? In the USA turnout is notoriously low for all elections. Even the

---

3 See in particular Sidney Verba and Norman H. Nie, *Participation in America: Political Democracy and Social Equality*, New York Harper and Row, 1972.

contest perceived by most people as the most significant — electing the President — hardly inspires a high level of mass participation. Since 1960 turnout has been declining, and now rarely exceeds 60 per cent for Presidential elections and 50 per cent for Congressional contests (Table 6.2). At the state and local levels turnout is even lower and can fall as low as 20 per cent. This seeming political apathy has long puzzled and disturbed American political scientists.

TABLE 6.2 *Turnout in Presidential and House Elections, 1930—78 (percentage of voting age population)*

Year	Presidential Elections	House Elections
1930	—	33.7
1932	52.4	49.7
1934	—	41.4
1936	56.9	53.5
1938	—	44.0
1940	58.9	55.4
1942	—	32.5
1944	56.0	52.7
1946	—	37.1
1948	51.1	48.1
1950	—	41.1
1952	61.6	57.6
1954	—	41.7
1956	59.3	55.9
1958	—	43.0
1960	62.6	58.5
1962	—	45.4
1964	61.9	57.8
1966	—	45.4
1968	60.9	55.1
1970	—	43.5
1972	55.4	50.9
1974	—	36.1
1976	54.4	49.5
1978	—	35.1
1980	51.8	45.4
1982	—	40.9

Sources: Adapted from various sources including various editions of the *Statistical Abstract of the United States*, Washington DC, US Government Printing Office.

Explanations usually fall into one of two categories — institutional and ideological/psychological. The institutional barriers to voting are, in fact, considerable, although claims that the formidable *number* of elections reduces turnout are probably erroneous. After all, turnout at Presidential elections remains low in spite of their relative infrequency and the disproportionate amount of publicity and attention paid to them by political parties and the media. More significant are America's voter registration laws. Under the laws of individual states voters must themselves make the decision to register and most states apply minimum residency requirements. Although for Presidential elections this requirement has been reduced by Congress to only 30 days, the fact remains that in a mobile, open society many people fail to register or to register in time. Indeed only about 71 per cent of eligible voters were registered in 1980.[4] Unlike most European countries, there is no automatic nationally organized compulsory registration system and recent studies have shown that were such a system introduced, turnout may increase by between 10 per cent and 12 per cent.

Even an increase of this magnitude would not bring the USA up to the 70—90 per cent turnout levels characteristic of Western European countries, so we must look beyond institutional factors for an explanation of low voting levels. The most common alternative explanation is that it is simply not rational to vote when the choice offered is so limited. Certainly the relative absence of well defined and deep rooted social cleavages articulated by class, ethnic or regionally based parties reduces the direct and immediate interest the voter has in ensuring that 'his' or 'her' party is represented in government. American parties and candidates rarely promise social revolution; nor do they often promise to defend well defined sectional, class, religious or ethnic interests. Given this, it is not so surprising that turnout is low compared with (say) a country such as the Netherlands where the religious divide between the Protestant and Catholic populations has traditionally been articulated by distinctive political parties.

To say that it is not *rational* to vote does, however, make certain assumptions about peoples' perceptions of parties and elections. It implies, indeed, a rather sophisticated electorate who weigh up the costs and benefits of voting for a particular party or candidate. Yet the first surveys of the American voter found just the opposite: most non-voters were apathetic and ill informed

4   Of a sample of voters, *New York Times/CBS New Poll*, November 1980.

about politics.[5] Rather than their non-participation being a rational calculation, it was a symptom of their isolation from political life. More recently, research has questioned this assumption and there is now evidence that both voters and non-voters are more sophisticated than was previously thought. They are, in particular, more ideological having a deeper appreciation of both issues and where individual candidates and parties stand in relation to issues. To understand this controversy properly, it is necessary to examine voting behaviour over several decades and to ask some more complex questions about the American electorate.

More Difficult Questions:
'The American Voter' Model and the New Deal Coalition

During the 1950s and early 1960s a number of studies were published whose findings established a 'model' of American voting behaviour. The unique contribution of this work was to explain the voting of individual citizens in terms of *psychological* orientations. By asking survey respondents how they felt about parties, candidates and issues and then relating these sentiments to actual political behaviour it was possible to built up a cognitive picture of how individuals thought about politics. The results were surprising, to say the least. In a more recent study, Nie, Verba and Petrocik[6] summarized the findings thus:

The American public had a remarkably unsophisticated view of political matters characterized by an inability to consider such matters in broad abstract terms... Citizens had inconsistent views when one looked across a range of issues...Most Americans had strong, long term commitments to one of the major political parties and this commitment served as a guide to their political behaviour...Citizens felt relatively satisfied with the political system and relatively efficacious.

Very few — a mere 2.5 per cent of the *American Voters'* sample were categorized as ideologues, or people who thought about politics in abstract terms. Most evaluated candidates and parties in terms of

5   This was a major conclusion of the most important of the early voting studies, Angus Campbell, Philip Converse, Warren Miller and Donald Stokes, *The American Voter*, New York, John Wiley, 1960.
6   Norman H. Nie, Sidney Verba and John R. Petrocik, *The Changing American Voter*, Cambridge, Massachusetts, Harvard University Press, enlarged edition, 1979, Chapter 2. The main works summarized were: *The American Voter, op. cit*; Gabriel Almond and Sidney Verba, *The Civic Culture*, Princeton, University Press, 1963; Robert A. Dahl, *Who Governs?* New Haven, Yale University Press, 1961; David E. Apter (ed.) *Ideology and Discontent*, New York, Free Press, 1964.

the benefits they brought to social groups (42 per cent) or in terms of the 'nature of the times' (24 per cent). In other words most voters had little sense of 'left' and 'right' or the role that parties and candidates might play in moving society in a particular direction. Instead, immediate or recent events or simple promises by politicians to lower taxation, say, or to increase social spending influenced voters. Reinforcement of this analysis was provided by studies showing that voters were often inconsistent in their views across issues. Some citizens favouring increased social spending also wanted a reduced role for government in society; anti-communists were not always in favour of an increased role for the United States as international policeman. Most importantly of all, when attitudes on all issues were examined it was not possible to find any pattern consistent with a coherently thought out ideology, whether liberal, conservative, socialist or whatever.[7]

The image projected, therefore, is one of a rather ill-informed voter who thinks rather little about politics. However, in one important respect American voters were found to be consistent: in their attachment to political parties, voters displayed enduring loyalties. Labelling this phenomenon, *party identification*, voting analysts discovered that people acquired a positive or negative psychological attachment to a party early in childhood which remained with them throughout their lives. In essence citizens were *socialized* by family and other social cues into thinking of themselves as Democrats or Republicans, a phenomenon which may account for the fact that 78 per cent of respondents to a 1958 survey had the same party identification as their parents.[8] Not all voters were found to be strong party identifiers. Some identified less clearly with a party, while others considered themselves either independent or independently supportive of one or other of the parties (Table 6.3).

We will discuss this changing pattern of party identification later, but for now note the consistency of Democratic support which constitutes a clear majority for most of the period (Strong, Weak and Independent Democrats). As these figures are for voting in Presidential elections they raise an interesting question: how is it that the Republicans managed to win in 1952 and 1956 (Table 6.4) given the inbuilt Democrat majority implied by the preponderance of Democratic identifiers?

---

7 Philip Converse, 'The nature of belief systems in mass publics', in David E. Apter (ed.) *Ideology and Discontent*, p. 543.
8 *The American Voter, op. cit*, p. 147.

TABLE 6.3   Party Identification, Percentage Distribution, 1952–82

Party Identification	1952	54	56	58	60	62	64	66	68	70	72	74	76	78	80	82[a]
Strong Democrat	22	22	21	23	21	23	26	18	20	20	15	17	15	15	18	
Weak Democrat	25	25	23	24	25	23	25	27	25	23	25	21	25	24	23	48 (Democrat)
Independent Democrat	10	9	7	7	8	8	9	9	10	10	11	13	12	14	11	
Independent Independent	5	7	9	8	8	8	8	12	11	13	13	15	14	14	13	26 (Independent)
Independent Republican	7	6	8	4	7	6	6	7	9	8	11	9	10	10	10	
Weak Republican	14	14	14	16	13	16	13	15	14	15	13	14	14	13	14	
Strong Republican	13	13	15	13	14	12	11	10	10	10	10	8	9	8	8	26 (Republican)
Apoliticals/Don't Know	4	4	3	5	4	4	2	2	1	1	2	3	1	3	3	

Source: Center for Political Studies, University of Michigan.

Note:

[a] Figures for 1982 are taken from a Gallup Poll, 25–28 June 1982. They are not strictly compatible with the Michigan figures and are included only as a guide to post-1980 trends.

Survey question: 'Generally speaking, do you usually think of yourself as a Republican, a Democrat, an Independent, or what? If a Republican or Democrat, would you call yourself a strong or not very strong Republican or Democrat? If Independent, do you think of yourself as closer to the Republican or Democratic Party?'

In answering this question political scientists have stressed that party identification is very much a psychological orientation to politics. There may be elections when voters deviate from their normal identification because of the particular appeal of the candidate (as was the case in the 1950s with Dwight Eisenhower) or because of the importance of certain issues (for example law and order in 1968). Obviously, however, the Democratic majority must come from somewhere; it cannot be purely psychological. The answer is that there have been certain periods in American history when rapid social and economic changes have forged new political coalitions. During these periods orientations towards parties change as the parties themselves come to represent an emergent social group or region. By implication, during these years of turbulence, the voter is indeed guided by the issues and by objective economic and social circumstances. Political scientists have called such transitions periods of *re-alignment* when new electoral majorities are built. Between 1896 and 1928 the Republican Party reigned supreme. Urbanization, depression, the naturalization and integration of new immigrant groups and the emergence of an organized working class transformed party politics during the 1920s and early 1930s, however, and culminated in the resounding Democratic victory of 1932 (Table 6.4). From the late 1920s the Democrats became the party associated with the urban working class, trade unions and the underprivileged. The near invincibility of what was to be called the New Deal coalition was assured because of the support guaranteed by the traditionally Democratic South. By the mid-1930s the intellectual establishment and many members of an insecure middle class had joined the coalition resulting in the *maintaining* elections of 1936, 1940, 1944 and 1948. Not until incumbent Democrats (most notably Harry Truman) began to support civil rights for Southern Blacks did the first cracks in the majority appear (in 1948).

The Republican victories of 1952 and 1956 were, according to the scholars, *deviating* elections. In other words, the Democrats remained the 'natural' majority party, but the specific circumstances of these elections allowed the Republicans to triumph. Eisenhower was an avuncular, charismatic war hero; in contrast, Adlai Stephenson, the Democratic candidate, projected an aloof, intellectual and narrowly Eastern establishment image. This personality contrast was, above all, responsible for the Republican victories. Significantly, these successes were only partly repeated at the Congressional level. Following Republican victories in 1946 and 1952, after 1954 Congress was firmly controlled by the Democrats.

The Decline of Partisanship and the New Deal Coalition

This neat and appealing theory of electoral behaviour seemed to be reinforced by the 1960 and 1964 Presidential elections. Democratic victories returned, with the Republicans reverting to their normal status as the minority party. However, from about 1964 onwards a number of developments appear which in total present a rather serious challenge to the accepted theory. In particular we note the following:

Partisanship declines. A popular interpretation of Richard Nixon's victory in 1968 was that it heralded a new Republican majority.[9] More citizens were suburban, middle class and conservative, so the Republicans should find themselves ascendant. Moreover, the South, so long solidly Democratic, could no longer tolerate the integration-ist policies of Democratic Presidents.

Superficially, the 1972 election seemed to reinforce these trends (Table 6.4). Yet 1968 and 1972 were not classic *re-aligning elections* like 1932. The number of Republican party identifiers far from increasing decreased slightly during these years (Table 6.3) and the Democrats retained their dominance of Congress. Similarly at the state level there was little evidence of an unstoppable Republican surge. Note, however, that Democratic Party identification also declined during the 1960s. This fact, together with the rise of Inde-pendent identifiers has led some commentators to speculate that what was occurring was party *de-alignment*, or the slow demise of party identification as a key indicator of political preference. We will return to this point later. Further evidence of declining partisanship was provided by the rise in 'ticket splitting' or the increasing ten-dency for voters to divide their loyalties between candidates of different parties. Often, voters supported Presidential candidates from one party but Congressional or state candidates from another.

Increasing evidence of ideological voting. In their 1976 work, *The Changing American Voter*, Nie, Verba and Petrocik discovered that from about 1964 voters showed a significantly increased consistency in their views on domestic and foreign policy issues. Unlike the rather unthinking citizen portrayed by *The American Voter*, the public appeared more able to see the connections between issues,

9   See, in particular, Kevin Phillips, *The Emerging Republican Majority*, New York, Double-day Anchor, 1970.

TABLE 6.4 *Presidential Election Results, 1928–80*

Year	Presidential Candidates	Party	Electoral vote	Popular vote	Percentage share	No. of States won[a]
1928	Herbert Hoover	Republican	444	21,392,190	58.2	42
	Alfred E. Smith	Democratic	87	15,016,443	40.8	6 (all Southern)
	Norman Thomas	Socialist	0	267,420	1.0	0
32	Franklin D. Roosevelt	Democratic	472	22,821,857	57.3	42
	Herbert Hoover	Republican	59	15,761,841	39.6	6 (all North Eastern)
	Norman Thomas	Socialist	0	884,781	2.2	0
36	Franklin D. Roosevelt	Democratic	523	27,751,597	60.7	46
	Alfred M. Landon	Republican	8	16,679,583	36.4	2 (Maine and Vermont)
	Norman Thomas	Socialist	0	187,720	0.5	0
40	Franklin D. Roosevelt	Democratic	449	27,244,160	54.7	38
	Wendell L. Wilkie	Republican	82	22,305,198	44.8	10
	Norman Thomas	Socialist	0	99,557	0.2	0
44	Franklin D. Roosevelt	Democratic	432	25,602,504	52.8	36
	Thomas E. Dewey	Republican	99	22,006,285	44.5	12
	Norman Thomas	Socialist	0	80,518	0.2	0
48	Harry S. Truman	Democratic	303	24,179,345	49.5	32
	Thomas E. Dewey	Republican	189	21,991,291	45.1	12
	J. Strom Thurmond	States' Rights Dem.	39	1,176,125	2.4	4 (all Southern)
	Henry A. Wallace	Progressive	0	1,157,326	2.4	0
	Norman Thomas	Socialist	0	139,572	0.2	0
52	Dwight D. Eisenhower	Republican	442	33,936,234	55.2	40
	Adlai E. Stevenson	Democratic	89	27,314,992	44.5	8 (all Southern)

Year	Candidate	Party	Electoral College	Popular vote	%	States
56	Dwight D. Eisenhower	Republican	457	35,590,472	57.4	41
	Adlai E. Stevenson	Democratic	73	26,022,752	42.0	7 (all Southern)
60	John F. Kennedy	Democratic	303	34,226,731	49.9	23[b]
	Richard M. Nixon	Republican	219	34,108,157	49.6	26
64	Lyndon B. Johnson	Democratic	486	43,129,484	61.1	46
	Barry M. Goldwater	Republican	52	27,178,188	38.5	5 (Southern and Arizona)
68	Richard M. Nixon	Republican	301	31,785,480	43.3	32
	Hubert M. Humphrey	Democratic	191	31,275,166	42.7	14
	George C. Wallace	American Independent	46	9,906,473	13.5	5 (all Southern)
72	Richard M. Nixon	Republican	520	47,169,911	61.3	49
	George McGovern	Democratic	17	29,170,383	37.3	2 (DC and Massachusetts)
	John G. Schmitz	American	0	1,099,482	1.4	0
76	Jimmy Carter	Democratic	297	40,830,763	50.1	24
	Gerald R. Ford	Republican	240	39,147,973	48.0	27
	Eugene J. McCarthy	Independent	0	756,631	1.0	0
80	Ronald Reagan	Republican	489	42,951,145	51.0	46
	Jimmy Carter	Democratic	49	34,663,037	41.0	5
	John B. Anderson	Independent	0	5,551,551	7.0	0

Notes:

a From 1960 includes Alaska and Hawaii. From 1964 includes Washington DC.

b 15 Electoral College votes were cast for segregationist candidate Harry F. Byrd, including 8 in Mississippi which he effectively 'won'.

parties and candidates and to view the world in terms of broad ideological categories such as 'liberal' or 'conservative'. Certainly, Presidential elections took on a more ideological stance after 1964. The Goldwater–Johnson contest of that year was clearly a conflict between conservative and liberal as were the later contests between Humphrey, Nixon and Wallace and, more especially, between McGovern and Nixon. In 1976 there was a marked decline in ideological voting, almost certainly because the two candidates projected rather bland images and few issues clearly divided them. 1980 saw a return to a clear-cut choice, however, with the conservative Ronald Reagan facing an incumbent President, Jimmy Carter, identified – albeit reluctantly on his part – with the liberal cause.

Declining partisanship and the rise of what has been called 'issue voting' raises a number of questions. One of the most important of these we addressed in the last chapter – the failure of the political parties to exploit the new interest in politics by providing coherent and ideologically consistent programmes to the electorate. Indeed to a European observer the combination of more ideological voters but declining parties and partisanship should be slightly baffling. Surely parties should be stronger in such a context? But as was pointed out in Chapter 5, the complexity of the issues dominating the political agenda together with recent changes in American society, have made it impossible for the parties to know what to say and to whom. Recall that in order to win, American political parties have to build broad coalitions of support. And research has shown that although there has been a rise in ideological thinking among the electorate, it hardly dominates. The price of presenting to voters an unequivocally ideological programme was revealed in 1972, when George McGovern's evangelizing liberalism was rewarded by a landslide victory for his Republican opponent. So, rather than parties and issues coinciding and thus strengthening partisanship, the opposite has been happening. Issues (and sometimes individual candidates) have gained importance independently of parties and have often done so in a way which seriously damages a party's fortunes. Hence in 1968 and 1972 Vietnam and the 'social issue' dominated – a combination of law and order, civil rights and civil liberties. Liberals within the Democratic party found themselves seriously at odds with some of the traditional Democratic supporters on these questions. Southerners were conservative on civil rights and a large number of blue-collar workers were consistently conservative on Vietnam and the social issue. This combination helps explain Richard Nixon's victories in 1968 and 1972. Nixon's success seemed to herald the beginning of the end for the New Deal coalition. At the level of Presidential elections the South was moving rapidly into the Republican camp, and the now dominant social issue divided rather than united Democrats.

Some have argued that Ronald Reagan's 1980 victory was in a different category. He won, so the theory goes, because his economic policies coincided nicely with what the electorate wanted. Disillusioned with high levels of public spending, budget deficits and inflation the public had acquired an *ideological* aversion to liberal or Keynesian economics. Ronald Reagan's promise of a new prosperity based on free-market principles offered an irresistible alternative. Concomitant with the success of this issue appeal came a revival of the Republican Party, and because the Party became identified with 'Reaganomics' some commentators claimed that a permanent realignment was under way.

Yet as Table 6.3 shows, the number of Republican identifiers did not increase markedly in 1980. Moreover, the public's attitudes on economic issues are not as unambiguously ideological as the more optimistic of the Republican supporters claimed. Of course everyone wants a healthy economy, but if the price of low inflation — the major objective of Reagan's programme — is high unemployment then large sections of Republican support are likely to fall away. This is exactly what happened during the 1982 mid-term elections when Republican candidates associated with the administration's economic policies fared particularly badly. All this suggests that 1980 was far from being a re-aligning election, and that although the New Deal coalition is now seriously weakened, the Democrats continue to be the more successful of the two major parties at the Congressional, state and local levels.

PARTISANSHIP, ISSUES, CANDIDATES AND IDEOLOGY: WHERE DO WE GO FROM HERE?

We have so far only touched on the major controversies in the study of American voting behaviour. Unfortunately, many questions remain unresolved, although we can conclude certain points with some degree of confidence.

A Responsible Electorate

It may be that the times have changed rather than the electorate. As long ago as 1966, V. O. Key argued in his book *The Responsible Electorate*[10] that voters were far from being the fools which the currently fashionable studies implied that they were. Instead, the apparent apathy of the 1950s could be explained by the simple fact that the electorate was presented with little choice between parties and candidates. Earlier in American history, and especially during the New Deal period, the choice was clearer and people voted 'rationally' or for the party or candidate most likely to deliver on the controversial issues of the day. And, crucially, the issues *were* relatively clear with industrial workers and the underprivileged identifying strongly with the Democrats on economic questions. By way of contrast, the 1950s were almost 'issueless', or those issues considered important, such as foreign policy, united rather than divided parties and voters. The new issues of the 1960s and 1970s certainly had divisive consequences and generally raised the ideological temperature of American politics. However, we should be wary of overstressing this ideological element. As was emphasized in the last chapter, Americans have never been divided by ideology in quite the same way as have Europeans. For a blue-collar worker to support the American war effort in Vietnam and to be critical of equal opportunity and welfare policies during the 1960s hardly transforms him into something equivalent to the archetypal ideological voter found in many European countries — a Communist industrial worker in France or a Roman Catholic in Northern Ireland, for instance. Indeed by the late 1970s the American industrial worker was probably *less* 'ideological' as the social issue receded and was replaced by economic issues which produced much less clear-cut ideological divisions (Figure 6.1). How, after all, do you choose between unemployment and inflation? Or between large budget deficits and severely reduced government spending.[11] Some commentators on the 1980 Presidential election made instant claims of party re-alignment and the emergence of a majority Republican Party. Yet just two years later the Democrats regained 26 seats in the House, and 7 Governorships (giving the Democrats control of 34 state houses). The electorate may consider economic questions the important ones, but *within* the economic issue there is great complexity and, often, confusion.

10   Cambridge, Massachusetts, Harvard University Press.
11   The difficulties of pinning down what a particular issue means to the electorate are discussed in Nie, Verba and Petrocik, Chapters 8–10 and Chapter 18.

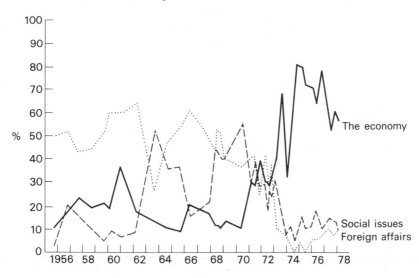

FIGURE 6.1   *Public Perceptions of the Nation's Most Important Problem, 1955–78*

Source: *Public Opinion*, Vol. 1, No. 2, May/June 1978 (based on Gallup, Hankelovich and Roper Polls). © American Enterprise Institute.
Note: Data are based on responses to the question: 'What do you think is the most important problem facing the country today?'

A Changing Electorate

This implies that the electorate as well as the issues have changed. Perhaps this is obvious. It would be naive to claim that somehow issues change independently of the electorate; there must be interaction between the two as constantly shifting demographic and social forces create new issues and remove others from the policy agenda. In the last chapter we noted how suburbanization, increasing levels of education and a changing occupational structure had affected the party system. More specifically, the following changes have occurred.

1.   Voters are better educated and more sophisticated. Free from the ties of 'solidaristic' communities where family and job determine political views, they are better able to make rational choices between candidates and issues. It follows that voters are more ideological, but only in the sense that they appreciate the linkages between issues and note inconsistencies in the programmes and policies of parties and candidates.

2.   Younger voters are even less attached to traditional party cues than older voters. By implication, therefore, the electorate will become increasingly fickle and critical as the new age cohorts move up. This new sophistication may help account for declining turnout as voters become disillusioned with politicians they know to be inconsistent in their views and unable to deliver promises made during election campaigns.

3.   Region is much less accurate a guide to voting than it used to be. During the first half of this century the South was solidly Democratic and until the 1930s New England was solidly Republican. Today the South is not unlike the rest of the country — at least at the Presidential level where it has been more often Republican than not in recent elections. At the state and local levels, the South remains predominantly Democratic, although most Southern Democrats are conservatives and have much more in common with Northern Republicans than with Northern Democrats.

   The West now appears to be consistently Republican in Presidential elections, although at the Congressional and state levels the Democrats continue to do well in some parts of this region. What we can conclude is that irrespective of party label — which as we found in the last chapter is not always an accurate guide to political attitudes — West and South are more conservative than the North and North East. This is at least in part because the West and South have attracted middle-class, higher income voters working in newer, high growth, high technology industries. But we should be wary of implying the emergence of a new conservative coalition based on the South and West. The South is still significantly poorer than any other region and must surely still have the potential for electing populist or liberal candidates. And the largest state in the West (and indeed in the USA) California, is by no means consistently conservative. If anything, its politics can be characterized only in terms of their volatility or unpredictability.

4.   Candidates and their stand on particular issues have become more important as voting cues. Evidence from the voting studies of the 1950s and '60s suggested that especially charismatic or appealing candidates could overcome party ties (as did President Eisenhower in 1952 and 1956) but they were exceptional or 'deviant' cases. By the early 1980s it would be quite foolhardy to make such a claim. At almost any level, an appealing candidate can now defy national trends. Conversely a candidate lacking in charisma or the right public image can ensure the victory of even a slightly more attractive

opponent, as with Richard Nixon's victory over George McGovern in 1972. In one sense the rise of candidate voting is quite easy to explain. The more sophisticated, calculating voter of the 1980s is more likely to choose between candidates much as he/she might between issues. Moreover, the decline of partisanship and party organization has given great impetus to politicians with the resources to create their own personal organizations and followings. Bolstered by access to the media – and especially television – candidates can often 'create' images for themselves independently of political parties. Thus in 1968 a 'new' Richard Nixon was projected by the media, and in 1980 Ronald Reagan was presented as a strong, wise, yet moderate candidate. We will return to this question later in our discussion of Members of Congress and Presidents.

But assessing the impact of candidates is not as easy as suggested. How do we know that it was the candidate appeal of Nixon (or the negative appeal of McGovern) as opposed to candidates' identification with certain issues which accounted for the 1972 result? Surely, the two are inseparable? Or have American politics become so bland that the mere promotion of moderation, strength of personality, or sex appeal is sufficient to win an election? Unfortunately, we cannot answer these questions definitively.[12] What can be said is that most candidates *do* take stands on issues – even if they do so without a whole-hearted commitment to one side or the other. Or, in the case of state and local candidates, they confine themselves strictly to constituency questions. In other words, image is rarely enough. Some policy substance or position-taking has to be added to ensure victory. It seems probable, for example, that Gerald Ford's 1976 and Jimmy Carter's 1980 defeats can in part be attributed to their failure to become identified with particular issues. Instead they had acquired somewhat wishy-washy images associated with weakness and indecision when dealing with the major issues of their Presidencies. In contrast, in 1976 Jimmy Carter had been identified with open, good government and Ronald Reagan's 1980 campaign was built on the twin pillars of economic recovery and strength in foreign policy.

5. Finally, we should note the very high and consistent support for the Democrats among black and some other minority voters. In 1980 a staggering 86 per cent of non-Whites[13] voted Democrat,

12   For a good discussion of this question, see Herbert Asher, *Presidential Elections and American Politics: Voters, Candidates and Campaigns since 1952*, Holmewood, Illinois, Dorsey Press, 1976, Chapters 5 and 6.
13   Non-Whites includes Blacks, American Indians and citizens of oriental origin, but not Hispanics. Blacks constitute easily the largest group in this category.

1 per cent up on 1976 and against the national trend (Table 6.1). Two conclusions can be drawn from these figures. Either the vast majority of Blacks perceive themselves to be the direct beneficiaries of Democratic policies, or they display a remarkable sense of group solidarity. On the former point, Democrats are more supportive of the civil rights and welfare policies from which many Blacks benefit. But by no means all Blacks are direct beneficiaries of these policies and the high support for the Democrats implies that the party is always unambiguously in favour of welfare and civil rights, which is certainly not the case. More feasibly, most Blacks feel a strong sense of racial solidarity and vote Democrat because they know that many of their number are more likely to benefit from Democratic policies than from Republican measures. No other social group of significant size shows such solidarity which speaks volumes for the very special and troubled status of Blacks in American history and present-day society.

We can conclude then, that, minority groups apart, the behaviour of the American electorate is now much more volatile and difficult to predict than during the 1950s and 1960s. Voters are also more sophisticated, better informed and more likely to make their electoral choices according to rational criteria — such as candidates' stand on issues — than before. The great paradox is that these apparently encouraging trends for democracy have emerged alongside declining parties and falling turnout — developments which have inspired a number of observers to ask the most fundamental question of all: does the electoral process provide the voters with a means of real control over policy makers?

NON-ELECTORAL POLITICAL PARTICIPATION

As earlier implied, elections must by their very nature represent limited means of control over those forming and implementing policy. A considerable degree of centralized political power is necessary even for a relatively low level of economic efficiency and social justice. With centralized power, individual citizens casting their votes in periodic elections can only hope to exercise an occasional veto influence over those at the apex of the constitutional system. This applies even in state and local elections where voters, although closer to the office holders, are still several steps removed from day-to-day decision making.

TABLE 6.5   *Percentage Engaging in 12 Different Acts of Political Participation*

Type of political participation	*Percentage*
1. Report regularly voting in Presidential elections	72
2. Report always voting in local elections	47
3. Active in at least one organization involved in community problems	32
4. Have worked with others in trying to solve some community problems	30
5. Have attempted to persuade others to vote as they were	28
6. Have ever actively worked for a party or candidate during an election	26
7. Have ever contacted a local government official about some issue or problem	20
8. Have attended at least one political meeting or rally in last three years	19
9. Have ever contacted a state or national government official about some issue or problem	18
10. Have ever formed a group or organization to attempt to solve some local community problem	14
11. Have ever given money to a party or candidate during an election campaign	13
12. Presently a member of a political club or organization	8

Number of Cases: weighted   3,095
unweighted   2,549

Source: Participation in America: Political Democracy and Social Equality by Sidney Verba and Norman H. Nie, New York, Harper & Row p. 31. © 1972 Sidney Verba and Norman H. Nie. Reprinted by permission of Harper & Row Publishers, Inc.

But elections are just one of a number of means whereby citizens can influence the decision makers. As Table 6.5 shows, participation extends to a number of other activities, particularly those associated with the local community. Historically, the local community was the primary focus of political life with both formal and informal access to local officials being the very essence of American democracy. In many respects this holds true today with some 30 per cent of a sample of citizens having worked on community problems and 20 per cent having contacted a local official (Table 6.5). For most Americans, then, non-electoral participation involves contact with local officials or community leaders over such questions as school management, zoning[14] public works projects and law enforcement. This is a continuing, constantly changing interactive process. It is also perceived by all parties to be highly legitimate, and local policies *are* created, modified and vetoed through citizen involvement. Of course this process is not equivalent to direct or pure democracy. The earlier noted biases against participation by lower income groups, women and ethnic minorities remain, and virtually no apparently local policy issue is entirely local today. Federal and state funding of local programmes ensures that local political activity is but one of a number of influences at work. Nonetheless, the importance of local community activity should not be underestimated — especially in the light of the very high percentage of citizens (14 per cent) who have directly helped *form* a group or organization to solve a local community problem (Table 6.5).

There are two further varieties of political participation which Table 6.5 either excludes or refers to only obliquely. The first involves the activities of national interest groups. As Chapter 11 will show, there is hardly an area of economic or social life that is not influenced by interest groups. How representative or democratic groups are is a point we will cover later, but as earlier implied, interest group membership and loyalties do cut across party allegiances so their activities must be considered an additional part of the representative process.

Second, there are all those political actions usually viewed as external to the established channels of political access: demonstrations, marches, boycotts and, more rarely, acts of political violence and terror. Clearly the latter are evidence of the breakdown of democratic processes and at the national level, at least, have been remarkably rare in the USA. In recent history they have been confined to the actions of isolated individuals (assassinations, hijacks) or have been precipitated by a single, sometimes ephemeral issue (the Vietnam War, Black rights). At the local level the picture is somewhat different. Until the 1960s political violence was a relatively common feature of some parts of Southern society with the black population being the victims of often systematic intimidation and random violence. Rarely, however, has local political violence been motivated by a desire for regime change. More often the motivation has been the assertion of authority over a politically and

14 Zoning is equivalent to local land-use planning powers in European countries and involves the division of land into different use-types: residential, industrial, commercial, recreational.

socially subordinate minority group. Often, these illegal acts were implicitly endorsed by the legitimate authorities.

More difficult to evaluate are acts of political protest — demonstrations, marches, boycotts, political strikes. These are very much a part of American life and at certain times have played a crucial role in politics. Starting in the 1940s and reaching a crescendo in the early 1960s these were precisely the methods successfully employed by the civil rights movement, a fact which must help explain the greater sympathy shown by the Black community for these types of political activity (Table 6.6).

TABLE 6.6 *Protest Attitudes by Race*

Percent of Buffalo, New York, citizens who say it is wrong to	Whites	Blacks
Go with a group to protest to a public official	19	8
Attend protest meetings	29	8
Join in a protest march	52	14
Join in public street demonstrations	62	21
Riot if necessary to get public officials to correct political wrongs	83	62

Source: Adapted from Lester W. Milbrath and M. L. Goel, *Political Participation*, 2nd edn, New York, Rand McNally, 1977, p. 15.

Other than civil rights, however, it is difficult to find an issue where protest was both successful and broadly accepted as legitimate, and even the civil rights movement helped inspire the urban riots of the 1960s which aroused bitter controversy and, eventually, a 'backlash' from many Whites. This is not to deny that protest has been influential. In many instances — over unemployment in the 1930s and the Vietnam War in the 1960s — clearly it has. But it is almost impossible to *measure* its influence, or in some cases, to judge whether it actually helped or hindered the cause in question.[15]

What we can conclude is that protest is very much a last resort. Only when the unambiguously legitimate means of access are either unavailable or exhausted do individuals and social groups take recourse to protest. In some cases, such as Southern Blacks in the 1950s and early '60s, they had no choice because within Southern

15 But see Michael Lipsky, 'Protest as a political resource' in Kenneth M. Dolbeare (ed.) *Power and Change in the United States*, New York, John Wiley, 1969.

states normal channels of access were closed. But even in this example, the movement needed and received vital support from established political actors and institutions in the North. In other cases — protest over the Vietnam War or nuclear energy, for example — some argue that direct political action was illegitimate because normal channels of access were available and the democratic process took its course. This last point demonstrates nicely the problems involved in discussing political participation. As emphasized, 'the democratic process' — whether electoral or through interest group activity — must always be an imperfect representative mechanism. Some individuals and social groups will win or lose more than others; some have disproportionately greater access and hence greater political power than others. What is perhaps remarkable about the American system is that in spite of the obvious biases in the system in favour of certain interests and classes, there is a broad acceptance of basic constitutional arrangements. Protest and political violence are comparatively rare. Most Americans accept the legitimacy of the established channels of political access — elections and the activities of interest groups.

FURTHER READING

The best analysis of political participation in the USA is Sidney Verba and Norman H. Nie, *Participation in America: Political Democracy and Social Equality*, New York, Harper and Row, 1972. For a discussion of recent changes in electoral behaviour, see Norman H. Nie, Sidney Verba and John R. Petrocik, *The Changing American Voter*, Cambridge, Massachusetts, Harvard University Press, enlarged edition, 1979. A good guide to Presidential elections is Herbert Asher, *Presidential Elections and American Politics: Voters, Candidates and Campaigns since 1952*, Holmewood, Illinois, Dorsey Press, 1976. *Elections in America* by Gerald M. Pomper and Susan S. Lederman, New York, Longman, 2nd edition 1980, is a good introduction to elections generally. For an analysis of the 1980 Presidential election, see Austin Ranney (ed.) *The American Elections of 1980*, Washington, American Enterprise Institute, 1981.

CHAPTER 7

US Legislators
and Their Constituents

Congress has declined into a battle for individual survival.
Each of the Congressmen and each of the Senators has the
attitude: 'I've got to look out for myself'. If you remember the
old best advice you ever had in the Army, it wound up with:
'Never Volunteer.' This applies to Congress, and so we have very
few volunteers. Most of them are willing only to follow those
things that will protect them and give them the coloration
which allows them to blend into their respective districts or
their respective states. If you don't stick your neck out, you
don't get it chopped off.
Senator William B. Saxbe (Republican, Ohio),
quoted in David Mayhew, Congress, The Electoral Connection

The US Congress is usually — and accurately — referred to as the
most powerful legislature in the world. While a common trend in
other democratic countries has been the rise of powerful executives
and the relative decline of assemblies and parliaments, the Congress
has been remarkably successful in maintaining its independence from
executive influence. This is not to deny that the powers and functions of Congress have changed over time. Clearly they have, and
the particular way in which the institution operates today is very
different even from 20 years ago. But throughout its history, Congress
has remained an essentially autonomous institution. Even during
periods of executive ascendancy — most recently during the Johnson
and Nixon years — Congress never became the mere instrument of
Presidents.

The independence of Congress derives in part from its constitutionally defined powers and in part from the particular way in which

DOONESBURY   by Garry Trudeau

the American party system has evolved. Constitutionally, Congress was given three main powers, all of which remain important today. First, all legislative power is vested in the House of Representatives and the Senate, and within this broad function Congress is given special powers to appropriate monies, to raise armies and regulate interstate commerce. Second, Congress has a constitutionally established right to declare wars and ratify treaties. Finally, the Senate is empowered to approve appointments by the President to the judiciary and executive branch and the House can impeach executive officers for wrong-doing. In addition, from very early in its history, Congress established the right to oversee and investigate the behaviour of the executive. In total these powers are awesome, especially when it is remembered that originally Congress was expected both to initiate and to approve legislation. As with other legislatures around the world, Congress has largely (although by no means entirely) forfeited the responsibility for initiating legislation to the President. Unlike most other assemblies, however, Congress retains an independent power to approve legislation, appropriate monies and generally oversee the executive branch.

The simplest explanation of this autonomy is the distinctive constituency base which individual members of Congress enjoy. In contrast to parliamentary systems, the electoral fortunes of Presidents and legislators are not directly linked. Presidents can, and often do, face a legislature dominated by a party other than their own. But this constitutional arrangement has been reinforced by the nature of the American party system. It is certainly possible to imagine a system characterized by bicameralism and the separation of powers where political party ties are strong and the electoral fortunes of legislators are interdependent with those of the executive. Only rarely has this been the case in the history of the United States. Much more common is a very loose party relationship between the President and members of Congress, with the legislators remaining essentially independent.

REPRESENTATION AND CONGRESS

The sort of party government associated with parliamentary systems greatly restricts the representative function of individual legislators. In Britain, for example, the individual member of Parliament is largely tied, through party discipline in the House, to the policies of either government or opposition. Crucially, his or her electoral survival depends on an official party endorsement.[1] So while MPs may exercise some independent pressure on party leaders or governments, it is strictly limited. Clearly, this close organic link between executive and legislator limits the representative function of MPs. The electorate may benefit, at least in theory, from the coherent

---

1 Only very exceptionally do British MPs survive the removal of party endorsement, they may survive on personal appeal for one election, but rarely longer.

programmes and policies which party government produces, but the interests of individual constituencies do tend to become subordinated to national policy objectives. Curiously, British MPs are quick to insist that they come closest to what is called *trustee* representatives, that is, they are elected by the people on trust to exercise their own judgment. They arc not *delegated* to carry out a specific programme, to the letter, and without discretion. In reality they are closer to being *party* delegates than trustees. Members of Congress are patently not delegates either in the sense of being slaves to a party programme or in the sense that they are mandated by their constituents to carry out specific policies. Indeed, the idea of a representative being a direct delegate of the people has relatively few applications in modern industrial societies. In small communities — and possibly in early New England town meetings — such a concept has meaning. But no member of Congress can accurately and continuously carry out the wishes of diverse and volatile electorates. Even if he or she knew what the electorate wanted, the individual member of Congress has but limited powers to influence what is a complex national policy process.

In truth, members are much closer to being trustees of their electorates. They are elected on the promise that they will exercise their judgment on behalf of their constituents' interests. And should they fail in the opinion of the electorate to defend and promote these interests, they are punished in subsequent elections. If members of Congress are not delegates, neither are they representative in the *microcosmic* sense. In fact by this measure they could hardly be less representative. An overwhelming majority of Senators and Representatives are White, middle-aged, middle-class and male. In the 97th Congress (1981–3) no fewer than 266 of the 539[2] members were lawyers, with a further 127 identified as businessmen or bankers. Very few (19) were women or members of ethnic minorities (17 were Black, 5 Hispanic and 3 Japanese Americans).

To claim that members approximate most closely to a trustee form of representation is accurate, but tells us very little about the precise linkages between legislators, constituency and party and how these have changed over time. Over the last 20 years, for example, it is commonly asserted that party has weakened its influence on members even further, with constituency pressures on the ascendant.

2   There are 435 members of the House of Representatives, 100 Senators, 3 delegates (District of Columbia, Guam, Virgin Islands) and a Resident Commissioner from Puerto Rico. The latter four cannot vote on the floor but can serve as committee members.

The remainder of this chapter will be devoted to these questions and also to a preliminary discussion of the links between constituency influences on members of Congress and their work within the House and the Senate.

CONGRESSIONAL ELECTIONS

Representatives are elected every two years, Senators every six (with one third elected every two years). This simple fact helps account for what are some starkly contrasting trends in the electoral dynamics of the two Houses, but there are also some common trends. Let us examine these first.

The spread of direct primaries

As with Presidential elections, primaries are now the major means whereby members of Congress win their party's nomination for office. One major consequence of the demise of party conventions (the standard 19th-century form of nomination) has been to weaken the role of political parties in the nomination process. By being able to appeal directly to the electorate, the Senator or Representative now owes much less allegiance to local and national party figures.

The 'Localization' of Congressional elections

Related is the shift towards local party organization and candidate-centred electoral organizations. Even when parties are active in election campaigns they tend to be locally oriented rather than nationally oriented organizations. Local issues often dominate and, increasingly, candidates establish their own organizations which are independent of both local and national parties.

Personalized campaigns

Campaigns have become more personalized, more media-conscious and more expensive. As Thomas Mann has shown, members now take campaigning much more seriously even than just 20 years ago. How an individual legislator projects him or herself to the voters is seen as having a sometimes crucial influence on the outcome of the election.[3]

3 Thomas E. Mann, 'Elections and change in Congress', in Thomas E. Mann and Norman J. Ornstein (eds) *The New Congress*, Washington, DC, American Enterprise Institute, 1981, pp. 32–54.

Political consultants advising on campaign strategy and media usage have emerged as a new and necessary breed of political animal.[4] Concomitant with what might be called the professionalization of campaigning, has occurred a rapid rise in the cost of elections. Mann reports that in 1978 prospective House candidates required a minimum of $200,000, while in the Senate few candidates spent less than $1 million.[5] Ten years previously most House candidates spent less than $25,000. The rapidly rising cost of campaigning is partly a result of the 1976 Federal Election Campaign Act which limited political party contributions and contributions by individuals but which put no limit on candidates' own contributions and also encouraged the growth of political action committees (PACs). PACs are committees set up usually by unions, corporations or citizen's groups specifically to promote a particular policy position or candidates supporting such positions. Contributions to PACs should be voluntary, although in effect they have become the virtual equivalent of direct union or corporate support for particular candidates (For further discussion, see Chapter 11.) From the point of view of launching a new campaign, however, PACs are almost certainly not as important as the personal financial standing of the candidate. Richard B. Cheney, a Republican Congressman from Wyoming, has put the point nicely:

My own experience in 1978 is illustrative. Because of my background, I could raise campaign funds more easily than most of my Freshmen colleagues in the House. Yet, I had to come up with $50,000 out of my own pocket to finance the primary effort. I had to risk everything. I had to make the race. So did my opponents. Because I won, I was able to recover my original investment. My primary opponents, who made similar commitments, sunk virtually everything they had in a losing cause. In the general election, my Democratic opponent, whose net worth was in excess of $1 million, spent some $80,000 of his own funds in a losing effort. The proper conclusion, I believe, is that the limitations on contributions has placed a higher premium than ever before on candidates who are able and willing to invest their personal wealth in a race. A person who has no assets simply cannot afford to participate.

Now, I know some will say, but what about the PACs? Haven't they taken up the slack? Hasn't the rapid expansion in the number of political action committees made more funds available? The answer is, yes, more money is

4 See Larry Sabato, *Political Consultants and American Democracy*, New York, Basic Books, 1982.
5 Mann, *op. cit*, p. 46.

available, but usually not until it is clear who the winner is going to be. From the perspective of the candidate looking for financial support, the PACs are relatively slow and often timid.[6]

Democrat dominance

In spite of several Republican Presidential victories, Democrats continue to dominate the House (Table 7.1) and, until 1980, the

TABLE 7.1 *National Popular Vote and Seats Won by Democrats, House of Representatives 1946—82*

Year	Per cent of all votes	Democratic seats
1946	44.3	43.3
1948	51.6	60.6
1950	48.9	54.0
1952	49.2	49.1
1954	52.1	53.3
1956	50.7	53.8
1958	55.5	64.9
1960	54.4	60.0
1962	52.1	59.4
1964	56.9	67.8
1966	50.5	57.0
1968	50.0	55.9
1970	53.0	58.6
1972	51.7	55.8
1974	57.1	66.9
1976	56.2	67.1
1978	53.4	63.7
1980	50.4	55.9
1982	55.9	61.8

Source: Various, including *Congressional Quarterly Almanac* and *Weekly Reports.*

Senate. And even the 1980 Senate results, with the Republicans holding 53 seats to the Democrats' 46, hardly reflects the landslide victory enjoyed by Ronald Reagan. The major reason for this pattern is the continuing majority of the Democratic identifiers in the

6 Richard B. Cheney, 'The law's impact on Presidential and Congressional election campaigns', in Michael J. Malbin (ed.) *Parties, Interest Groups and Campaign Finance Laws,* Washington, DC, AEI, 1980, pp. 245—6.

population (see Chapter 6, Table 6.3). Although this majority has decreased recently, it has not been accompanied by a parallel Republican surge. The Democrats also benefit from being the majority party in another sense. For in single-member district first-past-the-post electoral systems majority parties usually score more constituency victories than would be expected from their aggregate popular vote (Table 7.1). Democrats also dominate state legislatures which are responsible for drawing up the boundaries of Congressional districts. Although the Courts have been active on the question of malapportionment (Chapter 12 pp. 251 and 262), a considerable amount of discretion remains — especially over the *shape* of constituencies rather than the balance of population between districts.

Regional Convergence

While at the Congressional level the Democrats continue to do better than would be expected from Presidential election results, they have lost what was the solid support of the Southern states. As we noted in the last chapter, the electorate is now more volatile and no one region can be labelled as unequivocally Republican or Democratic. Figures 7.1 and 7.2 demonstrate this point well. In the House regional party solidarity has tended to break down, with Southern Democrats and Mid-western and North East Republicans declining in relation to representation from other regions. Similar, although not identical trends have occurred in the Senate.

These common trends can be contrasted with the very different patterns which apply to incumbency and turnover of members between the two Houses. As Table 7.2 shows, of those seeking re-election to the House a remarkably high and generally rising percentage are re-elected (93.7 per cent in 1978). Incumbency clearly has its advantages. The contrast with the Senate is stark, where in 1978 only 60 per cent of those seeking re-election were successful. What accounts for this difference? Most important is the relative status of the two Houses. Senators are elected for six years; they represent whole states — which can mean over 23 million people in the case of California, and being a Senator can lead to higher things, certainly a Cabinet post and possibly even the Presidency. In contrast House members are elected every two years, they represent relatively small constituencies (around half a million people) and the rewards of office are modest. Above all, re-election efforts exact their price on most members. As noted, they are expensive and involve intense campaigning. True, incumbents are usually rewarded

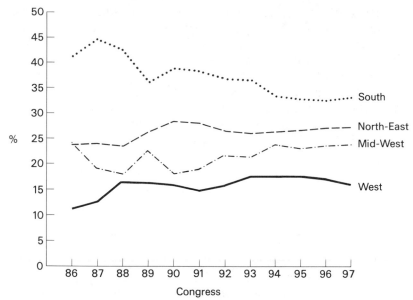

FIGURE 7.1   *Percentage of Democratic Members of the
House of Representatives, 1959–81, by Region*

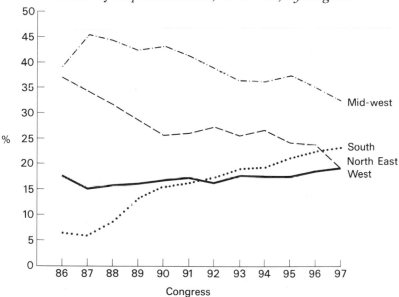

FIGURE 7.2   *Percentage of Republican Members of the
House of Representatives, 1959–81, by Region*

Source: Congressional Quarterly Almanacs (various years) and Weekly Reports.

with success, a fact which accounts for the decline in the number of genuinely competitive seats. Probably only one quarter of seats are now seriously contested (not withstanding primary challenges). Yet incumbent members cannot afford to drop their guards. When seeking re-election they must look like winners, project themselves on television and generally work very hard indeed.

Given the electoral advantages of incumbency, the rise in the number of Representatives not seeking re-election might seem surprising (Table 7.2). But with the rewards of the job low and the

TABLE 7.2   *House Incumbents Re-elected, Defeated or Retired, 1946–82*

| | | Sought Re-election | | | | Re-elected | |
Year	Retired[a]	Total	Defeated in primaries	Defeated in general election	Total	Percentage of those seeking re-election	Percentage of House membership
1946	32	398	18	52	328	82.4	75.4
1948	29	400	15	68	317	79.2	72.9
1950	29	400	6	32	362	90.5	83.2
1952	42	389	9	26	354	91.0	81.4
1954	24	407	6	22	379	93.1	87.1
1956	21	411	6	16	389	94.6	89.4
1958	33	396	3	37	356	89.9	81.9
1960	26	405	5	25	375	92.6	86.2
1962	24	402	12	22	368	91.5	84.6
1964	33	397	8	45	344	86.6	79.1
1966	22	411	8	41	362	88.1	83.2
1968	23	409	4	9	396	96.8	91.0
1970	29	401	10	12	379	94.5	87.1
1972	40	390	12	13	365	93.6	83.9
1974	43	391	8	40	343	87.7	78.9
1976	47	384	3	13	368	95.8	84.6
1978	49	382	5	19	358	93.7	82.3
1980	34	398	6	31	361	90.7	83.0
1982	40	393	10	29	354	90.1	81.4

Source: John F. Bibby, Thomas Mann and Norman J. Ornstein, *Vital Statistics on Congress 1980*, Washington DC, American Enterprise Insitute; 1982 data from *National Journal*, 6 Nov. 1982. © AEI.
Note:
a   Does not include persons who died or resigned from office before the election.

costs high, many simply give up and move back into legal practice or on to a job in state government or business. Predictably, few Senators give up their seats voluntarily and most Senate places are hotly contested. This might not seem to square up with the 10 Senators who chose to retire in 1978 (Table 7.3). But some of these were old or in ill health (Senators are generally older than Representatives).

TABLE 7.3   *Senate Incumbents Re-elected,*
Defeated or Retired, 1946—82

Year	Retired[a]	Sought Re-election				
		Total	Defeated in primaries	Defeated in general election	Total re-elected	Re-elected as % of those seeking re-election
1946	9	30	6	7	17	56.7
1948	8	25	2	8	15	60.0
1950	4	32	5	5	22	68.8
1952	4	31	2	9	20	64.5
1954	6	32	2	6	24	75.0
1956	6	29	0	4	25	86.2
1958	6	28	0	10	18	64.3
1960	5	29	0	1	28	96.6
1962	4	35	1	5	29	82.9
1964	2	33	1	4	28	84.8
1966	3	32	3	1	28	87.5
1968	6	28	4	4	20	71.4
1970	4	31	1	6	24	77.4
1972	6	27	2	5	20	74.1
1974	7	27	2	2	23	85.2
1976	8	25	0	9	16	64.0
1978	10	25	3	7	15	60.0
1980	5	29	4	9	16	55.2
1982	3	30	0	2	28	93.3[b]

Source: John F. Bibby, Thomas Mann and Norman J. Ornstein, *Vital Statistics on Congress 1980*, Washington DC, American Enterprise Institute; 1982 data from *Congressional Quarterly Weekly Report* 6 Nov. 1982. ©AEI.
Notes:
a Does not include persons who died or resigned from office before the election.
b This very high figure is generally taken to be exceptional. In many cases incumbents won by very narrow margins.

LEGISLATORS AS RATIONAL ACTORS

Senators and Representatives' determined efforts to get elected or re-elected essentially involves an interaction between the candidate and the constituency. While not unimportant, party ties and contacts have long since ceased to dominate the nomination and campaign process. But this electoral interaction is not simply one of candidate projection and media promotion. Members are also required to tend to the needs and interests of their constituencies — a job which in the American context is both complex and demanding.

Political scientists have attempted to characterize these efforts in terms of rational choice analysis. David Mayhew, for example, in his stimulating and influential book *Congress: The Electoral Connection*,[7] argues that members of Congress are motivated by just one thing: re-election. All their behaviour inside and outside Congress is shaped by this simple drive. A major *a priori* assumption here is that members *can* affect their re-election chances. While Mayhew accepts that there are limits to what a Representative or Senator can do to please his or her constituents — no individual legislator can, after all, banish unemployment or solve the energy problem — he does identify three broad strategies which can improve re-election chances. He or she can, first, advertise by spreading his or her name and reputation and generally creating a favourable image. Exposure on television and in the local press can be important, and unlike the Washington/New York press, local newspapers are generally sympathetic to members of Congress.[8] Sometimes members go to unusual lengths in their efforts at self-promotion. Mayhew reports Charles Diggs Jr (Democrat, Michigan) as running a radio programme with himself as 'combination disc jockey-commentator and minister', and Daniel Flood (Democrat, Pennsylvania) apparently is 'famous for appearing unannounced and often uninvited at wedding anniversaries and other events'.[9]

Probably more significant is *credit claiming* or convincing constituents that the member has 'delivered the goods'. This is nothing new, of course, indeed 'pork barrel' politics is part of American folklore. Pork barrel politics almost always involves particular rather

---

7 New Haven, Connecticut, Yale University Press, 1974.
8 While there are no genuinely national newspapers in the USA, the *New York Times*, *The Wall Street Journal* and *Washington Post* act as forums for national debate.
9 Both quotes from Mayhew, *op. cit*, p. 51.

than collective benefits to constituents. It would be very difficult for an individual member of Congress to claim credit for having reduced the rate of inflation, which everyone benefits from. Much more likely is he or she to benefit from helping direct federal investment (for example on a military installation or community development project) to his or her constituency. As we shall see later, the internal structure of power in Congress, not least the absence of strict party discipline facilitates just such distributions.

Finally, members benefit from *position taking* or being identified positively in the minds of constituents with a particular policy position. A predominantly Roman Catholic or Fundamentalist Christian constituency would be gratified by public pronouncements or actual legislative action by their Congressman against abortion. New York's large Jewish community would expect their Congress person to take a pro-Israeli stance, and so on. Most recently, legislators have formed caucuses to promote or defend a particular constituency interest. Typical examples are the House Automobile Task Force and the Steel Caucus, both of which strive to counteract economic decline in these industries.

Senators and Representatives have always tended their constituencies, but in recent years the pressures to do so have increased considerably. We have already noted the decline of political party influence — one potentially major bulwark against an intimate constituency/legislator relationship. Less obvious is the impact of a number of political and technological changes on the information flow between the electorate and member. On the members' side, free mailing privileges, together with computerized mailing lists, enable legislators not only to send out a vast volume of letters (Senate offices, for example, send out about 1 million letters a month),[10] but also to *target* mail to particular groups of constituents. So if a legislator wants to publicize his anti-abortion stand to all Roman Catholics and evangelical Christians in his district he can do so. He can even hone down the target group to a particular neighbourhood or block. Not all legislators have this facility, but it is spreading fast. On the constituents' side, interest groups and political action committees increasingly 'rate' the legislative voting record of individual members. These group ratings enable groups and, via publicity back home, constituents, to identify their members as

10   See Michael J. Robinson, 'Three faces of Congressional media', in Mann and Ornstein (eds), *The New Congress, op. cit*, pp. 55—96.

'liberal', 'conservative', pro- or anti-environmental protection, labour, affirmative action or whatever.[11]

Predictably, Senators are less exposed to such highly focused pressures than are Representatives, but Mayhew contends they are just as instrumental in their quest for re-election as House members. There is undoubtedly a great deal of validity to the rational choice approach. Any observer of the Washington scene would have to concede that members are increasingly preoccupied with constituency matters. Richard Fenno, who spent several months with Congressmen as a participant observer, has dubbed these activities 'home style'.[12] Fenno also noted another phenomenon, however, which does cast some doubt on the rational choice thesis. The longer House members remained in Congress, the more concerned they became with Washington affairs and less diligent they became in their pastoral constituency work. The implication here is that there are forces at work in the lives of members of Congress other than the simple drive to win re-election. It may be, of course, that these other forces complement rather than compete with constituency pressures. Most voters have very little knowledge of what Representatives and Senators actually do in Washington. And given that the electorate is not so naive as to expect an individual member to transform society, a steady flow of positive messages linked to advertising, credit claiming and position taking may be enough to convince voters that 'their' Representative or Senator is doing a good job.

Undoubtedly there are a number of activities important to the legislators which do not seriously conflict with constituency duties. On some issues — especially foreign policy or technical financial questions — constituents do not have well formed opinions. Yet if members devote themselves to such issues, possibly they are at least indirectly neglecting their re-election chances by not putting their time to the most effective use. The rational choice theorists' answer here is simple: members devote time to non-constituency questions because the internal dynamics of the House (or Senate) demand it. As separate and individual political actors they can achieve very little for the voters. So in order (say) to ensure the siting of a federal installation in their constituency, they are obliged to form *coalitions* with other members. Naturally, coalition formation

---

11   An excellent and comprehensive sample of ratings can be found in Michael Barone and Grant Ujifusa, *The Almanac of American Politics 1982*, Washington DC, Barone and Co, 1982.
12   Richard E. Fenno Jr, *Home Style: House Members in their Districts*, Boston, Little Brown, 1978.

involves give and take. It is necessary for a legislator to spend time on apparently nonrelevant legislative activity, in order to win support on those issues which are directly relevant. This is called *log-rolling* or the bargaining, vote trading and exchange of favours which has long been a characteristic of Congress. As long ago as 1885 Woodrow Wilson, then an academic observer of Congress, noted:

It is principally in connection with appropriations that what has come to be known in our political slang as 'log-rolling' takes place. Of course the chief scene of this sport is the private room of the Committee on Rivers and Harbors, and the season of its highest excitement the hours spent in the passage of the River and Harbor Bill. 'Log-rolling' is an exchange of favors. Representative *A* is very anxious to secure a grant for the cleaning of a small watercourse in his district, and representative *B* is equally solicitous about his plans for bringing money into the hands of the contractors of his own constituency, whilst representative *C* comes from a seaport town whose modest harbor is neglected because of the treacherous bar across its mouth, and representative *D* has been blamed for not bestirring himself more in the interest of schemes of improvement afoot amongst the enterprising citizens of his native place; so it is perfectly feasible for these gentlemen to put their heads together and confirm a mutual understanding that each will vote in Committee of the whole for the grants desired by the others, in consideration of the promise that they will cry 'Aye' when his item comes on to be considered.[13]

Today, of course, it is not the Committee on Rivers and Harbors, but any one of the 113 standing workgroups (committees and sub-committees) in the Senate and 170 in the House which dominate day-to-day legislative business (figures are for the 96th Congress, 1979–80).[14] We will return to log-rolling and the work of Congressional committees later. For now it is important to stress that although persuasive, the rational choice view of the work of Congress has its limitations. It assumes that legislators can know what the interests of his or her constituency are. Often this is difficult. Some districts are socially, ethnically and economically diverse. A Senator from Washington State may not need any prompting when voting on legislation affecting the two industries — lumber and aerospace — which dominate that state. But it is much more difficult for Senators from California, representing diverse and politically volatile populations, to respond in this way.

13 Woodrow Wilson, *Congressional Government*, New York, Meridian Books, 1956, p. 121.
14 Ironically, however, 'water' continues to generate a mass of pork barrel legislation, mainly because dams and other water projects are widely supported by rural Congressmen and by the Army Corps of Engineers who build them.

More serious is the implication in the rational choice approach that members of Congress are mere automatons responding to constituency demands. There is no place for ideology, party or individual preferences. Yet a wealth of empirical evidence exists to suggest that at one point or another in a legislator's life all of these can be — and usually are — important. As suggested, party influences are weak by European standards, but that does not mean they do not exist. Democrats have some policy positions and perspectives in common, as have Republicans. The next chapter will show, indeed, how party leadership within each House can be crucial in determining the outcome of legislation. Similarly, appeals by a President to his fellow party members in Congress can be effective. Lyndon Johnson used the Democratic majorities in the House and Senate to great effect when pushing through his Great Society social and civil rights programme. More recently, Ronald Reagan appealed directly to party solidarity when endeavouring to persuade the Republican Senate to support his economic reforms in 1981–2. Assured of Republican minority support in the House, victory there was sealed by the additional support of conservative Democrats.

The existence of 'conservative' and 'liberal' groupings shows the importance of ideology. In itself this need not be significant — members may after all be simply mirroring their constituents' view — but constituencies are not always easily labelled conservative or liberal, and it is not uncommon for an established conservative or liberal member to represent a constituency which cannot accurately be described as either. Legislators are also influenced by other members and by their staff. In other words, in the context of a legislative process which is both fragmented and complex, they are exposed to a number of pressures and influences. Constituency demands may be on the ascendant but this does not mean that we should reduce the role of legislators to the vote-getting machines implied by some political scientists.

In sum, members are exposed to many influences. Given the importance of their constituents' preferences in deciding their electoral survival, it is unlikely that members will do anything directly to antagonize the voters. And, if particularly vulnerable or in a marginal seat, they may indeed devote all their energies to re-election. For some, and particularly members of the Senate, however, political life becomes much more complex, with constituency, party, committee, interest group and ideological pressures competing for the members' favour.

THE WORK OF MEMBERS OF CONGRESS

The changing pattern of influence on members has had important consequences on the internal structure of power in each House — and these changes will be analysed in the next chapter. A useful way to link discussion of the activities of members outside and inside the legislature is to examine the typical workload of legislators and the support in staff, offices and other services provided for them.

Clearly Representatives and Senators are not 'lobby fodder' as British MPs are often labelled. They have little choice but to take note of the needs and demands of their constituents and to act on them. Part of this function involves formulating and monitoring a mass of complex legislation. Given the sheer volume of legislation (some 25,000 bills are introduced every session, but only about 600 become law) most members specialize in a particular policy area, often but not always related to their constituents' interests. Senator William Fulbright, for example, was for many years Chairman of the Senate Foreign Relations Committee. In this job he took a predominantly liberal stance, especially on the conduct of the Vietnam War — not a strategy which was linked in any obvious way to the interests of his rural and conservative constituency, Arkansas. Most of the crucial legislative work is conducted in the committees and subcommittees, yet as Table 7.4 shows, Representatives spend rather little of their awesome 11-hour day directly on committee work. The remainder is devoted to a number of tasks — but in particular answering mail and consulting with aides. To assist the legislator perform all these functions, Congress has voted for itself a quite extraordinary number of services. Office space, furnishings, stationery and postal allowances are generous. And all communication with constituents, primarily by mail, is free for Senators and Representatives are given generous mailing privileges. All of these benefits pale into insignificance compared with the provisions made for Congressional staff. In 1979, a staggering 23,528 people worked for Congress including, in the House, 7,067 personal aides and in the Senate 3,612. So each Representative has approximately 16 people working for him or her and each Senator enjoys the assistance of no fewer than 36 aides. Some of these positions are secretarial, but many are professionals including some (about two for each member in the House and five in the Senate) directly assigned the job of drafting

TABLE 7.4 *A Representative's Average Day*

	Minutes	Hours
In the House chamber		2.53
In committee/subcommittee work		1.22
Hearings	26	
Business	9	
Mark ups	42	
Other	5	
In his/her office		3.19
With constituents	17	
With organized groups	9	
With others	20	
With staff aides	53	
With other Representatives	5	
Answering mail	46	
Preparing legislation, speeches	12	
Reading	11	
On telephone	26	
In other Washington locations		2.02
With constituents at Capitol Hill	9	
At events	33	
With leadership	3	
With other Representatives	11	
With informal groups	8	
In party meetings	5	
Personal time	28	
Other	25	
Other		1.40
Total		11.16

Source: US House of Representatives, Commission on Administrative Review, *Administrative Reorganization and Legislative Management*, 95th Congress, 1st session, 1977, H. Doc. 95–232: pp. 18–19.

and amending legislation.[15] In addition 2000 staff work for House committees and over 1200 for Senate committees. Over the last 20 years there   has been a rapid increase in the number of sub-committees, reflecting both an increase in the legislative workload and

15   See Michael J. Malbin, 'Delegation, deliberation, and the new role of Congressional staff', in Mann and Ornstein (eds), *The New Congress, op. cit,* pp. 134–77.

the increasing independence of members of Congress and staff have risen correspondingly. Finally, members benefit from the work of a number of support agencies such as the Library of Congress (5390 staff) and the General Accounting Office (5303). Of course these support agencies are rarely directly involved in legislation, but their presence does reinforce the claim that probably uniquely among world assemblies,[16] Congress has acquired a formidable permanent bureaucracy.

So we can conclude that the typical member is a man or woman under pressure. But American national legislators are also uncommonly independent of party and executive, and to help them perform their legislative duties and retain this independence, they are uniquely privileged with staffing and other bureaucratic support. But the important questions remain. How does Congress influence the policy process? To what extent does it check executive power? Most important, is Congress truly the 'people's branch' in the sense that it expresses the democratic wishes of the population?

FURTHER READING

David Mayhew's *Congress: The Electoral Connection*. New Haven, Yale University Press, 1974 catalogues the ways in which members of Congress tend to their constituencies. *Home Style*, Boston, Little Brown, 1978 by Richard E. Fenno Jr is a book rich in anecdote on the same theme. Congressional elections are examined in Morris P. Fiorina, *Congress: Keystone of the Washington Establishment*, New Haven, Yale University Press, 1977, but see also Thomas E. Mann and Norman J. Ornstein (eds), *The New Congress*, Washington DC, American Enterprise Institute, 1981, Chapter 2.

16   Michael Malbin notes that the next most heavily staffed legislature is the Canadian Parliament, with a mere 3300 staff, *ibid*, p. 135.

CHAPTER 8

ongress as Policy Maker

Let me say this about Congress....A Congress is not a President
....A Congress should not be a President....A Congress should
be nothing more, nothing less than what it is: a reflection of the
will of our people and the problems that disturb them and the
actions they want taken. The Congress ought to improve its
ability to serve that function.

Senator Edmund S. Muskie (Democrat, Maine) 1975,
quoted in John L. Steele (ed.) The Role of Congress II:
Study of the Legislative Branch, 1975

It is impossible for either the internal or the foreign policy of
great states to be strongly and consistently carried out on a
collegial basis. Collegiality unavoidably obstructs the prompt-
ness of decision, the consistency of policy, the clear responsibility
of the individual, and ruthlessness to outsiders in combination
with the maintenance of discipline within the group.

Max Weber, Theory of Social and Economic Organizations

As was stressed in Chapter 3, Congress was originally intended to be
the key institution in the federal government. It was only through
Congress that the people were given a direct control over policy.
Members of the House of Representatives were directly elected,
Senators, President and Vice-President were not. Moreover Congress
was meant to formulate and pass laws — the President's main job
being merely to implement them. Popular control of government
was of course limited by the Presidential veto and the territorial base
of appointed Senators. But it was the House of Representatives
which controlled the purse strings and it was Congress as a whole
which stood, as legislature, at the apex of the constitutional system.

The actual functioning of the institution never quite worked as intended. In 1804 the Constitution was amended to facilitate direct election of the President, and as the country grew and demands on government increased, President and executive took on the major responsibility for formulating legislation. This trend has occurred in almost every country and is an almost inescapable consequence of the vast information and manpower resources available to modern executive bureaucracies, but not to legislatures. Yet unlike some national legislatures, Congress retains quite formidable power. It remains an indisputably important actor in the policy process. It is also an institution whose powers and internal operations are constantly changing. The main purpose of this chapter is to analyse the nature and significance of these changes so that an accurate understanding of the policy-making role of Congress in the 1980s can be achieved.

THE FUNCTION OF CONGRESS

As indicated in Chapter 7, the first and most general function of Congress is one of representation. At its simplest this means that members of Congress are held accountable for their actions through the electoral process. In complex societies the citizen/representative relationship must necessarily be limited, however, so when we talk of the 'representative function of Congress' we are actually referring to a number of different functions, most of which are at least one removed from the direct influence of the voters. So the business of formulating and passing laws — the legislative function — involves constant interaction between members, and between members and staff, interest groups, executive officials, the courts and the media. Clearly the individual voter's influence in this process is limited, although as we have already established, the constant threat of electoral defeat does oblige US legislators to tend to the general pastoral needs of their constituencies. A second major function of legislatures, and especially the Congress, is to oversee the executive branch. Constitutionally and by convention, Congress has a number of established oversight powers. It controls finance, so appropriations bills originate in the House of Representatives and have to be approved by both Houses. As we will develop later, it is the President who actually produces the annual budget, so the appropriations process is an opportunity for Congress to approve, modify or criticize the executive's spending plans and also to monitor them during implementation. The Senate also approves Presidential appointments and both Houses have power to investigate inefficiency or wrong-doing in the executive branch. Finally, Congress has the power to veto all administrative reorganizations in the executive branch. Before we look at these functions in detail, it is necessary to outline the formal structure of power in the two Houses.

Two major foci of power exist — committees and party leadership. Table 8.1 lists the standing committees and subcommittees of the 97th Congress, together with their chairmen. Committees have always been central to the business of legislation in Congress and if anything their importance has increased over the years. As Table 8.1 shows, the permanent committees are distinguished by function, and as government has become more complex, so the number of committees and subcommittees has proliferated. Consolidation and reorganizations have occurred, but it is never long before the need for another work-group emerges. Both internal and external pressures are at work to increase this need. Internally, individual legislators build reputations by specializing in a particular subject. Often this specialization is linked to constituent needs. Moreover, Congress' own bureaucracy has to match developments in the executive branch, and as departments and agencies have increased in number and function, so Congress has been obliged to respond. Often this is a two-way street. Member's career and constituency needs may benefit from executive fragmentation which legislation often encourages.

It is in the committees that the business of framing, amending and rejecting legislation occurs. Most committees *authorize* legislation while others provide funds to *finance* programmes. Hence the Appropriations, House Ways and Means, Senate Finance and the Budget Committees are concerned with approving income (taxation) and expenditure bills. We will examine the budgetary process in more detail in Chapter 13. By no means are all committees equal in power. The above named finance committees are particularly prestigious and influential, especially so in the case of the House Appropriations Committee (which is the source of all appropriations bills), the House Ways and Means and Senate Finance Committees (which are responsible for tax bills) and the Budget Committees. Of the authorizing committees, the Senate Foreign Relations is of central importance in foreign policy, while the Agriculture, Banking and Judiciary Committees are prominent in both Houses. An equivalent hierarchy applies to most subcommittees with, for example, the House Appropriations Subcommittee on Defense being markedly more important than the subcommittee responsible for the District of Columbia. Because the House of Representatives is a larger and, by tradition, a more formal body than the Senate, a number of complex rules have been formulated to govern day-by-day business. The Rules Committee is responsible for interpreting these regulations and in particular for helping to decide which bills, and in what form, come before the floor of the House. This power to withhold bills or to allow them to proceed only if certain amendments or provisions are omitted or included gives the Rules Committee considerable political clout. Indeed during the late 19th and early 20th centuries, the Rules Committee was at the very centre of Congressional power. Today, although it continues to perform a gatekeeper function, it is less powerful, in part because the House is less formal than it was (of which more later) and in part because the Committee tends to be the voice of the majority party leadership rather than being an independent source of power in Congress.

Clearly, membership of committees is an important determinant of the status and influence of individual Representatives and Senators, and accordingly the processes whereby members are selected to sit on committees and eventually selected as chairmen have long been the subject of debate and controversy. The most basic rule is that the party with a majority in the Chamber automatically achieves a majority in the committees, with the minority party represented in rough proportion to its delegation in the Chamber as a whole. Committee and subcommittee chairmen are drawn exclusively from the majority party. In both House and Senate, members are allowed to sit on a maximum of two committees, although House members assigned to the important Rules, Ways and Means and Appropriations Committees are not normally permitted further assignments. In both Houses party committees selected by party caucuses (meetings of all party members in each House) choose the members of the standing committees. This process is predictably political, with seniority, experience, reputation and connections being the main determinants of assignments. Since the 1950s the Senate has ensured that all freshmen (new) Senators are given at least one major committee assignment (the so-called 'Johnson Rule' introduced under the influence of the then Senator majority leader Lyndon Baines Johnson). By winning prestigious committee jobs, members can enhance their institutional reputations, gain access to legislative programmes of direct interest to their constituents, and, occasionally, attract

TABLE 8.1 *Senate and House: Standing Committees and Subcommittees, 97th Congress, 1981—2*

Senate Committees	Chairman (all Republicans)	Number of Subcommittees
Agriculture, Nutrition and Forestry	Jesse Helms N. Carolina	8
Appropriations	Mark Hatfield Oregon	12
Armed Services	Strom Thurmond S. Carolina	6
Banking, Housing and Urban Affairs	Jake Garn Utah	7
Budget	Peter Domenici New Mexico	None
Commerce, Science and Transportation	Bob Packwood Oregon	6
Energy and Natural Resources	James McClure Idaho	6
Environment and Public Works	Robert Stafford Vermont	4
Finance	Robert Dole Kansas	9
Foreign Relations	Charles Percy Illinois	7
Governmental Affairs	Toby Roth Delaware	8
Judiciary	Strom Thurmond S. Carolina	9
Labor and Human Resources	Orrin Hatch Utah	7
Rules and Administration	Charles Mathias Maryland	None
Veterans' Affairs	Alan Simpson Wyoming	None

House Committees	Chairman (all Democrats)	Number of Subcommittees
Agriculture	Eligio De La Garza Texas	8
Appropriations	Jamie Whitten Mississippi	13
Armed Services	Melvin Price Illinois	7

TABLE 8.1 *continued*

House Committees	Chairman (all Democrats)	Number of Subcommittees
Banking, Finance and Urban Affairs	Fernand St Germain Rhode Island	8
Budget	James Jones S. Oklahoma	None
District of Columbia	Ronald Dellums California	3
Education and Labor	Carl Perkins Kentucky	8
Energy and Commerce	John Dingell Michigan	6
Foreign Affairs	Clement Zablocki Wisconsin	8
Government Operations	Jack Brooks Texas	7
House Administration	Augustus Hawkins California	6
Interior and Insular Affairs	Maurice Udall Arizona	6
Judiciary	Peter Rodino New Jersey	7
Merchant Marine and Fisheries	Walter Jones N. Carolina	5
Post Office and Civil Service	William Ford Michigan	7
Public Works and Transportation	James Howard New Jersey	6
Rules	Richard Bolling Missouri	2
Science and Technology	Don Fuqua Florida	7
Small Business	Darren Mitchell Maryland	6
Standards of Official Conduct	Louis Stokes Ohio	None
Veterans' Affairs	Sonny Montgomery Mississippi	5
Ways and Means	Dan Rostenkowski Illinois	6

Source: **Congressional Quarterly**

national attention.[1] During the first two years of the Reagan Administration, for example, Congressman James R. Jones (D. Oklahoma) assumed a pivotal position as Chairman of the House Budget Committee. Although he opposed most of the Administration's economic policies, Jones was able to straddle party positions by proposing alternative, but by no means opposite, policies and by maintaining a friendly relationship with Pete Domenici, the Republican Chairman of the Senate Budget Committee.

Within individual committees and subcommittees status is no less important, with the chairman of each work-group at the very top of the pecking order. From 1911 until the early 1970s, both ranking within committees and the assertion of power by the chairman over committee members was determined by seniority. Longevity of service on committees, therefore, was the first and final criterion for advancement. Naturally, this gave an enormous advantage to the majority party, the Democrats and particularly to members from safe seats which in the period in question meant mainly conservative Democrats from the one-party South. Indeed, the caricature image of elderly white-haired Southerners lording it over all and sundry on Capitol Hill was not so far from the truth, as such figures as Richard Russell of Armed Services, Russell Long of Finance and James Eastland of Judiciary in the Senate and Carl Vinson of Armed Services, and Howard Smith of Rules in the House, testified.

Chairmen were, and indeed still are, powerful because of their control of the agenda. They can decide the order in which bills are discussed, the timing of committee meetings, the frequency of public hearings and the management of bills on the floor of the House. They used also to have a major say in the number and composition of subcommittees, together with the selection of subcommittee chairmen. Since the early 1970s a number of reforms have removed committee chairmen from the very pinnacles of power, although they remain very powerful members of Congress. But they now no longer have complete control of the work and membership of subcommittees which, as we will expand upon later, have considerable independent influence. Moreover, seniority is not now the only criterion for advancement within committees. In 1975 the House Democratic caucus, caught up in a general atmosphere of reform, removed three of the most powerful committee chairmen at a stroke (Wight Patman of Texas — Banking and Currency, W. R. Poage of

---

1 See Richard Fenno Jr, *Congressmen in Committees*, Boston, Little Brown, 1973, for a vivid account of committee politics.

Texas — Agriculture, and F. Edward Herbert of Louisiana — Administration). In fact, seniority remains central to any promotion within committees. The crucial difference now is that chairmen are obliged to treat subcommittee chairmen (and committee members generally) more as equals than as feudal vassals. This is part of a general democratization and dispersal of power in both the House and (to a lesser extent) the Senate which we will return to later.

In addition to the standing committees in each House, a number of other work-groups exist, the most important of which are the Conference Committees. These are, simply, *ad hoc* bodies created to reconcile the differences that occur in the House and Senate versions of the same piece of legislation. Membership is drawn from those members in each House who have been most closely involved with the legislation — usually the relevant committee members — who then vote *en bloc* so as to represent the wishes of their Chamber. A great deal of politicking goes on in conference with bills often amended considerably, and not always in line with the wishes of the House or Senate as a whole. Conference decisions can, however, be rejected by a subsequent vote on the floor of each Chamber and sent back to the committee. (See Figure 8.1 p. 157.) Finally, *ad hoc* committees can be formed by the Speaker of the House to reconcile standing committees with overlapping jurisdictions, and select committees appointed by presiding officers can be created in either House to expedite a particular problem, often in association with a Congressional investigation.

The second focus of power in Congress is the party leadership. In the House the key figures are the Speaker and Minority Leader and the key groups are the party caucuses, in particular the majority party caucus. The Speaker of the House used to have quite awesome formal power. Until 1911, he was also Chairman of the Rules Committee and he appointed committee chairmen. This combination enabled speakers to control the flow of legislation on to the floor. Concentration of such power in the personage of one particularly assertive speaker, Joseph Cannon, led to a revolt in 1910—11 which resulted in the removal of the Speaker's control of the Rules Committee and of committee assignments. But the Speaker retains considerable authority. He continues to help control the flow of legislation, recognizes who is to speak on the floor, can create *ad hoc* committees, gives advice on assignments to conference and select committees, helps in assigning bills to committees and he votes in the event of a tie. While the Speaker has the greatest formal power of any individual in the House, his potential informal power is much greater. As both leading parliamentarian and party leader he can become a crucial link between other centres of power — particularly committee chairmen — as well as be the person most able to muster often disparate party forces behind a particular bill or the programme of a President. Whether these powers are utilized to the full depends on the personality, capabilities and political skills of the incumbent.

In recent years, for example, the office has come full circle as incumbents have changed. Between 1940 and 1960 the office was dominated by the forceful and highly political Sam Rayburn (with breaks in 1947—8 and 1953—4 when the Republicans had a majority in the House). Between 1961 and 1978 first John McCormack and then Carl Albert became Speakers, neither of whom had the skills or the charisma of Rayburn. The most recent incumbent, however, is the highly partisan yet politically astute Tip O'Neil, who has returned the office at least partly to its former status.

After the Speaker, the most important offices are the majority and minority floor leaders, who are elected by the party caucuses and whose main job is to monitor and organize party business on the floor of the House. In fact the Minority Leader is often a more crucial figure than the Majority Leader, largely because the Speaker is the effective majority spokesman. Robert Michel (pronounced 'Michael'), the most recent Minority Leader, has seen his position and importance increase with the Republicans in control of both the Senate and the Presidency. Finally, both parties appoint whips to help control floor business. These are in no way equivalent to British Parliamentary whips. they have no effective sanctions at their disposal to oblige members to toe the party line (if there is one!). Instead their job is to persuade, negotiate, bargain and cajole members into broad agreement on particular items of legislation.

The party caucus meets infrequently and then usually to agree on procedure rather than to discuss substantive policy issues. As important today are the informal caucuses which have emerged over the last 20 years. Most important are the Democratic Study Group representing liberal Democrats, the Southern caucus, or 'Boll Weevils', which crosses party lines and is generally conservative in orientation and the equally conservative Republican Study Group.

Leadership in the Senate roughly parallels that in the House, but there are some important differences. Unlike the House, the presiding officer, the Vice-President of the United States, has few powers. Neither, indeed, has the President Pro-Tem who normally presides over day-to-day business. Real power lies with the majority and minority leaders, although even they can often do little to control the behaviour of just 100 fiercely independent Senators. Again, much depends on the personality of the incumbents. Some Majority Leaders such as Lyndon Johnson (1955–60) built reputations as power brokers, as has the most recent incumbent, Republican Howard Baker, whose management of the Republicans' fragile majority in 1981–3 showed great political skill. Others, however, including recent Leaders such as Mike Mansfield (1961–78) and Robert Byrd (1977–81) have either been unwilling or unable to assert authority over fellow party members.

So far in our discussion we have concentrated on describing the formal powers of committees and party leaders. This tells us little about the dynamics of the policy-making process, however, and how the institution can be assessed in terms of its performance and effectiveness. One way to examine these questions is first to look at the validity of the *criticisms* which have been directed at Congress over recent years, and then to discuss the reform measures adopted in response to these criticisms.

CONGRESS UNDER FIRE

At least since the Second World War Congress has been the subject of sometimes intense criticism. Very generally we can divide these criticisms into two broad categories – those which are historically specific and those which identify structural features of Congress which persist through time. Of course, the two sets of critiques are related, especially as the institution is constantly changing, but this simple distinction does facilitate a more subtle understanding of how the institution works.

1. *Perhaps the most common and persistent criticism is that Congress is fragmented and unresponsive; that it is not a 'coherent' policy-making body but instead a forum for the defence and promotion of disparate, unrelated interests.* That the policy-making process in Congress is fragmented cannot be disputed. Power is dispersed to committees and subcommittees and the legislative process itself is cumbersome. When a bill is introduced it faces a formidable number of potential veto points before it actually becomes law and this is true even of those bills which are part of the President's programme, have substantial support in Congress, and are recognized as important public questions. Figure 8.1 shows the major obstacles that confront

any bill when introduced into Congress. Committee action is the most difficult stumbling block, with only about 10 per cent of bills actually reported out. The Presidential veto is a much rarer barrier, but it is frequently exercised on important items of legislation. Even less common are successful attempts to override a veto. Indeed between 1945 and 1975 Presidents vetoed 251 bills, and Congress overrode just 31 of these. Of these 31, 12 occurred during the Presidency of Gerald Ford when an overwhelmingly Democratic Congress, still bristling from the Watergate experience, not only rejected much of the President's legislation, but also pushed through some of its own social reform measures in the face of Ford's opposition (see Chapter 9, p. 189). The President can also exercise a *pocket veto* by failing to sign a bill passed within the last 10 days of a legislative session.

Figure 8.1 also omits reference to the Senate *filibuster* — a debating device which, although used infrequently, has ended the life of several controversial bills. Filibustering is the practice, allowed only by Senate rules, of speaking in unlimited debate and eventually forcing the opposition to back down. During the 1950s and 1960s many civil rights bills were killed by this method, with segregationist Southern Senators speaking for many hours against the reform measures. A device does exist for ending a filibuster known as a *cloture* (or closure) rule; this can be invoked to end debate if three-fifths of the Senators agree. Between 1917 (when the Cloture Rule was introduced) and 1978 140 cloture votes were taken, of which just 41 were successful.

In the House, the Rules Committee can constitute a further barrier to the passage of a law. Until 1975, Southerners dominated the Committee and frequently refused to grant rules to bills they disliked, irrespective of the support the measures may have won in the legislative committees. Again liberal, and especially civil rights legislation was the victim. In 1975, however, the Democratic caucus voted to give the Speaker the power to appoint Rules Committee members. As a result, although the Committee can still stop bills, it acts more in accordance with the general wishes of the House — and particularly with the relevant legislative committee — than before. Interestingly, debate on the floor used to be one of the least significant aspects of the legislative process, for by the time a bill reached this stage it was already roughly in its final form. Recent reforms, however, have increased floor activity with individual legislators now more able to attach riders and amendments to bills. Floor *votes* can also be crucial, of course.

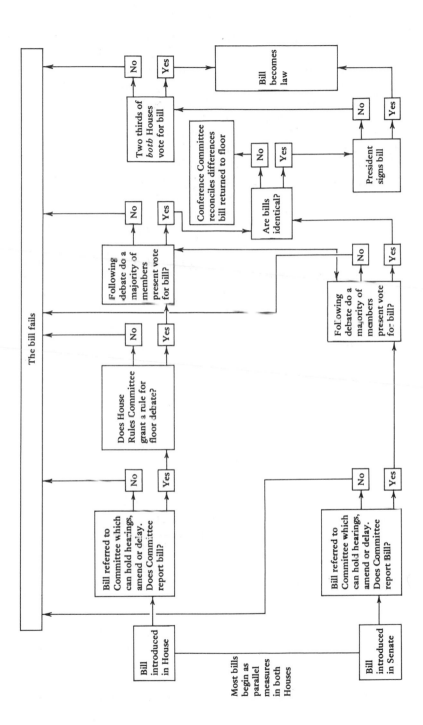

FIGURE 8.1   *How a Bill Becomes Law: the Obstacle Course for Legislation in Congress*

Figure 8.1 gives the slightly misleading impression that bills either proceed past a number of legislative hurdles or are simply killed off. The reality is that most bills are non-starters because they lack the support of key members — although some are initiated simply to attract public attention to an issue — and the remainder embark on a course which is beset with problems and pitfalls. But these do not always involve the possibility of a sudden death. As likely are the possibilities of amendment and delay. Delay can occur at almost any stage of the process, but it is in the committees that bills most often become buried, sometimes never to reappear. Given that Congress has a heavy workload and is constantly under pressure, delaying a bill is often an expedient course to follow. For a bill's supporters, including Presidents, this can be highly frustrating.

Few bills emerge from Congress in the precise form that they entered. They are amended — sometimes dramatically — from their original form, and this amendment process is the very essence of Congressional politics, for it is by changing the detailed provisions of bills that Congressmen can indulge in *log-rolling*, or the exchange of favours which is so crucial to their electoral survival. So items are added to or deleted from bills in accordance with bargains struck between key legislators, usually within, or between committees. Committee hearings, open to public scrutiny, also allow organized interests to air their views and generally to advertise particular points of view. And of course executive departments and agencies usually have a crucial interest (with positions to defend or promote) in the detail of legislation. Finally, committees may compete one with the other, for as can be inferred from the list of committees in Table 8.1, there are a number of areas where overlapping jurisdictions occur.

When all these influences are at work, as they are in major items of legislation, the potential for delay, obstruction and even confusion can be appreciated. A classic example of what can happen to a vital piece of legislation is provided by President Carter's energy programme introduced in Congress in 1977. Carter's programme, involving as it did changes in oil and gas pricing and taxation, conservation in homes and factories and an increase in coal consumption, automatically concerned several Congressional committees (Finance, Ways and Means, Interior, Banking, Currency and Urban Affairs plus a number of subcommittees), but also members from competing constituencies (the energy rich West versus the energy poor North East), the oil, gas and coal interests, and organized consumer interests intent on higher taxes for the then highly profitable oil companies. After a long and sometimes acrimonious process, the bill failed. And this in spite of the importance of the issue, general public support for energy reforms, President and Congress controlled by the same party, and determined efforts by the House Speaker, Tip O'Neill, to drive the legislation through.[2] To be fair, President Carter's liaison with Congress was poor, but there have been remarkably few occasions when a major legislative package has not been delayed or obstructed by Congress. The early New Deal and Great Society (89th Congress, 1965–6) periods are usually mentioned as the notable exceptions (See chapter 13, pp. 272–3). Some have argued that the first two years of the Reagan administration were also characterized by a responsive and responsible Congress, but the President by no means had it all his own way, and by the end of 1982, Congress was beginning to assert a more independent position, especially on economic policy.

Perhaps, indeed, Congress should assert its independence. How else, after all, could it be responsive to the demands of public opinion and voters? There are two answers to this question. The first, which is highly controversial, is the simple fact that in a complex and pluralistic society beset with urgent domestic and international problems, democratically elected executives should not have to face open resistance from the legislative branch. Executives in most Western states are relatively free from such pressures, and may be, as a result, more able to respond effectively to crisis. We will return to this contentious point in Chapter 13. The second response is more relevant to the argument in this section: fragmentation of power in Congress, multiple veto points and open access by myriad interests to centres of power render the institution *inefficient*. In other words it cannot be responsive because its decision-making structure is clumsy, slow and confused. When it does appear to 'work', it is to resist change and pander to special rather than collective or public interests. Our brief survey of the legislative process suggests that there is considerable truth to this charge. Certainly more than one generation of House and Senate members have been aware of it, for they have repeatedly attempted to reform the institution. Before we examine these reforms, we should mention some of the other criticisms levelled at Congress.

---

2 Appreciating the jurisdictional battles which the legislation would inspire, O'Neil actually created an *ad hoc* committee to handle the bill, consisting of key members from the relevant standing committees. O'Neil's ploy worked, but the resulting bill was quite incompatible with the Senate version. Events in the Senate went rather differently, with petty amendments, filibustering, and jurisidictional disputes dominating.

2. *Congress has failed to perform the oversight function effectively.* In addition to passing legislation, Congress is charged with the job of overseeing the executive or holding the President, executive departments and agencies accountable for their actions. The appropriations process in part involves this job and this will be dealt with elsewhere (Chapter 13, pp. 285–92). In addition Congress is responsible for monitoring executive appointments, holding formal investigations into the executive branch, and, as a last resort, it has the authority to impeach executive officers. The Constitution requires the Senate to approve Presidential appointments, but it is not a power which the Senate has used in the strictly 'moral' sense, i.e. rooting out inefficient, incompetent or corrupt appointees. As often, Senators are concerned to ensure that incumbents in the 1529 major posts subject to Senate confirmation (in 1977) are men and women who are sympathetic to the legislators' political or constituency interests, or who are likely to defend an organized interest (such as labour or business) which Senators are known to identify with. The appointment process is, in other words, not unlike the legislative process – it is highly politicized and subject to similar constituency interest group pressures.[3] Only rarely are appointees rejected or obliged to withdraw. In 1976, for example, only 10 appointees were rejected or had to withdraw – the highest in the whole post-1961 period – out of a total 1529 nominations.[4] So Congress is accused of two failings in this area. First it favours many appointees not because they are likely to serve the public interest, but because they will support particular or special constituency and group interests. And second that, independently of this problem, it has failed to root out some of the more obvious and colourful examples of incompetent Presidential nominations. The Nixon administration was littered with such cases. But even the Carter Presidency was able to produce its Bert Lance (the Budget Director who was eventually obliged to resign following exposure of illegal banking practices).

The investigative power of Congress consists of investigations by the standing committees, the work of special or select committees created for the specific purpose of enquiring into a particular problem, and the work of the General Accounting Office (GAO). GAO auditing of the executive spending is a continual process with the Office reporting its findings to Congress. Congress can also require

---

3　For an excellent analysis of this subject, see G. Calvin Mackenzie, *The Politics of Presidential Appointments*, New York, Free Press, 1981.
4　*Ibid*, Table 8-1, p. 177.

the GAO to investigate a particular programme or agency at any time. Standing committee investigations involve public hearings into alleged executive inefficiency or wrong-doing. One of the most famous was the Army–McCarthy hearings by the Senate Government Operations Permanent Investigations Subcommittee into communist influence in the Army, the CIA and Department of State. Subcommittee Chairman Joseph McCarthy became notorious as a red-baiter in this role, and his unfair and intimidating methods led eventually to his censure by the Senate in 1954.[5]

More typical are the several instances when Congress has created a select committee specifically to investigate a subject of public concern. In recent years, for example, the Senate Select Committee on Campaign Practices – known popularly as the (Sam) Ervin Committee after its Chairman – won great public attention through its enquiries into the Watergate scandal. This in turn spawned further investigations into the security agencies (FBI, CIA, Defense Intelligence) the legality of whose activities had been questioned during the Watergate exposures. Other notable Congressional investigations include enquiries into racketeering in trade unions, safety in atomic power stations, the conduct of the Vietnam War and standards in the pharmaceutical industry.

Note that it is not only government activities which come under Congressional scrutiny – although it is usually investigations into the executive branch which arouse the most feeling and controversy. The reason for this is simple: investigations (and oversight generally) raise awkward questions about where executive power begins and ends. With the rise of big government and the vast bureaucracy which accompanies it, Congress has found it increasingly difficult to perform the oversight function because it has limited access to exactly what goes on within the executive. Information is a valuable commodity and one jealously guarded by Presidents and their bureaucrats. Even though Congress can subpoena witnesses and documents, Presidents have repeatedly refused or been extremely reluctant to hand over information. In recent years they have claimed 'executive privilege' to certain information. Unfortunately this concept has no clear constitutional status, so the legality of withholding information remains an open question. Since Watergate and Richard Nixon's unprecedented reluctance to furnish evidence to Congressional

---

5 The institution of red-baiting, if not the actual practice, continued with the work of the House Unamerican Activities Committee (later the Internal Security Committee) until its abolition in 1975.

committees (he withheld information at least 19 times on matters unrelated to Watergate), Presidents have been more pliant. But the executive continues to hold the trump card because the sheer volume and technical complexity of documentation often makes it difficult for a hard pressed committee even to know what to ask for.

Finally, Congress has the power to impeach executive officers. Impeachment is a formal accusation of wrong-doing which the House of Representatives carries out, while the Senate actually tries and convicts impeached officials. But on only 12 occasions has the House used this power, and on only four has the Senate convicted. One President, Andrew Johnson, was formally impeached although the Senate failed to convict, and of course the House Judiciary Committee voted articles of impeachment against Richard Nixon, who resigned before further action could be taken. Again, Congress has been accused of tardiness and indecision in this general area. The main criticism is that the impeachment process is so cumbersome and formalized that it is rarely used. Critics also point to the continuing evidence of executive wrong-doing which shows that impeachment is not an adequate deterrent. (Although the cumbersome impeachment process has also been praised for preventing hasty and partisan attacks on individual officials and politicians.)

In addition to these structural criticisms, Congress is at any one time criticized for its specific failure to deal with a contemporary crisis or problem. Or, observers infer that a structural feature of the institution is permanent when it is only temporary. So in the 10 years following the Second World War it was common to accuse Congress of excessive partisanship. And indeed the red-baiting committees of the late 1940s and early 1950s did in part represent Republican attempts to indict the activities of past or present Democratic administrations. By the late 50s and early 1960s the charge was somewhat different: Congress was dominated by conservative, segregationist Southerners. Following the reforms of the 1970s, the criticism has shifted once again. Now the accusation is that Congress is the creature of increasingly vocal and influential special and public interest lobbies. This is hardly a new accusation, however, and it is one we will return to in Chapter 11. These shifting criticisms show not only that the policy agenda is constantly changing, but also that the institution is too. Some of these institutional changes result from conscious reforms adopted in response to the catalogue of criticisms outlined above.

REFORM AND CHANGE IN CONGRESS

The major criticisms of Congress prevalent in the late 1960s and early 1970s stressed two failings: legislative business was dominated by a few mainly Southern committee chairmen, and in its dealings with the executive, Congress was failing to provide either realistic policy-making alternatives or to check the burgeoning growth of executive power. Commentators had long noted that, if these problems were to be solved, political party organizations in the two Houses would have to take the lead. Indeed if we think in terms of centralizing and decentralizing influences, party and party leadership are clearly centralizing forces, while the committee structure essentially disperses power. Party voting has not been strong in Congress since the 1890–1910 period, when over half the roll calls (votes on the floor) involved 90 per cent of one party voting differently from 90 per cent of the other.[6] As Table 8.2 shows, even by the weakest measure of party unity — the percentage on which a majority of voting Democrats opposes a majority of voting Republicans — less than half of the roll-call votes in the 1954–79 period show any party cohesion. And even on these occasions only between approximately 50 per cent and 80 per cent of members from the same party voted together.[7] Note also that what little party unity there was declined markedly in the House from the mid-1960s to the early 1970s. But this simple index hardly gives an accurate picture of the frustration which liberal Democrats increasingly felt at the way in which conservative Southerners dominated committee business and the legislative agenda. By the early 1970s this frustration had reached such a point that a number of sweeping reforms were introduced, reaching a crescendo in 1975 following the election of the unusually liberal post-Watergate Congress in 1974. The major changes were.

(1)   In 1970 the House ended non-recorded teller voting and switched over to electronic voting on all roll calls. As a result the *number* of roll calls increased dramatically from 177 in 1969 to 541 in 1978.

(2)   In 1973 all bill drafting in committee was opened to public scrutiny, so exposing to organized interests and constituents the precise policy preference of members.

6   John F. Bibby, Thomas E. Mann and Norman J. Ornstein, *Vital Statistics on Congress 1980*, Washington DC, American Enterprise Institute, p. 97.
7   *Ibid*, Table 8-4.

TABLE 8.2   *Votes in Congress Showing Party Unity,*
1954—79 (per cent of all votes)

Year	House	Senate
1954	38	47
1955	41	30
1956	44	53
1957	59	36
1958	40	44
1959	55	48
1960	53	37
1961	50	62
1962	46	41
1963	49	47
1964	55	36
1965	52	42
1966	41	50
1967	36	35
1968	35	32
1969	31	36
1970	27	35
1971	38	42
1972	27	36
1973	42	40
1974	29	44
1975	48	48
1976	36	37
1977	42	42
1978	33	45
1979	47	47

Source: Congressional Quarterly Almanac, various years.
Note: Data indicate the percentage of all recorded votes on which a majority of voting Democrats opposed a majority of voting Republicans.
Reproduced from Bibby, Mann and Ornstein, *Vital Statistics on Congress 1980*, Table 8-3.

(3)   The Democratic caucus in the House voted in 1971 to permit 10 or more members to demand a special vote on a disputed committee chairman assignment. In 1975 all nominees for chairmen were subject to an automatic secret ballot by caucus members.

(4)   Also in 1975 the caucus voted to give the Speaker the power to appoint Rules Committee members, subject to caucus approval.

(5) Since 1973 all Democratic House members have been guaranteed a major committee assignment and since 1974 committee assignments have passed from the Ways and Means Committee (traditionally dominated by Southerners) to the party's Steering and Policy Committee.

(6) Subcommittees have been greatly strengthened and increased in number by a number of measures, beginning with the 1970 Legislature Reorganization Act. In 1973 the subcommittees were provided with a 'Bill of Rights' which gave to the full committee caucus the power to set subcommittee jurisdictions and select chairmen. Subsequently, subcommittees have been allocated extra staff.

(7) Although the number of formal changes in the Senate have been fewer than in the House, reforms have taken the same general direction and in some cases have been quite radical. Committee meetings have been opened up to the public, the Democratic caucus' power has been strengthened in relation to the nomination of committee chairmen, and it is now much easier to end a filibuster than it was in the early 1970s. Also, the committee structure has been rationalized with the number of committees reduced and some overlapping jurisdictions eliminated.

All these reforms were designed to speed up the legislative process and to weaken the entrenched power of committee chairmen. By so doing, members hoped to make Congress a more effective policy-making body and therefore enhance its position in relation to the executive. In fact, in the wake of the abuse of executive power represented by the conduct of the Vietnam War and Watergate, Congress passed a number of laws specifically designed to curb such excesses and to strengthen the legislative branch. The two most important of these measures were the following.

The 1973 War Powers Act

Overriding a Presidential veto, Congress acted in 1973 to limit President's ability to conduct war without the prior approval of Congress. Under this law the commitment of US armed forces could occur only if Congress declared war or authorized the use of forces or if the President acted in a national emergency. During emergency actions, Presidents were required to win Congressional support after 60 days, and a further 30 days could be granted. After the 90-day period Congress could act to stop the use of troops in a law which is not subject to a Presidential veto.

The 1974 Budget and Impoundment Control Act

A perennial complaint of Congress watchers in the post-war period was the failure of the institution to match the executive's budget-making capacity. Presidents presented annual budgets which had effectively become national policy programmes. Congress, in contrast, seemed unable to see the budget as a coherent whole. Indeed it dealt with finance in an incremental, piecemeal way, reflecting the fragmentation characteristic of bicameralism and the appropriations process. The 1974 Act attempted to compensate for these problems by creating budget committees in each House and a Congressional Budget Office to provide specialized technical information for both chambers and allow Congress to compete with the President as budget maker.

We will expand on executive/congressional relations in Chapters 9 and 13. But for now, what have been the main effects of these reforms? Little was expected from them as they were being adopted; by the early 1980s, however, they had helped to contribute to what are now recognized as profound changes in the institution, as titles such as *The New Congress* and *The Decline and Resurgence of Congress* suggest. The main changes can be summed up quite simply: power in Congress is now even more dispersed than it used to be, but the institution is more professional, more concerned with the details of the legislative process and with oversight of the executive. Finally Congress is just as conservative as it used to be — although not quite in the same ways as during the reign of the Southern Democrats.

The reform movement was fuelled by two main forces — the increasing electoral independence of individual members from party and regional ties which a more rapid turnover of members and other changes had produced, and the already noted disillusionment with the institution's ability to deal with executive power. Chapter 7 showed just how much constituency pressures have increased and how electoral success now depends less on traditional party organization and more on personal resources. In order to 'deliver the goods' to constituents, members needed two things: more control within Congress over legislation and more control over the executive policy-making process. The reforms have gone a long way towards the achievement of both objectives. Almost every legislator now has a power base in Congress, with the proliferation of near independent subcommittees facilitating this dispersal of authority. The erstwhile czars of Capitol Hill — Southern Democratic committee chairmen — have been replaced by myriad centres of power with individual legislators even better placed to defend and promote constituent and pressure group interests.

In one sense Congress is more efficient — after all, the flow of legislation has greatly increased and committees do expedite bills more rapidly than before. But subcommittee proliferation has cancelled out many of the rationalizations, and scheduling bills on the floor is now a more complex and cumbersome process than ever before. In other words, Congress remains an institution where blockages, delays and vetoes can happen at several stages in the legislative process. As a result it retains an inbuilt conservative bias — it is easier to prevent things happening than to pass bills, even though the absolute number of bills passed has increased in recent years. Partly as a result of this institutional characteristic, although also because of the electoral changes outlined in Chapter 7, a conservative coalition continues to exercise considerable influence. Until the early 1970s this consisted of Southern Democrats and Northern Republicans. Today it consists of Southern Democrats and Republicans from every region. President's Reagan's quite impressive legislative successes in economic policy during 1981 and 1982 were possible only because this coalition was able to organize support in both Houses behind the President's programme. He was, of course, aided by a Republican controlled Senate (which has, independently of party, become more conservative in recent years). But victory in the House testifies to the strength of the coalition.

Yet we should be wary of inferring too much from Reagan's early successes. Congress today almost certainly reflects the moods and wishes of the nation more accurately than for many years. This is a direct result of a new, much more intimate Congressman/constituency relationship and the easier access to legislators which organized interests now enjoy. During the 1978—81 period, public opinion appeared to move to the right and Congress accurately mirrored this trend. But as we have already established, the American electorate is now highly volatile and issues are much less susceptible to a simple identification on a left/right political continuum than they used to be.

The central dilemma for Congress in the 1980s is, in fact, the same dilemma of the 1950s and 1960s: the institution may be responsive to *particularistic* interests in American society (individual constituents or constituencies and organized groups with political clout), but it remains a poor vehicle for the expression of the *public* or *collective interest*. Building coalitions in a highly fragmented institution involves many trade-offs with costs in terms of time, coherence, and efficiency mounting steadily as the legislative process lumbers on. If anything, these costs have increased with recent reforms as the number of power centres has multiplied. And although reform was initiated through party mechanisms, political party influence on legislation is now weaker. Given the ever more serious economic and international problems confronting the United States, the need for decisive and coherent policy making is now greater than ever. If Congress can contribute little in this area, then this role must be played by that institution traditionally associated with national leadership — the Presidency.

FURTHER READING

Among recent volumes on change in Congress, the best are: Thomas E. Mann and Norman J. Ornstein (eds) *The New Congress*, Washington, DC, American Enterprise Institute, 1981, and James L. Sundquist, *The Decline and Resurgence of Congress*, Washington DC, Brookings, 1981. The classic work on committees is by Richard Fenno Jr, *Congressmen in Committees*, Boston, Little Brown, 1973. For a good analysis of Congressional leadership, see Robert Peabody, *Leadership in Congress*, Boston, Little Brown, 1976. Facts and figures on the institution can be found in Congressional Quarterly's *Inside Congress*, Washington DC, latest edition, 1971, and also in John F. Bibby, Thomas Mann and Norman J. Ornstein, *Vital Statistics on Congress, 1980*, American Enterprise Institute, 1981.

CHAPTER 9

Presidential Power

The modern Presidency of the United States, as distinct from the traditional concepts of our highest office, is bound up with the survival not only of freedom but of mankind...The President is the unifying force in our lives...The President must possess a wide range of abilities: to lead, to persuade, to inspire trust, to attract men of talent, to unite. These abilities must reflect a wide range of characteristics: courage, vision, integrity, intelligence, sense of responsibility, sense of history, sense of humour, warmth, openness, personality, tenacity, energy, determination, drive, perspicacity, idealism, thirst for information, penchant for fact, presence of conscience, comprehension of people and enjoyment of life – plus all the other, nobler virtues ascribed to George Washington under God.

Nelson A. Rockefeller, Unity, Freedom and Peace, 1968

All over Europe, in the autumn of 1980, wherever people met to talk politics, there was only one topic of conversation: How on earth had a great country like the United States, filled with talented men and women, managed to land itself with two such second- (or was it third-?) rate presidential candidates as Jimmy Carter and Ronald Reagan?

Anthony King, in The American Elections of 1980, 1981

These two quotations pinpoint the central dilemma of the modern Presidency: in the American political system the President is the only national unifying force. He has, therefore, both awesome responsibilities and awesome power. But in recent years few incumbents have possessed the qualities necessary to carry out the job efficiently and responsibly. Every President since the mid-1960s is associated to a greater or lesser extent with failure. Lyndon Johnson was broken by the Vietnam War and Richard Nixon by Watergate. Gerald Ford was little more than a caretaker President and Jimmy Carter has been judged indecisive and politically inept. And although it is too early to make a final assessment of Ronald Reagan, he will surely not be deemed one of the great Presidents.

Curiously, this association of the office with mediocrity and the abuse of power is comparatively recent. Most texts on American government written during the 1950s and 1960s saw little wrong either with the nature of the office or with recent incumbents.[1] In retrospect the mid-century Presidents — Franklin Roosevelt, Harry Truman, Dwight Eisenhower and John Kennedy — do seem impressive figures. So what has happened since? There are three possible answers to this question which will constitute the major part of discussion in this chapter. First, it could be argued that an accumulation of changes in American society and polity have made the job almost impossible to perform satisfactorily. Second, the processes whereby Presidents are recruited may have changed in ways which preselect inappropriate Presidential candidates. Third, it could be simply that different — and inappropriate — personality types have occupied the office in recent years. Before we examine these claims in detail, it is necessary briefly to outline the formal and informal sources of Presidential power and to trace the growth of the modern presidency.

FORMAL SOURCES OF POWER

To a European observer, one of the most remarkable features of the American political system is the concentration of governmental functions in one institution, the Presidency. The Constitution is partly responsible for this, for it assigns to the Presidency the roles of chief executive, (Article 2, Section 1), commander in chief of the armed forces (Article 2, Section 2), chief diplomat (or the power to make treaties, Article 2, Section 2), chief recruiting officer to the executive and courts (Article 2, Section 2) and legislator (by making recommendations to Congress, Article 2, Section 3, and exercising the veto power under Article 1, Section 7). As was emphasized in Chapter 3, the Framers did not expect the President also to become chief legislator, but over the last 100 years he has assumed this

---

1 For a good review of this 'textbook' view of the Presidency see Thomas E. Cronin, *The State of the Presidency*, Boston, Little Brown, 2nd Edition 1980, Chapter 2.

crucial function. Finally, the President is Head of State, so must carry out all those diplomatic and ceremonial duties normally performed by constitutional monarchs (in Britain, the Netherlands) or presidents (in Israel, India and Italy).

Given this panoply of powers it is not surprising that we automatically think of periods in American history in terms of incumbent Presidents. The first years of the Republic are inseparable from the personality and influence of George Washington. Andrew Jackson's Presidencies are closely associated with the democratization of American politics and the rise of a modern two-party system. Abraham Lincoln's personal conduct of the Civil War effectively shaped a whole era in American history, while Woodrow Wilson was the first President to elevate the United States on to the world diplomatic and military stage. Since the New Deal period — itself synonomous with the personage of Franklin D. Roosevelt — every President has made a lasting imprint on both American and world politics. Of course Presidents are constrained, sometimes seriously, by a number of domestic and international forces, but within the United States, the chief executive is the natural and immediate focus of attention. As we saw in Chapters 7 and 8 it would be difficult to consider Congress a natural leader or decision maker. If anything, the opposite is true. Federalism fragments political power and authority even further, leaving the Presidency (and on rather rare occasions, the Supreme Court) as the sole unifying and centralizing influence in the system.

During the 19th and early 20th centuries, it was the constitutionally assigned powers in military, foreign and diplomatic policy which tended to raise the visibility of the office. Indeed, through exercising these powers some Presidents greatly expanded and even exceeded their constitutional authority. In 1803 Thomas Jefferson authorized the purchase of the Louisiana Territories from France (see Map 2.1, p. 9) without consulting Congress. Abraham Lincoln's conduct of the Civil War was almost authoritarian, involving as it did a blockade of the South, the suspension of *Habeas Corpus* and unauthorized increases in the size of the army and navy. Much later Woodrow Wilson asked for, and was given, broad powers under the 1917 Lever Act to seize factories and mines and fix prices to help the war effort. But government, and especially the federal government, played a relatively minor part in economic and social life during this period. An assertive Congress could, and often did, dominate the political agenda. Without the vast bureaucratic and logistical resources of the modern executive, those Presidents lacking political skills or unfortunate enough to preside over particularly difficult domestic events such as the recriminations and confusion characteristic of the post-Civil War period, were truly secondary political figures. From the New Deal period onward, no President has been able to take the back stage because the demands on the office have multiplied so dramatically.

All of the constitutionally assigned powers of the Presidency have been asserted as never before. Since World War II, commander in chief has meant control over several million men and women under arms and literally the power of life and death over mankind. As chief executive, modern Presidents are responsible for numerous programmes and policies affecting every aspect of society. As chief legislator, the President takes to Congress a package of programmes, together with budget requests, which effectively mould the national political agenda. As we catalogued in Chapter 4, the rise of federal grant programmes has meant that even local governments — those bodies so free from central control in the early Republic — now depend in part or in whole on the President's policies. Of course the President is constrained when performing these functions, and of course every industrial country has been required to centralize power in executives and greatly to expand the role of government. However, no Western country has acquired such formidable military and strategic power as has the USA, and in none has the role of the state been transformed in quite the way as in America. The USA is, after all, the country where the state has traditionally been weak in relation to society; where the market was considered the most appropriate mechanism for distributing resources (Chapter 2, pp. 28–30). Yet by the 1970s more than 30 per cent of national income was accounted for by government spending, and in some areas of economic and social life, the federal government had become a major source of income and support for large number of individuals, subnational governments and corporations. It could be argued that American institutional arrangements, especially federalism and the separation of powers, are ill suited to the sort of efficient and effective policy making needed in modern industrial society. If this is so, it increases the pressures on the executive even more, for to repeat the point, only the Presidency has a truly national constituency and only the Presidency is the natural coordinator and organizer of national policy.

INFORMAL POWERS

Given the President's position at the apex of the constitutional system, it is not surprising that the office has also attracted a number of informal powers or influences additional to those constitutionally assigned. These include his position as party leader, and as national and world leader. All three can provide Presidents with valuable extra resources, but they can also burden the office with extra duties and responsibilities. Being party leader certainly sounds grandiose and impressive enough — and in the British system, for example, being both Prime Minister and party leader is indeed a great political advantage. But as we have seen, American political parties are fragmented and weak. Only very rarely in recent history have Presidents been *guaranteed* party support in Congress, and lucky is the President who knows he can count on the support of governors, mayors and other party leaders in the federal system. This accepted, weak party ties are almost certainly better than none at all, and Presidents do use party connections to rally support (if not always successfully) during the nomination process and at mid-term elections. Party is also the vital cue available to Presidents when they make appointments to the executive branch. Without the myriad party contacts at congressional, state and local levels, it would be difficult to fill all the 50,000-plus jobs which are nominated annually. Presidents also use this process to pay off debts for electoral and other services rendered.

Americans expect something more than the efficient execution of policy from their Presidents; they also expect them to embody the spirit of the nation or, in Clinton Rossiter's term, to be the 'voice of the people'.[2] It should not be forgotten that the United States has relatively few symbols of national unity, such as the monarchy in Britain or a long established culture rooted in language and custom as in France. In some respects the institution of the Presidency helps fill this gap by providing Americans with a sense of national identity. When, at press conferences, an aide announces the entrance of 'The President of the United States', he is presenting a national symbol as well as chief executive, and the simple words of the announcement carry with them an almost religious respect that is notably missing

2 In the heady optimism of the late 1950s Clinton Rossiter's famous essay *The American Presidency*, New York, Harcourt Brace Jovanovich, 1960, listed five informal powers, some of which now look unachievable, if still sought after (1) voice of the party; (2) voice of the people; (3) protector of the peace; (4) manager of prosperity; (5) world leader (pp. 4–25).

when a British Prime Minister or German Chancellor appears in public.

In recent years, Presidents' role as national leaders has been reinforced by America's emergence as a world power, a fact amply demonstrated by President Kennedy's famous speech at the time of the Cuban missile crisis:

Let no one doubt that this is a difficult and dangerous mission on which we have set out. No one can foresee precisely what course it will take or what costs or casualties will be incurred. Many months of sacrifice and self-discipline lie ahead — months in which both our patience and our will will be tested, months in which threats and denunciations will keep us aware of our dangers. But the greatest danger of all would be to do nothing. The path we have chosen for the present is full of hazards, as all paths are; but it is the one most consistent with our character and courage as a nation and our commitments around the world. The cost of freedom is always high — but Americans have always paid it. And one path we shall never choose, and that is the path of surrender or submission.[3]

Such stirring rhetoric may seem inappropriate in the 1980s, but Presidents continue to project themselves as the spirit of the nation, as an examination of Jimmy Carter's speeches on energy or Ronald Reagan's on the economy would show. In other words, Presidents attempt to project themselves as defenders of the *public interest*. In contrast to the fragmentation and particularism of Congress and the federal system, they alone claim to see policy in terms of what is in the interest of the whole country. In this sense, they attempt to elevate themselves above party, special interests and even ideology. Of course they do not always succeed — indeed none of the last four Presidents have even come close to succeeding — but they are constantly striving for this very special status, and almost certainly the American public expect their Presidents to play this part. Indeed, the public are dramatically more aware of the Presidency (including the Vice-President) than other public offices and this consciousness is acquired early in life (Table 9.1).

As world leaders, recent Presidents have had to attenuate their styles and rhetoric in line with the relative decline of American power. But they retain a special status in the international system. Certainly what Presidents say and do is significantly more important than the speeches and deeds of British and Japanese Prime Ministers, German Chancellors and French Presidents. This crucial international status adds yet another dimension to Presidential power, and also to the pressures of the office.

3 Quotes in Robert F. Kennedy, *Thirteen Days*, Harmondsworth, Middx., Penguin, 1970, p. 37.

TABLE 9.1 *Awareness of Political Leaders on the Part of Adults and Children, 1969—70*

Office	Percentage correct by age		
	Adult	17	13
President (Nixon)	98	98	94
Vice-President (Agnew)	87	79	60
Secretary of State (Rogers)	16	9	2
Secretary of Defense (Laird)	25	16	6
Speaker of the House (McCormack)	32	25	2
Senate Majority Leader (Mansfield)	23	14	4
At least one Senator from own state	57	44	16
Both Senators from own state	31	18	6
Congressman from own district	39	35	11

Source: Fred Greenstein, 'What the President means to Americans', in James Barber (ed.) *Choosing the President*, Englewood Cliffs, New Jersey, Prentice-Hall, 1974, p. 125.

THE PRESIDENCY IN CRISIS

Presidential Selection

Returning to our original questions, it seems reasonable to hypothesize that the crisis of the modern Presidency is one of recruitment. It may be simply that the wrong men are being selected for the job. What is the nature of the Presidential nomination process? And why is it now the subject of such criticism? We can divide Presidential elections into four distinct phases: pre-primary, primary, convention and campaign.

Pre-Primary. It is often quipped that no sooner is a President elected than he has to start running for his second term. Although an exaggeration, this is not so far from the truth, for any candidate with even the slightest hope of winning nomination must plan his campaign several years ahead. In his build-up for the 1976 campaign, Jimmy Carter cultivated newspaper editors and political commentators more than a year before the convention. His strategy was simple: he had to raise his public visibility in order to neutralize the 'Jimmy who?' reaction whenever his name was uttered. Ronald Reagan announced himself more than two years before the 1980 election and by late 1982, ex Vice-President Walter Mondale was already grooming himself for the 1984 contest. Merely announcing early guarantees nothing, of course. Much depends on the political resources, reputation, experience and skill of the candidate. The times are also important. Jimmy Carter's extraordinary journey from obscurity to President between 1972 and 1976 owed much to the prevailing disillusionment with 'Washington' and established party candidates. More typically, candidates must win the support of key political figures if they are to have any chance. In 1980 Ronald Reagan was endorsed by many of the leading Republicans and 'king makers' of the political right; Gerald Ford notably lacked such support and was well advised to make an early retreat from the race. Edward Kennedy, in contrast, had failed to win the unequivocal endorsement of the Democratic establishment but soldiered on nonetheless. An incumbent President naturally enjoys a huge advantage in winning his party's nomination, and there is no instance in recent years of a President who wants to stand failing to secure nomination.

The Primaries. There was a time when a candidate with strong intra-party support could avoid the primary circuit. In 1968, for example, only 37.5 per cent of the votes cast by delegates at the convention were decided by primary election, the remainder were in the pocket of party caucuses. By 1980 this figure had risen to 74.7 per cent, thus making it absolutely essential for candidates to run in the primaries (see Table 5.2, p. 93). So Hubert Humphrey's strategy of depending on his very considerable Democratic party connections was successful in 1968, but suicidal even four years later when he entered the primaries late and was effectively beaten before the convention.

Today there are at least 35 primaries, starting with New Hampshire in February and concluding with California and a number of other states in early June.[4] Unfortunately, the precise technicalities of primaries defy simple description because each state decides the timing, voter eligibility and general organization of its primary elections. The most important formal distinction is between *closed primaries* operative in most states, which are open only to registered party members, and *open primaries* where voters can vote for either party, but not both, by asking for that party's ballot at the polling station. They do not, in other words, have to be registered as Democrats or Republicans to vote in that party's election. In those states

---

4 Puerto Rico is effectively first with its Republican primary scheduled in February, but it is not a meaningful guide to trends on the continental USA.

without primaries for Presidential nominations (all states have some form of primary for statewide elections) party caucuses decide delegate selection. Over the last 15 years, primaries have become more important not only because they have increased in number, but also because changes in party rules have had the effect of binding delegates more closely to candidates. There was a time when bargaining on the convention floor resulted in delegates switching their allegiance, so making the convention a key decision maker in the nomination process. Today the primaries proper play this role.

As candidates *must* enter the primaries they must have the political and financial and even physical resources to endure the long series of campaigns involved. They must also have the *time*, for staging a series of primary campaigns is effectively a full-time job. As will be developed later, this fact alone may preselect certain sorts of candidates. Recent elections have also shown how important it is for candidates to make a good start. There is what might be called a 'media bandwagon effect', where a particular candidate is identified as a winner and this itself provides an essential impetus to his campaign. This may constitute a disadvantage for candidates with key support in those large industrial states whose primaries come relatively late. Some commentators have even gone so far as to claim that Iowa (an early party caucus state) and new Hampshire (the first primary) hold the key to the fortunes of candidates — and these are hardly representative areas of the United States. Certainly Jimmy Carter did well in early contests in 1976 and 1980, which helped him to head off opponents with support in larger states. And in 1980 George Bush's late victories in such states as Michigan meant little when Ronald Reagan had already won most of the early primaries and therefore had accumulated a formidable number of delegate votes.

The Nominating Conventions. To foreigners, nothing better represents the sheer theatre of American politics than the nominating conventions. During the summer before the election several thousand party delegates meet to choose their Presidential and Vice-Presidential candidates in an apparently crazy few days of party festival. Although policy is discussed at conventions, they are as much a media event where candidates and their supporters strive to achieve maximum public exposure. There was a time when the conventions actually chose candidates for the general election, with several ballots required before a majority (until 1936 two-thirds in the Democratic convention) of all the delegates could agree on a candidate. During this period conventions were an accurate reflection of the vote trading and coalition formation typical of American politics generally. They were, in other words, highly political, involving deals, bargains and periodic deadlocks as party bosses switched their blocks of delegate votes or opted for a compromise candidate. In recent elections, however, the winning candidate is almost certainly identifiable before the convention begins as the primaries effectively decide the contest.

The spread of primaries was part of a general party reform movement prevalent in the late 1960s and 1970s. In the case of the Democrats, calls for reform were greatly aided by the events at the 1968 convention in Chicago when an old-style party organization nominated Vice-President Hubert Humphrey, a candidate associated with organized labour and Lyndon Johnson's conduct of the Vietnam War. But this was the period when the social issue (the war, minority rights, the liberalization of society) was on the ascendant, and traditional Democratic Party organizations were notably unsympathetic to the new movement. Following violent scenes outside the convention hall when the young, radicals and other excluded groups demonstrated against the old-style machine politics, the Party was plunged into a turmoil of recriminations.[5] The upshot was the appointment of a commission (the McGovern–Fraser Commission) to recommend changes in delegate selection. Since then the Party has never been free of commissions, reforms and debate on how best to organize itself.

McGovern–Fraser resulted in two major changes. From 1972, representation at conventions from minorities and under-represented groups — Blacks, women, youth — was greatly increased. Second, a system of proportional representation was recommended for primary elections. Previously, the person winning the primary took all the delegate votes ('winner take all'). McGovern–Fraser recommended that the delegates given to a candidate should be in proportion to his share of the vote. Between 1972 and 1980, the rules were modified further. From 1976 winner-takes-all elections were banished, but a minimum 15 per cent cut-off point was established to discourage frivolous candidacies. (It has since been set at a minimum of 15 per cent and maximum of 20 per cent.) The original McGovern–Fraser idea of quotas for under-represented groups has been replaced

5   For a graphic description of these harrowing events and the contrast with the Republican convention of that year, see Norman Mailer, *Miami and the Siege of Chicago*, London, Weidenfeld and Nicolson, 1968.

with affirmative action requirements,[6] and beginning in the early 1970s the rules governing selection of delegates to party caucuses have been gradually modified to 'open up' meetings and committees to rank and file members.

Very generally, these reforms (which are paralleled in an attenuated form in the Republican Party) have involved the struggle between old-style party professionals and a new breed of party activists which was discussed in Chapter 6. As we established, the new party activists have generally won out, yet it would be misleading to argue that somehow party influences are stronger as a consequence. In fact the opposite is true. Because delegates are now primarily chosen in primaries and are almost always tied to particular candidates, the voters, not party activists, decide the nomination. And given the rise of candidates' own vote-getting organizations, this effectively relegates political parties to a minor position in the nominating process. As James W. Caeser has put it:

Over the past fifteen years the nominating process has...been transformed from a mixed system, in which control over the nomination was shared by the people and the party organizations, to what can be termed a plebiscitary system in which the key actors are the people and the individual aspirants. Along with the emergence of this new institutional form has come a new method of generating support in presidential campaigns: 'popular leadership', or the attempt by individual aspirants to carve out a personal man's constituency by their own programmatic and personality appeals and by the use of large personal campaign organizations of their own creation. At the nomination stage, this form of leadership takes place entirely without the filter of traditional partisan appeals, as the nomination race is in effect a national non-partisan contest.[7]

Not only has the drive for more democratic procedures in party nominations weakened the influence of party, it has also failed to correct the non-representativeness of convention delegates. In 1972, the delegates were certainly younger and more radical than in 1968, but in ideological and programmatic terms they were *not* typical of the average Democratic voter.[8] By 1980, Democratic delegates

---

6 In the American context affirmative action means a determination to increase the representation (in employment, access to housing and other services) of women and minorities. It can mean quotas, but as often is interpreted as taking positive action to help the under represented.

7 James W. Caeser, *Presidential Selection: Theory and Development*, Princeton, New York, Princeton University Press, 1979, p. 5.

8 See Jeane Kirkpatrick, *The New Presidential Elite*, New York, Russell Sage, Twentieth Century Fund, 1976.

were markedly more female and Black than before, but they were also more middle-class and had fewer links with industrial trade unions and traditional Democratic party organizations and stronger links with the growing public sector unions. Increasing disquiet within the Party has moved some leading Democrats, including Terry Sanford, the ex-Governor of North Carolina, to call for a return to party control over nominations.[9] Indeed in March 1982 the Democratic National Committee accepted the recommendations of the latest commission to investigate the nomination process (the Hunt Commission). The major changes are:

(1)   a shortened primary season;
(2)   reform of the rule whereby delegates are bound or committed to candidates;
(3)   an increase in the number of delegates at the convention drawn from party and elected officials.

What actually happens in 1984 under these new rules remains to be seen. A shorter primary season is, however, unlikely because state laws, not party rules, decide the timing of primaries.

The Campaign. Before the campaign proper starts, nominated candidates have to choose their Vice-Presidential running mates. Unlike most recent activity on the floor of the convention hall, this remains a highly political process. Nominees use the opportunity to heal political wounds or to balance the ticket geographically or ideologically. In 1960 John Kennedy's choice of Lyndon Johnson helped to smooth relations between the two main contenders for the nomination; it also balanced the ticket between the urbane Catholic North Easterner and the more populist, Protestant Southerner. The choice is an important one, for although the office of Vice-President is not in itself very important, no fewer than four of the last nine Vice-Presidents eventually became Presidents themselves (Harry Truman, Lyndon Johnson, Richard Nixon and Gerald Ford). Occasionally things go terribly wrong. George McGovern's initial choice of Thomas Eagleton in 1972 had to be changed with indecent haste once it was revealed that Eagleton had received psychiatric treatment. In 1980, Ronald Reagan's first preference, Gerald Ford, proved politically tactless when Ford, not unsurprisingly, laid down

9 *A Danger of Democracy: The Presidential Nominating Process,* Boulder Colorado, Westview, 1981.

,certain conditions for acceptance including a demand that the Vice-President should be more an executive partner than subordinate.

Both the pre-convention and post-convention campaigns are expensive. Advertising, and particularly television advertising, takes the lion's share. Indeed spending on television has risen almost exponentially since the first major exposure of candidates during the 1960 campaign, when John Kennedy confronted Richard Nixon in live debates. What effect it has on the voters is, however, an open question. Some evidence exists to suggest that general television advertising has little, most voters apparently acquire positive or negative impressions towards candidates quite early on and then their perceptions are based on performance rather than image.[10] Nonetheless no candidate can afford to drop his guard and live televised debates between candidates at least have the potential for affecting public images. (For further details of campaign spending, see p. 183).

For most candidates a high level of public exposure is maintained by constant travel, usually by air, but still a candidate may hire a train to re-enact the famous whistle stop tours of an earlier era. Incumbent Presidents standing for re-election are usually less eager to engage in constant public image-building. They do, after all, enjoy the advantages of incumbency and can exploit their established position as statesmen. In 1972, for example, Richard Nixon appeared in public infrequently and relied instead on the prestige of the Presidential office when appealing to the voters.[11] Whatever the campaign strategy, all candidates continue during the last two or three months before the election to build political bridges, and to strengthen the coalition of support they must already have established to have won the nomination. To a European observer, the campaigns are remarkably free from reference to specific programmes and policies. Indeed candidates score points against opponents or make reference to very broad issues and ideological labels. Jimmy Carter was condemned by Reagan as indecisive and incapable of upholding American power and prestige abroad. Carter in turn branded Reagan an ideologue of the Right and insensitive to the needs of ordinary citizens. Attacking opponents may not be the only focus. Reagan promised in 1980 to 'get America back to work'. Richard Nixon in 1968 pledged that he would pursue 'peace

10 Thomas E. Patterson and Robert D. McClure, *The Unseeing Eye: The Myth of Television Power in National Elections*, New York, Putnam, 1976.
11 And also, as we now know, on the illegal activities of CREEP (the Committee to Re-elect the President).

with honour' in Vietnam. As we have already noted, the whole of the campaign, pre- and post-convention, has increasingly become an exercise dependent not on traditional party organization, but on *personal* party organization and in some cases simply on personal followings. Again, this demonstrates the general trend towards essentially non-partisan elections, the implications of which we will discuss later.

Presidential Selection: Faults and Foibles

Writing in 1981 and making direct comparisons with the selection process for British Prime Ministers, Anthony King listed eight apparently serious flaws in the 1980 Presidential selection process. It is worth repeating these:

(1) The two winners in the United States had entered politics in middle age, and neither had very much experience of government....

(2) Neither winner in the United States had ever served in any capacity in the national government, whether in Washington or overseas. Moreover, at the time of their nomination, neither held any public office whatsoever....

(3) The candidates in the United States were assessed and voted upon by party activists in some states but mainly by voters in primary elections. No special weight was attached to the views of those who had worked with the candidates or had had a chance to observe them at first hand....

(4) The campaigns of would-be presidential nominees in the United States last for a very long time.

(5) Campaigns for Presidential nominations in the United States involve an enormous amount of wear and tear on the part of the candidates and their families...

(6) The campaigns in the United States cost enormous sums of money, and the candidates and their staffs have to devote a great deal of time and effort to raising money.

(7) The process of selecting Presidential candidates in the United States is by no means an exclusively party process....

(8) Electoral considerations may have loomed large in the minds of many of the party regulars who attended party caucuses in 1976 and 1980, but they probably figured scarcely at all in the minds of most voters in the primaries.[12]

Many of the charges have already been implied in earlier sections. In sum, they add up to a serious indictment of recent party reforms

12 Anthony King, 'How not to select Presidential candidates: a view from Europe', in Austin Ranney (ed.) *The American Elections of 1980*, Washington DC, AEI, 1981, pp. 315–20.

and also those reforms in campaign finance which have almost certainly weakened candidates' ties with party organizations. Under the 1971 and 1974 Federal Election Campaign Acts, primary candidates receive matching federal funds up to a maximum of $5.5 million (in 1976). During the campaign proper a further subsidy is available ($21.8 million in 1976) provided candidates do not spend more than this from money raised from other sources. National and state local party committees can also spend a limited amount on the campaign (in 1976 $3.2m and $4.5m for each candidate respectively). Although these reforms have reduced the cost of total spending on Presidential elections, they have also reduced candidate dependence on grass-root party activists and organizations. So according to the critique, candidates are out of touch with the 'real' world of party organization and with day-to-day governmental activity.

Ronald Reagan and (in 1976) Jimmy Carter were 'unemployed' middle-aged (or even elderly) men with no experience of Washington and the wider international community. They owed their electoral success to an undisputed political acumen devoted to winning their party's nomination. This involved mobilizing a personal party following and exploiting the uniquely open — even populist — nature of the 'new' American nomination process. As the critique bluntly asserts, such a system encourages the candidacies of a breed of politicians — the 'unemployed', wealthy, ambitious and instrumental — who are much less likely to make good Presidents than those tested by peer group pressures and the rigours of many years experience in high office.

There is, without doubt, a great deal of truth to these charges. Certainly few successful European leaders have assumed office with as little experience of the world of high politics as did Ronald Reagan or Jimmy Carter. But we should be wary of extrapolating from such small a sample; the same accusation would, after all, be difficult to level at the other three 'failures' among recent Presidents — Lyndon Johnson, ex-Senate Majority Leader and Vice-President; Richard Nixon, ex-Congressman, Senator and Vice-President; and Gerald Ford, ex-House Minority Leader and established party man. Of course at least two old-style party candidates (Hubert Humphrey and Gerald Ford) did *lose* elections, which may vindicate the charges, but then so did George McGovern in 1972 (very much a non-party candidate) and Jimmy Carter in 1980 (an incumbent President with all the advantages that should bring). Final judgment on the Reagan Presidency should be reserved until a later date. But during his first two years of office he used his party connections in the House (via

Bob Michel, the Minority Leader) and in the Senate (through Howard Baker, the Majority Leader) to great effect. This performance is not quite what should be expected from a man whose election depended on popular appeal rather than party connections, and who had no experience of 'high politics' before coming to Washington. Finally, things do change very rapidly in American politics, and it may be that the reforms of the 1970s will be short lived. Already there are signs (the Hunt Commission recommendations) of some retreat from the new populism and at least a partial return to party control.

Nevertheless, we can conclude that the American Presidential selection process is far from ideal and has no doubt contributed to a succession of less than impressive Presidents. But the very considerable problems associated with the office in recent years also have their origins in forces beyond the technicalities of the selection process, and it is to these we must now turn.

The Presidency and Structural Changes in American Society

As suggested, reforms in the selection process reflect deeper changes in the party system and in American society generally. It could well be argued that almost irrespective of the quality of President, these and other developments have together made the job of chief executive much more difficult than ever before. We can identify three such developments, each of which has added to the burden of office.

The Decline of Party and the Rise of Issue Politics. In one sense condemnation of recent Presidential candidates because they have lacked close party ties and have failed to subject themselves to party peer group review is unfair, for if traditional party organizations have declined, candidates cannot be expected to have utilized this particular route to nomination. Once in the White House, however, the real problems of trying to govern in the absence of unifying party forces becomes painfully apparent. In Chapter 5 we listed the functions of political parties, and among the most important were the provision of institutional cohesion and a means to staff the government. Jimmy Carter is usually quoted as the classic case of a President who failed on both counts, largely because he came to Washington with very limited executive experience (as Governor of Georgia) and with few connections in the traditional world of the Democratic Party (the unions, the big cities, the North Eastern establishment). As a result, so the argument runs, his liaison with Congress was poor and his ability to fill key posts with the right men and women, wanting. Certainly, Carter had a rough time with Congress and was not personally inclined to create and nurture relationships with Congressional leaders. But he was not unique in experiencing difficulties with Congress. As we saw in Chapter 8, *all* Presidents have had such problems, including John Kennedy and even Franklin Roosevelt, both of whom had strong party contacts and support.[13] The difference now is that Congress is even more fragmented and party leadership even weaker than it used to be. The coalition building that is essential for legislative success is now correspondingly more difficult.

Worse still, the political vacuum left by the parties has in part been filled by 'issue politics', or the mobilization of political resources around particular issues and ideas. We will examine this phenomenon in more detail in Chapter 11, but even the most casual observer of the American political scene will be aware of the rise of the minority caucuses, pro- and anti-abortion leagues, women's caucuses, the nuclear freeze movement, the conservative coalition and so on. Each of these movements has its Congressional supporters and advocates within administrations and state governments. Issue politics have been aided by the growth of political action committees (PACs) devoted to ensuring the success of 'their' men or women in Congress or the defeat of their opponents. In 1982, for example, it is estimated that NICPAC (the National Conservative Political Action Committee) spent $214,000 trying to unseat the supposedly 'liberal' Senate Minority Leader, Robert Byrd, and $526,000 to defeat the more transparently liberal Edward Kennedy. PACs help build Congressmen's independence from party and administration, and therefore make the Presidents' job that much more difficult.

Issue politics has had a more subtle effect on the political agenda, however. For when policy is defined in terms of discrete issues or one-dimensional ideologies (such as 'conservatism'), the effect is to fragment decision making throughout the political system. Within the executive departments and agencies each issue or position has its supporters, so compounding the already problematical business of getting bureaucrats to implement policy (of which much more later). In sum, in the absence of strong party linkages, Presidents increasingly lack ideological and organizational 'connective tissue' when performing their duties — a fact which puts even more of a premium on the skills and political acumen of individual incumbents.

13 Roosevelt, for example, vetoed an unprecedented number of bills even if very few were subsequently overriden by Congress.

The Nationalization of Politics and Society. With improved communications and the spread of governments' responsibilities, the United States has become a much more centralized society over the last 20—30 years. Information is disseminated centrally by the three major television networks (NBC, CBS, ABC) and by the news services and syndicated columns of major newspapers. Economically, society is more centralized and nationalized with giant corporations providing the same goods and services uniformly throughout the country. It follows that the demands on governments have been centralized, with Washington increasingly the focus of political activity. Chapter 4's discussion of intergovernmental relations showed how state and local governments have become more interdependent with the federal government in recent years. And the same is true of unions, corporations, farmers and almost all those interests in society affected by federal government spending, regulation and arbitration. Naturally, the President is a major focus of all this attention, for he frames most major laws, draws up the budget and has the responsibility for implementing all laws. As chief executive, the President has to manage the vast bureaucracy responsible for these tasks, a bureaucracy which in terms of powers and complexity has grown considerably.

The Relative Decline of American Economic and Political Power. Although not always true, it does seem reasonable to suppose that governing is easier when a country's economy is growing in real terms and its status and power abroad is on the ascendant. Both applied in the case of the United States between 1942 and 1965. Since then, American international economic and military might have experienced sharp relative decline. Perhaps it is not entirely coincidental that the earlier period was associated with the era of 'successful' Presidents, while the latter has witnessed the incumbency of executive 'failures'. While it would be foolhardy to accept this argument in full — was Harry Truman, after all, a 'success' and is Ronald Reagan a 'failure'? — there is no question that the management of the economy and the exercise of military and diplomatic power abroad is *more likely* to be difficult during periods of decline.

The Vietnam War was the first major demonstration of the limits to American military power and it effectively broke one President (Lyndon Johnson) and led another (Richard Nixon) to commit a series of illegal acts, including the secret bombing of Cambodia and the unauthorized surveillance of opponents of the War. More recently, Jimmy Carter's handling of the Iranian Hostage situation dominated the final year of his Presidency, and provided a poignant reminder of the limitations of American might. For recent Presidents, ventures abroad have been problematical, for nothing increases Presidential popularity more instantly than successful — or even unsuccessful but bold — military and diplomatic forays overseas. John Kennedy's popularity soared during the Cuban Missile Crisis, as did Jimmy Carter's following the signing of the Begin/Sadat/Carter Camp David accords in 1979. When the USA is apparently 'humiliated' abroad as, eventually, with Vietnam, the hostage incident in Iran and perhaps over American inability to stop the spread of left-wing activity in Central America, it puts pressure on Presidents to do something about it. Whether the resulting actions are in the public interest or in the interests of world peace are, of course, another matter.

At home, managing the many distributional questions which are the very essence of the chief executive's job is obviously more difficult when the economy is stagnating or even contracting. In his book the *Zero Sum Society*,[14] Lester Thurow identifies this as the key problem of modern society. In other words, when the national cake stays the same size or diminishes, distributional questions become a zero sum game, or when one person gains another must lose, because there is a strict limit to the total mount of resources available. So if more women are employed fewer men must be, or if South Carolina receives an increase in federal aid, other states must suffer a decrease. Of course in reality the number of decision points in the distributional system means that it is more complex than this. Even so, no single individual is more centrally placed to make these distributional decisions than is the President. He is responsible for producing an annual budget amounting to over $700 billion, and for ensuring that this money is properly spent on literally thousands of programmes. Congress is, of course, also involved in this process and when it comes to contested distributions the courts become key actors. But neither Congress nor the courts are as politically visible as the President. Only the President is perceived as national leader and defender of the public welfare. Small wonder, then, that recent Presidents have experienced such difficulties, both in domestic policy and with defence spending, which naturally affects the amount available for domestic programmes. Add to this zero sum problem the increasingly strident demands of the single issue lobbies and the potential for conflict and failure can be appreciated. So no recent President has been able to balance

14 Harmondsworth, Middlesex, Penguin, 1981.

the budget (in 1982 Ronald Reagan, a fiscal conservative, presided over a deficit of more than $150 billion), or has come anywhere near satisfying the demands of all social groups. Take Ronald Reagan's 1981 tax cut measures. As passed by Congress, the cuts had a number of divisive consequences. They gave those earning between $15,000 and $20,000 a year (a majority of wage-earners) only $6 extra a week. But for the rich the benefits were sizeable — $90 a week for those earning $100,000 a year, $257 a week more for the super-rich in the $200,000-plus class. Organized labour were offended by this apparently unfair package, especially as it was accompanied by cuts in welfare and social security benefits. Together with tax cuts on corporate profits and increases in defence spending, this combination obliged Reagan to claw back some of the cuts with tax hikes during 1983. So the President's radical changes, which had been central to his 1980 electoral platform, ended up satisfying almost nobody.

In effect, these changes in society and politics have made the country less easy to govern. Pressures on the central institutions are greater while the ability to respond effectively has been weakened. For the Presidency this unfortunate combination has been particularly serious and helps explain the waxing and waning of Presidential power over the last 20 years. The era of the 'Imperial Presidency' coincided with the tail end of American hegemony, and also, of course, with the incumbency of two especially imperious Presidents. By the mid-1960s the office had grown enormously in power, and the pressures imposed by the Vietnam War and a declining economy tested the office to the full. The potential for the abuse of power was considerable. Unfortunately for the American people Lyndon Johnson and, particulularly, Richard Nixon fell to this temptation. The real importance of the Nixon period is not that the President, along with many of his aides and cabinet officers broke the law, but that the chief executive wielded power in such a way that raised very serious questions on where, exactly, Presidential power began and ended.

Richard Nixon impounded funds appropriated by Congress for programmes he disliked (Impoundment is the setting aside by the executive of funds appropriated by Congress). Towards the end of his Presidency he was exercising the veto power with almost debonaire abandon, and few of his vetoes were overridden by Congress. He invoked 'executive privilege' to justify the withholding of information from Congressional investigative committees and he nominated a number of men to official posts who were unqualified or otherwise unsuitable. Even before Watergate, Congress began to fight back, notably by rejecting two of his more outrageous Supreme Court nominees (see Chapter 12, p. 260). In 1972 the Congress attempted to control the President's discretion to make executive agreements — effectively treaties with foreign powers which could be concluded, sometimes in secret, without consulting the Senate. Under the Case Act all such agreements have to be submitted to Congress. More far-reaching was the 1973 War Powers Act passed by Congress over a Presidential veto which put limits on the President's power to commit troops overseas (see Chapter 8, p. 165). 1973 also saw Congress insist that the President's Director and Deputy Directors of the vital Office of Management and Budget be subject to Senate confirmation.[15]

Following Watergate, Congress asserted its power even more vigorously - in part because Watergate had precipitated a landslide victory for the Democrats in the 1974 mid-term elections. The Budget and Impoundment Control Act of 1974 obliges the President to report 'recission' to Congress when funds appropriated remain unspent. Congress then has to approve recission within 45 days. The same law created the Budget Committees in Congress to enable the legislature to play a more constructive part in the budget process (see Chapter 13, pp. 285–90). As can be seen from Table 9.2 Gerald Ford, as the unfortunate successor to Nixon, experienced unprecedented opposition from Congress, with nearly 23 per cent of his vetoes being overridden.

TABLE 9.2   *Presidential Vetoes of Public Bills, 1945–81*

	Total vetoed	Regular vetoes	Pocket vetoes	Congressional over-rides	Percentage of regular vetoes
Truman	83	54	29	11	20.4
Eisenhower	81	36	45	2	5.5
Kennedy	9	4	5	0	0
Johnson	13	6	7	0	0
Nixon	40	24	16	5	20.8
Ford	46	35	11	8	22.8
Carter	29	13	16	2	15.4
Reagan[a]	2	2	0	0	0

Source: Guide to Congress, Washington DC, 2nd edition, 1976, p. 626; *Congressional Quarterly Almanac*, 1980 and 1981.
Note:
a   1981 only. It is rare for Presidents to veto many bills during their first year in office.

15   The best history of the Nixon era is Jonathan Schell, *The Time of Illusion*, New York, Vintage, 1975.

Finally in 1976 Congress put considerable limits on the President's power to declare emergencies and assume special powers. Under the National Emergencies Act of 1976, Congress can terminate a declaration of emergency and all declarations must be reported to Congress, together with legal justifications for them.

Following the adoption of all these measures and the incumbency of an unusually unassertive President, Jimmy Carter, Presidency watchers began to talk of the *decline* of Presidential power and the resurgence of Congress. As we saw in Chapters 7 and 8, there can be no doubting that Congress has become more rather than less difficult for Presidents to deal with. However, Presidents retain an enormous fund of resources on which to draw. The next section concentrates on those resources not covered in early sections and on the ways in which successive Presidents have adapted to the pressures and problems associated with the office.

Two main resources can be identified — the public and the Presidential bureaucracy — to which a third, conceptually distinct resource, personality, can be added.

PRESIDENTIAL RESOURCES

The Public

It may seem paradoxical in the light of the foregoing discussion to view the public as a resource. Yet under certain circumstances it can be just that. As national leaders, Presidents can make direct appeals to the public through press conferences and special televised announcements. In some instances this amounts almost to a limited form of direct democracy. In 1981 and 1982, for example, Ronald Reagan made specific appeals to the public on television that they should write to their members of Congress expressing support for the President's economic policies. Both the tax and spending cuts were passed by narrow margins and it seems reasonable to assume that Reagan's pleadings had some effect — especially as many members cannot afford to ignore a sudden influx of constituency mail. Appeals to the public are not always successful, of course, as Richard Nixon's sometimes painful public attempts to hide his guilt over Watergate demonstrated. But earlier in his Presidency, Nixon had made highly effective use of this resource through his carefully constructed public lectures on American disengagement from Vietnam.

Although still a potentially powerful weapon, the public appeal resource is beset with problems and pitfalls. As was established in

Chapter 6, the American electorate is now highly volatile. Together with a growing cynicism with public institutions, not least the Presidency,[16] this had made the President's public appeals more risky than they used to be. During Ronald Reagan's first two years, it seems reasonable to infer that the public were willing to provide support during what was effectively a 'honeymoon' period. Following the mid-term elections when the Democrats made deep inroads into the conservative coalition in the House, such support will probably become more grudging with, possibly, the balance of public opinion shifting to the Congress rather than the President. This accepted, no other national institution — Congress, party, courts — can use the media quite like the President. He is, after all, just one man with a special national status. Given all the problems of governing in the 1980s, Presidents will continue to make direct appeals to the public, for it is one of the few, if imperfect, means whereby the fragmenting influences in American politics can be overcome.

Bureaucracy

As the job of President has become more demanding, so incumbents have adapted their administrative resources accordingly. All Presidents have had a *Cabinet* composed mainly of departmental heads at their disposal, but as we will see, the Cabinet is but one of a number of administrative devices available, most of which have been introduced during this century to help Presidents formulate and execute policy. In 1921 the Bureau of the Budget (now called the Office of Management and Budget) was established to help the President prepare the budget and coordinate spending policies. As can be seen from Figure 9.1, since then a number of other agencies have been created which collectively are known as the Executive Office of the President (EOP) (formally established by Franklin Roosevelt in 1939). Quite distinct from the Cabinet, the Executive Office consists of about 2,000 individuals directly accountable to the President. This figure includes about 500 people who actually work in the White House

---

16 Both during and immediately after Watergate public rating of the office sank to a new low with, in 1974, only 13 per cent expressing 'a great deal of confidence in the executive branch'. Quoted in Koenig, *op. cit*, p. 102. Since the mid-1970s public confidence in the office has increased a little, but ratings of individual Presidents have generally been low. Comparing Reagan with his predecessors, after 12 months in office, around 55 per cent of the public approved of the way he was handling his job as President, compared with 68 per cent for Eisenhower, 77 per cent for Kennedy, 69 per cent for Johnson and 61 per cent for Nixon. Both Ford (46 per cent) and Carter (52 per cent) fared badly by comparison. *Public Opinion*, Vol. 4, No. 6, December/January, 1982, pp. 30–1.

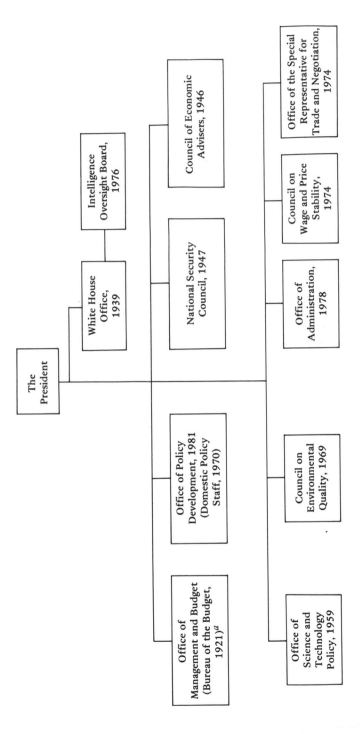

FIGURE 9.1   *The Executive Office of the President, 1982*

Source: Adapted from Hugh Heclo, 'The changing Presidential office' in Arnold Meltsner (ed.) *Politics and the Oval Office,* San Francisco, Institute for Contemporary Studies, 1981, p. 164.

Note:
a   Formally incorporated into the Executive Office in 1939.

as personal aides to the President — the White House Office in Figure 9.1. How Presidents actually use the EOP, and in particular the White House staff, has aroused bitter controversy over the last 20 years. A major criticism, inspired mainly by Watergate, has concerned the extent to which the staff has grown in recent years and has increasingly insulated Presidents from public opinion and political reality. A related theme centres on whether any personal bureaucracy can be an adequate administrative tool against the vast resources of executive departments and agencies and against a fragmented but powerful Congress.

There can be no disputing that some Presidents have used their staffs unwisely. Richard Nixon, in particular, relied heavily on just a handful of personal aides, eschewing most Cabinet officers, Congressional and party leaders. Three of his closest aides — John Erlichman, Bob Haldeman and Ron Zeigler, became so effective in acting as the President's mouthpieces, that they earned the sobriquet 'The Berlin Wall'. And in the Carter Presidency Stewart Eisenstadt, the domestic policy adviser, almost assumed the status of policy initiator and spokesman. Not that these are historically isolated examples. This century there are at least three other instances of staffers assuming national prominence and even notoriety as 'the powers behind the throne'.[17] Critics have argued that the very considerable power of personal staffs is undemocratic — they are, after all, unelected and few are subject to Senate confirmation. Personal staffs — and modern Presidents all have domestic, economic and foreign policy advisers, a press secretary, legal counsel, and staff responsible for liaison work with Congress — often overlap with members of other agencies within the EOP. Hence Presidents' national security advisers are also members of the National Security Council, a body consisting among others of the President, Vice-President and Defense and State Secretaries set up by Congress in 1947 to help the formulation of foreign policy and aid crisis management. In some instances, the National Security Adviser becomes more important than the Secretary of State, as was clearly the case with Henry Kissinger before he effectively 'deposed' the incumbent, William Rogers, and assumed the office of Secretary of State himself during Nixon's second term. Similarly the Director of the Office of Management and Budget can become a key figure, for the OMB is responsible for monitoring the spending of the various executive departments.

17 Colonel House with Woodrow Wilson, Harry Hopkins with Franklin Roosevelt and Sherman Adams with Dwight Eisenhower.

In 1980 Ronald Reagan's choice of Director, David Stockman, a bright young ex-Congressman, suggested strongly that the OMB Director would have direct responsibility for handling the budget and the cuts to be imposed on many of the departments and agencies.[18] In this sense, the OMB and its director resemble, although are by no means identical to, the British Treasury and Chancellor of the Exchequer.

How Presidents use the EOP and especially their personal staff varies greatly from administration to administration. Until Watergate it was common to contrast Franklin Roosevelt's style of creating an atmosphere of constructive competition with aides deliberately positioned to provide contrasting information and advice, with Eisenhower's tendency to delegate responsibility and Kennedy's emphasis on intelligence and *esprit de corps*.[19]

Since Watergate, however, there is evidence that whatever management strategy adopted by Presidents, they will experience serious command problems. Certainly, Presidents have felt obliged to innovate and reorganise the executive branch to improve management. Some Presidents have appointed 'chiefs of staff' specifically to help management of the White House — although two recent incumbents in this position, Bob Haldeman of Watergate fame and Hamilton Jordan in the Carter White House, whose private lifestyle attracted some attention, have not been the best advertisements for the job. Ronald Reagan appointed Martin Anderson as chief of the Office of Policy Development, a new unit replacing the Domestic Policy Office and embracing some responsibility for economic affairs. Anderson had a special status within the White House, particularly in helping smooth relations between Cabinet members. However he left the White House after only a short period and instead three of President Reagan's other staffers — Chief of Staff James Baker, President's Counsel Edwin Meese and Deputy Chief of Staff Michael Deever — acquired a special status and became more centrally placed than other staffers or individual departmental secretaries. A more radical ploy has involved attempts to institutionalize the delegation of power through strengthening the Cabinet. Although every President has had a Cabinet, the Constitution unambiguously assigns executive power to the President, so whether the device is used or not is a matter of great

18 Significantly, since 1973 the Director of OMB has been subject to Senate confirmation.
19 An excellent account of how different Presidents have used their staff is Richard Tanner Johnson's *Managing the White House*, New York, Harper and Row, 1974.

discretion. Its membership consists of the heads of the executive departments plus individuals assigned by the President himself. Re-invigorating the Cabinet is a natural option for Presidents to choose, because a major part of executive leadership involves control and management of the vast federal bureaucracy. Much of the work of personal staff involves liaison with this marasmus, and the closer the communications and finer the line of command, the better. So Presidents Nixon, Carter and Reagan pledged that they would strengthen their Cabinets. Nixon patently failed to do this, but Carter did in fact use the Cabinet quite frequently, as has Ronald Reagan. Indeed, during his first year in office President Reagan convened his Cabinet no less than 37 times, a very high figure in historical perspective.[20] It is too early to judge whether this will smooth relations between White House and the Executive Departments. As we will see in Chapter 10 a natural antipathy exists between the two, largely because departments and agencies have constituencies and interests of their own. Whatever the promises, Presidents generally resort to using their own (usually reliable) staff rather than risk giving real power to departmental secretaries, and recent history is littered with examples of conflict between powerful staffers or EOP members and departmental heads.

Presidents' urge to reorganize extends to other areas and has included a major reorganisation of the EOP by Jimmy Carter, who eliminated seven of the Office's administrative units. And both Jimmy Carter and Ronald Reagan promised to make greater use of their Vice-Presidents. Traditionally the position has meant little in itself, or 'not worth a pitcher of warm spit' as John Nance Garner, one of Franklin Roosevelt's Vice-Presidents, colourfully put it. Walter Mondale was, however, accorded a more central position in the Carter Administration than many previous Vice-Presidents, and George Bush, although hardly prominent in the Reagan Cabinet, has at least a degree of public visibility.

All these efforts demonstrate the increasingly difficult political environment in which Presidents have to work. As we have stressed time and again in earlier chapters, American politics has become increasingly fragmented in the post-war era. Together with the nationalization of political life, this has forced Presidents to manage numerous centres of political power each with its own policy

---

20 For a good discussion of recent developments in the Cabinet and in the National Security Council see A. J. Bennett, *American Government and Politics 1982: A Survey for Students*, Royal Hospital School, Ipswich, Suffolk, UK, 1982.

network. As Hugh Heclo has emphasized, staff and other administrative assistance helps, but cannot solve the central dilemma of the office:

Whoever the President and whatever his style, the political and policy bureaucracies crowd in on him. They are there in his office to help, but their needs are not necessarily his needs. Delegation is unavoidable; yet no one aide or combination of aides has his responsibilities or takes his oath of office. However much the President trusts personal friends, political loyalists, or technocrats, he is the person that the average citizen and history will hold accountable.[21]

Personality

While no one could deny the importance of changes in the nomination process and the political environment as determinants of change in the nature of the Presidency, some observers stress that the most crucial element in the office is the personality of the incumbent. With so much discretion attached to the job and such a premium on leadership skills — persuasion, manipulation, coercion, insight, charisma — personality is undoubtedly important. Indeed even the most casual student of American politics has a cognitive picture of certain Presidents — Truman as feisty and combative, Eisenhower as kind and avuncular, Kennedy as inspirational, and above all, perhaps, Richard Nixon as devious and insecure. Borrowing heavily from psychology, one political scientist, James Barber, has attempted to formalize the 'Presidential character' by classifying Presidents by personality type.[22] Barber's two dimensions are active–passive and positive–negative. Simplifying somewhat, the former describes how much *effort* Presidents put into the job and the latter how much enjoyment or *satisfaction* they get from it. The resulting four categories are shown in Table 9.3, along with the classification of a number of recent Presidents. The key types are Active/Positives, representing individuals who receive enormous satisfaction from being active in the job and Active/Negatives who put in intense effort but get little emotional reward for their pains. Beware, says Barber, of the Active/Negatives, who are likely to dig in when under pressure and display a sometimes paranoid inflexibility. Active/ Positives, in contrast, enjoy the cut and thrust of a highly demanding

21   Hugh Heclo, 'The changing Presidential office', in Arnold J. Meltsner (ed.) *Politics and the Oval Office*, San Francisco, Institute for Contemporary Studies, 1981, p. 177.
22   James David Barber, *The Presidential Character*, Englewood Cliffs, New Jersey, Prentice-Hall, 2nd Edition, 1977.

job and are likely to show that spirit of compromise and adaptability which is so essential to the politics of coalition formation. As with all simply psychological theories, Barber's typology is open to criticism.[23] *Events* often mould personality rather than the other way round. Who, after all, would have judged Lyndon Johnson 'inflexible' before he became so fatally obsessed with the war in Vietnam? And in many respects Richard Nixon, the epitome of the active/negative type according to Barber, was pragmatic and adaptable. Unlike Woodrow Wilson and Lyndon Johnson he had little moral commitment to causes or higher ideals. Moreover, to put Ronald Reagan (admittedly at the beginning of his Presidency) in the same category as Warren Harding and William Taft seems misguided, for *every* modern President has to be 'active'. This may not mean working 18-hour days, but it must at least mean being *psychologically* active or aware of events and political priorities.

TABLE 9.3   *Barber's Classification of Modern Presidents*

| | | Energy Level in the Job | |
		Active	Passive
Emotional attitude to satisfaction from the job	Positive	Franklin Roosevelt Harry Truman John Kennedy Gerald Ford Jimmy Carter	William Taft Warren Harding Ronald Reagan
	Negative	Woodrow Wilson Herbert Hoover Lyndon Johnson Richard Nixon	Calvin Coolidge Dwight Eisenhower

Source: Adapted from various sources including James David Barber, *The Presidential Character, op. cit,* and Louis Koenig, *The Chief Executive,* New York, Harcourt Brace Jovanovich, 4th edition, 1981, p. 345.

In sum, Barber's categories are not a very useful guide to Presidential *quality*. Highly successful and 'failed' Presidents are put in the same category (Franklin Roosevelt and Jimmy Carter as Active/ Positives, Dwight Eisenhower and Calvin Coolidge as passive

23 For a good critique, see Alexander L. George, 'Assessing Presidential character', in Aaron Wildavsky (ed.) *Perspectives on the Presidency*, Boston, Little Brown, 1975.

negatives),[24] and the changes earlier analysed, especially those associated with Presidential selection, appear to bear little or no relationship to Barber's idea of Presidential quality.

What the typology does do is force us to think more carefully about the impact of personality on the office. There is no disputing that some men have been more suited to the job than others and that, irrespective of events, changes in the selection process and in American society, this simple fact continues to hold true. All the evidence suggests, for example, that Ronald Reagan enjoys being President and has a talent for handling people around him which most other recent Presidents have lacked. This does not mean to say that history will judge him a great President or even that his record in dealing with Congress and the public will be deemed successful. But having a personality apparently suited to the job must at least help the incumbent come to terms with what possibly is the most demanding executive position in the modern world.

ASSESSING THE PRESIDENCY: PRESIDENTIAL POWER IN THE 1980s

When, in 1960, Richard Neustadt described Presidential power as the 'power to persuade', he accurately captured the need for Presidents to be successful bargainers, negotiators and manipulators.[25] Coalition building, in other words, is the very essence of the President's job, and incumbents must have the personal capacity not only to appreciate this fact (as Jimmy Carter constantly said he did) but also act accordingly (as Jimmy Carter repeatedly failed to do). Coalition-building skills are necessary at every level — within the White House, and in relations with executive departments, Congress, the media, interest groups and the public. Neustadt's famous essay was designed to show that formal command was not enough; that indeed it was sometimes quite limited, unless supplemented by the more subtle political skills involved in the art of persuasion.[26] To reduce almost all of the President's job to bargaining skills is, of

24 This pairing is particularly inappropriate given recent evidence claiming the high quality of Eisenhower's leadership. See Fred Greenstein, *The Hidden Hand Presidency: Eisenhower as Leader*, New York, Basic Books, 1982.

25 *Presidential Power*, New York, John Wiley, 1960.

26 Neustadt showed how the commands of Presidents on three occasions — Truman's sacking of General MacArthur, his decision to seize the steel mills in 1951 and Eisenhower's decision to send federal troops to Little Rock, Arkansas in 1954 — were as much a demonstration of failure rather than success, for they represented the failure of persuasion or the bargaining skills so crucial to the office, *ibid*. Chapters 2 and 3.

course to oversimplify. Constitutionally, the chief executive has immense power of command — not least as commander in chief — which he can exercise without a finely honed aptitude for bargaining. The Presidencies of Lyndon Johnson and Richard Nixon are proof enough of this. Yet both Presidents are now considered less than successful, and since the early 1970s the number of power centres and policy networks in the American system has increased considerably. Moreover, changes in the selection process, while perhaps not preselecting certain personality types among candidates, has certainly affected the nature of their party and political contacts and hence their access to major bargaining resources. Add to this the structural changes in society listed earlier and it is easy to appreciate why so many commentators complain of the office being 'overloaded'. In such a context, the premium on bargaining and leadership skills is greatly increased. One thing is sure: no matter how difficult the job becomes or how recent Presidents are judged by a fickle electorate — and one-term Presidents may now be the norm rather than the exception — the position of President of the United States will continue to attract enormous attention both in the USA and abroad. For to repeat the point yet again, alone in a highly fragmented political system, the Presidency is the natural coordinating institution of national leadership. Given the inherent power of the federal government over the lives of many millions of Americans and non-Americans, this must ensure that the very special status of the Presidency will continue.

FURTHER READING

Louis W. Koenig's *The Chief Executive*, New York, Harcourt Brace Jovanovich, 4th edition, 1981 is among the best of the textbook treatments of the Presidency, but see also Thomas E. Cronin, *The State of the Presidency*, Boston, Little Brown, 2nd edition, 1980. Presidential policy making is analysed in Richard Neustadt, *Presidential Power*, New York, John Wiley, Revised edition, 1976. See also Arnold J. Meltsner (ed.), *Politics and the Oval Office*, San Francisco, Institute for Contemporary Studies, 1981. Fred Greenstein's *The Hidden Hand Presidency: Eisenhower as Leader*, New York, Basic Books, 1982 should not be missed as it combines careful scholarship with a completely new interpretation of the Eisenhower period. For a stimulating, if highly contentious view of Presidential personality, see James David Barber, *The Presidential Character*, Englewood Cliffs, New Jersey, Prentice-Hall, 2nd edition, 1977. Presidential elections are covered in Herbert Asher, *Presidential Elections and American Politics*, Holmewood, Illinois, Dorsey Press, 1976. The best review of the 1980

Presidential elections is Austin Ranney (ed.), *The American Elections of 1980*, Washington DC, American Enterprise Institute, 1981.

CHAPTER 10

The Federal Bureaucracy

The fully developed bureaucratic mechanism compares with other organizations exactly as does the machine with the non-mechanical modes of production. Precision, speed, unambiguity, knowledge of the files, continuity, discretion, unity, strict subordination, reduction of friction and of material and personal costs — these are raised to the optimum point in the strictly bureaucratic administration.

Max Weber, Essays in Sociology

It's time for us to take a new look at our government, to eliminate waste, to release our civil servants from bureaucratic chaos, to provide tough management...

Jimmy Carter, 1976

Our Government has no special power except that granted it by the people. It is time to check and reverse the growth of government which shows signs of having grown beyond the consent of the governed. It is my intention to curb the size and influence of the federal establishment...

Ronald Reagan, 1981

Few areas of federal government activity come in for as much opprobrium as does the bureaucracy. As the Weber quote suggests, bureaucracies are supposed to work efficiently. Hierarchy, order, responsibility and professionalism are implied by the model of the 'rational' bureaucrat, yet according to public folklore, typical federal administrators are the very opposite of this. They are overpaid, inefficient and wasteful. Worse, they are often the creatures of special interests and occasionally they are simply corrupt. Surveys have shown, indeed, that the federal government is considered easily the most inefficient of all the major institutions in American society

(Table 10.1). While some of the more colourful charges levelled at the federal bureaucracy more closely resemble caricature than accurate portrait, the executive branch does seem unusually inefficient, fragmented and complex. So much so, indeed, that every President has pledged himself to simplify the executive branch and to root out wasteful and unnecessary programmes. Promises of this sort are popular with the electorate and no doubt Presidents genuinely believe that they can actually rationalize the bureaucracy.

TABLE 10.1 *Public Perception of Efficiency of Institutions, November 1981 (percentage)*

Institution	Not efficient and well run	Efficient and well run	Don't know
Federal government	74	20	6
Local government	49	43	7
Large business corporations	33	56	10
Private voluntary organizations	23	60	17
Small business corporations	20	70	10

Source: *Public Opinion*, Vol. 5, No. 1 (February/March 1982), p. 28. © American Enterprise Institute.

However, in spite of some changes, the complaints — and frustrated attempts at reform — continue. This issue raises a number of questions. Why is it that the executive branch attracts so much criticism? Is the criticism justified? To what extent *can* the federal bureaucracy be controlled and reformed? It may be that the structure and behaviour of the executive departments and agencies reflect other forces in American government which would have to be changed as a prelude to bureaucratic reform. Before we address these questions directly, it is necessary to provide some basic facts about the federal administration in the United States.

THE FEDERAL BUREAUCRACY: ORGANIZATION AND FUNCTION

The annual *US Government Manual* produces an organization chart of the government of the United States (Figure 10.1). While such charts can be misleading — they imply a hierarchical simplicity and equality between units at the same level which is far from reality — they do reveal the bare bones of the system. The most important distinctions are between the 13 executive departments, the independent

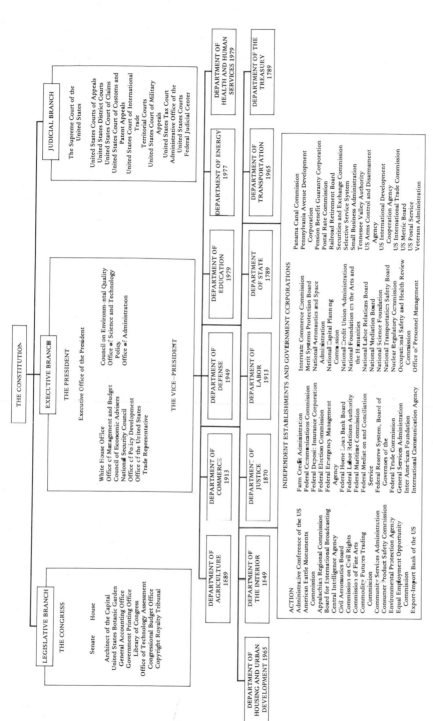

FIGURE 10.1   *The Government of the United States*

Source: Adapted from *US Government Manual 1981–2,* Washington DC, US Government Printing Office, 1981.

establishments and the government corporations. Executive or Cabinet departments are responsible for the major federal programmes, and their chiefs, the departmental secretaries, are directly answerable to the President. Given the growth in government over the last 50 years, Cabinet departments have not proliferated as might have been expected. In 1981 only six of the 13 departments were creations of the modern era and of these 1 (Defense) grew out of older departments and another 2 (Energy and Education) were threatened by the Reagan axe. In fact successive Presidents have worked hard to reduce the number of departments or to rationalize existing ones. In 1949 the Departments of War, Army, Navy and Airforce were combined in one Department of Defense. In 1971 President Nixon proposed 'the most far-reaching reorganization of the executive branch that has ever been proposed by a President of the United States'[1] by amalgamating seven Cabinet departments into four new ones. His plan was rejected by Congress, but both Jimmy Carter and Ronald Reagan have continued the campaign to simplify the departments. As already noted, Ronald Reagan went so far as to label the Departments of Education and Energy unnecessary and during 1982 bills were introduced into Congress proposing their abolition. Both were created by Jimmy Carter — the former because the existing Department of Health Education and Welfare was so large and cumbersome, and the latter as a direct response to the nation's energy crisis.

Most Presidents prefer a small, compact Cabinet so as to facilitate smooth policy making. Yet the number of departments for which they are responsible is but one of a number of management problems they have to face. Another involves the complexity characteristic of each department. This can be formidable, for with the possible exception of the Department of State (responsible for the foreign service and foreign policy) each department is itself a collection of different agencies and services, each with its own interests and constituents. So the Department of Housing and Urban Development (HUD) was created in 1965 by bringing together a number of existing agencies, most of whom retained some identity after the amalgamation. Subsequently, HUD was reorganized in an effort to blur the lines between the old agencies, but these tend to persist for as long as the function they perform persists. HUD's present (1981) organization is shown in Figure 10.2. Again the apparently simple hierarchical

---

1   Quoted in Otis L. Graham, *Toward a Planned Society: From Roosevelt to Nixon*, New York, Oxford University Press 1976, p. 209.

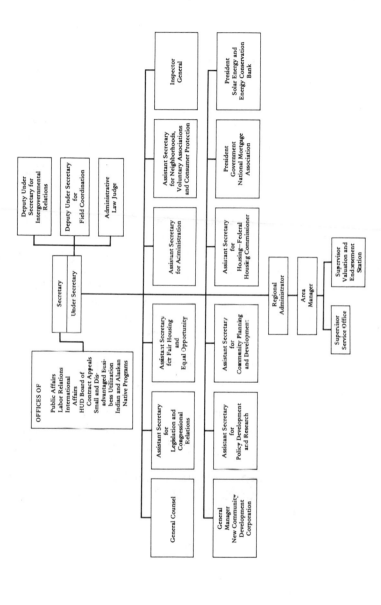

FIGURE 10.2 *Department of Housing and Urban Development*

Source: Adapted from *US Government Manual 1981–2*, Washington, DC, US Government Printing Office, 1981, p. 831.

structure belies a reality of considerable complexity and competition
— although the sheer number of different programmes does give
some sense to the complexity of what is one of the smaller (in terms
of money spent) departments. In almost all Cabinet departments
there is a horizontal division of responsibilities and a vertical division
organized geographically. So in Figure 10.2 much of the day-to-day
work of HUD is carried out at the regional and area levels. There
are ten standard federal regions and within these a number of area
offices, usually based on large cities. Figure 10.2 also allows us to
make some distinction between different sorts of bureaucrats. In
the American system, a crucial distinction exists between career
officials and political appointees. The latter consist of the executive
schedule appointments (Secretary, Under Secretary, Deputy Under
Secretary and Assistant Secretary positions as shown in Figure 10.2)
plus in the other agencies and corporations, administrators, commis-
sioners and so on. About 700 individuals are in this super league but
they are assisted by a further batch of political appointees drawn
from the 'supergrade' positions in the civil service. A number of
political appointees are also in lesser positions. This is the middle
management heart of American bureaucracy consisting of about
7,000 civil servants. Of these approximately 2,300 are political
appointees; the remainder are career civil servants. It is these career
officials who head the *bureaux* (or offices) in American administration which, placed at a level immediately below assistant secretary,
are crucial in running the day-to-day business of government policy.
While no one doubts the career status of the lower grades and the
political status of the executive schedule appointees (almost all of
whom are subject to Senate confirmation) this middle group of
7,000 have a somewhat ambiguous status — especially as some are
'quasi political' and exempt from many normal civil service procedures (competitive recruitment, tenure and so on).[2] This ambiguity
makes it particularly difficult for Presidents and Cabinet secretaries
to ensure that all the key positions are filled with personnel sympathetic to their policies and programmes.

The independent establishments and government corporations
(Figure 10.1) include a vast number of agencies performing numerous

2 The Civil Service Commission polices recruitment to the executive departments and
plays an especially crucial role in relation to these so-called non-career executives (NEAS).
Numbering about 600, this group is not subject to normal civil service procedures as they
are chosen by political appointees to carry out a policy-making role in the departments.
But the Civil Service Commission retains some control over their activities and status. For
a full discussion of these and related matters, see Hugh Heclo, *A Government of Strangers:
Executive Politics in Washington*, Washington DC, Brookings Institution, 1977, Chapter 2.

functions. A very general distinction can be drawn between government corporations (broadly equivalent to nationalized industries in other countries) which includes the US Postal Service and the Tennessee Valley Authority, and the regulatory agencies. But there are other institutions which fall into neither category, including the Veterans' Administration which, with over 200,000 employees, provides for the medical and other social needs of ex-servicemen, and the General Services Administration and Civil Service Commission which deal, respectively, with the provision of buildings, equipment and other services for the whole executive branch, and the recruitment of staff to the Cabinet departments. It is a little misleading to label all of these institutions 'independent' — the chief administrators (or in a few cases the boards of governors) are appointed by the President, subject to confirmation by the Senate. The President is also a key figure in helping decide the size of their budgets and in some cases he, or his Cabinet secretaries, take a very direct interest in their activities. This is patently the case with the Central Intelligence Agency (CIA) and with the International Communications Agency (formerly the US Information Service, which effectively acts as a propaganda service for the State Department).

However, the regulatory agencies are genuinely more independent as most of them were originally set up by Congress to act as nonpartisan organizations responsible for monitoring, controlling or regulating various aspects of economic and social life. Three waves of reform in American politics correspond to the three generations of regulatory agencies which exist. Between 1887 and 1915 a rising tide of reform sentiment led to the creation of agencies designed to tame the unacceptable economic and social activities of large corporations and natural monopolies, mainly the railroads. So during this period the Interstate Commerce Commission and Federal Trade Commission came into being. During the 1930s most of the reforms were inspired by the Depression and its consequences. Hence the Federal Deposit Insurance Corporation underwrites bank deposits to protect the public against bank failures, the Securities and Exchange Commission regulates the stock market and the National Labour Relations Board helps regulate industrial relations. The final wave of reform, during the 1960s and 1970s, was inspired by, among other things, concern at environmental pollution (leading to the Environmental Protection Agency which is, incidentally, *not* an independent agency but a cabinet level organization), civil rights (the Equal Employment Opportunity Commission), election malpractice (the Federal Election Commission) and consumer protection

(The Consumer Protection Safety Commission). These agencies have sometimes been given formidable powers by Congress to exercise administrative, legislative and judicial powers over corporations, unions and the public at large. Until the 1960s a common criticism was that they were anything but independent in the use of these powers. Instead the 'regulated controlled the regulators' or, to quote two celebrated cases, the Food and Drugs Administration was in the hands of the drug companies and the Interstate Commerce Commission was deferential to the needs of the truckers and railroads.

Although sometimes exaggerated, there is little doubt that many of the regulatory commissions had established a *symbiotic* relationship with what had become their clients.[3] They needed each other, the clients for guidance as how best to operate in (or dominate) the market, and the regulators to ensure political independence and to justify their bureaucratic *raison d'être*. During the 1960s and 1970s much greater public concern at the abuse of corporate power led to the newer agencies (such as the Environmental Protection Agency) establishing a more *adversarial* relationship with the regulated.[4] This, together with limited reforms in the older agencies and a general increase in the amount of regulation in American life — especially of corporations — has led to a backlash by the corporate world and their political allies, the Republicans.

Contrary to popular belief, the burgeoning responsibilities of the federal government, together with greatly increased expenditure, have not been matched by dramatic increases in the *number* of federal employees responsible for implementing programmes and policies. As can be seen from Figure 10.3, the number of federal employees has remained roughly the same over the last 30 years, the big increases in total government employment being accounted for by state and local governments. Indeed, starting with the Carter administration and continuing under President Reagan, the absolute number of federal/civilian employees has fallen, reaching around 2,700,000 by 1982. Recent reductions are part of the continuing campaign against big government, but the general failures of federal employment to rise in the post-war period takes more explaining. Part of the reason is the rapid increase in the number and size of grant-in-aid programmes to state and local governments. As we saw in Chapter 4, a fair percentage of the general increase in federal

3 See Murray Edelman, *The Symbolic Uses of Politics*, Urbana, Illinois, University of Illinois Press, 1964, for a good analysis of this point.
4 For a selection of case studies on regulation, see James Q. Wilson (ed.) *The Politics of Regulation*, New York, Basic Books, 1980.

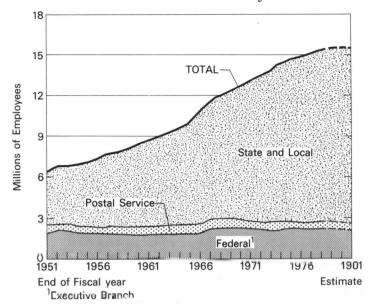

FIGURE 10.3 *Government Civilian Employment, 1951–81*

Source: Special Analysis Budget of the US Government, 1981, Special Analysis I, Washington DC, US Government Printing Office, 1981, p. 287.

spending derives from this source. Devolved programmes increase employment at the lower rather than federal level. Second, increased expenditure does not necessarily require more federal employees – although it has almost certainly led to what is a considerable expansion of the number of professionals in federal employment. Professionals are the middle grade employees – often scientists, or the highly trained personnel who have been increasingly recruited to help run more complex programmes, both old and new. In fact (the Post Office excluded) the federal government employs relatively few less qualified workers. State and local governments employ most of the lower grades (transport, hospital, municipal employees) and lower/middle grades (teachers, social workers, police and firemen). A more professional civil service is harder to control because it can more easily fall back on technical and highly specialised information when challenged by the public, Congress or the President.

THE BUREAUCRACY: HOW UNCONTROLLABLE?

Students of administrative behaviour are quick to identify certain characteristics of bureaucracy which are present whatever the political system involved or governmental function being performed. Some of these characteristics are labelled 'undesirable' — usually because they greatly reduce the accountability of bureaucrats to elected officials — and as government becomes larger and more complex so these undesirable features multiply. There is, of course, no reason to suppose that the United States is exempt from these trends. It is not, and that is problem enough. But critics go much further and argue that US government, and particularly the federal bureaucracy, has a number of additional, and uniquely American features which makes the problem of accountability a particularly serious one. Unfortunately, unravelling cause and effect is difficult in this area, especially in a country where 'federal government' and 'bureaucracy' often hold negative connotations. With so many Americans deeply prejudiced against government, it is important to treat with caution some of the more colourful critiques levelled against bureaucracy, regulation, 'Washington' and the civil service.

The task of the remainder of this chapter is, therefore, to outline the major criticisms directed at the federal bureaucracy, assess their validity and to record the ways in which Presidents, Congress, the courts and the public have attempted to increase their control over administrators.

THE INHERENT POWER OF BUREAUCRACY

Simple theories of both constitutional government and administrative behaviour assign little or no independent power or discretion to administrators. Their job is to implement laws. The legislature passes the laws and the chief executive is responsible for managing and directing the administrators in the implementation process. According to classical theories of administration, bureaucrats can do this effectively if they operate in line with certain basic principles — hierarchical command, specialization and delegation of duties. The elected chief executives are at the apex of this system, they alone give commands; bureaucrats may advise them; but it is not their job actually to give orders. Reality is, of course, very far from this ideal type. In most systems, bureaucrats have two main powers both of which can give them considerable control over the policy system.

Information

Bureaucrats act as administrative gatekeepers. When laws are being framed either by legislatures or executives, it is essential to find out what is achievable and what is not. A new law on lead levels in petrol, for example, needs to be carefully informed about a host of technical questions, including the efficiency of internal combustion engines, pollution levels, the car industry's ability to compete internationally once their products are adapted, and so on. Politicians are obliged to heed the advice of their officials on such technicalities, and the officials themselves can, up to a point, select and organize information according to their own preferences and prejudices, or in favour of one interest rather than another. They may, for example, advise the politicians that certain options are simply not possible for technical reasons. Examples of administrative gatekeeping in highly technical areas may sound understandable, and possibly exceptional. But almost *all* law making and implementation in modern industrial societies is technical and complex. From housing to transport to law enforcement to social security and defence, technical questions are paramount. No single President or Cabinet secretary can possibly absorb all this information — even with the assistance of professional staffs. They have to rely on their bureaucrats.

Clientelism

Clientelism is the word used to describe the sort of symbiotic relationships between bureaucrats and their customers referred to earlier. Again, it is not unique to American politics; to a greater or lesser extent it occurs everywhere. It is also an entirely understandable phenomenon. Consider the case of defence agencies and defence contractors. In those Western countries with sizeable defence industries (Britain, Germany, France, the USA) intimate relations exist between contractors and officials in defence departments. Defence officials have, therefore, a continuing interest in particular corporations and defence systems — and also, perhaps, in ensuring that defence spending remains at certain levels. These interests may or may not be the same as those of the administrators' political masters. But there can be no doubting the independent political influence of officials in this context. Information is, again, the crucial resource, but it is not merely technical information; it is this plus all the advantages which daily personal contact and shared values give to the official and which are often denied to the politicians.

As government has increased in size and scope, so clientelism has spread. In modern societies all bureaucracies have their customers whose interests and needs must be tended to, whatever the government in power or the values and preferences of elected politicians.

THE BUREAUCRATIC HYDRA:
A UNIQUELY AMERICAN PHENOMENON?

Scholars of comparative government often refer to the extent to which different political systems are characterized by 'strong' or 'weak' states. Almost invariably, the United States is categorized as a weak state. In other words, rather than government being unified, resolute and separated from the rest of society, it is fragmented, indecisive and infused with societal influence.[5] The aforementioned clientelism is a good indicator of the power and autonomy of the state. Although it exists everywhere, clientelism is likely to be more pervasive in weak state systems. In addition, weak states are characterized by competition between different parts of the administrative process. So sub-units — individual departments and agencies — display a marked degree of *autonomy* from the centre. They serve different interests and their officials do not all share the same values and policy objectives. We are not referring here to the absolute *size* of government. As noted, in terms of expenditure and function, American government is large by any standards. We are, rather, referring to the extent to which American government is fragmented and simply not amenable to central direction and control.

Much of recent criticism centres on this fact. Critics usually do not put the particular American situation in comparative context, but we have good reason to believe that the United States is different from many other countries; that certain institutional relationships make it especially difficult to exercise central control over public policy. Two basic critiques of American bureaucracy have been made in recent years — the 'iron triangle' and 'issue network' critiques.

5 For a good comparative analysis see Peter J. Katzenstein (ed.) *Between Power and Plenty: the Foreign Economic Policies of Advanced International States*, Madison, Wisconsin, University of Wisconsin Press, 1978.

Iron Triangles

Starting with books written by Douglass Cater and Leiper Freeman in the mid-1960s, came accusations that sub-governments working as iron triangles — congressional subcommittee, administrative bureau and special interest — were the dominant actors in American politics.[6] The analysis was simple: Congressional subcommittees provide the money and monitor regulations, the bureau actually hands over the money or enforces the regulation and the special interest is the beneficiary. All need each other and the system would break down without equal participation by all. Hence the 'iron triangle' metaphor. Empirical confirmation of sub-governments of this sort were readily at hand, especially in public works, defence, agriculture and water policy. Agriculture became a particularly appealing example with bureaux in the Department of Agriculture handing out subsidies to farmers who in turn had established intimate links with members of the several agricultural subcommittees. The triangle was 'iron' because it was impenetrable. The combined political clout of the leading sub-government actors was formidable with no individual President, public interest lobby or Congressional leader able to break the pattern of distribution and public expenditure which the triangle had moulded. While the empirical validity of this case was convincing for certain sorts of public policy, it was clearly inappropriate in other areas. Appreciating this fact, Ripley and Franklin refined the thesis in an important book published in 1976.[7] They pointed out that in what they call re-distributive domestic policy (where resources are taken from one group or class and given to another, as in social welfare programmes), Presidents and top level (politically appointed) officials as well as Congress as a whole play a more important part. And in some regulatory policies, bureaucracy and administration play a relatively small role. Other, more sophisticated refinements, were added by the authors to the sub-government theory, all of which demonstrated that the American administrative and political process is indeed unduly complex and often not amenable to simple, single-model characterizations.

6 Douglass Cater, *Power in Washington*, New York, Vintage, 1964; J. Leiper Freeman, *The Political Process*, New York, Random House, 1965.
7 Randall B. Ripley and Grace A. Franklin, *Congress, the Bureaucracy and Public Policy*, Holmewood, Illinois, Dorsey Press, 1976.

Issue Networks

A conceptually much simpler, yet almost certainly more accurate picture of administrative politics in America has been drawn by Hugh Heclo.[8] In his recent publications, Heclo has argued that as government programmes have grown in size and scope so they have generated new lobbies, interests and, simply, a larger number of active participants in the policy process. Moreover, the networks of politicking and lobbying which develop as a consequence are constantly adapting and changing. So it is very difficult accurately to categorize where the policy system begins and ends:

> The notion of iron triangles and sub-governments presumes small circles of participants who have succeeded in becoming largely autonomous. Issue networks, on the other hand, comprise a large number of participants with quite variable degrees of mutual commitment or of dependence on others in their environment; in fact it is almost impossible to say where a network leaves off and its environment begins.[9]

As a result of this much more open and volatile system, no erstwhile secure sub-government can afford to be complacent. The cosy relationships established between corporations and bureaucrats have been challenged by environmentalists, consumer protection advocates and other public interest lobbies (a point to be developed in the next chapter). The sub-governments continue to exist, of course, but they are increasingly buffeted by competing centres of power. Heclo does not view these developments as entirely negative – indeed there may be greater scope for executive leadership when the system is more open. But he does view with alarm the increasing complexity of government and the fact that direct democratic accountability is difficult to achieve when the 'real' decisions are taken, not by President and members of Congress, but by numerous additional political actors including bureaucrats, lobbyists, the media and political consultants.

To the foreign observer, what is interesting about these recent critiques of bureaucratic power, is that they are comments not on administrators and administrative agencies, but also on the whole

---

8 Hugh Heclo, *A Government of Strangers: Executive Politics in Washington*, Washington DC, Brookings Institution, 1977; also his 'Issue networks and the executive establishment', in Anthony King (ed.) *The New American Political System*, Washington DC, American Enterprise Institute, 1978.
9 Issue Networks, *ibid*, p. 102.

policy-making system. Many make the *a priori* assumption that more government is by definition a bad thing and that increasing public disenchantment with government derives from the constantly expanding volume of legislation and special regulations. Without commenting on the normative question of whether more government is good or bad, it is obviously the case that government, by whatever definition (number of policies, volume of regulations, amount of public expenditures) has increased in all modern industrial societies over the last 20 years. However, although criticism of big government has occurred in other countries, it has been particularly vocal in the USA — a country where as a percentage of GNP, government, although large, is hardly at the top of the international league table (see Chapter 2, Table 2.6). No doubt this can partly be explained in ideological terms. As we noted in Chapter 2, the USA has a long-established tradition of antagonism to government. But there are also important institutional differences between the USA and most other countries which may help us understand both academic and popular critiques of government in general and bureaucracy in particular.

Easily the most important is the independent role of Congress. Iron triangles and issue networks depend at least in part on an autonomous legislature and, within Congress, little legislatures (committees and subcommittees). Although this has long been appreciated — for example in 1970 Harold Seidman noted that 'meaningful improvements in executive organization and in the management of the Federal system...will depend in the final analysis on reorganization of the Congressional committee structure'[10] — it seems to have been partly forgotten amid all the talk of special interest politics, political action committees and the generally more complex and confusing pattern of government typical of the 1980s. Although it could be argued that autonomous legislative power increases accountability, it also greatly facilitates the sort of volatile issue network politics where no single actor in the policy process can ever fully understand what is going on, let alone control events. Arguably, this is the very antithesis of accountability.

A second unique feature of the American system is its openness. Access to Congress and Congressmen, as well as to officials at all levels, is remarkably easy compared with most other countries. Exploiting this fact, Washington has become a political consultants'

---

10 Harold Seidman, *Politics, Position & Power: The Dynamics of Federal Organization*, New York, Oxford University Press, 1st edition, 1970, p. 285.

and lobbyists' paradise. No interest, whether economic (corporations, unions), public interest (environment, consumer protection), or governmental (state and local governments) can afford to drop its guard by failing to make full use of the availability of policy makers. Again openness is at least partly a function of the proliferation of centres of autonomy or power. With subcommittees, bureaux, agencies and even individual officials competing with one another over particular areas of public policy, they are usually only too ready to make use of any resource which will enhance their autonomy further. In essence this means organized interests (together with their technical advisers, the lobbyists and consultants), and the media. A more open system has also, of course, been aided by the cathartic effects of the Watergate scandals. Freedom of information became a major public issue during the late 1960s and early 1970s, and the formal legal access of groups and individuals to government files and information was greatly strengthened as a result.[11] But these formal changes were almost certainly not as important in producing greater access as the changes in Congress, the party system and American society generally which earlier chapters have chronicled.

REFORM ATTEMPTS

Perhaps the most common recent response to the problem of big government and bureaucratic power is simply to propose a reduction in the size and complexity of government. In his 1982 State of the Union Message Ronald Reagan declared:

Together, we have cut the growth of new federal regualtions in half. In 1981, there were 23,000 fewer pages in the Federal Register, which lists new regulations, than there were in 1980...Together, we have created an effective federal strike force to combat waste and fraud in government. In just six months it has saved the taxpayers more than two billion dollars — and it's only getting started.[12]

As we noted earlier, the number of federal employees has been declining steadily since the late 1970s. Together with the Reagan

---

11   Under the 1966 and 1974 Freedom of Information Acts, Americans have the right to inspect all federal records. Certain information (for example relating to criminal investigation, defence or inter-office memos) can be denied, but citizens can appeal against refusals in the courts. The substantive freedom of access in the USA is dramatically greater than in most comparable countries, and especially than in the United Kingdom.
   Address to Congress, 26 January 1982, US Embassy Press Release, London, p. 3.

cuts, does this mean that Presidents are winning the battle against bureaucracy? Not necessarily. Federal employment may have fallen, but numbers are only loosely related to complexity and autonomy. Similarly, Ronald Reagan's reductions in *new* regulations does nothing to alter the fact of already established regulations, together with their policy networks. 'Waste and fraud' in the federal government undoubtedly exist, but this condemnation is more of a populist rallying cry than an attack on the central problems of complexity and autonomy. As we know, a number of Presidents have attempted to reorganize the executive branch, the most dramatic proposal being Richard Nixon's 1971 plan to create four 'super departments' — Natural Resources, Human Resources, Community Development and Economic Affairs. Other, less ambitious reorganizations have been attempted, some successfully, others not. Sometimes these involve the creation of new departments (HUD in 1965, Health, Education and Welfare (HEW) in 1953, the Department of Education in 1979). More common are *internal* reorganizations usually aimed at simplifying administration and reducing overlapping jurisdictions. Although well intentioned, reorganization is almost always a less than adequate reform measure. For one thing Congress is reluctant to approve reorganizations which affect its own internal distribution of power, and accordingly has vetoed the more far-reaching reforms. Committees and, increasingly, subcommittees, have a vested interest in the continuing autonomy of departments, bureaux and agencies. Secondly, internal reorganization often involves 'shuffling the same old drones into new hives' as Robert Sherrill has put it,[13] so no real change occurs (as with the HUD reorganization mentioned on p. 204).

What then, of Presidential appointments? Surely a political civil service provides the chief executive with a controlling mechanism denied to British Prime Ministers and other executives obliged to work with a career civil service. No doubt the approximately 700 top level posts which Presidents can fill with their own appointees helps, but not that much. As we noted in Chapters 5 and 9, the political party cues available to Presidents are weak, so he can never be assured that his appointees will follow his policies. As Hugh Heclo has shown, Washington is a 'government of strangers' where the cohering forces of party and loyalty to a President's programme are weak.[14] As serious, immediately below the political appointees

13 Robert Sherrill, *Why They Call it Politics: A Guide to America's Government*, New York, Harcourt, Brace Jovanovich, 3rd Edition, 1979, p. 230.
14 *A Government of Strangers, op. cit.*

at the bureau level are the career civil servants whose relationships with organized interests, Congressional committees, the media and political consultants and lobbyists are frequently deeply entrenched.

Ronald Reagan has been particularly concerned to use the appointment power to change bureaucratic behaviour and sometimes, an especially tough and determined agency or departmental head can effect real changes, but usually at the cost of considerable unpopularity. Two of President Reagan's most determined appointees, for example, James Watt, Secretary of the Interior, and Anne Burford, Head of the Environmental Protection Agency, decided to implement policies quite incompatible with the values and practices of their respective agencies. Mrs Burford, in particular, attempted greatly to weaken the enforcement of environmental protection laws. So serious was her clash with staff that many of them resigned and by early 1983 Anne Burford's own political future was in doubt.

Recognizing that reorganization and the appointment power are inadequate, successive Presidents have attempted to improve executive branch *management*, mainly in the budgetary area. So Lyndon Johnson experimented with the Planning Programming and Budgeting System (PPBS) and Richard Nixon with Management by Objectives (MBO). Both devices were designed to force administrators to clarify what programme objectives and their costings were. Predictably, each part of the administration was found to have its own objectives.[15] The problem was (and is) not managerial and technical, but essentially political.

More recently Jimmy Carter introduced zero based budgeting, which required departments and agencies to review programme spending and priorities from the bottom up on an annual basis, the aim being to stop spending drifting upwards incrementally from year to year. This may have helped, but new programmes and increased spending are all too easy to justify as necessary, and as we will see in Chapter 13, a fair proportion of federal spending is simply unavoidable.

One of the great paradoxes of the anti-government mood of the late 70s and early 80s was that individual Congressmen, echoing constituency demands, were the first to criticize the bureaucracy, while Congress as an institution remained a major bulwark against fundamental change. This accepted, Congress has acted in other ways to improve administration and the implementation of laws. The Budget Act of 1974 was specifically designed to provide Congress with more accurate and comprehensive information on government

15   See Richard Rose, *Managing Presidential Objectives*, London, Macmillan, 1976.

spending, and the Congressional Budget Office under the leadership of its highly effective Director, Alice Rivlin, has conducted a series of studies into executive programmes. *Evaluation* has become the key word in this context and it is now standard practice for new programmes to contain requirements that policies be evaluated to test their effectiveness and usefulness. Although much criticized, evaluation studies have forced both legislators and administrators to think more carefully about the basic objectives of programmes and policies. Even so, evaluation is by definition a normative and political exercise. Evaluating the Urban Development Action Grant programme (UDAG), for example, which provides assistance for private capital to develop commercial and industrial projects in central city areas, involves not only analysis of technicalities, but judgments on who benefits and loses from the programme. UDAG administrators in HUD, together with the private interests and local governments who benefit from UDAG, clearly have an interest in seeing that the evaluation exercise, even if conducted by 'outsiders', puts the programme in a favourable light.

Other oversight resources have been utilized by Congress in its attempts to control the bureaucracy. The General Accounting Office and Office of Technology Assessment have been more rigorous in providing an information base for evaluation. Congressional hearings into Presidential appointments have become more thorough and there has even been some flirtation with 'sunset' legislation. Another symptom of the populist revolt against big government, sunset laws require agencies or programmes to be renewed annually. If they are not fulfilling their purpose, they simply cease to exist. Such measures have not so far been adopted on a significant scale. Finally Congress has been increasingly diligent in securing *information* from the executive branch. Although partly successful, Chapter 9 showed that there are technical limits to both the quality and quantity of information which Congress can glean from the executive.

Finally, what of the courts? Surely they are well placed to curb the worst excesses of bureaucratic power. Certainly individual citizens can sue the government if they believe a constitutional right has been violated. It is quite common for the powers of an administrative agency to be delineated by the courts. During the 1978—9 Supreme Court term, for example, the Court outlawed the Federal Communications Commission's directive that cable systems should give citizen groups a certain number of channels (*FCC* v. *Midwest Video*; *ACLU* v. *FCC*). However Congress often gives to administrative agencies quasi-judicial powers. The USA has only a limited system of administrative courts, so recourse to judicial redress is very much up to the aggrieved individual. As we will discover in Chapter 12, this can be a long, complicated and expensive process. And of course, much of the criticism of bureaucracy centres not on administrative wrong-doing or abuse of power but on questions of efficiency, responsiveness and accountability.

CONCLUDING REMARKS – AND A WORD OF CAUTION

This review strongly implies that the Heclo analysis is valid. The system is characterized by numerous and highly volatile issue networks. These are not impenetrable because a more open policy system allows new forces and interests to influence even the most established 'iron triangles'. Environmentalists now fight the dams and water projects previously approved by the cosy triumverate of bureau (the Army Corps of Engineers), subcommittee and local communities.[16] These networks remain autonomous, however, not in the sense that they constitute closed policy systems, but because they are not amenable to central control. Finally, although bureaucrats and administrators continue to attract most of the public opprobrium (and most of the reform attempts), on their own, their powers would be quite limited. Congressional committee and subcommittee autonomy and open access to government are the other absolutely essential conditions which allow the policy network system to flourish.

Fragmentation, autonomy, complexity and openness are all adjectives which can be accurately employed to describe the federal bureaucracy. To the outside observer, however, some really very important characteristics of the policy-making system remain, which can be obscured by the pluralistic confusion which our analysis has so far implied. First, not all of the policy-making sub-systems can be characterized thus. As we will discover in Chapter 13, many aspects of foreign policy are made in a very different environment. Second, the distributional consequences of the generally pluralistic policy-making system are far from random. Intuitively, at least, it would be expected that multiple access and overlapping jurisdictions would

---

16   Although the Army Corps of Engineers is quoted as a classic case of a powerful bureau, it was not completely autonomous, for it competed with the Department of Agriculture, the Bureau of Reclamation and the Tennessee Valley Authority over control of water policy. See Arthur B. Maass, 'Congress and water resources', *American Political Science Review*, Vol. 44, September 1950, pp. 576–93.

have egalitarian consequences; all groups, interests, classes and regions would benefit. Yet reality is very different. As we will explore in Chapters 11 and 13, increasing access to policy makers does not necessarily result in a more equitable distribution of resources. Indeed in some crucial respects, a system of fragmented political power and open access to government actively discourages re-distributive policies or the transferral of resources from one group or class in society to another.

FURTHER READING

Randall B. Ripley and Grace A. Franklin provide a fascinating insight into the world of sub-governments in their *Congress, the Bureaucracy and Public Policy*, New York, Dorsey Press, 1976. The best study of senior civil servants is Hugh Heclo, *A Government of Strangers*, Washington DC, Brookings Institution, 1976. A series of case studies is provided by Francis E. Rourke (ed.) *Bureaucratic Power in National Politics*, Boston, Little Brown, 3rd edition, 1978. Case studies of regulation can be found in James Q. Wilson (ed.) *The Politics of Regulation*, New York, Basic Books, 1980.

CHAPTER 11

Organized Interests:
The Real Power?

Suppose you go to Washington and try to get at your government. You will always find that while you are politely listened to, the men really consulted are the men with the biggest stake — the big bankers, the big manufacturers, the big masters of commerce...The government of the United States is the foster child of special interests. It is not allowed to have a will of its own. It is told at every move: 'Don't do that; you will interfere with our prosperity'.
Woodrow Wilson, The New Freedom, Doubleday Page, 1913

Concededly, each interest group is biased; but their role...is not unlike the advocacy of lawyers in court which has proven so successful in resolving judicial controversies. Because our congressional representation is based on geographical boundaries, the lobbyists who speak for the various economic, commercial and other functional interests of this country serve a very useful purpose and have assumed an important role in the legislative process.
John F. Kennedy, 1956, quoted in Congressional Quarterly,
The Washington Lobby, 1979

Throughout American history, concern over the power of organized interests has never been far from the surface. Indeed the growth of the Republic can almost be described in terms of successive waves of populist revolt against the undue influence of organized groups, and in particular private corporations. Woodrow Wilson's characterization (above) came after more than 20 years of public disquiet at the operations of the big companies. During the 1920s corporate power was regarded more benignly, with capitalism flourishing as never before. The Depression transformed this image, however, and it was not until the 1950s that the benevolent view of private power returned. Most recently, the critique has returned to the centre of the political stage, with popular opprobrium directed at those companies responsible for high energy costs, pollution, consumer exploitation and discrimination against women and minorities. Criticism of other organized interests — labour, promotional groups — has been much more isolated and fragmented, although during the 1940s trade unions were under considerable attack with Congress eventually passing union-curbing legislation.

The critique of corporate power has two related strands. First, that large private companies are by their very nature ruthless and exploitative. This mainly populist view considers size to be the main problem. Break up large monopolies and oligopolies and something approaching 'fair' competition will emerge. Second, corporations have been criticized because they exercise power without accountability. They are not, in other words, answerable to democratically elected institutions. They can 'buy' Congressmen, bribe local, state and federal officials and generally manipulate democratic processes in their favour. We will return to these points later, but note that the most common critique of capitalism in Europe — that the private accumulation of wealth in business is *by definition* exploitative — has been quite rare in the United States.

The quote by John Kennedy represents the second, quite different, judgment on the role of organized interests in America. According to this view, groups are an essential part of the democratic process; that far from undermining representation, they aid it. Advocates of this position point to the multiple access points in the American system and the ways in which myriad organized groups are able to exploit these to their advantage. Crucially, because *all* classes, interests, ideological positions, regions, localities, and social groups *can* organize (even if some actually do not) to defend or promote their positions, the potential for fair or just policies is particularly great in the American system.

Much of the comment and discussion in this chapter will centre on these two contrasting perspectives and how valid they are in the early 1980s. Before we embark on this exercise, it is necessary to provide some basic information on interest groups in the United States.

INTERESTS, GROUPS AND LOBBYISTS

In all modern industrial societies, citizens band together to form organizations with social, economic and political aims. American group participation is high in comparative terms with some 62 per cent of the population being members of some voluntary association or other.[1] Of this number many (about one third) are inactive, however, and the organizations with the most active membership tend to be 'non-political' social clubs (youth groups, church related groups, fraternal organizations – Rotary, the Masons, the Lions – and so on), professional societies (representing doctors, lawyers etc.) and educational groups (parent–teacher associations, school and college fraternities). About 8 per cent of the adult population are active in political clubs and organizations – a similar figure to that for most social clubs. The organizations with the highest membership (17 per cent), although by no means the highest active membership, are the labour unions.[2] In addition to voluntary associations with individual membership, a number of groups exist representing corporate and governmental interests, such as trade, commerce and manufacturers' associations and state, local, county and regional government organizations. Finally, a number of *ad hoc* single issue groups exist at any one time, ranging from organizations to maintain American control of the Panama Canal, to proponents of a freeze on nuclear arms levels, to local groups created to stop the construction of a particular public works project.

All of these organizations can have a political dimension, obviously so in the case of corporate labour and *ad hoc* groups, but also with most social organizations. Chambers of commerce and professional associations, for example, frequently engage in political activity when laws and regulations affecting their members are introduced or existing laws are changed. As local, state and federal governments have legislated in almost every conceivable area of economic and social life over the last 30 years, it is not surprising that many erstwhile mainly social groups and associations have found themselves at the very centre of political controversy. The debate on gun control intimately involves the National Rifle Association (NRA); environmental pollution controls involve the Audubon Society and

1 Sidney Verba and Norman H. Nie, *Participation in America: Political Democracy and Social Equality*, New York, Harper and Row, 1972, p. 41.
2 *Ibid*, all figures are from Table 2.2, p. 42.

Sierra Club, and education cuts and school district consolidations, Parent—Teacher Associations.

Political scientists have long been engaged in the business of trying to classify interest groups and even now no completely satisfactory taxonomy exists. We have already drawn some distinctions (for example between voluntary associations with individual members and corporate groups) but as all of these can engage in political activity this distinction is not necessarily that helpful. For our purposes it is more useful to distinguish between three broad categories of organized group — economic, professional and promotional — to which we should add some comments on political action committees and lobbying.

ECONOMIC GROUPS

Business

When discussing business organizations, it is common to distinguish between the activities of individual corporations and those of peak associations (trade union confederations, employers and trade associations). In the United States, corporations tend to be both powerful and autonomous and frequently they exercise political power as independent units. So General Motors, the world's largest vehicle manufacturer, is a political force to be reckoned with in its own right as is International Telephone and Telegraph (ITT),[3] the major oil companies or many of the firms listed in the *Fortune 500*.[4]

In a famous study of business lobbying published in the 1960s, Bauer, Pool and Dexter concluded that the lobbying activities of individual firms were not an important influence on public policy.[5] The authors were, however, primarily concerned with Congress rather than executive departments and agencies. And state and local governments were not the subject of their study. Few dispute that corporations do wield enormous influence on lower level governments. Land, taxation, labour and public works policies are often moulded by corporate interests within states. Of course there is also competition between corporate interests, and between these and other organized groups, but in most locales business is the single

3 For an account of ITT's political activity, see Anthony Sampson, *The Sovereign State: The Secret History of ITT*, London, Coronet Books, 1974.
4 *Fortune* magazine produces an annual list of the 500 largest corporations in the USA.
5 Raymond Bauer, Ithiel de Sola Pool and Anthony Lewis Dexter, *American Business and Public Policy*, New York, Prentice-Hall, 1964.

most important influence. The precise extent of this power varies from area to area, with some states being effectively dominated by one corporation (such as with the Du Pont chemical corporation in Delaware); or by a few interests (until recently cattle and oil in Texas); while in others (New York, Michigan, California, Massachusetts) individual corporate power is much more diffuse and ameliorated by union and public interest group activity.

Moreover, since the 1960s there is overwhelming evidence that individual firms have taken a more active part in public policy making. Most major corporations now have Washington offices and employ professional lobbyists to advance and protect their interests. The size of business lobbying can partly be explained as a response to the increasingly strident and successful efforts of the new public interest lobbies devoted to environmental and consumer protection and to affirmative action in employment.[6] Since the mid-1970s, however, a more important spur to corporate political activity has been the worsening economic environment and increasing vulnerability of US corporations to foreign competition. Business now *needs* the federal government as never before to help protect it from overseas competition and a generally hostile economic climate.[7]

American business peak (or trade) associations have also been labelled 'weak' in the past. And certainly the influence of the major single industry associations (representing automobiles, rubber, textiles and so on) as well as the two major cross-industry organizations (the National Association of Manufacturers, and the US Chamber of Commerce) has historically been weak compared with equivalent organizations in such countries as Germany and Japan. Perhaps this should be expected, given the traditional strength of individual corporations in the USA which we noted in Chapter 2. Why, after all, should successful individual firms forfeit some of their independence to a trade association? Indeed, as recently as the 1950s both the NAM and Chamber of Commerce (which represents smaller firms) were regarded as of marginal influence in Washington. Both adhered to a sometimes unthinking anti-statist philosophy, and were notably less important than the sum of the political efforts of individual corporations. Since then, however, both organizations plus some new ones (the Business Round Table and a number of

6   See Graham K. Wilson, *Interest Groups in the United States*, Oxford, Oxford University Press, 1981.
7   See David H. McKay, 'Industrial policy and non-policy in the US', *Journal of Public Policy*, Vol. 3, No. 1, February 1983.

business Political Action Committees), have emerged as more respected spokesmen for corporate interests.[8] This is not to say that American business peak associations have assumed the status of equivalent groups in Germany, Japan or even Britain, but they are now more important than ever before. Again, this revival is linked to the general increase in group activity characteristic of the last 20 years. Before we leave our discussion of business interests, a word of caution should be expressed about any comparison between business activity in government during the 1950s and today. As earlier mentioned, the 1950s were an especially benign period in American politics. For much of the 50s and 60s, corporations were highly successful and entered the political arena only when necessary. Government policy was favourable towards them, and particularly towards the larger corporations.[9] Iron triangles and cosy relations with executive bureaux do not require lobbying as such, with all that this implies in terms of attention seeking and publicity. Only when competing or conflicting interests enter the fray is lobbying of the more visible kind necessary.

Trade Unions

American unions have traditionally been considered a relatively weak influence in the policy process. In comparative perspective this is undoubtedly true. Only about 22 per cent of the total labour force are affiliated to a union; the unions do not have the unequivocal support of a major political party, and unlike many union movements in Europe they lack ideological cohesion. Almost all the powerful union movements in history have been driven forward by some ideal vision of a new — usually socialist — society. Not so in the case of American unions which, although by no means un-ideological, are significantly more instrumental than their European counterparts. Interestingly, the period when unions were most ideological in the USA (the 1930s and early 1940s), coincided with the years of their most rapid growth and greatest political achievements.

Although relatively weak and divided, trade unions as a whole do constitute one of America's most important organized interests. The USA is, after all, a highly industrialized country and the unions

---

8 See Wilson, *ibid*, Chapter 4.
9 For example a negative relationship exists between corporate size and taxation levels — the bigger the corporation the lower the tax paid. See Lester M. Salamon and John J. Sigfried, 'Economic power and political influence: the impact of industry structure on public policy', *American Political Science Review*, Vol. 71, (1977) No. 2, pp. 1026–43.

represent more than 20 million workers. However, the relatively high political visibility of the unions has been achieved only slowly. The first unions in America of any significance were craft rather than industry oriented and eschewed any active involvement in politics. Known for the advocacy of *business unionism*, these unions formed the American Federation of Labor (AFL) in 1886 under the leadership of Samuel Gompers. As the name implies, business unionism involved workers perceiving themselves as a part of the capitalist environment. The union's job was, therefore, to bargain with employers in line with what employers could afford. If a company was doing well, then the workers would benefit. If it was not, low wages and lay-offs were to be expected. With over a million members, the AFL became an important representative of the skilled worker, but its limited approach became very obvious when the Great Depression struck. Industry wide unions (such as the United Steel Workers and United Mine Workers) formed rapidly during the Depression years and banded together in 1935 as the Congress of Industrial Organization (CIO). In contrast to the AFL, CIO unions saw themselves in an adversarial relationship with employers, and were strongly disposed to use political means to achieve better working conditions and higher wages.

Since the 1930s the CIO (and, following an amalgamation in 1955, the AFL/CIO) has lobbied hard in Washington over the whole range of public policies which affect workers and working conditions — union rights, social security, job training, vocational education, occupational health and safety, overseas trade relations and economic policy generally. Observers generally agree that in terms of organization, staffing and access, the AFL/CIO — mainly through its political organization, the Committee on Political Education (COPE) — has become one of the most coherent and visible of the Washington lobbies. As suggested in earlier chapters, the unions do have links with the Democratic Party, but formal affiliation has always been avoided (although for the first time, the AFL/CIO was, in 1983, planning to endorse a Presidential candidate, Walter Mondale, early in the campaign). This has almost certainly helped, rather than hindered, the AFL/CIO's public image. In recent years COPE's political interests have widened to include activity on a number of issues not directly related to members' interests, for example foreign policy and civil liberties. Generally — but by no means always — COPE is identified with a liberal political position.

Although the AFL/CIO's national political activities are important, it would be misleading to give the impression that the United States has a centralized and united union movement. In comparison with unions in many countries, the opposite is, if anything, true. Most union structures are highly decentralized, with local and state units often responsible for bargaining over wages and salaries. Moreover, some of the biggest and most powerful unions are not even members of the AFL/CIO, including the Teamsters (truckers), the largest teachers' union (the National Educational Association) and the United Auto Workers.

Over the last 15–20 years, there has been much talk about the decline of the unions as a political force. Certainly their membership (as a percentage of the labour force) has been falling and an occupational structure changing in favour of the tertiary sector has generally weakened the unions whose strength is traditionally rooted in the secondary (manufacturing) sector.[10]

Nonetheless, the unions remain highly visible in the Washington political scene. Graham Wilson has noted that this very visibility is a symptom of weakness, or the unions have so much to do in the pursuit of their interests that they are obliged to take a highly active part in politics.[11] While this is probably true, it should also be stressed that almost *all* interests have become more active at the national level in recent years. In effect the nature of the policy process is now such that no one group or sector can afford not to take part in the Washington bargaining and coalition-building game.

The Farmers

In most modern industrial countries, farmers occupy a special place in society. For strategic and/or electoral reasons they often exercise formidable political power, and in recent history American farmers have proved no exception. They are the recipients of massive subsidies designed to raise their incomes to a point at or beyond that necessary to keep production up. As in some other countries (notably within the EEC), this has sometimes resulted in overproduction and the need to destroy or store produce in order to keep prices buoyant. American farms are also among the most efficient in the world, being highly capital intensive and mechanized. Given the high rate

10   Although, since the 1960s, the level of unionization among *government* workers (many of them in manual jobs in hospitals and local government services– has increased, as the phenomenal growth of the American Federation of State, County and Municipal Employers (AFSCME) which now has over 1 million members, shows.

11   *Interest Groups in the United States, op. cit*, Chapter 3. For a good account of how the AFL/CIO operates as a lobby, see Congressional Quarterly, *The Washington Lobby, op. cit*, pp. 97–112.

of innovation and the general trend towards urban and suburban living over the last 60 years, it comes as no surprise to learn that the farm population declined from over 30 million in 1920 to under 10 million in 1970. Indeed, by 1980 a mere 4 per cent of the American workforce were employed in agriculture — a remarkably low figure, given the fact that the United States is easily the largest producer (and exporter) of foodstuffs in the world.

Given this, American farming organizations are perhaps rather less cohesive than would be expected. The largest group, the American Farm Bureau Federation (AFBF), has, until recently, actually preached the merits of disengagement of the state from the economy, including presumably the removal of farm subsidies. The National Farmers Union (NFU) has taken a pro-subsidy line, but its membership is smaller and more geographically concentrated (in the West and Mid-west). Nonetheless, the NFU is a lobbying force to be reckoned with and has achieved considerable status in Washington.

As the farm population has declined, so the electoral influence of farmers has fallen. During the late 19th and early 20th centuries, farmers virtually constituted a separate social class in the United States, a fact which helps explain the emergence of farm-based political movements, including the Populists, the Farmers Alliance and the Grange. However, these parties and organizations failed to establish permanent bases of social support and most have now passed into history.[12] More recently, farmers' influence in state legislatures has continued, although even here, re-districting and demographic change has produced a steady decline in the agricultural lobby. The same is true of Congress. At one time, many Congressmen were virtually elected by farmers. Not so today, when in most states and districts the farm vote is but one small voice among many.

In spite of the general weakness of the farming organizations, it would be misleading to suggest that farm interests are politically weak. A more accurate way to characterize them would be simply to see the larger farmers (or agribusiness, as it is called) as other corporations. Indeed general industrial and financial corporations do own a large number of agribusiness farms. No federal government could afford to see these interests or those of the numerous prosperous middle-sized farmer, seriously damaged. As with defence industries, food is strategically too important for this to happen. However, small farmers, and especially those working marginal land

12   The Grange remains an important farm lobby. For an account of the vain attempts to build an agrarian populism, see Grant McConnell, *The Decline of Agrarian Democracy*, Berkeley, University of California Press, 1953.

or producing products liable to sharp fluctuations in price, are genuinely weak — a fact shown by the occasional public demonstrations to which small farmers are sometimes obliged to resort.

Although receiving much less public attention than business or unions, professional groups have probably grown and improved their political status more rapidly than any other of the organized interests over the last 40 years. As educational standards have risen and the premium on expertise in a number of areas — particularly the law, medicine and education — has increased, so the professions have prospered. The role of the main lawyers' organization, the American Bar Association (ABA), will be developed in Chapter 12. The ABA not only acts as gatekeeper for those practising law, it is also a major source of information on legal standards and procedures. So the nomination of judges and changes in criminal and civil law depend in part on the opinions and position taken by the ABA. With some 500,000 lawyers in the USA, the central importance of the law in policy making, and the great overrepresentation of lawyers among state and federal legislators and officials, the ABA's opinions and interpretations must be taken seriously. As with other professional associations, *expert* opinion gives the ABA its special status. It is true that only about one half of all lawyers are ABA members, but its members include the more successful lawyers, whose expert, non-partisan opinions are highly respected.

The American Medical Association (AMA) performs a similar function for doctors. Again, not all doctors are members, but those who are tend to be among the more successful. For many years the AMA was famous for its fight against federal health insurance (or 'socialized' medicine) and from the 1940s to 1960s it was one of the most vocal and biggest spending of the Washington lobbies. It eventually lost the battle with the enactment of Medicare (medical insurance for the old) and Medicaid (medical aid for the poor) in 1965,[13] but it remains a major influence on all legislation affecting health care. Its political action committee (AMPAC) was actually the largest spender of all PACs during 1977 and 1978, contributing a total of $1,644,795 to federal candidates.[14] Generally, the AMA's

13 See Theodore R. Marmor, *The Politics of Medicare*, London, Routledge & Kegan Paul, 1970, for an account of the AMA's battle against Medicare.
14 Quoted in Congressional Quarterly, *The Washington Lobby*, *op. cit*, p. 75.

position has been conservative although, since the advent of federal (and state and local) health programmes, it has also sought to improve the position of those members working for governments or receiving government fees.

Other leading professional groups include some (the American Bankers' Association, the National Association of Home Builders, the National Association of Realtors) whose function is more economic than professional. They are no less important for this, of course. The Realtors (estate agents), for example, contribute large amounts of money mainly to Republican candidates, and generally lobby hard to ensure a growing housing market and low interest rates. At the state and local levels, the Realtors are highly active politically — especially in combating what they consider to be any unnecessary regulation of the housing market — whether it be through restrictive zoning laws, building codes, property taxes or fair housing statutes.[15]

In sum, professional associations often represent the rich and the powerful in American society. This can mean the maintenance of professional standards (as in law or medicine), but it can also mean the advancement of particular economic interests (lawyers, doctors, bankers, Realtors and so on).

PROMOTIONAL GROUPS

By promotional group is meant all those organizations devoted to promoting a particular cause or position. This can include a wide variety of groups ranging from the National Rifle Association (NRA), which champions the right of Americans to own firearms, to the National Association for the Advancement of Coloured People (NAACP), which represents Black Americans, to Common Cause, one of the new breed of public interest groups which fights for honesty and efficiency in government. Some of these groups are *ad hoc* and transitory as with the several organizations which emerged in opposition to the American presence in Vietnam, but most are at least semi-permanent.

In all democratic societies such groups exist, but in America they are particularly numerous and vocal. Why should this be so? One reason is undoubtedly the openness of the policy system.

15 The Realtors have made particularly strenuous efforts to prevent the passage of fair housing (anti-race, sex discrimination) laws at the local, state and national levels. See David H. McKay, *Housing and Race in Industrial Society*, London and New Jersey, Croom Helm, Rowman and Littlefield, 1977.

Promotional groups *know* that with enough organization, public support and media exposure they can influence members of Congress, executive officials and even judges. So in the 1960s Ralph Nader, the consumers' advocate, went about the business of exposing automobile safety standards with a single-minded determination. Eventually, his methods led to media and later Congressional investigations and culminated in stringent new standards imposed by law. Later, other groups mobilized to launch similar campaigns on environmental pollution, occupational safety and women's rights which led to new, often quite far-reaching, legislation. Common Cause, the 'clean government' public interest group, has supported the reform of the Congressional committee sytem, votes for 18-year olds, limits on electoral campaign spending, rationalizing government organization and improvements in voter registration.

Although the sudden blossoming of public interest groups in the 1960s and 1970s has surprised — and even worried — some commentators, it is not so difficult to explain in historical perspective. Middle class reform movements are, after all, hardly new to the United States. In Chapter 4 we saw how reformers attempted to 'clean up' the cities during the 19th century, and waves of middle-class moralism have frequently accompanied periods of rapid economic and social change in American history. The 1960s and early 1970s were just such a period, characterized as they were by rapid economic growth, social and political dislocation and, finally, evidence of corruption at the highest level. Moreover, as was chronicled in earlier chapters, this was also a period of party decline, and the increasing atomization of political power. In such an environment, coalition building around such popular issues as environmental protection or clean government became that much easier. This was also a policy context with no parallel in other countries, where, although the same issues have been raised to national prominence, they have tended to do so via political parties or through the operation of a consensus between political and economic elites.

Although public interest groups claim to present 'the public interest', in reality they are not value free and the policies they promote hardly have neutral distributional consequences. New environmental standards may help produce cleaner air and water, but they can also lead to higher prices. Reforming government sounds admirable enough, but reforms often have unexpected results, as did the 19th-century city reforms and campaign finance reforms of the 1970s. By the early 1980s, the public interest lobbies had passed from the very centre of the political stage, but they have by no means disappeared. Instead they have become yet another part of the complex and often confusing web of policy making which characterizes Washington today.

One final point: although our discussion of promotional groups has concentrated on the public interest lobbies, the same openness in the system and multiplicity of power centres is exploited by other promotional group. Hence the entrenched power of the National Rifle Association, which continues to block any meaningful attempt by the federal government to control citizens' access to and use of firearms. To the NRA the activities of numerous other promotional groups could be added. Of course the mere fact that a particular group is well organized and has access to decision makers does not always equal success. As we will develop later, certain groups and interests fail repeatedly. The policy system may be open and complex but it is not neutral.

POLITICAL ACTION COMMITTEES

In the sense that particular organized interests have formed Washington committees to fight for or against a particular item of legislation or the electoral success of an individual candidate, PACs are nothing new. Earlier we noted the efforts of the AMA's AMPAC to prevent the passage of Medicare in 1965, for example. Yet since the mid-1970s, PACs have spread to the point where in the 1980 election they contributed $55m of $239m spent by Congressional candidates, and their 1982 contributions were expected to reach $80m.[16] In addition, further vast sums are now spent by PACs in general efforts to defeat candidates or to support candidates separately from their personal campaign organizations. The rise of the 'electoral' PAC can be explained in the main by changes in campaign finance laws which, by putting restrictions on direct contributions by corporations and unions, have encouraged the big contributors to form committees which in turn can raise money from employees and/or members which is then passed on to (mainly) Congressional candidates. (Federal funding of Presidential candidates has effectively removed PAC influence from Presidential elections.) Fearing that PACs would become simply the 'fat cat' contributors by another name, Congress has amended the 1974 Federal Campaign Act to put further limits on PAC activity. In particular, each PAC cannot

16 *National Journal*, 7 August 1982, p. 1368.

contribute more than $5,000 to any one candidate's primary campaign, and a further $5,000 to his or her general election campaign. While this does not sound very much, it adds up as the figures quoted above for the 1980 and 1982 elections show. Moreover, there are no limits on PAC spending which does not go directly into the campaign coffers of candidates, so PACs can launch their own campaigns against or for particular politicians. In 1982, for example, NICPAC (the National Conservative Political Action Committee) spent $526,000 in an effort to unseat the liberal Senator Edward Kennedy in Massachusetts.

As can be seen from Table 11.1, private corporations have donated the largest sums to candidates, followed closely by associations (mainly professional groups such as the AMA) and the trade unions. Note also, however, that non-connected organizations easily raised the most money, much of which was devoted not to particular campaigns but to raising the salience of a political issue, ideological position or to painting a positive or negative picture of a candidate. Of these non-connected organizations, two ultra conservative groups raised by far the most money — NICPAC and the National Congressional Club which supports the maverick right-wing Senator from North Carolina, Jesse Helms. Together these two groups raised nearly $15m, only a very small proportion of which went directly to campaign organizations.

Table 11.2 shows that Labour contributes mainly to Democratic candidates (predictably) but corporations distribute their largesse more evenly between the two parties (perhaps less predictably). Direct campaign contributions from PACs have generally helped the Democrats rather than Republicans, but the overall impact of PAC activity has almost certainly been to help conservatives. This is mainly because conservative PACs are better organized, generally more professional and can (at least up to 1982) appeal to the strongly felt conservative sentiment so prevalent in many parts of the country.

Whatever the merits and de-merits of PACs — and Congress and public interest groups are constantly discussing how they should be reformed — their rise has brought out into the open most of the corporate, labour and association political funding which previously tended to be covert and often illegal. Also, by virtue of their ability to make direct appeals to the public on particular issues, PACs have almost certainly aided the rise of single interest politics and have

17 See *National Journal, op. cit.*

TABLE 11.1   *The Growth of PACs, 1977—82*

	Association	Corporate	Labour	Non-connected	Other	Total
1977—8						
January 1977—June 1978						
Raised	$18.4	$10.5	$13.5	$9.8	$1.8	$54.9
Contributed	3.5	2.6	3.7	0.6	0.5	10.9
January 1977—December 1978						
Raised	24.4	17.4	19.6	16.1	2.5	80.0
Contributed	11.3	9.8	10.3	2.8	1.0	35.2
1979—80						
January 1979—March 1980						
Raised	21.0	19.2	15.6	13.5	2.2	71.6
Contributed	3.9	5.7	3.6	0.7	0.5	14.2
January 1979—December 1980						
Raised	33.9	33.9	25.7	40.1	4.2	137.7
Contributed	15.9	19.2	13.2	4.9	2.0	55.2
1981—2						
January 1981—March 1982						
Raised	26.1	25.1	20.1	33.9	3.9	109.1
Contributed	6.4	9.0	5.0	1.5	0.9	22.8

Source: Federal Election Commission, reproduced in the *National Journal*, 7 August 1982, p. 1373. ©*National Journal*, 1982.
Note: Figures are in millions of dollars and show amount raised and contributed to candidates. Figures for January 1977—December 1978 and January 1979—December 1980 are for election years.

TABLE 11.2   *PAC Contributions to Candidates by Party, 1977—82*

	Association	Corporate	Labour	Non-connected	Other	Total
1977—8						
Democrats	$5.0	$3.7	$9.8	$0.8	$0.7	$19.9
Republicans	6.3	6.1	0.6	2.1	0.2	15.3
1979—80						
Democrats	7.0	6.9	12.4	1.5	1.1	28.9
Republicans	8.9	12.3	0.8	3.4	0.8	26.2
1981—2 (to March)						
Democrats	3.2	4.3	4.6	0.7	0.5	13.3
Republicans	3.1	4.7	0.4	0.7	0.4	9.4

Source: As for Table 11.1. ©*National Journal*, 1982.
Note: Figures are in millions of dollars.

helped further to weaken traditional political party organizations. Perhaps not surprisingly, Democrats have been more vocal in their criticisms of PACs than have Republicans. Indeed, by early 1983 both Walter Mondale and Gary Hart had announced that they would reject all PAC assistance for their 1984 Presidential campaigns.

THE WASHINGTON LOBBY

We have already referred to the 'traditional' interest groups — labour, business, agriculture, the professional associations — to which are added promotional groups and the activities of political action committees. But the Washington Lobby consists of much more than this. The executive branch itself lobbies Congressmen for support, as do state and local governments, either individually or through the US Conference of Mayors, Council of State Governments and other umbrella organizations (see Chapter 4, p. 70). Finally, foreign governments lobby Congress and executive alike. A recent *Congressional Quarterly* publication lists the Israeli, Arab, Korean and Taiwan Lobbies as the most significant in recent years.[18] Given that American foreign policy decisions affect virtually every country and also the openness of the American policy system, the presence of such interests should perhaps be expected.

All of these groups and interests employ consultants and professional lobbyists to collect information and to establish links with the key political actors in the policy system. The result is that Washington is a city alive with political activity, where it is difficult to distinguish between the 'insiders' (elected and appointed officials) and the 'outsiders' (lobbyists, media consultants, interest group leaders). Indeed the presence of policy networks with fluid memberships and constantly shifting agendas means that there are really only 'insiders'.

If anything resembles pluralistic decision making, then surely this does. Yet as earlier suggested, openness and accessibility hardly result in neutral policies or a distribution of public benefits which can be considered egalitarian. Let us develop this point further.

INTEREST GROUPS: FOR AND AGAINST

Returning to the questions posed at the beginning of this chapter, it is easy to appreciate why, in a society where economic individualism

18   *The Washington Lobby, op. cit,* pp. 129–66.

is much admired, a multiplicity of competing interest groups can be regarded as beneficial. In classical economics, equilibrium is reached when demand and supply match each other in a perfectly competitive market. An analogous situation in politics could prevail when groups (analogous to firms) compete with one another in a completely open political environment. The public interest (equilibrium) is hence achieved by the balancing of different interests. No policy, according to this theory, is likely to be completely against any one interest because its involvement in the system will ensure it modifies or amends policy at least partly in its favour.

These are, in essence, the theoretical assumptions of the 'traditional' group theorists, notably Arthur Bentley and David Truman.[19] Government's role in such a context is to *arbitrate* between competing interests. By implication, government exercises little independent power; it more resembles a cipher or sorting mechanism and ensures that the rules of the game are abided by.

The group theorists never claimed that in reality there was complete *equality* between groups (although that was the ideal), but they did maintain that if the interests of a particular section of society were seriously damaged, they would mobilize, organize and, through access to representative institutions, manage to do something to redress the balance. The rise of trade union power in the 1930s is often quoted as an example of such mobilization. Neither were the group theorists so naïve as to assume that *all* groups had access, even potentially. David Truman, for example, accepted that the position of the American Black population (in the 1950s) was exceptional because they patently lacked access to the policy-making process.

Classical group theory has since been criticized by scholars from almost every school of political thought. Public choice theorists have stressed the tendency in such a system for public expenditure (or the provision of public goods) to spiral ever upwards. The reasoning here is both simple and familiar. With open access to multiple decision-making centres, the potential for log-rolling is enormous. So if one group, sector, region, state or local government is the recipient of a federal programme, all the others will be too. Anthony Downs has put this nicely, labelling it the 'iron law of political dispersion': 'All benefits distributed by elected officials will be distributed to all parts of the constituency, regardless of the

---

19 Although they were never explicit about the analogy with economics. See Arthur Bentley, *The Process of Government*, San Antonio, Texas, Trinity University Press, 1949; David B. Truman, *The Governmental Process*, New York, Alfred Knopf, 1951.

economic virtues of concentrating them upon a few parts of the constituency.'[20] The result is, in fact, the very opposite of equilibrium or the 'optimal' in economics. Governments end up handing out far too much to various interests which leads to inefficiency and excessive government spending. This particular critique is currently popular. The solution is not to abolish groups, but drastically to reduce the role of government in economy and society. Predictably, advocates of this position view with alarm the decline of party, and the rise of single issue and special interest politics. Such changes have fragmented the system further and therefore increased the potential for log-rolling and yet more government programmes and regulations. But as we have already noted a number of times in earlier chapters, reducing the size and scope of government is easier said than done, especially given that organized groups and interests are now deeply entrenched in the policy system and most have some interest in maintaining the present pattern of expenditure.

Efficiency in resource distribution is the main concern of this essentially conservative critique. Critics on the left have been more interested in the consequences of the classical view for political, social and economic *equality*. They argue that groups are not just unequal, they are grossly unequal. Or, that there is a bias in the system which some groups are more able to exploit than others.[21] Business or corporate interests, in particular, are advantaged, while labour, the poor and minorities are disadvantaged. This brings us back to the populist condemnation of big business mentioned earlier. How much truth is there to this critique?

First we should note the obvious fact that in terms of its power to move capital, labour and resources around, business is in a unique position among major organized interests. Only government can exercise anything like an equivalent power; none of the other groups can. Instead they are confined to single issues, or particular geographical areas, or they exercise influence over just one sub-group of the population. Even Labour, with its mass membership and finely tuned lobbying machine has relatively few resources compared with business. It is, perhaps, testimony to the power of the corporations that most of them did not even consider it necessary to engage in overt lobbying until relatively recently, because the policy agenda generally favoured them. While the unions and other interests struggled

20 Anthony Downs, quoted in David H. McKay, 'Industrial policy and non-policy in the US', *op. cit*, p. 45.
21 The most eloquent exposition of this view remains E. E. Schattsneider's *The Semi-Sovereign People*, New York, Holt, Rinehart and Winston, 1960.

to get items discussed and legislated, business could often sit back and wait until it perceived its interests as threatened.[22] Business is privileged in another sense: it has access to large sums of money which can be used to 'lubricate' the policy-making system to its advantage. This is also true of unions and some other groups, but none have access to money in quite the way business has. Recent revelations of corruption in American corporate life (ITT, Lockheed) confirms that, quite apart from legal contributions to candidates, the long-established reputation of American corporations and business generally for undercover financial deals is still very much with us.[23]

Second, if we view society not in terms of discrete groups or organized interests, but in terms of social strata, there is very little evidence that the new politics of openness and accessibility have made very much difference to social and economic mobility. Those groups and classes at the bottom of the social heap 30 or 40 years ago are, generally speaking, still there. Changes in occupational structure have had some impact, but what many have called a 'transformation' of the political system has had little effect. Indeed, it is often the case that the more atomized and complex the decision-making system, the lower the potential for re-distributive policies. The two great social reform periods in recent history which laid the foundations of the welfare state — the New Deal and Great Society — coincided with what was virtually the antithesis of the new politics — strong Presidents, pliant Congresses and a public broadly agreed on the need for reform. To be fair, many re-distributive policies (counter recession and manpower retraining programmes, increased social security spending) were enacted during the Nixon and Ford years and if there is any validity to the public choice critique, greater access should result in more spending, whatever the distributional consequences. This accepted, in a period of fiscal stress, a fragmented political system almost certainly leads to re-sources being more thinly divided between groups, interests and classes, and those whose need is greatest are likely to find themselves relatively worse off.

Finally, the politics of distribution are now multi-layered and it

22 Keeping the policy agenda free of discussion of those issues which threaten the powerful has been called 'non-decision making', and the concept has inspired considerable controversy and empirical application. A good application is by Peter Bachrach and Morton Baratz, *Power and Poverty*, New York, Oxford University Press, 1970. For a theoretical discussion, see Stephen Lukes, *Power: A Radical View*, London, Macmillan, 1974.
23 For a discussion of the ways in which private power has been exercised throughout American history, see Grant McConnell, *Private Power and American Democracy*, New York, Alfred Knopf, 1967.

is not always adequate to perceive the system only in terms of social classes or strata. Environmental controls, equal opportunity for women and improved standards of occupational safety clearly benefit some people more than others, but there is no obvious relationship between the distributional impact of each of these reforms and those which traditional 'class based' policies (tax reform, welfare, social security) produce. In fact much of the assault on corporate power during the 1960s and 1970s involved policies of this sort. Middle-class reformers, outraged at pollution, consumer exploitation and discrimination, launched the new promotional groups which the corporations were then obliged to engage in battle. Meanwhile, the measures by which it is usual to gauge the living conditions of industrial workers, minorities and deprived social groups — income, access to housing and so on — changed very little.

It would be wrong to leave our discussion of organized interests without mentioning the serious structural problems which the American economy has been experiencing since the mid-1970s. Changes in the party system, Congress and the increasing accessibility of myriad groups to the major political institutions have all had consequences for economic management and industrial policy. Chapter 13 will expand on this question and whether meaningful control of the economy can be achieved in this new policy context.

FURTHER READING

Interest groups and lobbying cover such a wide area of political activity that no one book is a completely adequate guide. For a good account of recent developments in unions, business and farmers' organizations, see Graham K. Wilson, *Interest Groups in the United States*, Oxford, Oxford University Press, 1981. Grant McConnell's *Private Power and American Democracy*, New York, Alfred Knopf, 1967, remains one of the most stimulating books on groups in America. For an excellent analysis of the ways in which business has lobbied successive administrations, see Kim McQuaid, *Big Business and Presidential Power: From FDR to Reagan*, New York, William Morrow, 1982. For facts and figures, see Norman J. Ornstein and Shirley Elder, *Interest Groups, Lobbying and Policy Making*, Washington DC *Congressional Quarterly*, 1978.

CHAPTER 12

The Supreme Court
and Judicial Politics

We are very quiet there but it is the quiet of a storm centre.
Oliver Wendell Holmes, Associate Justice of the Supreme
Court, 1902—1932

....In a democracy, politics is a process of popular education —
the task of adjusting the conflicting interests of diverse groups,
...and thereby to the hostility and suspicion and ignorance
engendered by group interests...toward mutual understanding.
Felix Frankfurter, Associate Justice of the Supreme Court,
1939—62

In all societies, the courts play some political role. In liberal democracies where the independence of the judiciary is regarded as essential
to prevent the exercise of irresponsible executive (and sometimes
legislative) power, the political role of the courts as interpreters of
the law and as defenders of individual freedoms is well established.
In one-party states, courts are political in the quite different sense
that they are the instruments of a dominant executive. However,
there are also important distinctions within liberal democratic states,
the most crucial being the presence or absence of judicial review. As
was noted in Chapter 3, judicial review is long established in the
United States, the Supreme Court being the final arbiter of the
meaning of the Constitution. Hence, all laws passed by the state
and national legislatures, together with all executive actions, are
subject to review by the courts who judge their compatibility with
the Constitution. As the final court of appeal, therefore, the Supreme
Court has the legal power to declare any action by any other branch
of government, unconstitutional. As we will develop later, this

apparently awesome power is tempered by a number of factors, but in contrast to many other liberal democracies, there can be no disputing the evidence of what is enormous potential judicial power. In the United Kingdom, for example, the courts can review executive actions — but only by testing them in relation to the content of Acts of Parliament. This can produce sharp rebukes for governments as happened in the Thameside and Laker Airways cases and there is good reason to believe that the British courts are becoming more active in reviewing executive actions.[1] A Parliament controlled by the executive can, however, always reverse a judicial judgment as sovereignty lies not in the Constitution but in Parliament. In the United States, a decision of the Supreme Court involving the constitutionality of a statute or governmental action can be overturned only by constitutional amendment (or by the court itself, of course) and as was shown in Chapter 3, the amendment procedure is cumbersome and rarely used.

In fact, the Supreme Court uses its power of judicial review quite sparingly and much of the day-to-day business of the courts is concerned with interpreting the law, rather than making solemn declarations on the constitutionality of legislation. Even in non-constitutional areas, however, American courts are more active than their British equivalents, for the United States is a highly legalistic society. Recourse to the courts for redress of grievances is swift and ubiquitous in American life. Indeed, the country boasts a staggering half a million lawyers and judges, and among the occupational backgrounds of US Representatives and Senators lawyers outnumber all the other professions put together. A number of reasons could be suggested for this. As we have repeatedly stressed in this book, the USA is a country with a liberal tradition, and the ideology of economic liberalism implies a society made up of individuals rather than social classes, races or other social groups. Distinct and separate individuals acting as self-contained economic units are more likely to defend or promote their interests in the judicial market place rather than, as in many other countries, fall back on social class, family, ethnic group or simply custom and tradition for support. There is a danger of making too much of this, but the tendency for individuals to seek legal redress for poor medical care or a faulty consumer product, or for corporations to sue competitors or

---

1 For comparisons of the two legal systems and an account of the political role of the British courts, see Ian Budge, David McKay *et al*, *The New British Political System*, London, Longman, 1983, Chapter 7.

suppliers for patent violations or breach of contract is surely related to a pervasive economic liberalism.

In addition, the United States is infused with Constitutionalism. With a written constitution granting certain rights and freedoms to citizens, delineating a separation of powers and guaranteeing a federal system of government, disputes between individuals and government and between branches and levels of government must be arbitrated. Of course, in every political system disputes of this sort have to be resolved, but in few systems are rather rigidly delineated citizens rights, separation of powers, and federal arrangements married to a strong tradition of legalism and the institution of judicial review. As far as the political role of the courts is concerned, it is the presence of judicial review which marks out the American system as distinctive, and as the Supreme Court is the highest court in the land, it is the Court's judicial review function which has attracted the most attention. The bulk of this chapter will therefore be devoted to this subject.

THE AMERICAN LEGAL SYSTEM

For the vast majority of Americans, state courts are what matter, for of the approximately 10 million cases tried in the United States every year, the federal courts account for less than 2 per cent. State, municipal, county and other local courts have jurisdiction over state law — which means that in any one state the vast majority of criminal and civil law cases from mugging to property disputes, to divorce to homicide are initiated and concluded within the state system. As can be seen from Figure 12.1, however, federal courts can play a crucial part in state law because, if a decision by the highest state courts of appeal is controversial and if the case involves a federal question then it can be appealed to the US Supreme Court. Effectively, this gives the Supreme Court the power to interpret and judge state law, for 'a federal question' can mean almost anything that is contentious or controversial. In law it means any state court decision which is potentially incompatible with federal law or with the US Constitution. If, for example, a state high court, hands down a decision extending the power of state police to search a suspect's house for evidence, this would have to be compatible with the 4th Amendment of the Constitution which prohibits unwarranted search and seizure. Only the US Supreme Court can judge whether the state law is unconstitutional or not.

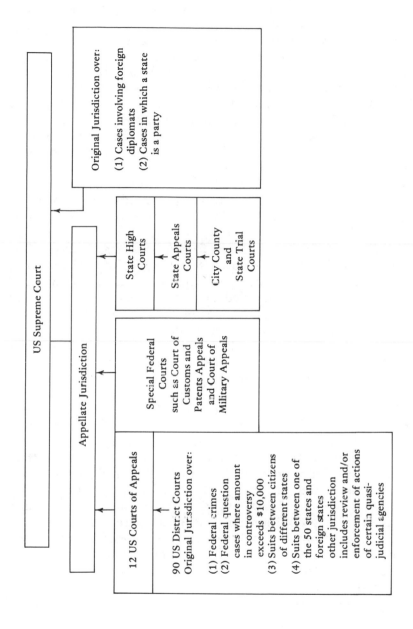

FIGURE 12.1   *Organization of the US Court System*

In one sense, the Supreme Court's power of judicial review over state law is its most important function. Without it, the country would cease to be a united nation state. Instead, a loose confederacy would prevail with each state going its own way in economic and social affairs. The power to review state high court decisions is part of the *appellate* jurisdiction of the Court. In addition, the Court hears cases on appeal from within the federal court system. As shown in Figure 12.1, most federal cases originate in the federal district courts (90 in number) whose decisions can be appealed to one of the twelve crucial Courts of Appeals, and thence to the Supreme Court. The Court[2] also has original jurisdiction on a number of minor areas such as cases involving ambassadors.

Most citizens involved in federal litigation, therefore, have contact with the District Courts which are responsible for cases involving federal criminal and civil law. Compared with state law, federal criminal law is limited to very few areas, the most notable being bank robbery, kidnapping, currency forgery and assassination. Most of the work of the District Courts is in the area of civil law, with taxation, regulation and civil rights and liberty cases dominating. Few of these cases are appealed and those that are, are usually settled in the Appeals Courts which on a day-to-day basis are the most important judicial policy makers in the country.

They are not, however, the key judicial policy makers because their decisions can always be overruled by the Supreme Court.

As can be seen from Figure 12.2, the District Courts' caseload has shown an inexorable increase over the last few years, and in the period since about 1966 the number of civil cases commenced has increased particularly rapidly. A greatly expanded federal role in part accounts for this, and although the precise relationship between spreading federal legislation and litigation is hard to establish, there is no doubt that the legislation listed in Figure 12.2 has greatly increased the caseload of both the District Courts and Appeals Courts (Figure 12.3). By 1978 the overload of the courts had reached crisis proportions and Congress increased the number of district judges from 281 to 398 and appeals judges from 62 to 97. Thus far, the Supreme Court has been immune from such changes in spite of efforts to create a National Court of Appeals to screen petitioners to the Court.

As Figure 12.3 shows, the Court has also experienced a sharp

---

2 For the remainder of the chapter Supreme Court and the Court will be used interchangeably.

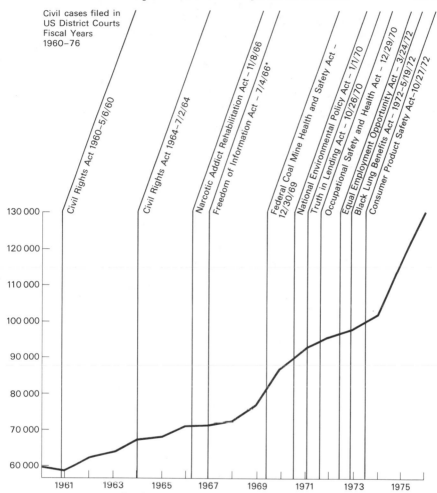

Civil cases filed in
US District Courts
Fiscal Years
1960–76

Civil Rights Act 1960–5/6/60

Civil Rights Act 1964–7/2/64

Narcotic Addict Rehabilitation Act – 11/8/66

Freedom of Information Act – 7/4/66*

Federal Coal Mine Health and Safety Act –
12/30/69

National Environmental Policy Act – 1/1/70

Truth in Lending Act – 10/26/70

Occupational Safety and Health Act – 12/29/70

Equal Employment Opportunity Act – 3/24/72

Black Lung Benefits Act – 1972–5/19/72

Consumer Product Safety Act–10/27/72

130 000
120 000
110 000
100 000
90 000
80 000
70 000
60 000

1961   1963   1965   1967   1969   1971   1973   1975

FIGURE 12.2   *Civil Cases Filed in US District Courts
Fiscal Years 1960–76*

Source: as reproduced in Linda E. Demkovich, 'The clogged federal courts – who are the culprits?', *National Journal*, 2 November 1978, p. 233. ©*National Journal*, 1978.
Note: * Effective 7/4/67.

rise in its caseload, though not as dramatic an increase as in lower courts. Increases in the number and use of law clerks (each Justice has three clerks assigned to him or her and the Chief Justice four), and

3 For a discussion of this point see Richard Hodder-Williams, *The Politics of the US Supreme Court*, London, Allen & Unwin, 1980, Chapter 2.

improved administration of the Court by the present Chief Justice, Warren Burger, probably account for the institution's ability to manage. As with lower courts, new legislation in civil rights and liberties, and in the general area of federal regulation largely account for the new demands on the Court. So like the Congress and Presidency, an ever expanding federal role has produced new pressures on the Supreme Court which have made its operations more complex and difficult and, crucially, more politically visible.

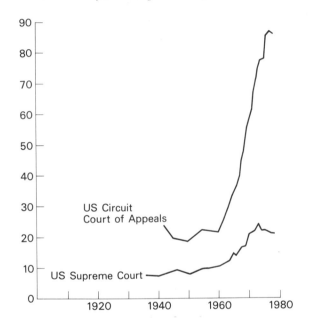

FIGURE 12.3 *Cases Docketed in Federal Appellate Courts per Million Population*

Source: Advisory Commission on Intergovernmental Relations, *The Federal Role in the Federal System: The Dynamics of Growth*, Washington DC, ACIR, 1980, Figure 91.

THE SUPREME COURT: DECISION MAKING

Each year about 150 cases are actually decided by the Supreme Court, and while most of these will be of relatively minor political or constitutional import, some will have profound consequences for the American polity and society. Since 1950, for example, the Court has decided that racially separate educational and other facilities are inherently unequal; that almost exact mathematical equality should be applied to the size of state legislative and Congressional disticts; that indigent arrested persons should be provided with the services of a lawyer at the government's expense; that tapes of Presidential conversations were not so private as to be protected by executive privilege and therefore could be used in Court against Presidential staff acused of dishonesty; and that the bussing of schoolchildren to achieve racial integration is constitutionally required to overcome a historical pattern of legally imposed educational segregation. The very fact that all of these decisions have aroused intense controversy demonstrates their political significance — and the question of how far and in what ways the Court can hand down decisions which are at odds with public opinion or with the other branches of government is a topic we will return to later. Clearly, *how* the Court makes decisions is important. How does it decide which cases to hear? What criteria does it employ when deciding a case?

It is misleading to talk of *the* Supreme Court. Rather than being a unified organic body, the Court consists of nine individuals each with his or her (in 1981 Sandra Day O'Connor was the first woman to be appointed to the Court) quite distinctive view of law, politics and society. Justices are appointed by the President with the advice and consent of the Senate. Unlike other executive appointments, they are appointed for life. Once on the Court then, they are free from the political, financial and other pressures which insecurity of tenure inflicts on most political actors. Of course, only a small percentage of cases coming before the Court are actually heard; most are denied review or, in the language of the Court are denied *certiorari*. *Certiorari* is, simply, that act whereby the losing party in the lower court appeals the record of the case to the Supreme Court so that details of the case can be made 'more certain'.[4] More than 90 per cent of cases are appealed in this way, in most of the remainder the Court is required to hear cases by a statutory appeals process.[5] The granting or denial of *certiorari* is clearly an important decision and the court is legally beholden to no-one to justify which cases are heard and which are not. From a strictly legal perspective, the criteria for granting *certiorari* are relatively easy to identify. Loren Beth lists seven:

4 For a good discussion of this point, see Loren P. Beth *Politics the Constitution and the Supreme Court*, New York, Harper and Row, 1962, Chapter 3.
5 The most important class of cases here are those where *state* high court decisions declare a federal law unconstitutional, or where the constitutionality of state law is in doubt.

(1)   How fundamental is the constitutional (or other) issue presented by the case?

(2)   How many similar cases have been or are being litigated?

(3)   Is there a conflict of opinion in the lower courts on this particular issue?

(4)   Does a lower court decision seem to conflict with an earlier Supreme Court decision?

(5)   Is there a significant individual right involved?

(6)   Haw the lower court departed significantly from the accepted and usual course of judicial proceedings?

(7)   Does the case involve the interpretation of a statute never before construed?[6]

At least four of the nine justices have to agree to grant *certiorari* — a fact which strongly implies that the decision is not so clear cut as the list suggests. Indeed, not one of points (1) to (7) is completely unambiguous or not open to serious disagreement or argument. How many cases in the civil rights and liberties areas — a good proportion of the total — do *not* involve a significant individual right? Almost certainly none. Similarly, many cases claim to involve a 'fundamental constitutional issue', yet few of these are granted *certiorari*. The fact is that while points (1) to (7) may be a legally correct list of criteria, it tells us very little of the political context in which decisions are taken. Why did it take until the 1940s and 1950s before the Court started regularly to hear civil rights cases? Why did it take to the 1960s for criminal defendent's rights cases to come to the fore, and until 1973 for the Court to deliberate on the constitutional status of abortion?

There are two possible answers here. First, that the philosophy and outlook of the justices changes over time, either as a result of turnover or because individual justices change their minds; and second, that the political and social context in which the Court operates has changed over time, thus forcing certain issues on to the judicial policy agenda which were previously excluded. Taking the second point first it is certain that the Court is influenced by the broader society. In the civil rights area, the Second World War 'nationalized' a number of social issues and brought into sharp focus both for Whites and Blacks the injustices of segregation in the American South. Publicity on conditions in the South was advanced by a number of interest groups, in particular the National

6   Beth, *ibid*, pp. 31–2.

Association for the Advancement of Coloured People (NAACP) who also acted as a judicial interest group by providing financial and legal support for litigants involved in civil rights cases.[7]

Although it is impossible to measure the influence on the Court of the 'social and political environment' or of the work of interest groups intent on promoting a particular cause or defending a special interest, the justices are undoubtedly swayed by such factors, at least in terms of letting them influence the policy agenda, or what sort of cases are actually heard.

But it would be misleading to leave the impression of a Court granting *certiorari* only to classes of cases currently subject to public attention. Many cases are heard when the public pressure is minimal or absent. Re-apportionment, for example, was not a matter of intense public debate when the Court implied in the famous 1962 case, *Baker* v. *Carr*, that the Tennessee State Legislature was constitutionally bound to organize its legislative districts according to the principle of mathematical equality. Later, in *Reynolds* v. *Sims* (1964), the Court made re-districting mandatory. Also, the business of getting a case before the Supreme Court is long and hard. It may be years from the time a case is first filed in the District Court before it eventually reaches the Supreme Court. Such a process does not always lend itself to instant decision making in response to public or interest group pressure.

The judicial agenda is also influenced by the philosophies and attitudes of the justices themselves. Generally speaking, a decision not to hear a case which in some way does meet one or more of the criteria (1) to (7) and which is currently controversial, is a conservative decision. It can reflect a justices' desire to keep the Court out of the 'political thicket' by leaving a lower court's decision or judicial precedent to settle the matter. The fact that the Court did not hear many civil rights cases in the 1920s and 1930s might be explained in this way, as might more recent Courts' reluctance to get involved in cases involving economic policy. We should be wary here, however, for so far discussion has been confined to the influences shaping the Courts' policy agenda, i.e. which cases are heard and which are not. Naturally, the crucial question is, how does the Court decide those cases granted *certiorari*? Even the most conservative justice would have to recommend the issue of a writ of *certiorari* when a Circuit Court of Appeals had decided a case which

---

7 For a good account of the early lobbying efforts of the NAACP see Clement E. Vose, *Caucasians Only*, Berkeley and Loss Angeles, University of California Press, 1967.

fundamentally contradicted judicial precedent as represented by an earlier Supreme Court decision. More interesting are those instances when the Court decides to uphold such a radical departure from precedent, or decides that a particular act of Congress or executive action is unconstitutional.

One basic fact must be appreciated when discussing the Court as a political actor — it uses its power sparingly. It exercises *judicial self restraint* (although as we shall see some Courts have been more restrained than others). It follows the doctrine of 'assumption of constitutionality'. In other words, it will use its power of judicial review very selectively, arguing a case on procedural grounds when it can, rather than declaring a law unconstitutional. Indeed, between 1789 and 1937 just 77 national laws were invalidated, although between 1937 and 1977 the rate increased considerably. This accepted, as with the granting of *certiorari* the political and social environment and the judicial philosophy of individual judges will determine the way in which these important decisions go.

As noted earlier, the Supreme Court consists of nine individual justices and the final decision of the Court reflects the interaction of the opinions of these nine people. The formal decision-making process goes like this. Once *certiorari* is granted, the justices first receive written and then hear oral argument from the lawyers on both sides of the case. Later a case conference is convened at which the justices, sitting in private, make a preliminary decision. Five of the justices must agree to constitute a decision and one of these will be assigned to write the majority opinion. If the Chief Justice is part of the majority he or another majority member assigned by him will write the opinion. If the Chief Justice is part of the minority, the most senior member of the majority will make the assignment. Once the assignments have been made, the opinion of the Court is written. This can take many weeks to complete and once published the names of other members of the majority may be added to it. However, some members, while they may agree with the author of the opinion of the Court, may do so for *different* reasons, in which case they will write *concurring* opinions. Finally, those in the minority may choose to write a dissenting opinion, or even a number of dissenting opinions. Usually members will join just the majority or dissenting opinion, but it is quite possible for the Court to publish up to nine separate opinions: an opinion of the Court, four concurring opinions which may support the Court opinion on four different grounds, and four dissenting opinions which dissent on four different grounds. In the celebrated 1978

Bakke decision which limited the use of racial quotas to discriminate positively in favour of minorities when admitting them to university courses the Court published no less than six separate opinions.[8] In this case — and this often applies when the justices are split — the variety of concurring opinions made it difficult to infer the exact meaning of the Court's decision — an outcome possibly preferred by the Court in this politically sensitive and technically complex area.

To the more casual observer of the judicial process, how a justice decides in a particular case may seem obvious. Precedent, and a careful interpretation of congressional statutes would be the immediate answer. Naturally, the justices do refer to precedent and they do spend much of their time interpreting legislation. In this respect their behaviour is little different from that of the British House of Lords (the highest court of appeal in Britain). But even reference to precedent can be problematical. What historical precedents are there for cases involving electronic bugging? Or genetic engineering? Or racial quotas, for that matter? Very few that could be considered even vaguely relevant. And interpreting statute law when it involves overruling executive actions can be politically sensitive, to say the least. In both instances the courts have very considerable discretion not only to follow precedent, but to create it; not only to interpret statutes, but to direct the executive branch to change policy. When the formidable power of judicial review is added, the discretion available to the Court widens dramatically. Again, the reflex response to the question 'what guides the Court when it uses judicial review?' is: the Constitution. But as was stressed in Chapter 3, there is very little in the Constitution that is unambiguous and the Supreme Court has reversed itself on a number of occasions when interpreting Constitutional provisions.

If the justices cannot rely on precedent or the literal meaning of statutes or constitutional provisions, what does guide their judicial opinions? This is a complex and difficult question. We have already mentioned the political and social environment and there can be no disputing that the Court has been influenced by pressures from public opinion, Presidents and interest groups. Instances of such pressures will be recorded later. Partly independently of such forces however, different Courts and justices have acquired reputations for being 'conservative' or 'liberal', 'active' or 'passive'. These labels

---

8 For a good account of this and associated cases see Alan P. Sindler, *Bakke, Defunis and Minority Admissions: The Quest for Equal Opportunity*, New York, Longman, 1978.

often refer to the jurisprudence or legal philosophy adhered to by different justices. Certainly, no self-respecting Supreme Court justice would rationalize his decision in terms of 'political pressures' or 'political expedience' — even if these were truly the main influences. Instead, justices would indeed refer to the Constitution and the ways in which the wording of the Constitution should be interpreted. By so doing they are obliged to look not only at the actual wording of the document but also to the meanings and motives behind the words. If, along with such a 'positivist' approach, the justice also believes that the Court has an unbending duty always to 'discover' the Constitution's true meaning, then an activist Court is implied. For relating the events in a particular case to the true meaning of the Constitution and then testing whether (say) a law on internal subversion is reconcilable with the Constitution, invites the Court to declare on the constitutionality of that law. Such was the approach of the two outstanding jurists of the early part of this century, Oliver Wendell Holmes and Louis Brandeis. In a number of celebrated cases both argued that some federal and state laws on internal subversion were incompatible with the 1st Amendment's general prohibition of laws abridging freedom of speech[9] — although they accepted that absolute freedom of speech was clearly not intended by the Framers of the Constitution. In Justice Holmes's famous example, 'the most stringent protection of free speech would not protect a man in falsely shouting fire in a theater and causing a panic' they argued that if the 1st Amendment was to mean anything, some principle inherent in the provision must be detected and invoked. By this reasoning, Holmes elaborated the 'clear and present danger test', or 'the question in every case is whether the words used in such circumstances are of such a nature as to create a clear and present danger that they will bring about the substantive evils that Congress has a right to prevent'. Of course, problems remain here — discovering exactly when the danger is clear and present must in part be a subjective exercise — perhaps especially so when Congress (or a state legislature) has passed a law attempting to prevent subversion in time of war. Indeed, Holmes and Brandeis sometimes believed there was a clear and present danger, as they did in the *Schenck* case[10] from which the above quotation is taken. But the very fact of attempting to find some principle inherent in the Constitution implies a legal philosophy which is largely independent of the

9 See Henry J. Abraham, *Freedom and the Courts*, New York, Oxford University Press, 1977.
10 *Schenck* v. *United States (1919)*.

vagaries of social and political pressures prevailing at any one time.

In marked contrast, one of the most prominent jurists of the 1940s and 50s, Felix Frankfurter, believed that the representatives of the American people — Congress and President — should be left to interpret the Constitution, the Court's involvement being confined to mediating disputes between the branches or between federal and state governments. Even then, Frankfurter argued, the Court should attempt to *balance* the various competing interests in society rather than search for some 'inherent principle' or 'higher meaning' behind the wording of the document. Clearly, a passive Court is implied by this approach, or one which steers clear of politics, letting representative institutions sort out conflict in society. The activism of Holmes and Brandeis and the passivity of Frankfurter represent two of the more coherent of a number of philosophical positions taken by the Court and the labels 'active' and 'passive' 'liberal' and 'conservative' usually correspond to the perceived philosophy of the Court at a particular time. We should not, however, be deceived into thinking of different Supreme Courts as representing distinct and coherent philosophies. To repeat, nine individuals make the decisions and each may vary quite dramatically in outlook.

Some Courts, then, have lacked an identifiable philosophy. More important, it is impossible to separate the decisions of the justices from the political and social environment in which they operate. The 'positivism' of Holmes and Brandeis with its search for a consistency and justice inherent in the Constitution, irrespective of political and social pressures, failed to dominate even the Court on which they sat, let alone been the main approach of subsequent Courts. Like any other political institution, the Court has to interact with society and polity. It is subject to a number of pressures and constraints. What makes the institution so interesting, however, is the mix of judicial philosophy and external constraint which has produced an ever-changing political role for the Court in American history. The remainder of this chapter will be devoted to studying this role, by analysing the constraints on the Court's power and in particular by asking whether the institution can be the equal of the other branches of government.

THE COURT AND POLITICAL POWER

There can be no doubting that Supreme Court decisions have political impact. From the momentous *Marbury* v. *Madison* decision in 1803 when, by declaring Section 13 of 1789 Judiciary Act unconstitutional, Chief Justice John Marshall effectively established judicial review, through to the landmark civil rights cases of the last 30 years, the attention of public and polity alike has been riveted by the political implications of the Court's decisions. But as earlier suggested, this does not mean that these solemn judicial deliberations take place in isolation from society. On the contrary, many have argued that the Court rarely deviates from the prevailing weight of political or public opinion; that, in fact, its main function has been to legitimize dominant political influences, and when it has gone against these it has soon found itself in trouble of one sort or another. In one rather obvious sense this is true, for courts depend on their authority rather than naked power. They have no police force or army — or even bureaucrats — to enforce their decisions. For this they have to depend on the other branches of government. Perhaps the most dramatic example of the dangers inherent in fundamentally disagreeing with the other branches of government was the 1857 *Dred Scott* case. In this the Court effectively declared unconstitutional the 1820 Missouri compromise which gave Blacks free status in those states in the Louisiana Purchase North of the Missouri. If Blacks were to revert to slave status in these Northern states, a forced extension of the culture and values of the South was implied, a change completely unacceptable to Lincoln and the dominant Republican Party. The decision was never enforced because the Civil War soon followed, as did the 14th Amendment which specifically granted equal legal status to all citizens. For the other branches of government simply to ignore the Court is the most serious challenge to its power, for once ignored, its authority and legitimacy are undermined. Without these it loses all influence. After the Civil War the Court did, in fact, soon reassert its authority and it has never been seriously undermined since. But there have been ebbs and flows of judicial power, crises of confidence and periods of intense controversy. A useful way to study these is to document the constraints or limitations on the court's power, or to record those instances when the scope and substance of judicial decisions have, in one way or another, been circumscribed.

Constitutional Amendment

Amending the Constitution to overturn the Court is the ultimate legal weapon available to the other branches and to the states. As we know, however, amendments have been few and far between and just four have been employed to overrule the Court. In one of these — the 26th Amendment ratified in 1971 to extend the vote to 18-year olds — the Court's *Oregon* v. *Mitchell* (1970) decision was overturned, although the Amendment would almost certainly have been considered necessary whatever the stance of the Court. Another (the 11th Amendment which prohibited a citizen of one state to sue the government of another state) has passed into historical obscurity.[11] Only two amendments stand out as changes crucial to preserve the integrity of the union and the smooth running of government — the 14th Amendment which overturned *Dred Scott*, and the 16th Amendment sanctioning a federal income tax. Ratified in 1913 when the need for increased defence spending was widely perceived as necessary, the 16th Amendment overturned the 1895 *Pollock* v. *Farmers' Loan and Trust* decision which had declared a graduated federal income tax unconstitutional.

Congressional Control

The Constitution grants remarkably wide discretion to Congress over the composition and organization of the federal judiciary. Article 3 states, quite simply: 'The judicial power of the United States shall be vested in one Supreme Court, and in such inferior Courts as the Congress may from time to time ordain and establish.' So Congress has the power to determine the size and administration of the federal machinery of justice. Additionally, the Constitution specifically gives to Congress discretion over the Court's appellate jurisdiction and implicitly, at least, over the number of justices and when the Court should actually sit. Only rarely, however, has the Congress exercised these very substantial discretionary powers. Easily the most important item of legislation in these areas is the 1789 Judiciary Act which established the Courts' power to review state court decisions denying federal rights to citizens. Apart from this, Congress has regularly increased the number of federal judges and courts (the latest increases in District and Appeals Court judges occurred in 1978) in line with population and caseload increases, and the number of Supreme Court justices fluctuated between six and ten until 1870, since when it has remained at nine. During the 1930s, President Roosevelt attempted to increase the size of the Court to overcome opposition to his New Deal legislation, but Congress was disinclined to tinker with the

11   Although the Supreme Court decision which sanctioned such cases, *Chisolm* v. *Georgia* (1793) aroused great controversy at the time.

Court in this way (see p. 259 below). By the 1930s the figure of nine justices was regarded as almost a part of the Constitution.

If Congress has been reluctant to alter the Court's composition and jurisdiction, it has shown little hesitation in reversing Court decisions via statutory reversals, or legislating to invalidate a particular judicial interpretation of federal law. Between 1946 and 1968, for example, some one hundred and eleven roll-call votes in Congress reversed Court statutory interpretations. Few of these were of great import, however, and of course Congress cannot touch those decisions which are based on *constitutional* interpretation. Perhaps Congress' most important function in relation to the Supreme Court is as a forum for public opinion. Senators and Congressmen quite frequently openly attack the Court or even introduce bills designed to curb its power. During the 1950s and 1960s for example, Southerners incensed at the Court's desegregation decisions, and conservatives at its civil liberties and re-appointment decisions, regularly did both. More recently, the 'pro-life' lobby in Congress has attempted to change the law on abortion, following the Court's liberal *Roe* v. *Wade* decision in 1973. While these attempts may fail, we cannot claim that constant attacks in the national legislature have no effect on the justices. In some contexts they may well influence the Court, especially if the justices are effectively isolated in their policy position, as was the case in 1937 when few sources of power or influence in American society sided with the Court.

Presidential Control

Presidents have two main means whereby they can influence the Court. First and most important, via the appointment power; and second, by appealing to public or Congressional opinion to reinforce their opposition to or support for a particular position. All federal judges are political appointees and the vast majority nominated by a President share his political party label if not his total political and social philosophy. In the case of District and, to a lesser extent, Appeals Court nominations, Presidents are guided by the advice and influence of the Senate (via the confirmation power) but also by state and local party leaders and dignitaries. Supreme Court judges are in a quite different category, their nomination being very much a matter of Presidential preference. Broadly speaking, Presidents have appointed justices whose political views are similar to their own. This does not mean to say that Presidents deliberately manipulate an appointment in order to change the complexion of the Court —

although often they do — nor does it mean that they are always successful in their attempts to change the Court's outlook and philosophy.

Obviously, they are circumscribed by chance, for although a vacancy on the Court has on average come up about every two years, some Presidents have been denied the privilege of receiving their 'quota' of two nominations. In his four years as President, poor Jimmy Carter made no appointments, while in his first three years in office Richard Nixon made four. Interestingly, it was President Carter who explicitly stated an intention to remove political considerations from the appointment of all federal judges, although as far as the Supreme Court was concerned his pledge went untested.

On two occasions in recent history, Presidents have been given and taken the opportunity to try and change the political complexion of the Court. Roosevelt did so after 1937 and Nixon after 1969. In Roosevelt's case, the Court had repeatedly struck down New Deal legislation on the grounds that it was an unconstitutional exercise of the Interstate Commerce Clause. In the face of the possible collapse of his economic recovery programme, Roosevelt attempted to 'pack' the Court by asking Congress to increase the number of justices by one for every existing justice over 70 years old, up to a maximum of 15. His strategy was clear — to tip the ideological balance of the Court away from the so-called 'Four Horsemen of Conservatism' (Justices Butler, McReynolds Sutherland and Van Devanter) towards a more liberal stance. He failed in the Court-packing plan largely because by the time it reached the critical stage in a not too enthusiastic Congress one of the conservatives, Van Devanter, had retired. Roosevelt then proceeded to fill this and other vacancies which came thick and fast during the next few years with 'New Dealers' or Justices sympathetic to an enhanced federal role in economy and society. He was remarkably successful. Almost all of his nine appointees toed the New Deal line and the Court kept well out of economic affairs during the 1937–53 period.[12]

The other quite dramatic instance of political use of the appointment power occurred during the first two years of the Nixon administration. One of Richard Nixon's 1968 campaign pledges had been to replace the liberals of the Warren Court with 'strict constructionists' or conservatives less prone to the advancement of civil rights and liberties characteristic of the Warren era. He was given a golden

---

12 And in many respects the Court still keeps out of major economic controversies, especially those relating to federalism, see Chapter 4.

opportunity to do just this, for four vacancies occurred during the 1969—71 period. One of these was for Chief Justice and the President lost no time in nominating Warren Burger, Chief Judge of the District of Columbia Court of Appeals to the position. Burger, a conservative Republican from Minnesota remains Chief Justice today.[13] Nixon's next two nominees ran into serious trouble in the Senate. Only rarely in the 20th Century have Supreme Court nominations been rejected and it is a remarkable testimony to Nixon's political insensitivity that his second and third nominations, Clement Haynsworth and Harold Carswell were voted down in the Upper Chamber. Both were undistinguished as jurists and Carswell, in particular, had acquired a dubious record on civil rights in the Southern Courts from which he hailed. Their rejection illustrates well the simple fact that Presidential discretion over appointments is limited. A President may nominate a conservative or a liberal, but not an incompetent or a bigot. A Senate judiciary committee well versed by the American Bar Association, leading jurists and interested groups will see to that. Richard Nixon did, however, succeed with his next three appointments, Harry Blackman, Lewis Powell and William Rhenquist. Rhenquist was a solid conservative (but a respected jurist) while the others were known at least as moderately conservative.

There can be no doubt that the Burger Court is very different from the openly liberal Warren Court and that this is partly a function of personnel changes. But Presidents can never be sure that, once appointed, a justice will fulfil expectations. Appointed for life to the most respected forum in the land, many justices change their political philosophies once on the Court. Such was the case with Earl Warren, one-time conservative Republican governor of California, expected by his patron President Eisenhower to continue the self restraint of the Stone and Vinson Courts. In civil rights and liberties and re-apportionment he did just the opposite. And although the Nixon appointees have generally moved the Court to the right they have hardly done so in a coherent and consistent manner. Liberal civil rights and liberties decisions did not suddenly cease in 1971,

---

13 The Chief Justice position became vacant quite fortuitously for Nixon. President Johnson had nominated Abe Fortas as Warren's successor, but during the Senate hearings into Fortas' suitability it was revealed that, among other things, in 1966 he had received a $20,000 fee from a millionaire who at the time was being investigated (and later was convicted) for fraud. See Bob Woodward and Scott Armstrong, *The Brethren: Inside the Supreme Court*, New York, Simon and Schuster, 1979, Prologue.

even if they have become infrequent and interspersed with more conservative judgments.[14]

Public and Political Opinion

So the appointment power must by definition be limited because, even when Presidents have made appointments, they have no direct control over the justices once they are on the Court. They can, of course, appeal to Congress (as with the Court-packing plan) or to public opinion, but once this happens the independent influence of the President is lost. As we noted in earlier chapters, public opinion is hard to define and almost impossible to measure. Scratch beneath the surface and what most commentators mean by public opinion is a particular configuration of political power, expressed either through representative institutions or through organized groups. If we accept this approach, we can confidently state that only very rarely in American history has the Court challenged a dominant climate of opinion. Between the Civil War and 1932, for example, the Court acquired the reputation for defending the burgeoning capitalist interests of the period by striking down both state and federal legislation designed to regulate industry or protect workers from exploitation. The regulation of interstate commerce did not, the Court argued, extend to such things as federal laws regulating child labour. Or, more importantly, entitlement of 'due process of law' under the 14th Amendment did not extend to *state* attempts to regulate industrial and commercial life. It only applied directly to federal–citizen relationships. As a result, between 1900 and 1937 some 184 decisions invalidated state regulatory provisions.[15] To be fair, a number of state laws were also upheld during these years, but the general stance of the Court was anti-regulation or anti-government 'interference'. Crucially, however, so generally was public opinion, at least until 1932. Most Presidents, Congress and many state legislatures accepted the Supreme Court's judgments with relative equanimity. It was not until the coming of the Great Depression in the early 1930s that the climate of opinion changed dramatically. And when the Court began regularly to strike down federal New Deal legislation it became politically isolated. Within two years, and following intense pressure from unions,

---

14 See Woodward and Armstrong, *ibid*, also Richard Hodder-Williams, 'Is there a Burger Court?' *British Journal of Political Science*, Vol. 9, Part 2, 1979.
15 Quoted in Hodder-Williams, *The Politics of the US Supreme Court, op. cit*, p. 138.

Congress and President,[16] the Court had made its 'switch in time that saved nine' and thereafter followed rather than led the other branches in the general area of economic policy.

During the 1940s and up to about 1957, the Court was deferential to Congress and President on questions of national security. In case after case the Court accepted the restrictions placed on citizens by the 1940 Smith Act, the 1950 McCarren Act and in the case of the Japanese Americans by executive *fiat*.[17] Not until the late 1950s when public fears about communist subversion began to subside did the Court begin to relax the restrictions on communists and others perceived to be subversive.

Even in civil rights it would be difficult to argue that the Court was acting in isolation from broader political and public opinion. *Brown* v. *Board*, the landmark 1954 decision, which argued that racially separate facilities in education and other facilities were inherently unequal, may have been highly unpopular in the South, but it was welcomed in the North by many members of Congress, and was not unpopular with the President. What can be claimed for *Brown*, is that it helped push opinion towards the de-segregation of the South — although enforcement problems apart (of which more later) it was not until 1964 that Congress, goaded on by a determined and proselytizing President, passed the first major federal civil rights act.

The apportionment decisions of the early 1960s, extending the principle of representation according to mathematical equality, first to state legislatures and then to Congressional districts, were probably more widely unpopular with politicians than the civil rights decisions. But they were not unpopular with the public, most of whom stood to gain from a removal of the bias in representation towards rural areas. And how could state and national politicians justify the gross inequities that had accumulated over time? This is not to deny that the Court was a genuine innovator in this area,[18] however, as it was in the realm of criminal defendents'

---

16 See Beth, *op. cit*, Chapter 6.

17 The Smith Act made it unlawful to advocate the overthrow of the US Government and the McCarren Act required 'subversive organizations' to register with the Subversive Activities Control Board. In 1942 West Coast Americans of Japanese origin (many of them citizens) were arbitrarily interned in concentration camps by the Governor of California (ironically Earl Warren, later the champion of individual freedom on the Court) as a threat to internal security. The Court failed to hear the cases arising from this until 1944 and then argued them on procedural rather than constitutional grounds.

18 It is interesting to note that the Burger Court has modified the original apportionment decisions to allow community of interest as well as population to determine the size of districts.

rights. Starting with *Gideon* v. *Wainright* in 1963 and continuing through to Earl Warren's resignation in 1969, the Court handed down a remarkable succession of decisions granting defendents the right to state-provided counsel, access to police files, extending the freedom from unlawful search and seizure and generally providing much greater protection to arrested persons. Coming as they did during the disruptions of the 1960s, these changes were welcomed only by what eventually was a diminishing band of liberals.

Undoubtedly, the Warren Court moved well ahead of public opinion in this area. Perhaps predictably, the Burger Court has not continued the crusading spirit of the Warren era. It has trod cautiously, and in both civil rights and liberties has been careful to qualify some of the more dramatic decisions of the 1960s. This does not, however, represent a sudden break from the past; many of the earlier decisions have been upheld, and the anger and frustration of police forces, local and state governments, as well as many sections of the public at large at the procedural and substantive protection given to defendents, continues.

Often the Court cannot predict what the impact of its decisions on public opinion will be. The Warren Court, for example, handed down a decision on abortion in 1973 (*Roe* v. *Wade*) which looked like a model of careful, pluralistic judicial decision making. The Court effectively outlawed all state laws which prohibited abortion during the first three months of pregnancy, liberalized them during the next three months and banned abortions during the last ten weeks. This apparently reasonable compromise has, however, been seized by the pro-life anti-abortion special interest groups and branded as a further example of the federal courts undermining public morals and the sanctity of family life. Little doubt exists that the decision precipitated debate and political controversy on an issue whose salience increased enormously during the 1970s. The Court's decisions on capital punishment which although laying down pretty strict guidelines have effectively left to the states the final decision on when (and how) a person should be executed, have also aroused great controversy. In both instances, debate on the issues have been passed on to the broader political stage. But they have hardly left the judicial policy agenda. Controversy on where individual rights begin and end must by necessity concern the courts, and given governments' intimate involvement both in granting and denying rights to citizens (indeed in exercising a power over life and death in the two examples cited above), the courts involvement must also continue.

We can conclude that only rarely has the Court consciously moved against prevailing public and political opinion, and when it has done so, it has not been for long. Two important qualifications have to be applied to this generalization. First, the Court has been reluctant to challenge or has never for long challenged a programme or policy supported by the other branches, and which is perceived to be crucial to the integrity of the union (the status of slavery in the North), national security in wartime or 'emergency' conditions ('subversion' in the two World Wars and afterwards) or to the running of the economy (the New Deal legislation). When, however, there is no consensus on a policy — especially when Congress and President are in serious disagreement — then the Court plays a central role in arbitrating the conflict. We have two dramatic examples of the Court playing just such a role in recent history. In 1951 President Truman seized the nation's steel mills on the grounds that industrial disputes were undermining production and the Korean War effort. The Court quickly condemned the seizure as an unconstitutional infringement on the legislative powers of Congress. In 1974, the Court declared that executive privilege did not protect President Nixon's taped conversations which could be used in the Courts and Congress to investigate the Watergate wrong-doings. On both occasions Congress was unsympathetic to the President's position and, significantly, so was broader public opinion.

The second qualification to the Court's deference to prevailing public and political opinion is that when it does challenge them in areas involving the behaviour of myriad individuals, rather than a few institutions or political leaders, it tends to experience serious problems in enforcing its decisions or in predicting their precise impact on public opinion.

Lack of Enforcement Powers

As noted earlier, without their own police force, army or bureaucracy, the Courts cannot enforce their decisions unless their authority is accepted by those who do exercise coercive powers. Moreover, the Supreme Court depends on lower courts (federal and state) to implement its decisions and these may not always interpret or accept the Court's judgments in an unambiguous fashion. The most celebrated examples of judicial recalcitrance and obstruction involved the enforcement of civil rights in the South. Following *Brown* v. *Board's* 1954 directive that Southern schools should desegregate 'with all deliberate speed', Southern District courts were assigned the job of enforcing the order. Appointed by Presidents on the advice of local politicians and party faithfuls, District judges reflect local conditions, interests — and prejudices. Very few of the Southern District judges of the 1950s and 60s were integrationists and most resisted — mainly through delays of one sort or another — the order to desegregate. In fact, not until 1969 in the *Alexander* v. *Holmes County Board of Education* decision — some fifteen years after *Brown* — did the Supreme Court finally make it mandatory to desegregate immediately,[19] and by then, of course, the Court was supported by the not inconsiderable weight of the 1964 Court Rights Act with its array of compliance and enforcement procedures.

More rarely, a state or local political actor may openly defy a Court order as happened in Little Rock, Arkansas in 1957 when Governor Faubus used the local militia forcibly to prevent Black children from entering a high school. Only the eventual use of federal troops on the instruction of President Eisenhower, enabled the Black children to enter the school. Much more common is evasion of the directives of the Supreme Court, not only by other courts or by outright defiance, but through ignorance, deception or the simple fact that complete enforcement is technically impossible to achieve. Such has been the case with criminal law decisions like *Miranda* and *Gideon* which laid down strict procedures for the interrogation of suspects. As research has shown, arrested persons often do not know their rights, police officers are frequently ignorant of the correct procedures, and even when informed can compromise them. Similarly, the decisions of the early 1960s outlawing special prayers and bible reading in public schools (*Engale* v. *Vitale*, *Abington School District* v. *Schempp*) as infringements of the 1st Amendment's freedom of religion clause, have proved very difficult to enforce.

Conclusion

It is often argued that the greatest limitation on the political power of the Court is 'judicial self-restraint' or a conscious decision by the justices to avoid the political thicket by deferring to the other branches (or to public opinion) rather than causing great controversy by departing from the dominant opinion. Our earlier discussions suggest strongly that this is true, although self-restraint is more a

19 For an excellent account of the tactics of Southern District judges see Jack Peltason *58 Lonely Men*, New York, Harcourt Brace Jovanovich, 1961.

matter of political common sense than, as some jurists have argued, something which can be justified solely on philosophical grounds. Judges may search for a 'higher principle' inherent in the Constitution, or they may be convinced that government 'interference' in the economy is always a bad thing. Sooner or later, however, they have to take cognizance of the political and social environment in which decisions are made. As we noted, the Supreme Court is seriously constrained by this environment; it is not an institution apart from politics, but one which is an organic part of the polity and society.

If the Court rarely challenges the dominant political forces in society, what use then is the institution of judicial review? From our discussion we can identify three crucial functions: (a) The Court arbitrates between federal and state law. In terms of the stability and integrity of the union this is undoubtedly its most important function; (b) Judicial review provides the Court with an apparently neutral point of reference (the Constitution) for arbitrating between the different branches of government — although historically this has tended to work only when one branch (the executive) is relatively isolated from Congressional and public opinion; (c) Judicial review can help defend individual freedoms under the Bill of Rights and 14th Amendment. Of course, there have been numerous occasions when the Court has clearly failed to defend such freedoms, as with the internment of the Japanese Americans in 1942. But — and this is the strongest argument in favour of judicial review under bills of rights — the legislative and executive branches would have denied these freedoms even in the absence of judicial review. Its presence is usually beneficial, therefore, in the sense that when it deviates from the other branches it does so by favouring the individual. As the civil rights and especially civil liberties cases of the 1950s and 1960s demonstrate, this can involve quite radical, if sometimes temporary, departures from prevailing political and public opinion.

Finally, how has the Court responded to the much more fragmented polity and society characteristic of the 1970s and 1980s? In a word, uncertainly. As suggested, the Burger Court is cautious and pragmatic, yet even this prudential stance hardly guarantees the avoidance of controversy. Issue politics, combined with the increasingly technical nature of cases, can produce a situation where the Court hands down decisions which are highly contentious. Issue politics produces odd, unpredictable political coalitions where it is almost impossible to please everybody. The Court's decisions on abortions and capital punishment, for example, involved issues where the subsequent lines of opposition and support were complex and unpredictable. In some other areas — campaign finance for instance (see p. 235) — the technicalities of the question are so formidable that the Court has produced decisions whose consequences have been unexpected, and perhaps undesirable.[20]

Throughout all these changes the Supreme Court and the whole judiciary strives to perform what is perhaps its most vital function — the legitimization of the system in the eyes of the citizenry. In the words of Felix Frankfurter:

A gentle and generous philosopher noted the other day a growing 'intuition' on the part of the masses that all judges, in lively controversies, are 'more or less prejudiced.' But between the 'more or less' lies the whole kingdom of the mind, the difference between the 'more or less' are the triumphs of disinterestedness, they are the aspirations we call justice...The basic considerations in the vitality of any system of law is confidence in this proximate purity of its process. Corruption from venality is hardly more damaging than a widespread belief of corrosion through partisanship. Our judicial system is absolutely dependent upon a popular belief that it is as untainted in its workings as the finite limitations of disciplined human minds and feelings make possible.[21]

To perform this function adequately the Court cannot deviate too much from the mainstream of political opinion, a fact which has not been lost on many recent justices, including most on the present Court.

FURTHER READING

The best single introduction is Henry J. Abraham, *The Judicial Process*, New York, Oxford Univeristy Press, 1980. A good non-American interpretation of the Supreme Court is Richard Hodder-Williams, *The Politics of the US Supreme Court*, London, Allen & Unwin, 1980. For a vivid journalists' account of how the Court operates, see Bob Woodward and Scott Armstrong, *The Brethren: Inside the Supreme Court*, New York, Simon and Schuster, 1979. For a more detailed factual account, see Elder Witt (ed.) *Congressional Quarterly's Guide to the United States Supreme Court*, Washington DC, Congressional Quarterly,

20   For example in *Buckley* v. *Valeo* (1976) the Court accepted that organizations could spend as much as they liked to support or defeat candidates, so long as the money did not go directly into candidates' campaigns. As a result PACs launching hugely expensive media campaigns for or against individuals have become a feature of American politics.
21   Quoted in David F. Forte, *The Supreme Court in American Politics*, Lexington, Massachusetts, D. C. Heath, 1972, pp. 93–4.

1979. The best analysis of the Court and civil rights and liberties is Henry J. Abraham, *Freedom and the Court*, New York, Oxford University Press, 3rd edition, 1977.

CHAPTER 13

The Style and Substance
of Policy Making

The crisis of our cities is the crisis of the modern United States. Seventy percent of all Americans now live in or close to cities. The number grows each year. So the fate of the city and the future of our country are one and the same thing.
O. C. James and L. D. Hoppe, Urban Crisis in America, 1969

Today the administration is proposing a national recovery plan to reverse the debilitating combination of sustained inflation and economic distress which continues to face the American economy. Were we to stay with existing policies, the results would be readily predictable: a rising government presence in the economy, more inflation, stagnating productivity, and higher unemployment...The program we have developed will break that cycle of negative expectations. It will revitalize economic growth, renew optimism and confidence, and rekindle the nation's entrepreneurial instincts and creativity.
Ronald Reagan, February 1981

Historically, the test for American statesmanship should therefore be not how long it manages to cling to a deteriorating and overextended hegemony, but how well those liberal domestic and international arrangements it has fostered can adapt themselves to the stresses of the more plural order. In other words, the real test of American statesmanship is whether the postwar world system can survive the relative decline of American Power.
David Calleo, The Imperious Economy, 1982

It would be easy to infer from earlier chapters that decision making in the American political system is so fragmented and dispersed that the resulting policies are simply not amenable to simple characterization; that the open and pluralistic nature of the system produces a politics of confusion and unpredictability. While there is no doubt a great deal of truth to this, it would be wrong to leave the analysis without enquiring further into the nature and consequences of policy making in the United States. The purpose of this last chapter is, therefore, to add perspective and balance to earlier conclusions by examining how policy making has developed in three important areas — urban, economic and foreign policy. Discussion will particularly focus on the following three questions:

(1) To what extent do policy systems differ in style and substance one from the other?

(2) How does policy develop over time? How do changes in administration and the domestic and international environment change the ways in which policy is formulated and implemented?

(3) Related is the crucial question of the role that political institutions and processes play in the policy system. To what extent do institutional relationships mould public policies as opposed to broader structural forces in economy and society? This question is important because if institutions' independent role is limited, then so is the potential for institutional reform. In other words, it may be that, whatever the institutional context, governing a large complex industrial society such as the United States would be a difficult business.

Obviously we cannot provide definitive answers to these questions, and obviously our discussion of each of the policy areas must, of necessity, be brief. Because we can only touch on some of the main issues involved, references to more detailed analyses will be provided when appropriate.

URBAN POLICY AND URBAN PROBLEMS:
THE PERPETUAL AMERICAN DILEMMA

Foreign observers of the American scene have long been struck by the contradictions which American cities seem to represent. The USA is the world's richest country, yet many of its urban areas are characterized by poverty, racial unrest and a dangerous criminality. At the same time, the downtown areas of many cities with their towering skyscrapers and general resilience appear almost as monuments to the success of capitalism and the 'American Way.' Certainly the United States has urbanized rapidly and by no means always unsuccessfully. Most Americans live comfortably in suburban or semi-rural settings and general standards in housing and urban amenity have improved dramatically in the last 30 years.

Yet for most of recent history, the country has also had serious urban problems. During the 19th and early 20th centuries overcrowding and squalor in the burgeoning industrial cities was the major problem. During the 1930s stagnation and poverty became the dominant themes, while most recently urban problems have become associated with the fortunes of racial and ethnic minorities. As with other areas of social life, federal administrations — but also state and local governments — have become increasingly involved in urban society, so that today literally hundreds of federal programmes and policies contain an urban dimension. What are the characteristics of these programmes and the policy processes which have produced them? We can identify three general features.

1. *Urban Policies are extensive, but complex and hard to define.* With more than 70 per cent of Americans living in urban areas, almost all of domestic policy has an urban dimension — a fact which has led many commentators to condemn attempts to formulate a 'national urban policy' as meaningless. But we can distinguish between those policies which have been designed mainly as urban programmes and those which are part of general social or economic policy with an urban dimension. Table 13.1 lists some of the more important of these programmes. It excludes civil rights policies, which from the 1960s onwards had an increasing impact on urban as opposed to Southern, mainly rural, areas. Table 13.1 also excludes specific reference to a number of federal law enforcement, health, social services, public works, housing and education programmes which in total have had an important impact on urban residents. Moreover some programmes have changed enormously over time as eligibility requirements and political conditions have changed (of which more later). Finally, the table excludes those state and local policies with an urban dimension. Since the mid-1960s these have increased in number and significance, often in parallel to federal initiatives.

2. *Urban policies tend to be* ad hoc, *reactive and selective rather than planned, strategic and comprehensive.* At first glance, the programmes listed in Table 13.1 might lead the reader to think that federal governments have planned to intervene in urban society in

TABLE 13.1　*Major Domestic Federal Programmes*
Affecting Urban Areas

Primarily Urban Policies	*General Policies with an Urban Dimension*
1937　Housing Act (established public housing)	1934　Housing Act (established federal mortgage guarantees)
1949　Housing Act (provided grants to cities for urban renewal)	1935　Social Security Act (created old age, disability and unemployment insurance and welfare payments)
1954　Housing Act (urban renewal)	1964　Economic Opportunity Act (a package of anti-poverty programmes)
1964　Urban Mass Transportation Act	
1965　Creation of the Department of Housing and Urban Development	1964　Food Stamp Programme created
1966　Model Cities Act (demonstration programme for urban revival)	1965　Medicare and Medicaid (medical care for the old and the poor)
1968　Housing Act (subsidies for lower income housing)	1965　Elementary and Secondary Education Act (aid for schools in poorer areas)
1974　Community Development Act (consolidation of a number of urban programmes into one block grant, housing subsidies reorganized)	1972　Revenue Sharing (general fiscal aid for states and cities)
1977　Urban Development Action Grants (urban renewal grants for private development)	1975　Comprehensive Employment and Training Act (CETA, training and employ-ment creation for lower level governments)
	1976　Counter Cyclical Revenue Sharing (supplemental fiscal aid for areas of high unemployment)

some comprehensive manner. If anything the opposite is true. Most policies have emerged as a result of lobbying, bargaining and coali-tion building with successive administrations reacting to constituency and other pressures rather than legislating comprehensive programmes based on coherent party platforms. There are, admittedly, two par-tial exceptions to this rule. In the mid/late 1930s Franklin Roosevelt's

New Deal produced a series of social policies which were certainly comprehensive in contemporary context. The 1935 Social Security Act laid the foundations of the modern welfare state in the USA, and the 1937 Public Housing Act created the precedent of direct federal aid for local governments, even if the programme itself was (and remains) very small. Similarly during the mid-1960s Lyndon Johnson's War on Poverty and civil rights 'revolution' had a clear urban dimension and resulted in a number of important new programmes, notably Medicare, Medicaid, educational assistance and housing subsidies. But even the New Deal and Great Society periods were hardly equivalent to (say) the British Labour government's comprehensive social policies adopted between 1945 and 1950. The rhetoric may have been stirring, but the resulting policies were, initially at least, quite limited. Welfare and social security began as selective programmes with narrow eligibility criteria and, in the case of welfare, great discretion remaining with the states. Food stamps was never intended as a large programme and eligibility requirements for Medicare and Medicaid were also limited. What is true is that most of those programmes involving transfers to individuals (food stamps, welfare, social security, medical aid) have grown very rapidly, often from humble beginnings.[1] Hence in 1964 only about 350,000 Americans were in receipt of food stamps. By 1976 this figure had reached a staggering 18.5 million. The reason for this, and equivalent increases in other programmes, is simple. Presidents and Congress have limited control over transfer payments, which tend to rise with increases in unemployment and in line with demographic changes. Moreover, the pressures from social groups and the courts to expand eligibility criteria have been considerable. This said, non-contributory welfare payments are almost certainly more susceptible to cuts than contributory social security benefits (unemployment insurance, pensions, disability allowances and Medicare) which most Americans accept as *rights*. For the poorer inhabitants of the inner cities this is significant, for those most in need have often never been members of the workforce, so for them welfare is their main means of support. Recent cuts in the welfare and food stamps programmes have had serious consequences for

---

1   Although what was originally the main welfare programme, Aid for Families with Dependent Children (AFDC), has grown much less rapidly and is now small in comparison with most social security programmes. For a good history of welfare in the United States see Walter I. Trattner, *From Poor Law to Welfare State*, New York, Free Press, 1979.

such people, among whom families headed by Black females have suffered the most.[2]

The vast array of grants to state and local governments which have some impact on the urban physical environment have, if anything, evolved in an even more erractic and *ad hoc* manner than have transfer payments policies. Numerous federal departments and agencies are involved and there is now hardly any aspect of urban life which is not affected by federal funding. So complex is this network of aid that no-one knows for sure what its extent and influence is. When, in 1977, President Carter attempted to formulate a national urban policy, he first asked his staff to measure where and how exactly the money was used. All the aides (and the Department of Housing and Urban Development) could do however was to provide broad aggregate statistics. These are provided in Table 13.2 (which also includes some transfer payments). The exercise was, in other words, a very hit and miss affair, with the eventual total of 47 billion dollars constituting more than 60 per cent of all grants to state and local governments.

The point is that in their day-to-day activities, departments, agencies and bureaux operate in terms of *individual programmes* rather than in terms of the spatial or social impact of particular policies. Most administrations simply do not know what the consequences of their policies for urban areas and specifically for distressed inner cities are. Why should they, when Congressional directives and the needs of clients (state and local governments) concentrate their attention on budgeting and distributional questions which only rarely include evaluative criteria based on urban distress and urban need?

Non-transfer payment grant programmes have not grown as rapidly as welfare and social security but they have certainly become much more susceptible to budgetary cuts. This is particularly true of capital expenditure programmes which tend to have less well established networks of clients and lobbyists. Indeed, during 1981–2 President Reagan singled out capital spending on housing, sewage treatment, and community development for particularly intensive budget reductions. He also attempted to cut the more vulnerable (in political terms) of the welfare programmes, especially food stamps.[3]

2   Forty five percent of such families living in inner cities were below the official poverty line in 1977, *The President's National Urban Policy Report 1980, Executive Summary*, Washington DC Department of Housing and Urban Development, 1980, Table ES-3.
3   For a radical critique of this latest round of welfare cuts, see Frances Fox Piven and Richard A. Cloward, *The New Class War: Reagan's Attack on the Welfare State and its Consequences*, New York, Pantheon, 1982.

TABLE 13.2 *Grants to Metropolitan Areas, 1977*[a]
millions of dollars

Function	
National Defence	25
Energy	15
National Resources and Environment	3,689
Agriculture	140
Commerce and Housing Credit	10
Transportation	4,905
Community and Regional Development	3,777
Education, Training, Employment and Social Services	11,602
Health	7,909
Income Security	8,503
Veterans Benefits and Services	21
Administration of Justice	628
General Government	30
General Purpose Fiscal Assistance	6,220
Total	47,474

Source: Department of Housing and Urban Development
Note:
a Estimated

But as pointed out in Chapter 4, no President can transform the pattern of intergovernmental aid which has developed over the last 30 years. Too many individual interests, whether local, state or federal, are involved in a complex of policy networks. Policy networks, lobbying and Congressional log-rolling tend, of course, to protect all recipients of federal funds, irrespective of need. So affluent as well as distressed cities, small as well as large jurisdictions will continue to receive federal funds even if some cuts are implemented. However, there is some evidence that in the context of a slowly diminishing federal cake, the poorer cities will suffer disproportionately. Why should this be so?

First, as their local tax bases have fallen in the context of falling populations, declining industries and increasingly *dependent* populations, poorer cities have come to rely on intergovernmental — mainly federal — aid. In 1979, for example, 68.4 per cent of Buffalo's total revenue, 63.8 per cent of Newark's and 49.1 per cent of Detroit's came from intergovernmental aid.[4] Although deriving from a number

4 US Census Bureau, *City Government Finances*, 1978–9, Washington, DC, 1980.

of programmes, this aid is needed for the provision even of minimal services in education, law enforcement and the physical upkeep of the city. Any expenditure cut is therefore serious for such localities.[5] Second, with declining and dependent populations, the political clout of these areas is limited.

Congressional re-districting is slowly reducing older urban areas' representation and, crucially, the cities' interests are no longer championed by a national administration.

3. *Democratic Presidents have attempted to rationalize the confusing pattern of aid to cities and urban areas, but with little success.* The first significant recognition that the federal government had a major responsibility for the welfare of large cities came with the creation of HUD in 1965. Designed to add coherence to the already burgeoning number of programmes, HUD ended up as an amalgam of various agencies rather than a coherent Cabinet department (for further discussion, see p. 204). In 1977 Jimmy Carter made a much bolder effort to formulate a national urban policy by attempting to fulfil his campaign pledge to the US Conference of Mayors that he would be 'a friend, an ally and a partner in the White House'. By this time the extreme complexity of federal intervention was appreciated and Carter experimented with an interdepartmental device which became known as the Urban and Regional Policy Group (URPG). Led by Patricia Harris, the HUD Secretary, the URPG's aim was to coordinate all the major domestic agencies responsible for urban policy. Although this initiative began as an experiment in Cabinet government, responsibility soon passed to the White House (in particular to Stuart Eizenstat of the Domestic Policy Staff) and to a few officials in HUD.[6] The demise of the Cabinet experiment can be explained in the main by the reluctance of individual departments to forfeit power to HUD, 'turf protection dominated', as two observers put it.[7] Moreover although Agriculture, Commerce, Transportation, Energy and a number of other agencies were involved, the Defense Department and General Services Agency, which together are responssible for the siting of almost all federal buildings and installations, were not. What eventually transpired was a document, *Cities and*

5 For discussion of this and related questions, see John P. Blair and David Nachmias (eds), *Fiscal Retrenchment and Urban Policy, Urban Affairs Annual Reviews*, Vol. 17, Berkeley and Beverly Hills, Sage, 1979.
6 For a fascinating account of this policy process, see Harold L. Wolman and Astrid E. Merget, 'The Presidency and policy formulation: President Carter and the urban policy', *Presidential Studies Quarterly*, Vol. 10, No. 3, Summer 1980.
7 *Ibid*, p. 409.

People in Distress, and a list of policies which were anything but comprehensive and coherent in nature. Some $10 billion in additional urban spending was proposed, but budgetary and Congressional constraints ensured that almost none of this increase was accepted. To be fair, President Carter's urban policy did initiate a general review of programmes and from 1978 there were some efforts to 'target' money towards more distressed areas. But, in sum, little was achieved.

President Carter's attempt at a coherent urban policy involved a number of familiar problems which earlier chapters have catalogued and which apply not just to urban but also to many other policy areas. The policy system is fragmented and complex, particular interests have autonomous power resources rooted in Congressional committees and administrative agencies and bureaux. Information is a jealously guarded bureaucratic prerogative. Presidents only have so much time and energy for any one problem.

There is no evidence that urban problems will somehow solve themselves. On the contrary, as recessions hit the economy with increasing frequency and the number of inner-city residents outside of the labour force spirals ever upwards, they are likely to get much worse. All Presidents of whatever party or ideological persuasion will have to confront this dilemma − and since the 1970 Housing and Urban Development Act, Presidents have been required to produce a biennial National Urban Policy Report. But for the Democrats, the intractability of urban problems is particularly serious. Democrats continue to *need* the electoral strength of the big cities − declining though it is − and as we established in Chapter 6, racial minorities are overwhelmingly Democratic in sympathy. This almost certainly makes coalition building more difficult for Democrats than for Republicans. For urban aid involves a zero sum game with some areas and social groups losing as the cities gain. Worse still, a *coherent* urban policy must involve the whole range of domestic social and economic policy and would force an interconnectedness between different programmes which only a singularly powerful President informed by an ideology of social reform could bring. Such a prospect is remote, to say the least.

MANAGING ECONOMIC CHANGE

As recently as 10 years ago, a section on economic policy in a textbook on American politics would not have been considered necessary. Today it is essential. Not since the 1930s have economic issues dominated the policy agenda as they do now. Abroad, America's standing has declined in a new and often hostile international economic order. At home, inflation and unemployment have become intractable problems prompting successive administrations to promise both to get the country 'back to work' and to reduce apparently ever increasing budget deficits. It hardly needs stressing that the state of the economy is vitally important, not only for the economic role of governments in society and the ways in which they tax citizens and allocate expenditure, but also for the health of the polity. Societies subject to high inflation and unemployment are usually less politically stable than those where economic growth is accompanied by steady prices and full employment. Small wonder, then, that economic policy has come to dominate the agenda of the 1980s. Governments, moreover, are now irrevocably involved in economic affairs. Some 33 per cent of Gross Domestic Product is accounted for by government expenditure; federal regulation of industrial and commercial affairs from environmental protection to anti-monopoly law is widespread; and by manipulating aggregate levels of expenditure and taxation and altering the supply of money in the economy, all federal governments now accept the need to 'manage' the economy. Regulation has been discussed elsewhere (Chapter 10), and this section's aim is to study economic management policies and in particular to identify those forces which shape the economic policy-making agenda.

State and Economy in the United States

As Chapter 2 emphasized, the traditional view of the United States is of a country where the state plays a relatively minor role. In contrast to the burgeoning welfare states and mixed economies of Europe, convention has it that Americans prefer market to public mechanisms to distribute goods and services in society. By most simple quantitative measures this view has some validity. The United States is low on scales measuring the percentage of GNP accounted for by public expenditure and of taxation's share of GNP. Note also, however, that America is closer to such countries as France, Germany and Canada than it is to Japan, so we might be better advised to label Japan rather than the United States as the 'exception' (Table 2.6, Chapter 2). And although the trend in expenditures has been upwards (Table 13.3), there has been no dramatic change since the late 1950s, the increase being from about 27 to 33 per cent of GNP.

Of course if a longer time span is taken, then the growth of public expenditure has been dramatic. In 1930 the percentage of GNP accounted for by public expenditure was less than 10 per cent. Much of the increase since then is a result of massively enhanced defence spending and, since the late 1950s, of the partial replacement of defence expenditure with spending on a range of domestic programmes (Figure 13.1, p. 282).

TABLE 13.3 *Federal Surplus or Deficit and Federal Debt as a Percentage of GNP and Percentage of GNP in the Public Sector, Selected Years 1956—77*

Year	Surplus or Deficit (current dollars, billions)	Total Accumulated Federal Debt As % of GNP	% GNP in Public Sector
1959	−12.9	61.1	26.9
1964	−5.9	51.4	27.7
1969	+3.2	40.6	30.5
1974	−3.5	35.8	32.4
1975	−43.6	37.8	34.9
1976	−74.1	39.3	33.5
1977	−57.2	39.2	32.9

Sources: ACIR, *The Federal Role in the Federal System: The Dynamics of Growth*, Washington DC, ACIR, 1980 and Dennis S. Ippolito, *The Budget and National Politics*, San Francisco, Freeman, 1978, Table 1-5, p. 33.

Whatever the relative position of the USA, the sheer size of the government budgets should not be underestimated. In 1981 the federal government alone spent over 600 billion and total expenditures of all governments came to over 800 billion. As in every other developed economy, therefore, American governments — and particularly the federal government — have enormous potential power over economic activity. By increasing spending and lowering taxation the economy can be stimulated. Conversely lower spending and higher taxes can lower the level of economic activity. Used in this way, fiscal policy is a major tool of *macro*-economic policy. Other tools include control over credit and money supply, both of which are currently in fashion as means of fighting inflation.

American government affects the economy in a number of other ways, most of which can be contained under the general description of *micro*-economic policy. Micro-economic policy is concerned not with pulling fiscal and monetary levers to affect the general direction in which the economy moves, but rather with a range of policy instruments which affect the specific behaviour of individuals, firms, sectors and regions. Hence, industrial policy, labour relations, education, training and regional and urban policy are typical micro-economic tools. Regulatory policy can also be a micro-economic device, although as we saw in Chapter 10, it is often motivated by non-economic considerations such as the promotion of equality or the protection of the environment. It hardly needs mentioning that this range of macro- and micro-policies are not perceived by policy makers as a coherent set of interrelated instruments. Neither do they always complement each other according to some coherent economic rationale. If anything the very opposite applies. Politicians and bureaucrats are not in agreement as to which policy should be applied at any particular time; and the policies themselves often compete with rather than complement one another; or as the economists would put it, *trade-offs* exist between (say) industrial policy and taxation, or between inflation and unemployment.

When attempting to identify the scope and limitations of economic policy in any society both institutional and ideological factors are important. How do these constrain economic policy making in the United States?

Ideology and economic policy

As our discussion in earlier chapters showed, ideology plays an important part in shaping the policy agenda or in influencing which issues or alternative policies are available for debate and discussion at any one time. In most Western countries economic policy has been influenced by three distinct philosophies, each of which has its defenders among economists as well as its political champions. On the right, economic liberals look to the market for salvation. In the centre, Keynesians believe that when the market fails to provide full employment and steady growth, governments should step in and via increased spending and borrowing stimulate demand. On the left socialists place the market in a subordinate position in relation to a public sector which would plan the allocation of resources in society. Socialist solutions are effectively excluded from the policy agenda in the United States. They carry connotations of collectivism unacceptable in a society so infused with economic individualism. Most debate in recent years has involved clashes between liberals and Keynesians. Much of the politics of economic policy, then, centres on levels of taxation and spending, and on the extent to which credit and the money supply should be controlled. Prior to 1933 liberal economics dominated, it was not until the New Deal and the Second World War that federal governments began to 'borrow and spend their way out of trouble', either to stimulate a depressed economy or to produce war materiel on a massive scale. To the economic liberal high levels of government expenditures are bad enough, even if they are covered by taxation. But deficit spending and loose money supply policies are even worse, for these lead directly to inflation and, so the argument runs, eventually to disaster. Economic liberals' antipathy even to government expenditure adequately financed by taxation derives from their conviction that the market is the most efficient allocator of resources. When governments allocate they do so wastefully and inefficiently. Of course, the liberals accept that governments have to play some role, especially in defence. But the essence of their philosophy is to reduce what has become a very intrusive role in society and always to ensure that what expenditure remains is covered by taxation.

During the 1930s and 1940s Keynesian thinking dominated, and successive federal governments ran up large deficits, the peak being reached in 1943 when in one year a $54.8 billion deficit amounted to some 35 per cent of GNP. Interestingly, although most of the post-war period is usually labelled 'Keynesian', total federal debt as a percentage of GNP declined steadily until 1974, although it has risen somewhat since (Table 13.3). If debt has been declining, spending certainly has not. Moreover, there has been a sharp tendency towards increased domestic rather than defence spending (Figure 13.1). To the economic liberal the latter may be justifiable, the former rarely is. The liberal position was given further stimulus by the events of the early and mid-1970s. During the 1971—3 period loose money supply policies were accompanied by steep rises in commodity prices, culminating in the 1973—4 fourfold increase in oil prices. This both fuelled inflation and wrought serious damage on the supply side of the economy. Producers, in other words, found their costs increasing rapidly. Their incentive to produce and invest was greatly undermined, resulting in a drop in output and rising unemployment. The ensuing recession convinced many in the Ford and Carter administrations that the way back to economic health lay in re-creating the right production and investment environment — low taxes, inflation and interest rates. This, they argued, could only be achieved if governments avoided over-stimulating demand through expenditure and borrowing. But neither President was very successful in keeping government spending down, and when elected in 1980, President Reagan made a much stronger pledge to cut expenditure, borrowing and taxes and therefore provide an amenable investment environment. We will examine how Ronald Reagan's new economic programme has fared later.

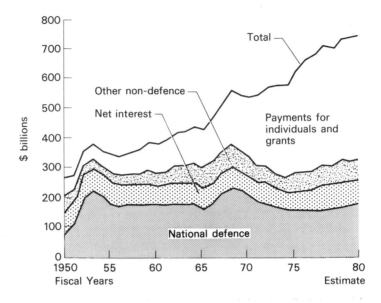

FIGURE 13.1   *Federal Outlays in Constant 1978 Dollars, in Fiscal Years 1950–82*

Source: *The Budget of the United States in Brief, Fiscal Year 1982* Washington DC, Government Printing Office, 1981, p. 19.

Although by the early 1980s we can conclude that liberal economics were on the ascendant, there was certainly no consensus on policy. Many on the left of the Democratic Party and in the labour unions continued to advocate Keynesian solutions, and most commentators remained wary of the *political* feasibility of monetarist solutions, whatever their economic merits. In addition many political leaders are concerned about the social consequences of expenditure cuts. As established in earlier chapters, federal, state and local governments are now irrevocably involved in the business of providing a wide range of economic and social services whether they like it or not. The tension between this plain fact and the prevailing liberal economic philosophy is considerable and unlikely to disappear in the immediate future.

The liberal—Keynesian conflict in economic policy is essentially about macro-economic management. What then of the relationship between ideology and *micro*-economic policy? In some respects, adopting interventionist micro-strategies to solve economic problems is more of a challenge to liberal ideology than is Keynesian demand management. For industrial or regional policy assumes that governments can and should interfere with individual economic actors or sectors by providing incentives, subsidies, loans or guidance. Perhaps for this reason, the United States has less consciously planned and developed industrial, regional and labour market policies than any comparable country. Indeed there *is* no federal industrial or regional strategy worth the name, and training and manpower policies are more ameliorative *ad hoc* measures than true labour market strategies. Japan and France, by way of contrast, have had highly developed industrial policies involving centrally coordinated resource and investment planning. In Japan's case industrial planning by sector involves close linkages between government, corporations and unions.[8] Such corporatist arrangements are quite alien to the American way of doing things.

Three further points on micro-policy should be noted. First, industrial or labour market policies need not involve great expenditure. Economic planning and coordination by sector or region can have profound effects on research and development investment and general economic performance. In the USA, planning of this sort simply is not on the policy agenda; it is not ideologically acceptable. Second, what *is* acceptable in the USA is the regulation of corporations, unions and industries, not primarily in order to enhance economic efficiency or improve international competitiveness, but to remove unfair competition and monopoly practices, or to promote employment opportunities and protect the environment. From a strictly economic point of view it is probably the case that such regulatory policies inhibit efficiency and prevent the best possible return on investment. Third, although there are no conscious or coherent federal micro-economic policies, there are, as our discussion of urban policy demonstrated, certainly plenty of policies. In fact, literally hundreds of programmes exist in each of the areas usually accepted under the general heading of micro-economic policy. Crucially, however, most are *ad hoc* in nature, having evolved as a result of the lobbying and bargaining process outlined in earlier

8   See Peter J. Katzenstein (ed.) *Between Power and Plenty. The Foreign Economic Policies of Advanced Industrial States*, Madison, Wisconsin. University of Wisconsin Press, Chapter by T. J. Pempel.

chapters. Often the federal government is lured into the area for strategic and political reasons – the rescue of Lockheed and Chrysler during the 1970s come immediately to mind. But more common are the host of policies from loans provided by the Small Business Administration to aid for nuclear power development, to employment creation programmes for poor cities and rural areas to investment incentives for commercial and industrial development which may have a specific economic purpose but which are *not* linked one with the other or are part of a broader strategy or design.[9]

Institutions and economic policy

The relationship between ideology and political and social institutions has inspired debate within social science for many years. In American politics, for example, whether federalism is a cause of a limited federal planning and coordinating role in society, or whether it has been maintained as a result of the power of liberal ideology has never been resolved. Whatever the causal directions, there can be no doubting that institutional arrangements continue to have a profound effect on economic policy making. Indeed, some would argue that the institutional constraints are such that no administration can effectively manage the American economy. What are the constraints?

Federalism and Localism. Chapter 4 referred to competitive interdependence in US intergovernmental relations and showed how the federal government is now locked into a symbiotic relationship with lower level governments. So, although federal governments hand out vast sums of money to states and localities, it is no easy thing to withdraw this largesse in line with economic imperatives. State and local governments have multiple channels of access to officials in Washington and formidable political resources can be harnessed to defend federally funded programmes. Of course to a greater or lesser extent this goes on everywhere, but the institution of federalism gives to individual states added legal weight in their efforts to maintain federal funding. Federalism also encourages 'highest common denominator' options when funds are being allocated. In other words, federal governments find it very difficult to discriminate between states according to some rational economic principle. When providing regional economic or research and development aid, for

---

9   See David H. McKay, 'Industrial policy and non policy in the United States, *Journal of Public Policy*, Vol. 3, No. 1, February 1983.

example, who gets what depends more on lobbying, criteria of equity or mere chance than on the needs of the economy. The failure to develop a coherent micro-economic strategy must in part be related to this phenomenon.

State and local governments also have independent revenue sources, which can weaken the scope and substance of federal fiscal policy. Federal revenues account for only about 60 per cent of all government income in the USA, the remainder deriving from state and local sales, property and income taxes. Constitutionally, and in marked contrast to the situation in a country like Britain, the federal government cannot *directly* affect these revenues. It is easy to make too much of this point, however. Runaway spending by sub-national governments is uncommon. Many state constitutions prohibit deficit spending and the bulk of government debt in the USA is incurred at the federal level. But in a rather indirect sense the fiscal goings on of state and local governments does affect federal budgets, for their fiscal problems, together with opposition by publics to increased state and local taxes, can lead to calls for federal revenues to fill the gaps left by tax limitation measures. Some commentators have, indeed, pointed to the paradoxical possibility that antipathy towards impersonal government and high taxes will lead to greater centralization and an enhanced role for the most criticized government of all — the federal government.

Separation of Powers. When studying economic policy making in the USA, foreign observers usually look first to the budgetary process and in particular to the conflicts between Congress and President which the spending power produces. Given the American concern with macro-policy and with controlling spending, this is perhaps not surprising. Indeed, as Chapters 7—10 showed, battles over spending are the very essence of both Presidential and Congressional politics. Much of the conflict derives from a simple constitutional fact: Congress, and in particular the House of Representatives, was given the power to raise taxes and appropriate monies for the executive branch to spend. As the role of the government has expanded, so the need for institutional mechanisms to coordinate and control spending have also increased. So both President and Congress have improved and streamlined their budgetary bureaucracies, each intent to provide the other branch with a coherent spending and taxing policy.

On the executive side, the first important item of legislation was the 1921 Budget and Accounting Act which created the Bureau of the Budget, a bureaucracy designed to provide improved budget advice and review for the President. At first, the Bureau of the Budget was intended to help control spending — an objective in line with the prevailing *laissez faire* or liberal philosophy that spending was essentially a bad thing. All changed with the coming of the New Deal, when under the leadership of Franklin Roosevelt the Bureau became a partisan for increased spending in opposition to an often hostile Congress. The Bureau was also formally incorporated into the Executive Office of the President during this period and its staff increased from 40 to over 600. The next significant law was the 1946 Full Employment Act, a piece of legislation which effectively endorsed Keynesian demand management by pledging the federal government to full employment policies. Among other measures, the Act created the Council of Economic Advisers, a further White House innovation but this time designed to encourage Presidents to pursue 'rational economic policies to foster and promote free competition, to avoid economic fluctuations or to diminish the effects thereof, and to maintain employment, production, and purchasing power'. The 1946 Act also mandated the President to produce an annual Economic Report to document economic performance over the past year and to provide Congress with a programme for the coming year.

Since 1946, successive Presidents have experimented further with the budget machinery, usually in order to inject rationality into burgeoning federal budgets. Lyndon Johnson ordered the adoption of planning–programming–budgeting systems, effectively a technique to link spending with preconceived planning priorities. Jimmy Carter, in turn, adopted zero base budgeting, or budget plans organized from the bottom up according to spending limits rather than according to specific programme objectives. The latter adapts spending to (say) the construction of so many miles of interstate highway or to a particular objective in the space programme and thus tends towards expenditure rising incrementally. The point about these and other innovations is that they reflect Presidents' growing concern with the sheer size of the budget and the need to present Congress with a coherent spending plan.

Congress has responded with its own innovations. The 1946 Act, for example, created a Joint Economic Committee consisting of seven Senators and seven Congressmen to provide Congress with a total view of the economy and aid the legislature's response to Presidential initiatives. More recently, the 1974 Budget Reform Act created a Congressional Budget Office, together with Budget Committees, to provide each House with a coherent view of budget making and instil a sense of spending priority, rather than proceed as had been the case in the past on an incremental basis. Judging by the first few years of the new Budget process Congressional control has improved but the fundamental problems of budget making remain. These are simply that Congress' role is negative rather than positive. Or, as we discovered in Chapter 9, 'the President proposes and Congress disposes'. Economic management is first and foremost an executive responsibility. Until the reforms, the role of Congress was confined to trimming, tinkering or otherwise modifying the President's budget on an *ad hoc* basis, and the Appropriations Committees were the major centres of power. Since the 1974 Act, however, power has in part passed to the Budget Committees which, as can be inferred from Figure 13.2, have now assumed the position of central budget decision makers in Congress. During the first years of the Carter Presidency the system seemed to work well, but then the economy was growing rapidly and deficits actually ended up lower than expected. Since 1980 the situation has been transformed by deepening recession, with deficits far exceeding expectations (Table 13.4). This period has also seen the most radical and frenzied activity in the politics and procedures of Congressional budget making ever experienced.

This started in the first few weeks of the Reagan Administration, when the President submitted major changes for spending in 1982, 1983 and 1984. Large increases in defence spending and cuts in domestic programmes were proposed. Parallel, quite radical cuts in taxation were also introduced into Congress. On the budget side, a new resolution known as Gramm-Latta I (After Delbert L. Latta, the ranking Republican on the House Budget Committee and Phil Gramm, a leading Democratic conservative on the Committee) actually instructed 15 House Committees and 14 Senate Committees on how their budgets would be slashed over the next three years. The amounts involved − $36, $47 and $56 billion in each of these years − were huge. Finally, the resolution was framed in such a way that any subsequent supplementary appropriations would be very difficult to achieve.[10] In reaction to these draconian measures, Congressional committees submitted a mass of new legislation designed to reassert traditional Congressional power. The Administration, fearing a sudden increase in spending, accepted a modified resolution (Gramm-Latta II) which was finally passed, very speedily in August.

10   For a full discussion, see Robert W. Hartman, 'Congress and budget making', *Political Science Quarterly*, Vol. 97, Fall 1982.

October—December: Congressional Budget Office submits five-year projection of current spending as soon as possible after October 1.

November 10: President submits current services budget.

December 31: Joint Economic Committee reports analysis of current services budget to budget committees.

Late January: President submits budget (fifteen days after Congress convenes).

Late January—March: Budget committees hold hearings and begin work on first budget resolution.

March 15: All legislative committees submit estimates and views to budget committees.

April 15: Budget committees report first resolution.

May 15: Committees must report authorization bills by this date.

May 15: Congress completes action on first resolution. Before adoption of the first resolution, neither house may consider new budget authority or spending authority bills, revenue changes, or debt limit changes.

May 15 through the 7th day after Labor Day: Congress completes action on all budget and spending authority bills.

● Before reporting first regular appropriations bill, the House Appropriations Committee, 'to extent practicable,' marks up all regular appropriations bills and submits a summary report to House, comparing proposed outlays and budget authority levels with first resolution targets.

● CBO issues periodic scorekeeping reports comparing congressional action with first resolution.

● Reports on new budget authority and tax expenditure bills must contain comparisons with first resolution, and five-year projections.

● 'As possible,' a CBO cost analysis and five-year projection will accompany all reported public bills, except appropriation bills.

August: Budget committees prepare second budget resolution and report.

September 15: Congress completes action on second resolution. Thereafter, neither House may consider any bill or amendment, or conference report, that results in an increase over outlay or budget authority figures, or a reduction in revenues, beyond the amounts in the second resolution.

September 25: Congress completes action on reconciliation bill or another resolution. Congress may not adjourn until it completes action on the second resolution and reconciliation measure, if any.

October 1: Fiscal year begins.

FIGURE 13.2　*Congressional Budget Deadlines*

Source: *Congressional Quarterly Almanac*, Vol. XXXI, 1975, Washington, DC, Congressional Quarterly Inc, 1976, p. 918.

TABLE 13.4   *Outlays and Revenues under Congressional Budget Resolutions and Actual Outcomes, Fiscal Years 1977–82*

Item	Date conference agreement	Outlays[a]	Revenues[a]	Deficit
Fiscal 1977				
First resolution	5/13/76	413.3	362.5	50.8
Second resolution	9/16/76	413.1	362.5	50.6
Actual	—	401.9	356.9	45.0
Overrun or shortfall[b] (−)	—	−11.4	−5.6	−5.8
Fiscal 1978				
First resolution	5/17/77	461.0	396.3	64.7
Second resolution	9/15/77	458.3	397.0	61.3
Actual	—	449.9	401.1	48.8
Overrun or shortfall[b] (−)	—	−11.1	4.8	−15.9
Fiscal 1979				
First resolution	5/17/78	498.8	447.9	50.9
Second resolution	9/23/78	487.5	448.7	38.8
Actual	—	493.7	465.9	27.7
Overrun or shortfall[b] (−)	—	−5.1	18.0	−23.2
Fiscal 1980				
First resolution	5/24/79	532.0	509.0	23.0
Second resolution	11/28/79	547.6	517.8	29.8
Actual	—	579.6	520.0	59.6
Overrun or shortfall[b] (−)	—	47.6	11.0	36.6
Fiscal 1981				
First resolution	6/12/80	613.6	613.8	0.2[c]
Second resolution	11/20/80	632.4	605.0	27.4
Actual	—	657.2	599.3	57.9
Overrun or shortfall[b] (−)	—	43.6	−14.5	58.1
Fiscal 1982				
First resolution	5/12/81	695.5	657.8	37.7
Second resolution	11/19/81	695.5	657.8	37.7
Actual[d]	—	725.3	626.8	98.6

Source: Congressional Budget Office, reproduced in Hartman, 'Congress and Budget Making', *Political Science Quarterly*, 97, Fall 1982, Table 1, p. 86.
Notes:
a   Actual outlays and revenues in each year use the definitions in force at the time. In fiscal 1982 the actual reflects new definitions adopted after the budget resolutions for that year were voted.
b   From first resolution.
c   Surplus.
d   Estimated in *Budget of the United States Government, Fiscal Year 1983*, pp. 2–14.

Although the final bill imposed less extensive cuts than those originally planned, this particular budget experience was almost the antithesis of the slow, incremental, deliberative process for which Congress is famous and which Figure 13.2 implies. In retrospect, we can conclude that President Reagan was fortunate to have the support of three key groups in Congress – the conservative Republicans, conservative Southern Democrats (the 'Boll weevils') and, crucially, moderate Republicans (the 'Gypsy Moths'). It was this coalition which also helped the Administration achieve quite startling tax cuts in the same session (see p. 188). Always a fragile arrangement, signs of collapse were evident even by late 1981, and during 1982 the Administration was much less successful in handling Congress. We can confidently predict that the more Democratic House elected in 1982 will prove even more difficult to manage.

Moreover, within Congress the 'traditional' centres of budgetary power, the appropriations committees and subcommittees, have begun to reassert their influence. The events of 1981 were, in other words, exceptional. Underneath all the dramatic events of those first few months of the new Administration, the policy networks, clientelism and fragmented and autonomous centres of power which earlier chapters have described did not somehow miraculously disappear. What the 1981 experience does show is that Congress is now at least capable of rapid response to Presidential economic initiative. It also demonstrates the growing influence of the Office of Management and Budget which, under the leadership of David Stockman, assumed a very central position as both designer and manager of government spending priorities.[11]

As can be seen from Table 13.4, the Administration's 1981 successes hardly solved the economic problem. On the contrary, deficits continued to increase and have done ever since. This is partly because the Reagan Administration combined hefty tax cuts with more modest reductions in expenditure (and real increases in defence spending). More importantly, certain areas of expenditure are almost impossible to cut. Entitlement programmes (Medicare, social security) increase automatically and to Presidents and Congress alike are almost electorally sacrosanct. And even the more vulnerable programmes – welfare, grants to state and localities – have their champions at all levels. With world recession deepening during the

---

11 Although even Stockman's glittering reputation was tarnished somewhat following the publication of a magazine article which revealed his misgivings about the rationality of the policy process. See William Greider, 'The education of David Stockman', *Atlantic Monthly*, December 1981.

1981—3 period, the economic and social needs of the population and lower level governments increased, while the capacity of the economy to generate tax revenue deteriorated. In essence, the national economy has been suffering from structural fiscal problems not unlike those we earlier identified as characteristic of distressed cities. Already by late 1982 the calls for a reversal of Administration policy were rising audibly, and included proposals to levy a 5 per cent tax on petrol to finance public works and create employment, as well as increasingly strident demands that defence spending be cut. Indeed in early 1983, the Administration heeded this advice with Defense Secretary Casper Weinberger accepting the need for at least some trimming of the defence budget.

The economic malaise of the early 1980s highlighted another important institutional relationship which is peculiarly American: the unique political position of the American central bank, the Federal Reserve System. Created in 1913, the Federal Reserve is a 'decentralized' central bank consisting of 12 Federal Reserve Districts governed by a Board in Washington. Congress deliberately gave the Board some autonomy from the President and in recent years, the Chairmen of the Board have asserted their independence to some effect. This is important because the Federal Reserve has special responsibility for implementing monetary policy, and in particular for setting interest rate levels. With budget deficits increasing, the most recent Chairman, Paul Volcker, has insisted on controlling the money supply through a policy of high interest rates. Although at first the Reagan Administration accepted the Federal Reserve's policy in this area, by late 1982 serious disagreement had emerged between Volcker and Donald Regan, the Treasury Secretary. Volcker continued to insist on a tight money policy, while some members of the Administration wanted some relaxation to help lift the economy out of recession. In other countries central banks, if not the creatures of executives, are significantly less autonomous than the Federal Reserve System.

In many respects the economic policy-making system resembles the urban policy system. In both, the chief executive has the major responsibility for policy formulation and implementation, and in both he faces competition from other centres of power — notably Congress, executive departments and agencies, state and local governments and organized interests. There are, however, some important qualitative differences between the two policy areas. Economic policy is obviously more important in the sense that most other domestic and foreign policies depend on it. All parties and politicians have an interest in economic performance and all believe that the federal government has to play a key role in economic management. They may disagree — sometimes radically — on what that role should be but no-one disputes the need for economic policy. Urban policy, in contrast, is not considered a legitimate concern of the federal government by many on the right. The great paradox of urban policy is the incontrovertible fact of dozens of federal programmes with an urban dimension existing in the absence of any central coordination and control. Control problems apply to economic policy too, of course, but not in quite the same way. Measures of performance — inflation, growth, interest rate levels, unemployment — exist to provide a focus of activity for policy makers, as does the budgetary process itself. Nonetheless, macro-economic management is shared between at least three major institutions — Presidency, Congress and Federal Reserve — which is highly unusual in comparative context. And micro-economic policy making is as confused and incoherent as urban policy. What the two policy systems do share in common is that both are attempting to solve apparently intractable problems. Most other countries are experiencing similar difficulties of economic and social management, but in few are institutional arrangements organized in such an apparently inefficient manner. We will return to this point later.

MANAGING FOREIGN AFFAIRS

Over the last 50 years the United States has been transformed from one of six or seven world powers with a standing army of under 200,000 and few foreign alliances or military bases, into a country with a military machine of 3 million men and women under arms (1.5 million of whom are stationed overseas), alliances with nearly 50 countries and an almost unrivalled military and diplomatic status and capacity. From being isolationist and contemptuous of the 'corruption' and imperialism of the old European powers, the United States is, in spite of recent reverses, now itself in a position to exploit and dominate other countries and, unlike the pre-war powers, literally to determine the fate of all mankind.

The country's political processes and institutions have not always handled these new responsibilities well. Indeed one school of thought argues that a country infused with a past characterized by a combination of isolationism and idealism is ill suited to playing the role of world policeman. Certainly, there have been many foreign and military policy mistakes in the post-war era, including the Vietnam

War, which caused serious domestic conflict and terrible suffering and instability throughout Indo-China. This section will not, however, concentrate on normative questions of fortune and folly in American foreign policy. Instead our discussion will focus on the policy-making process and on the constraints imposed on foreign policy by institutional arrangements and public opinion.

The Institutional Context

As with urban and economic affairs, it is somewhat misleading to refer to an American foreign *policy*, for there are at least three distinct types of foreign and defence policy. There is, first, strategic foreign policy or the general stance of the United States in relation to other countries over time. Scholars have been quick to identify two competing themes in the post-war period — realist and idealist. Realism[12] is, simply, the pursuit of 'national self interest' and is associated with international power politics and the implementation of policies which have clear military, diplomatic or economic benefits. Idealism, in contrast, injects a moral or normative element into policy as such Presidential rhetoric as 'making the world safe for democracy' or achieving 'peace with honour' in Vietnam implies. We will return to these two characterizations of strategic policy later. Although strategic policy is influenced by the broader society and polity, its main institutional context is the Presidency, National Security Council and State Department.

Second, crisis management is a crucial part of foreign policy. Since the last war, the Berlin airlift, Suez, the Cuban missile crisis, the Gulf of Tonkin incident, a number of subsequent military actions in Indo-China, American reactions to military activity in the Middle East and the Iranian hostage crisis, have all involved the United States in quick crisis management decisions.[13] Generally the Presidency and National Security Council are the institutional focus of these decisions, although the longer the crisis drags on the more likely are Congress and the public to become involved. Just this happened with the year long Iranian hostage crisis in 1979—80.

Third, logistical or structural defence policy involves the deployment of billions of dollars worth of materiel and several million personnel around the globe. As we established in earlier chapters,

---

12   The classic account of the realist position is by Hans J. Morgenthau, *In Defense of the National Interest*, New York, Alfred Knopf, 1951.
13   For a good account of post-war foreign policy, see James A. Nathan and James K. Oliver, *United States Foreign Policy and World Order*, New York, 1976.

this process entails voters, organized interests (defence contractors), state and local governments and Congressional committees, as well as the more obvious institutions of Department of Defense and Presidency. While this policy system is much more open and accessible than strategic and crisis management policy, it is almost certainly less fragmented and pluralistic than the processes associated with urban or economic policy. Oligopolistic defence industries are protected by government contracts,[14] and the defence budget has a powerful base of support in Congress.

These three contrasting institutional settings for foreign and defence policy do impinge on one another. Logistics and weapons systems can influence strategic thinking (the Cruise missile) and crisis management (the Iranian hostage crisis), while strategic considerations are obviously important determinants of logistical policy. Similarly, crisis management is profoundly affected by the strategic context. During the Cuban missile crisis, for example, President Kennedy referred constantly to the infringement of an American sphere of influence (the Western hemisphere) which was a long established part of American foreign policy.

How has decision making in each of these policy areas changed over time? Perhaps obviously, crisis management has always primarily been the prerogative of the President and his closest aides in the National Security Council. Quick response requires tightly knit decision-making structures and as commander in chief, the President has the constitutional as well as political position to assume the leadership of such structures. Not that this means that the President, together with his aides, are completely insulated from the outside world during a crisis and make their choices according to strictly rational criteria. As Graham Allison has shown in his brilliant study of the Cuban missile crisis, at least three competing models of decision making can be used to explain the events of the crisis, two of which put great premium on outside information and political and bureaucratic procedures and pressures.[15] But crisis management is, compared with other policy-making processes in American government, remarkably free from political and societal pressures.

14 The big eight arms contractors, Boeing, General Dynamics, Grumman, Lockheed, McDonnel Douglas, Northrop, Rockwell International and United Technologies receive almost one third of defence contracts and most depend on government contracts for their survival. For an account of the defence establishment, see Adam Yarmolinsky, *The Military Establishment: Its Impacts on American Society*, New York, Harper and Row, 1971.
15   Graham T. Allison, *Essence of Decision: Explaining the Cuban Missile Crisis*, Boston, Little Brown, 1971.

The main development in strategic foreign policy making has been the gradual centralization of power in President and National Security Council, at the cost of State Department influence. This has shown itself most graphically in the eclipse of some recent Secretaries of State in the shadow of National Security advisers — most notably Henry Kissinger and Zbigniew Brzezinski. As recent research has shown, Presidents have increasingly eschewed State Departments and their Secretaries, because they can represent independent sources of authority and control over particular issues and areas. Certain countries or policy options are championed within the Department and it is simply not convenient for Presidents to have to join battle with the professional bureaucrats when foreign policy is formulated.[16] White House/Departmental antagonism occurs in other areas, of course, but within foreign policy Presidents do at least have the option of, if not ignoring the State Department, at least of by-passing it. For State effectively has no domestic constituency, and its officials are unusually neutral and apolitical, versed as they are in the arts of diplomacy and moderation.[17] So while Presidents may find it almost impossible to disregard the Departments of Defense, Agriculture or Commerce, they can almost do this in the case of State. Foreign policy is also more insulated from the other 'traditional' centres of power in American government. House and, particularly, Senate Foreign Relations Committees are important forums for discussion and criticism, but their function is qualitatively different from (say) those of the Armed Services and Agriculture Committees with their entrenched relationships with big spending bureaux and powerful corporate clients.

In other words, foreign policy decision making is different. Within the White House the NSC is uniquely important, and a consistency and coherence is almost certainly more achievable in foreign affairs than in many domestic areas. It may be, of course, that clarity and coherence can lead to greater errors of judgment and strategy and that more pluralistic arrangements would lend to greater moderation. Perhaps. But it should be noted that in *cross-national context*, American Presidents are *not* particularly free from institutional and political constraints in foreign policy making. Public and Congressional opinion has been exerted on Presidents with increasing intensity since the events of Vietnam and Watergate. Earlier chapters have catalogued some of these constraints, including the 1973 War Powers

16   See Bert A. Rockman, 'America's Department of State: irregular and regular syndromes of policy making', *American Political Science Review*, Vol. 75, No. 4, December 1981.
17   *Ibid*, pp. 924–5.

Act. President Reagan's 1983 remark, when he heard of British Prime Minister Thatcher's carefully disguised visit to the Falklands that he 'couldn't even go to church in secret' reveals a great deal. Presidents and their policy makers are constantly exposed to public scrutiny; they may be able to secrete themselves away in the NSC and plan general strategy. They may also be relatively free from direct and immediate Congressional or bureaucratic pressure. But they still have to operate in the context of the American political system, with all that this applies in terms of openness and accessibility. So individual ethnic groups such as Americans of Polish or Jewish origin constantly monitor the Administration policy towards Poland or Israel. Right-wing caucuses, such as Jesse Helm's National Congressional Club, campaign strongly in favour of a hard line towards Moscow. On the left, anti-nuclear groups have grown particularly rapidly since 1980, with a number of towns and cities endorsing a freeze on nuclear weapons. Since the Vietnam War, the involvement of American troops in counter insurgency wars abroad has become especially difficult because of the ever present potential for serious domestic political opposition.

In sum, decision making in American foreign policy is constrained by the political environment to a much greater extent than equivalent policy making in countries such as Britain. But in the strictly American context foreign, and to a lesser extent defence policy, is relatively centralized and coherent.

American Foreign Policy under Pressure

Turning to the substance of foreign policy, the most striking development of recent years has been the slow demise of the idealist school and its replacement by a more realist vision of America's interests. Although some historians dispute that American foreign policy was ever idealist, the rhetoric of the Kennedy and Johnson years, when the United States role as world policeman was projected as part of a moral crusade, has now largely passed from political debate. Today even a conservative Republican Administration tends to couch its policies in terms of the country's economic and political interests, and when Presidents do justify policy in terms of moral imperatives — as with American support for Guatemala and El Salvador — it carries little conviction. Not only the rhetoric of politicians but actual policy has changed. The USA now deploys troops in active fighting abroad only very reluctantly. Foreign aid has gradually been reduced and is increasingly tailored to American economic and strategic interests rather than to the needs of recipient states. Even relations with NATO and the European powers have sometimes become strained as officials perceive a conflict of interests between the USA and its allies. These changes parallel the gradual erosion of American political and economic hegemony. No longer is the United States in a position to rescue ailing European economies (as with the Marshall Plan) or to act as military and economic saviour of the Third World. Indeed, many poorer countries view America as an adversary rather than benefactor.

None of this is to deny the enormous power which the United States continues to wield, especially in military affairs. But the period of hegemony is over. The relationship between these changes and the institutional setting of foreign and defence policy is complex. A less dominant world position probably makes the business of crisis management more difficult. Draconian solutions such as those employed in the Lebanon in 1958 and over Cuba in 1962 are less viable, as the Iranian hostage crisis showed. This may not, of course, always be a bad thing. Strategic policy making is also likely to be more problematical, for in a more interdependent world where American power is strictly circumscribed, calculating exactly what is in America's best interest becomes a more complex exercise. Policy towards the Middle East, for example, has become immeasurably more difficult since the rise of Arab power through OPEC. Indeed, it is now often hard to distinguish between military/strategic concerns and economic interest. The performance of the economy affects America's capacity to provide foreign aid or respond to crisis with military force. Perhaps more crucial is that with some 20 per cent of GNP now accounted for by imports and exports, the economy is interlocked with those of other countries as never before. As a result, decisions taken on strictly political or strategic grounds — discouraging Western firms from participating in the Soviet gas pipeline, for example — can have important economic consequences.

This interdependence often makes it difficult to distinguish clearly between different policy systems, and there is no doubt that it makes the business of government more burdensome. Given the external constraints imposed by interdependence and the internal pressures resulting from a fragmented and open political system, it is not surprising that Presidents have sought to centralize decision making in the White House and National Security Council. Unfortunately we cannot easily pass judgment on this development (which, in any case, represents only a relative and partial change towards centralization). For in a world fraught with tensions and dangers, the costs of policy errors and misjudgments can be startlingly high, and the relationship between 'rational' policy making and institutional arrangements is obscure. As Bert Rockman has put it:

> The problem of reconciling 'the persistent dilemmas of unity and diversity' remains to be solved as much in the foreign policy sphere as in the domestic one, especially as the distinction between these areas erodes. In unity lies strategic direction and clarity, but also the dangers of monocled vision. In diversity lies sensitivity to implementation and to nuance, but also the dangers of producing least common denominators.[18]

CODA: THE FUTURE OF THE AMERICAN POLITICAL ECONOMY

Since the mid-1970s an increasing number of commentators have expressed serious doubts about the capacity of the American political system to deal with a world characterized by low rates of growth, high unemployment, a sometimes ruthlessly competitive international trading environment and an uneasy military balance between East and West. Most of the misgivings have centred on the particular institutional arrangements of American governments or on broader questions of ideology. Both in this and earlier chapters we have made reference to these critiques, which, very generally, can be divided into three related themes.

1. Politics in the United States is too pluralistic. Open access to multiple centres of power ensures that public goods are distributed inefficiently. Institutionally, this means that the separation of powers, federalism and a weak party system prevent central direction and control. As a result, the sort of tough decisions needed to cope with economic dislocation and world instability cannot easily be made in the American context. Another way of putting this, perhaps, is to argue that the US system is simply too democratic. All social groups, jurisdictions and corporations have *some* influence on policy and need to be 'bought off' before anything actually gets done. This leads to inefficient and often excessive public expenditure.[19] In other countries strong central executives, unitary government and cohesive political parties are better able to direct economy and

---

18 *Ibid*, p. 925.
19 See Lester Thurow, *The Zero Sum Society*, Harmondsworth, Middlesex, Penguin, 1981; David Calleo, *The Imperious Economy*, Cambridge, Massachusetts, Harvard University Press, 1982.

society decisively and efficiently.[20] Related are claims that the United States has a 'weak state' system, or that government policy is a result of myriad societal influences, rather than being imposed on society by a strong government or by a state which has nurtured a corporatist consensus with leading economic actors within society.[21] This pluralistic indecision and confusion may not be damaging when there is little need for state action. But, so the argument runs, in an interdependent world where governments in all of the competing economies play crucial roles, the United States is at a serious disadvantage for *strategic* thought and action are all but impossible in a pluralist context.

2. A slightly different critique dwells on the gap between promise and performance characteristic of the American system. In other words, the dominant beliefs and values in the United States – liberty, equality, participation – lead to expectations which cannot be met by the institutional framework of politics.[22] The political system is not particularly efficient at translating the demands which these values encourage into actual policies and programmes. Again, the USA is different from many other countries in this respect. In few countries are egalitarianism and opportunity so deeply embedded in the national culture, and in few do these values persist even when the economy is declining and the ability of the system to meet public demands is so painfully inadequate. Proponents of this view point to the disintegrating parties, failed Presidents, capricious Congress and, above all, declining trust in government as evidence of the malaise.

3. Critics on the left are more concerned with the consequences of a declining capitalism and fragmented political system for social and political equality. With a diminishing national cake and a political

20 Although critics on the right advocate the disengagement of government rather than plead for a strong state, see Ezra Solomon, *Beyond the Turning Point: the US Economy in the 1980s*, San Francisco, W. H. Freeman, 1982; also Peter Duignan and Alvin Rabushka, *The United States in the 1980s*, London and Stanford, Croom Helm, Hoover Institution, 1980.

21 See Peter J. Katzenstein (ed.) *Between Power and Plenty*, Madison, Wisconsin, University of Wisconsin Press, 1978, chapters by Katzenstein and Krasner. For a general comparative perspective on the role of the state in industrial policy, see David H. McKay and Wyn Grant, 'Industrial policies in OECD countries: an overview', *Journal of Public Policy*, Vol. 3, No. 1, February 1983.

22 The most virulent statements of this view are presented in Nathan Glazer and Irving Kristol (eds) *The New American Commonwealth*, 1976, 10th Anniversary Issue of *The Public Interest*, New York, Basic Books, 1976. For a more recent analysis, see Samuel P. Huntington, *American Politics: The Promise of Disharmony*, Cambridge, Massachusetts, Harvard University Press, 1981.

system which puts great premium on distributing largesse according to political access and lobbying power, rather than according to criteria of social justice or need, the position of those already disadvantaged will surely deteriorate, and the prospects for racial minorities look especially bleak.[23] In partial contradiction of the promise/performance critique, advocates of this position see little prospect for improvement because of the pervasive strength of the dominant ideology which diverts the deprived masses from collective action by immersing them in a culture of shallow consumerism and misguided self reliance.[24]

Although the normative base of each of these three critiques is quite distinctive — the first dwells on questions of economic efficiency, the second on problems of legitimacy and political control, and the third on equality and justice — all are pessimistic about the capacity of American government to adapt to a new domestic and international environment by providing its citizens with an acceptable degree of economic security and social justice. How much credence can be attached to these critiques?

We must, first, acknowledge that the American political system has been experiencing particularly serious problems in recent years. Earlier chapters catalogued the difficulties which each and every one of the main political institutions has confronted, and our discussion of urban, economic and foreign policy confirmed that in a fragmented and open political system, both 'efficient' and 'just' policy making is remarkably difficult to achieve. While acknowledging this, we should be wary of too unqualified an acceptance of these three interpretations. They are, first of all, not always mutually compatible. The radical critique assumes a passivity on the part of the masses which is directly disputed by those who see increasingly strident public demands as the source of social disharmony. In comparative perspective, the latter perspective seems slightly misplaced. By most measures (regime and governmental stability, politically motivated violence, the strength of radical political parties) the USA is remarkably stable, and the populace has accepted economic

23   See Frances Fox Piven and Richard A. Cloward, *The New Class War: Reagan's Attack on the Welfare State and its Consequences, op. cit.* Interestingly, the American left is primarily concerned with questions of equality and justice, rather than with more theoretical or abstract issues, thus reflecting the influence of peculiarly American ideas on radical thinking.

24   For a summary of this perspective, see Ira Katznelson and Mark Kesselman, *The Politics of Power: A Critical Introduction to American Government*, New York, Harcourt, Brace Jovanovich, 2nd edition, 1979.

dislocation and the decline of American power with relative equanimity.[25] Second, problems of economic dislocation and governmental overload are hardly unique to the USA. Indeed, one country, the UK, which with unitary, party government patently lacks some of the institutional disadvantages of America, is experiencing just as serious a crisis. Admittedly, like America, Britain has a liberal tradition which militates against a dominant state, but the relationship between the strength of the state and an 'effective' political and economic system is uncertain. Conservative analyses suggest, indeed, a negative relationship between the strength of the state and economic efficiency — although they provide little realistic guidance on how the state can disengage from its present extensive if often chaotic role.

Discussion of governmental 'effectiveness' involves competing values. A truly successful economy able to adjust to technological change and a highly competitive international trading environment, may be incompatible with a democracy built on individualism and pluralism. Democracy, participation and accountability are desirable objectives in themselves and, to many, some sacrifice in political or economic efficiency is justified in order to achieve them.

Unfortunately, however, the trade-offs between accountability and effectiveness and between equality and efficiency are complex and difficult. It may even be that in the context of global economic interdependence and rapid technological change, the fragmented and pluralistic political system which characterizes the United States militates against both efficiency *and* responsiveness and equality. If this is so, radical reform of the American system is urgently needed. While recent experience should lead us to be pessimistic about the prospects for reform, American social and political institutions have, at various times in the past displayed an impressive adaptiveness. The crucial question for the last years of the twentieth century is whether the individualism and enterprise which for so long enabled the United States to achieve both economic success and political stability, can continue to facilitate adaptation to change.

---

25 To be fair, this is partly acknowledged by the relevant literature, which stops short of truly pessimistic conclusions. Samuel Huntington, for example follows his often depressing analysis with a surprisingly encouraging last few pages (*op. cit*, Chapter 8). Writing within a culture infused with self reliance and optimism, American critics usually do end on a hopeful, constructive note.

The Constitution
of the United States

[PREAMBLE]

We the people of the United States, in order to form a more perfect union, establish justice, insure domestic tranquility, provide for the common defense, promote the general welfare, and secure the blessings of liberty to ourselves and our posterity, do ordain and establish this Constitution for the United States of America.

ARTICLE 1 [THE LEGISLATURE]

Section 1

All legislative powers herein granted shall be vested in a Congress of the United States, which shall consist of a Senate and House of Representatives.

Section 2

1. The House of Representatives shall be composed of members chosen every second year by the people of the several States, and the electors in each State shall have the qualifications requisite for electors of the most numerous branch of the State legislature.
2. No person shall be a representative who shall not have attained to the age of twenty-five years, and been seven years a citizen of the United States, and who shall not, when elected, be an inhabitant of that State in which he shall be chosen.

3. Representatives and direct taxes[1] shall be apportioned among the several States which may be included within this Union, according to their respective members, which shall be determined by adding to the whole number of free persons, including those bound to service for a term of years, and excluding Indians not taxed, three-fifths of all other persons.[2] The actual enumeration shall be made within three years after the first meeting of the Congress of the United States, and within every subsequent term of ten years, in such manner as they shall by law direct. The number of representatives shall not exceed one for every thirty thousand, but each State shall have at least one representative; and until such enumeration shall be made, the State of New Hampshire shall be entitled to choose three, Massachusetts eight, Rhode Island and Providence Plantations one, Connecticut five, New York six, New Jersey four, Pennsylvania eight, Delaware one, Maryland six, Virginia ten, North Carolina five, South Carolina five, and Georgia three.

4. When vacancies happen in the representation from any State, the executive authority thereof shall issue writs of election to fill such vacancies.

5. The House of Representatives shall choose their speaker and other officers; and shall have the sole power of impeachment.

Section 3

1. The Senate of the United States shall be composed of two senators from each state, chosen by the legislature thereof,[3] for six years; and each senator shall have one vote.

2. Immediately after they shall be assembled in consequence of the first election, they shall be divided as equally as may be into three classes. The seats of the senators of the first class shall be vacated at the expiration of the second year, of the second class at the expiration of the fourth year, and of the third class at the expiration of the sixth year, so that one-third may be chosen every second year; and if vacancies happen by resignation, or otherwise, during the recess of the legislature of any State, the executive thereof may make temporary appointments until the next meeting of the legislature, which shall then fill such vacancies.[4]

3. No person shall be a senator who shall not have attained to the

---

1 See the Sixteenth Amendment.
2 Partly superseded by the Fourteenth Amendment.
3 See the Seventeenth Amendment.
4 See the Seventeenth Amendment.

age of thirty years, and been nine years a citizen of the United States, and who shall not, when elected, be an inhabitant of that state for which he shall be chosen.

4. The Vice-President of the United States shall be President of the Senate, but shall have no vote, unless they be equally divided.

5. The Senate shall choose their other officers, and also a President *pro tempore*, in the absence of the Vice-President, or when he shall exercise the office of President of the United States.

6. The Senate shall have the sole power to try all impeachments. When sitting for that purpose, they shall be on oath or affirmation. When the President of the United States is tried, the chief justice shall preside: and no person shall be convicted without the concurrence of two-thirds of the members present.

7. Judgment in cases of impeachment shall not extend further than to removal from office, and disqualifications to hold and enjoy any office of honor, trust or profit under the United States: but the party convicted shall nevertheless be liable and subject to indictment, trial, judgment and punishment, according to law.

Section 4

1. The times, places, and manner of holding elections for senators and representatives, shall be prescribed in each state by the legislature thereof; but the Congress may at any time by law make or alter such regulations, except as to the places of choosing senators.

2. The Congress shall assemble at least once in every year, and such meeting shall be on the first Monday in December, unless they shall by law appoint a different day.

Section 5

1. Each House shall be the judge of the elections, returns and qualifications of its own members and majority of each shall constitute a quorum to do business; but a smaller number may adjourn from day to day, and may be authorized to compel the attendance of absent members, in such manner and under such penalties as each House may provide.

2. Each House may determine the rules of its proceedings, punish its members for disorderly behavior, and, with the concurrence of two-thirds, expel a member.

3. Each House shall keep a journal of its proceedings, and from time to time publish the same, excepting such parts as may in their

judgment require secrecy; and the yeas and nays of the members of either House on any question shall, at the desire of one-fifth of those present, be entered on the journal.

4. Neither House, during the session of Congress, shall, without the consent of the other, adjourn for more than three days, nor to any other place than that in which the two Houses shall be sitting.

Section 6

1. The senators and representatives shall receive a compensation for their services, to be ascertained by law, and paid out of the Treasury of the United States. They shall in all cases, except treason, felony and breach of the peace, be privileged from arrest during their attendance at the session of their respective Houses, and in going to and returning from the same; and for any speech or debate in either House, they shall not be questioned in any other place.

2. No senator or representative shall, during the time for which he was elected, be appointed to any civil office under the authority of the United States, which shall have been created, or the emoluments whereof shall have been increased during such time, and no person holding any office under the United States shall be a member of either House during his continuance in office.

Section 7

1. All bills for raising revenue shall originate in the House of Representatives; but the Senate may propose or concur with amendments as on other bills.

2. Every bill which shall have passed the House of Representatives and the Senate, shall, before it become a law, be presented to the President of the United States; if he approve he shall sign it, but if not he shall return it, with his objections to that House in which it shall have originated, who shall enter the objections at large on their journal, and proceed to reconsider it. If after such reconsideration two-thirds of that House shall agree to pass the bill, it shall be sent, together with the objections, to the other House, by which it shall likewise be reconsidered, and if approved by two thirds of that House, it shall become a law. But in all such cases the votes of both Houses shall be determined by yeas and nays, and the names of the persons voting for and against the bill shall be entered on the journal of each House respectively. If any bill shall not be returned by the President within ten days (Sundays excepted) after it shall have been

presented to him, the same shall be a law, in like manner as if he had signed it, unless the Congress by their adjournment prevent its return, in which case it shall not be a law.

3. Every order, resolution, or vote to which the concurrence of the Senate and House of Representatives may be necessary (except on a question of adjournment) shall be presented to the President of the United States; and before the same shall take effect, shall be approved by him, or being disapproved by him, shall be repassed by two thirds of the Senate and House of Representatives, according to the rules and limitations prescribed in the case of a bill.

Section 8

1. The Congress shall have the power to lay and collect taxes, duties, imposts, and excises, to pay the debts and provide for the common defense and general welfare of the United States; but all duties, imposts, and excises shall be uniform throughout the United States;

2. To borrow money on the credit of the United States;

3. To regulate commerce with foreign nations, and among the several States, and with the Indian tribes;

4. To establish an uniform rule of naturalization, and uniform laws on the subject of bankruptcies throughout the United States;

5. To coin money, regulate the value thereof, and of foreign coin, and fix the standard of weights and measures;

6. To provide for the punishment of counterfeiting the securities and current coin of the United States;

7. To establish post offices and post roads;

8. To promote the progress of science and useful arts, by securing for limited times to authors and inventors the exclusive right to their respective writings and discoveries;

9. To constitute tribunals inferior to the Supreme Court;

10. To define and punish piracies and felonies committed on the high seas, and offenses against the laws of nations;

11. To declare war, grant letters of marque and reprisal, and make rules concerning captures on land and water;

12. To raise and support armies, but no appropriation of money to that use shall be for a longer term than two years;

13. To provide and maintain a navy;

14. To make rules for the government and regulation of the land and naval forces.

15. To provide for calling forth the militia to execute the laws

laws of the Union, suppress insurrections and repel invasions;

16. To provide for organizing, arming, and disciplining the militia, and for governing such part of them as may be employed in the service of the United States, reserving to the States respectively the appointment of the officers, and the authority of training the militia according to the discipline prescribed by Congress;

17. To exercise exclusive legislation in all cases whatsoever, over such district (not exceeding ten miles square) as may, by cession of particular States, and the acceptance of Congress, become the seat of the government of the United States, and to exercise like authority over all places purchased by the consent of the legislature of the State in which the same shall be, for the erection of forts, magazines, dockyards, and other needful buildings; and

18. To make all laws which shall be necessary and proper for carrying into execution the foregoing powers, and all other powers vested by this Constitution in the government of the United States, or in any department or officer thereof.

Section 9

1. The migration or importation of such persons as any of the States now existing shall think proper to admit, shall not be prohibited by the Congress prior to the year one thousand eight hundred and eight, but a tax or duty may be imposed on such importation, not exceeding ten dollars for each person.

2. The privilege of the writ of *habeas corpus* shall not be suspended, unless when in cases of rebellion or invasion the public safety may require it.

3. No bill of attainder or *ex post facto* law shall be passed.

4. No capitation, or other direct, tax shall be laid, unless in proportion to the census or enumeration hereinbefore directed to be taken.[5]

5. No tax or duty shall be laid on articles exported from any State.

6. No preference shall be given by any regulation of commerce or revenue to the ports of one State over those of another: nor shall vessels bound to, or from, one State be obliged to enter, clear, or pay duties in another.

7. No money shall be drawn from the treasury, but in consequence of appropriations, made by law; and a regular statement and account of the receipts and expenditures of all public money shall be published from time to time.

5   See the Sixteenth Amendment.

8. No title of nobility shall be granted by the United States: and no person holding any office or profit or trust under them, shall, without the consent of the Congress, accept of any present, emolument, office, or title, of any kind whatever, from any king, prince, or foreign State.

Section 10

1. No State shall enter into any treaty, alliance, or confederation; grant letters of marque and reprisal; coin money, emit bills of credit; make anything but gold and silver coin a tender in payment of debts; pass any bill of attainder, *ex post facto* law, or law impairing the obligation of contracts, or grant any title of nobility.

2. No State shall, without the consent of the Congress, lay any imposts or duties on imports or exports, except what may be absolutely necessary for executing its inspection laws: and the net produce of all duties and imposts laid by any State on imports or exports, shall be of the use of the treasury of the United States; and all such laws shall be subject to the revision and control of the Congress.

3. No State shall, without the consent of Congress, lay any duty of tonnage, keep troops, or ships of war in time of peace, enter into any agreement or compact wigh another State, or with a foreign power, or engage in war, unless actually invaded, or in such imminent danger as will not admit of delay.

ARTICLE 2 [THE EXECUTIVE]

Section 1

1. The executive power shall be vested in a President of the United States of America. He shall hold his office during the term of four years, and, together with the Vice-President, chosen for the same term, be elected, as follows:[6]

2. Each State shall appoint, in such manner as the legislature thereof may direct, a number of electors, equal to the whole number of senators and representatives to which the State may be entitled in the Congress: but no senator or representative, or person holding an office of trust or profit under the United States, shall be appointed an elector.

The electors shall meet in their respective States, and vote by

6 See the Twenty-second Amendment.

ballot for two persons, of whom one at least shall not be an inhabitant of the same State with themselves. And they shall make a list of all the persons voted for, and of the number of votes for each; which list they shall sign and certify, and transmit sealed to the seat of the government of the United States, directed to the president of the Senate. The president of the Senate shall, in the presence of the Senate and House of Representatives, open all certificates, and the votes shall then be counted. The person having the greatest number of votes shall be the President, if such number be a majority of the whole number of electors appointed; and if there be more than one who have such majority, and have an equal number of votes, then the House of Representatives shall immediately choose by ballot one of them for President; and if no person have a majority, then from the five highest on the list the said House shall in like manner choose the President. But in choosing the President, the votes shall be taken by States, the representation from each State having one vote; a quorum for this purpose shall consist of a member or members from two-thirds of the States, and a majority of all the States shall be necessary to a choice. In every case, after the choice of the President, the person having the greatest number of votes of the electors shall be the Vice-President. But if there should remain two or more who have equal votes, the Senate shall choose from them by ballot the Vice-President.[7]

3. The Congress may determine the time of choosing the electors, and the day on which they shall give their votes; which day shall be the same throughout the United States.

4. No person except a natural born citizen, or a citizen of the United States, at the time of the adoption of this Constitution, shall be eligible to the office of President; neither shall any person be eligible to that office who shall not have attained to the age of thirty-five years, and been fourteen years a resident within the United States.

5. In case of the removal of the President from office, or of his death, resignation, or inability to discharge the powers and duties of the said office, the same shall devolve on the Vice-President, and the Congress may by law provide for the case of removal, death, resignation, or inability, both of the President and Vice-President, declaring what officer shall then act as President, and such officer shall act accordingly, until the disability be removed, or a President shall be elected.[8]

7   Superseded by the Twelfth Amendment.
8   See the Twentieth Amendment and the Twenty-fifth Amendment.

6. The President shall, at stated times, receive for his services a compensation, which shall neither be increased nor diminished during the period for which he shall have been elected, and he shall not receive within that period any other emolument from the United States, or any of them.

7. Before he enter on the execution of his office, he shall take the following oath or affirmation: 'I do solemnly swear (or affirm) that I will faithfully execute the office of President of the United States, and will to the best of my ability, preserve, protect and defend the Constitution of the United States.'

Section 2

1. The President shall be commander in chief of the army and navy of the United States, and of the militia of the several States, when called into the actual service of the United States; he may require the opinion, in writing, of the principal officer in each of the executive departments, upon any subject relating to the duties of their respective offices, and he shall have power to grant reprieves and pardons for offenses against the United States, except in cases of impeachment.

2. He shall have power, by and with the advice and consent of the Senate, to make treaties, provided two-thirds of the senators present concur; and he shall nominate, and by and with the advice and consent of the Senate, shall appoint ambassadors, other public ministers and consuls, judges of the Supreme Court, and all other officers of the United States, whose appointments are not herein otherwise provided for, and which shall be established by law; but the Congress may by law vest the appointment of such inferior officers, as they think proper, in the President alone, in the courts of law, or in the heads of departments.

3. The President shall have power to fill up all vacancies that may happen during the recess of the Senate, by granting commissions which shall expire at the end of their next session.

Section 3

1. He shall from time to time give to the Congress information of the state of the Union, and recommend to their consideration such measures as he shall judge necessary and expedient; he may, on extraordinary occasions, convene both Houses, or either of them, and in case of disagreement between them with respect to the time

of adjournment, he may adjourn them to such time as he shall think proper; he shall receive ambassadors and other public ministers; he shall take care that the laws be faithfully executed, and shall commission all the officers of the United States.

Section 4

The President, Vice-President, and all civil officers of the United States, shall be removed from office on impeachment for, and conviction of, treason, bribery, or other high crimes and misdemeanors.

ARTICLE 3 [THE JUDICIARY]

Section 1

The Judicial power of the United States shall be vested in one Supreme Court, and in such inferior courts as the Congress may from time to time ordain and establish. The judges, both of the Supreme and inferior courts, shall hold their offices during good behavior, and shall, at stated times, receive for their services, a compensation, which shall not be diminished during their continuance in office.

Section 2

1. The Judicial power shall extend to all cases, in law and equity, arising under this Constitution, the laws of the United States, and treaties made, or which shall be made, under their authority; to all cases affecting ambassadors, other public ministers and consuls; to all cases of admiralty and maritime jurisdiction; to controversies to which the United States shall be a party; to controversies between two or more States; between a state and citizens of another State,[9] between citizens of different States, between citizens of the same State claiming lands under grants of different States, and between a State, or the citizens thereof, and foreign States, citizens or subjects.
2. In all cases affecting ambassadors, other public ministers and consuls, and those in which a State shall be party, the Supreme Court shall have original jurisdiction. In all the other cases before mentioned, the Supreme Court shall have appellate jurisdiction, both as to law and to fact, with such exceptions, and under such regulations as the Congress shall make.

9 See the Eleventh Amendment.

3. The trial of all crimes, except in cases of impeachment, shall be by jury; and such trial shall be held in the State where the said crimes shall have been committed; but when not committed within any State, the trial shall at such place or places as the Congress may by law have directed.

Section 3

1. Treason against the United States shall consist only in levying war against them, or in adhering to their enemies, giving them aid and comfort. No person shall be convicted of treason unless on the testimony of two witnesses to the same overt act, or on confession in open court.
2. The Congress shall have power to declare the punishment of treason, but no attainder of treason shall work corruption of blood, or forfeiture except during the life of the person attained.

ARTICLE 4 [INTERSTATE RELATIONS]

Section 1

Full faith and credit shall be given in each State to the public acts, records, and judicial proceedings of every other State. And the Congress may by general laws prescribe the manner in which acts, records and proceedings shall be proved, and the effect thereof.

Section 2

1. The citizens of each State shall be entitled to all privileges and immunities of citizens in the several States.
2. A person charged in any State with treason, felony, or other crime, who shall flee from justice, and be found in another State, shall on demand of the executive authority of the State from which he fled, be delivered up, to be removed to the State having jurisdiction of the crime.
3. No person held to service or labor in one State under the laws thereof, escaping into another, shall, in consequence of any law or regulation therein, be discharged from such service or labor, but shall be delivered up on claim of the party to whom such service or labor may be due.

Section 3

1. New States may be admitted by the Congress into this Union; but no new State shall be formed or erected within the jurisdiction of any other State; nor any State be formed by the junction of two or more States, or parts of States, without the consent of the legislatures of the States concerned as well as of the Congress.

2. The Congress shall have power to dispose of and make all needful rules and regulations respecting the territory or other property belonging to the United States; and nothing in this Constitution shall be so construed as to prejudice any claims of the United States, or of any particular State.

Section 4

The United States shall guarantee to every State in this Union a republican form of government, and shall protect each of them against invasion; and on application of the legislature, or of the executive (when the legislature cannot be convened) against domestic violence.

ARTICLE 5 [AMENDMENT PROCESS]

The Congress, whenever two-thirds of both Houses shall deem it necessary, shall propose amendments to this Constitution, or, on the application of the legislature of two-thirds of the several States, shall call a convention for proposing amendments, which, in either case, shall be valid to all intents and purposes, as part of this Constitution when ratified by the legislatures of three-fourths of the several States, or by conventions in three-fourths thereof, as the one or the other mode of ratification may be proposed by the Congress; Provided that no amendment which may be made prior to the year one thousand eight hundred and eight shall in any manner affect the first and fourth clauses in the ninth section of the first article; and that no State, without its consent, shall be deprived of its equal suffrage in the Senate.

ARTICLE 6 [DEBTS, SUPREMACY]

1. All debts contracted, and engagements entered into, before the

adoption of this Constitution, shall be as valid against the United States under this Constitution, as under the Confederation.

2. This Constitution, and the laws of the United States which shall be made in pursuance thereof; and all treaties made, or which shall be made, under the authority of the United States, shall be the supreme law of the land; and the Judges in every State shall be bound thereby, anything in the Constitution or laws of any State to the contrary notwithstanding.

3. The senators and representatives before mentioned, and the members of the several State legislatures, and all executive and judicial officers, both of the United States and of the several States, shall be bound by oath or affirmation to support this Constitution; but no religious test shall ever be required as a qualification to any office or public trust under the United States.

ARTICLE 7 [RATIFICATION]

The ratification of the conventions of nine States shall be sufficient for the establishment of this Constitution between the States so ratifying the same.

Done in Convention by the unanimous consent of the States present the seventeenth day of September in the year of our Lord one thousand seven hundred and eighty-seven, and of the independence of the United States of America the twelfth. In witness whereof we have hereunto subscribed our names.

[Names omitted]

ARTICLES IN ADDITION TO, AND AMENDMENT OF, THE CONSTITUTION OF THE UNITED STATES OF AMERICA, PROPOSED BY CONGRESS, AND RATIFIED BY THE LEGISLATURES OF THE SEVERAL STATES, PURSUANT TO THE FIFTH ARTICLE OF THE ORIGINAL CONSTITUTION.*

[The first 10 Amendments were ratified 15 December 1791, and form what is known as the 'Bill of Rights']

AMENDMENT 1 [FREEDOM OF RELIGION, SPEECH, ASSEMBLY, PETITION]

Congress shall make no law respecting an establishment of religion, or prohibiting the free exercise thereof; or abridging the freedom of

---

* Amendment 21 was not ratified by state legislatures, but by state conventions summoned by Congress.

speech, or of the press; or the right of the people peaceably to assemble, and to petition the Government for a redress of grievances.

AMENDMENT 2 [RIGHT TO BEAR ARMS]

A well regulated Militia, being necessary to the security of a free State, the right of the people to keep and bear Arms, shall not be infringed.

AMENDMENT 3 [QUARTERING OF SOLDIERS]

No Soldier shall, in time of peace be quartered in any house, without the consent of the Owner, nor in time of war, but in a manner to be prescribed by law.

AMENDMENT 4 [SEARCH AND SEIZURE]

The right of the people to be secure in their persons, houses, papers, and effects, against unreasonable searches and seizures, shall not be violated, and no warrants shall issue, but upon probable cause, supported by Oath or affirmation, and particularly describing the place to be searched, and the persons or things to be seized.

AMENDMENT 5 [CRIMINAL PROCEDURAL RIGHTS]

No person shall be held to answer for a capital, or otherwise infamous crime, unless on a presentment or indictment of a Grand Jury, except in cases arising in the land or naval forces, or in the Militia, when in actual service in time of War or public danger; nor shall any person be subject for the same offence to be twice put in jeopardy of life or limb; nor shall be compelled in any criminal case to be a witness against himself, nor be deprived of life, liberty, or property, without due process of law, nor shall private property be taken for public use, without just compensation.

AMENDMENT 6 [CRIMINAL COURT PROCEDURES]

In all criminal prosecutions, the accused shall enjoy the right to a speedy and public trial, by an impartial jury of the State and district wherein the crime shall have been committed, which district shall have been previously ascertained by law, and to be informed of the nature and cause of the accusation; to be confronted with the witness against him; to have compulsory process for obtaining witnesses in his favor, and to have the Assistance of Counsel for his defence.

AMENDMENT 7 [TRIAL BY JURY IN COMMON LAW CASES]

In suits at common law, where the value in controversy shall exceed twenty dollars, the right of trial by jury shall be preserved, and no fact tried by a jury, shall be otherwise reexamined in any Court of the United States, than according to the rules of the common law.

AMENDMENT 8 [BAILS, FINES AND PUNISHMENT]

Excessive bail shall not be required, nor excessive fines imposed, nor cruel and unusual punishments inflicted.

AMENDMENT 9 [RIGHTS RETAINED BY THE PEOPLE]

The enumeration in the Constitution of certain rights, shall not be construed to deny or disparage others retained by the people.

AMENDMENT 10 [RIGHTS RESERVED TO THE STATES]

The powers not delegated to the United States by the Constitution, nor prohibited by it to the States, are reserved to the States respectively, or to the people.

AMENDMENT 11 [SUITS AGAINST THE STATES]

[Ratified 7 February 1795]

The judicial power of the United States shall not be construed to extend to any suit in law or equity, commenced or prosecuted against one of the United States by Citizens of another State, or by Citizens or Subjects of any Foreign State.

AMENDMENT 12 [ELECTION OF PRESIDENT AND VICE-PRESIDENT]

[Ratified 27 July 1804]

The Electors shall meet in their respective states and vote by ballot for President and Vice-President, one of whom at least, shall not be an inhabitant of the same state with themselves; they shall name in their ballots the person voted for as President, and in distinct ballots the person voted for as Vice-President, and they shall make distinct lists of all persons voted for as President, and if all persons voted for as Vice-President, and of the number of votes for each, which lists they shall sign and certify, and transmit sealed to the seat of the government of the United States, directed to the President of the Senate; The President of the Senate shall, in presence of the Senate and House of Representatives, open all the certificates and the votes shall then be counted; The person having the greatest number of votes for President, shall be the President if such number be a majority of the whole number of Electors appointed; and if no person have such majority, then from the persons having the highest numbers not exceeding three on the list of those voted for as President, the House of Representatives shall choose immediately, by ballot, the President. But in choosing the President, the votes shall be taken by states, the representation from each state having one vote; a quorum for this purpose shall consist of a member or members from two-thirds of the states, and a majority of all the states shall be necessary to a choice. (And if the House of Representatives shall not choose a President whenever the right of choice shall devolve upon them, before the fourth day of March next following, then the Vice-President shall act as President, as in the case of the death or other constitutional disability of the President.—)* The person

---

* Superseded by Section 3 of the Twentieth Amendment.

having the greatest number of votes as Vice-President, shall be the Vice-President, if such number be a majority of the whole number of Electors appointed, and if no person have a majority, then from the two highest numbers on the list, the Senate shall choose the Vice-President; a quorum for the purpose shall consist of two-thirds of the whole number of Senators, and a majority of the whole number shall be necessary to a choice. But no person constitutionally ineligible to the office of President shall be eligible to that of Vice-President of the United States.

AMENDMENT 13 [ABOLITION OF SLAVERY]

[Ratified 6 December 1865]

Section 1

Neither slavery nor involuntary servitude, except as a punishment for crime whereof the party shall have been duly convicted, shall exist within the United States, or any place subject to their jurisdiction.

Section 2

Congress shall have power to enforce this article by appropriate legislation.

AMENDMENT 14 [CITIZENSHIP, DUE PROCESS, EQUAL PROTECTION]

[Ratified 9 July 1868]

Section 1

All persons born or naturalized in the United States, and subject to the jurisdiction thereof, are citizens of the United States and of the State wherein they reside. No State shall make or enforce any law which shall abridge the privileges or immunities of citizens of the United States; nor shall any State deprive any person of life, liberty, or property, without due process of law; nor deny to any person within its jurisdiction the equal protection of the laws.

Section 2

Representatives shall be apportioned among the several States according to their respective numbers, counting the whole number of persons in each State, excluding Indians not taxed. But when the right to vote at any election for the choice of electors for President and Vice-President of the United States, Representatives in Congress, the Executive and Judicial officers of a State, or the members of the Legislature thereof, is denied to any of the male inhabitants of such State, being twenty-one years of age,* and citizens of the United States, or in any way abridged, except for participation in rebellion, or other crime, the basis of representation therein shall be reduced in the proportion which the number of such male citizens shall bear to the whole number of male citizens twenty-one years of age in such State.

Section 3

No person shall be a Senator or Representative in Congress, or elector of President and Vice-President, or hold any office, civil or military, under the United States, or under any State, who, having previously taken an oath, as a member of Congress, or as an officer of the United States, or as a member of any State legislature, or as an executive or judicial officer of any State, to support the Constitution of the United States shall have engaged in insurrection or rebellion against the same, or given aid or comfort to the enemies thereof. But Congress may by a vote of two-thirds of each House, remove such disability.

Section 4

The validity of the public debt of the United States, authorized by law, including debts incurred for payment of pensions and bounties for services in suppressing insurrection or rebellion, shall not be questioned. But neither the United States nor any State shall assume or pay any debt or obligation incurred in aid of insurrection or rebellion against the United States, or any claim for the loss or emancipation of any slave; but all such debts, obligations and claims shall be held illegal and void.

---

* Changed by Section 1 of the Twenty-sixth Amendment.

Section 5

The Congress shall have power to enforce, by appropriate legislation, the provisions of this article.

AMENDMENT 15 [THE RIGHT TO VOTE]

[Ratified 3 February 1870]

Section 1

The right of citizens of the United States to vote shall not be denied or abridged by the United States or by any State on account of race, color, or previous condition of servitude—

Section 2

The Congress shall have power to enforce this article by appropriate legislation.

AMENDMENT 16 [INCOME TAX]

[Ratified 3 February 1913]

The Congress shall have power to lay and collect taxes on incomes, from whatever source derived, without apportionment among the several States, and without regard to any census or enumeration.

AMENDMENT 17 [DIRECT ELECTION OF SENATORS]

[Ratified 8 April 1913]

The Senate of the United States shall be composed of two Senators from each State, elected by the people thereof, for six years; and each Senator shall have one vote. The electors in each State shall have the qualifications requisite for electors of the most numerous branch of the State legislatures.

When vacancies happen in the representation of any State in the Senate, the executive authority of such State shall issue writs of election to fill such vacancies: *Provided*, That the legislature of any

State may empower the executive thereof to make temporary appointments until the people fill the vacancies by election as the legislature may direct.

This amendment shall not be so construed as to affect the election or term of any Senator chosen before it becomes valid as part of the Constitution.

AMENDMENT 18 [INTRODUCTION OF PROHIBITION]

[Ratified 16 January 1919]

Section 1

After one year from the ratification of this article the manufacture, sale, or transporation of intoxicating liquors within, the importation thereof into, or the exportation thereof from the United States and all territory subject to the jurisdiction thereof for beverage purposes is hereby prohibited.

Section 2

The Congress and the several States shall have concurrent power to enforce this article by appropriate legislation.

Section 3

This article shall be inoperative unless it shall have been ratified as an amendment to the Constitution by the legislatures of the several States as provided in the Constitution, within seven years from the date of the submission hereof to the States by the Congress.*

AMENDMENT 19 [WOMEN'S RIGHT TO VOTE]

[Ratified 18 August 1920]

The right of citizens of the United States to vote shall not be denied or abridged by the United States or by any State on account of sex.

Congress shall have power to enforce this article by appropriate legislation.

---

* Repealed by Section 1 of the Twenty-first Amendment.

[Ratified 23 January 1933]

Section 1

The terms of the President and Vice-President shall end at noon on the 20th day of January, and the terms of Senators and Representatives at noon on the 3d day of January, of the years in which such terms would have ended if this article had not been ratified; and the terms of their successors shall then begin.

Section 2

The Congress shall assemble at least once in every year, and such meeting shall begin at noon on the 3d day of January, unless they shall by law appoint a different day.

Section 3

If, at the time fixed for the beginning of the term of the President, the President elect shall have died, the Vice-President elect shall become President. If a President shall not have been chosen before the time fixed for the beginning of his term, or if the President elect shall have failed to qualify, then the Vice-President elect shall act as President until a President shall have qualified; and the Congress may by law provide for the case wherein neither a President elect nor a Vice-President elect shall have qualified, declaring who shall then act as President, or the manner in which one who is to act shall be selected, and such person shall act accordingly until a President or Vice-President shall have qualified.

Section 4

The Congress may by law provide for the case of the death of any of the persons from whom the House of Representatives may choose a President whenever the right of choice shall have devolved upon them, and for the case of the death of any of the persons from whom the Senate may choose a Vice-President whenever the right of choice shall have devolved upon them.

Section 5

Sections 1 and 2 shall take effect on the 15th day of October following the ratification of this article.

Section 6

This article shall be inoperative unless it shall have been ratified as an amendment to the Constitution by the legislatures of three-fourths of the several States within seven years from the date of its submission.

AMENDMENT 21 [REPEAL OF PROHIBITION]
[Ratified 5 December 1933]

Section 1

The Eighteenth Article of Amendment to the Constitution of the United States is hereby repealed.

Section 2

The transportation or importation into any State, Territory, or possession of the United States for delivery or use therein of intoxicating liquors, in violation of the laws thereof, is hereby prohibited.

Section 3

This article shall be inoperative unless it shall have been ratified as an amendment to the Constitution by conventions in the several States, as provided in the Constitution, within seven years from the date of the submission hereof to the States by the Congress.

AMENDMENT 22 [LIMITATION OF PRESIDENTIAL TERMS]
[Ratified 27 February 1951]

Section 1

No person shall be elected to the office of the President more than twice, and no person who has held the office of President, or acted as President, for more than two years of a term to which some other person was elected President shall be elected to the office of the President more than once. But this Article shall not apply to any person holding the office of President when this Article was proposed by the Congress, and shall not prevent any person who may be holding the office of President, or acting as President, during the term within which this Article becomes operative from holding the office of President or acting as President during the remainder of such term.

Section 2

This article shall be inoperative unless it shall have been ratified as an amendment to the Constitution by the legislatures of three-fourths of the several States within seven years from the data of its submission to the States by the Congress.

AMENDMENT 23 [PRESIDENTIAL ELECTIONS FOR THE DISTRICT OF COLUMBIA]

[Ratified 29 March 1961]

Section 1

The District constituting the seat of Government of the United States shall appoint in such manner as the Congress may direct:

A number of electors of President and Vice-President equal to the whole number of Senators and Representatives in Congress to which the District would be entitled if it were a State, but in no event more than the least populous State; they shall be in addition to those appointed by the States, but they shall be considered, for the purposes of the election of President and Vice-President, to be electors appointed by a State; and they shall meet in the District and perform such duties as provided by the Twelfth Article of Amendment.

Section 2

The Congress shall have power to enforce this article by appropriate legislation.

AMENDMENT 24 [POLL TAX ABOLISHED]
[Ratified 23 January 1964]

Section 1

The right of citizens of the United States to vote in any primary or other election for President or Vice-President, for electors for President or Vice-President, or for Senator or Representative in Congress, shall not be denied or abridged by the United States or any State by reason of failure to pay any poll tax or other tax.

Section 2

The Congress shall have power to enforce this article by appropriate legislation.

AMENDMENT 25 [PRESIDENTIAL DISABILITY AND VICE-PRESIDENTIAL VACANCIES]
[Ratified 10 February 1967]

Section 1

In case of the removal of the President from office or of his death or resignation, the Vice-President shall become President.

Section 2

Whenever there is a vacancy in the office of the Vice-President, the President shall nominate a Vice-President who shall take office upon confirmation by a majority vote of both Houses of Congress.

Senate 3

Whenever the President transmits to the President pro tempore of the Senate and the Speaker of the House of Representatives his written declaration that he is unable to discharge the powers and duties of his office, and until he transmits to them a written declaration to the contrary, such powers and duties shall be discharged by the Vice-President as Acting President.

Section 4

Whenever the Vice-President and a majority of either the principal officers of the executive departments or of such other body as Congress may by law provide, transmit to the President pro tempore of the Senate and the Speaker of the House of Representatives their written declaration that the President is unable to discharge the powers and duties of his office, the Vice-President shall immediately assume the powers and duties of the office as Acting President.

Thereafter, when the President transmits to the President pro tempore of the Senate and the Speaker of the House of Representatives his written declaration that no inability exists, he shall resume the powers and duties of his office unless the Vice-President and a majority of either the principal officers of the executive department or of such other body as Congress may by law provide, transmit within four days to the President pro tempore of the Senate and the Speaker of the House of Representatives their written declaration that the President is unable to discharge the powers and duties of his office. Thereupon Congress shall decide the issue, assembling within forty-eight hours for that purpose if not in session. If the Congress, within twenty-one days after receipt of the latter written declaration, or, if Congress is not in session, within twenty-one days after Congress is required to assemble, determines by two-thirds vote of both Houses that the President is unable to discharge the powers and duties of his office, the Vice-President shall continue to discharge the same as Acting President; otherwise, the President shall resume the powers and duties of his office.

AMENDMENT 26 [VOTE FOR 18-YEAR OLDS]

[Ratified 1 July 1971]

Section 1

The right of citizens of the United States, who are eighteen years of age or older, to vote shall not be denied or abridged by the United States or by any State on account of age.

Section 2

The Congress shall have power to enforce this article by appropriate legislation.

PROPOSED AMENDMENT [EQUAL RIGHTS FOR MEN AND WOMEN]

[Proposed 22 March 1972]

Section 1

Equality of rights under the law shall not be denied or abridged by the United States or by any State on account of sex.

Section 2

The Congress shall have power to enforce, by appropriate legislation, the provisions of this article.

Section 3

This amendment shall take effect two years after date of ratification.

PROPOSED AMENDMENT [TREATMENT OF THE DISTRICT OF COLUMBIA]

[Proposed 22 August 1978]

Section 1

For purposes of representation in the Congress, election of the President and Vice-President, and Article 5 of this Constitution, the District constituting the seat of government of the United States shall be treated as though it were a State.

Section 2

The exercise of the rights and powers conferred under this article shall be by the people of the District constituting the seat of government, and as shall be provided by the Congress.

Section 3

The Twenty-third Article of Amendment to the Constitution of the United States is hereby repealed.

Section 4

This article shall be inoperative, unless it shall have been ratified as an amendment to the Constitution by the legislatures of three-fourths of the several States within seven years from the date of its submission.

The States and Regions, Actual and Projected Population Changes 1960–2000

See table on pp. 330–331

APPENDIX 2   *The States and Regions, Actual and Projected Population Changes, 1960–2000*
(Thousands and Percentage Change)

	1960	1970		1980		1990		2000	
NORTH EAST	**48,988**	**54,289**	**+10.8**	**54,585**	**+ 0.5**	**57,136**	**+ 4.7**	**59,014**	**+ 3.3**
New England	**10,509**	**11,847**	**+12.7**	**12,348**	**+ 4.2**	**13,389**	**+ 8.4**	**14,238**	**+ 6.3**
Maine	969	994	+ 2.5	1,125	+13.2	1,278	+13.6	1,410	+10.3
New Hampshire	607	738	+21.5	921	+24.8	1,054	+16.6	1,165	+10.5
Vermont	390	445	+14.1	511	+15.0	562	+10.0	605	+ 7.7
Massachusetts	5,149	5,689	+10.5	5,737	+ 0.8	6,209	+ 8.2	6,601	+ 6.3
Rhode Island	859	950	+10.5	947	– 0.3	1,030	+ 8.8	1,102	+ 7.0
Connecticut	2,535	3,032	+19.6	3,108	+ 2.5	3,257	+ 4.8	3,356	+ 3.0
Middle Atlantic	**38,479**	**42,442**	**+10.3**	**42,237**	**– 0.5**	**43,747**	**+ 3.6**	**44,776**	**+ 2.4**
New York	16,782	18,241	+ 8.7	17,557	– 3.8	17,650	+ 0.5	17,616	– 0.2
New Jersey	6,067	7,171	+18.2	7,364	+ 2.7	7,882	+ 7.0	8,297	+ 5.3
Pennsylvania	11,319	11,801	+ 4.3	11,867	+ 0.6	12,174	+ 2.6	12,300	+ 1.0
Delaware	446	548	+22.8	595	+ 8.6	646	+ 8.6	684	+ 5.9
Maryland	3,101	3,924	+26.5	4,216	+ 7.5	4,791	+13.6	5,299	+10.6
DC	764	757	– 1.0	638	–15.7	604	– 5.3	580	– 3.9
MID WEST	**51,619**	**56,591**	**+ 9.6**	**58,854**	**+ 4.0**	**61,799**	**+ 5.0**	**63,745**	**+ 3.1**
Great Lakes	**36,225**	**40,263**	**+11.1**	**41,670**	**+ 3.5**	**43,537**	**+ 4.5**	**44,675**	**+ 2.6**
Ohio	9,706	10,657	+ 9.8	10,797	+ 1.3	11,047	+ 2.3	11,110	+ 0.6
Indiana	4,662	5,195	+11.4	5,490	+ 5.7	5,716	+ 4.1	5,852	+ 2.4
Illinois	10,081	11,110	+10.2	11,418	+ 2.8	11,824	+ 3.6	12,082	+ 2.2
Michigan	7,823	8,882	+13.5	9,258	+ 4.2	9,797	+ 5.8	10,131	+ 3.4
Wisconsin	3,952	4,418	+11.8	4,705	+ 6.5	5,151	+ 9.5	5,498	+ 6.7
Great Plains	**15,394**	**16,328**	**+ 6.1**	**17,184**	**+ 5.2**	**18,262**	**+ 6.3**	**19,070**	**+ 4.4**
Minnesota	3,414	3,806	+11.5	4,077	+ 7.1	4,390	+ 7.7	4,613	+ 5.1
Iowa	2,758	2,825	+ 2.5	2,913	+ 3.1	'3,053	+ 4.8	3,153	+ 3.3
Missouri	4,320	4,678	+ 8.3	4,917	+ 5.1	5,197	+ 5.7	5,414	+ 4.2
North Dakota	632	618	– 2.3	653	+ 5.6	698	+ 6.9	732	+ 4.9
South Dakota	681	666	– 2.1	690	+ 3.6	724	+ 4.9	748	+ 3.3
Nebraska	1,411	1,485	+ 5.2	1,570	+ 5.7	1,711	+ 9.0	1,824	+ 6.6
Kansas	2,179	2,249	+ 3.2	2,363	+ 5.1	2,488	+ 5.3	2,585	+ 3.9

SOUTH	50,649	57,584	+13.7	69,900	+21.4	79,961	+14.4	88,334	+10.5
South Atlantic	21,648	25,450	+17.6	31,494	+23.7	37,088	+17.7	41,788	+12.8
Virginia	3,954	4,551	+17.6	5,346	+14.9	6,129	+14.6	6,780	+10.6
West Virginia	1,860	1,744	− 6.2	1,950	+11.8	2,079	+ 6.6	2,182	+ 5.0
North Carolina	4,556	5,084	+11.6	5,874	+15.5	6,657	+13.3	7,310	+ 9.8
South Carolina	2,383	2,591	+ 8.7	3,119	+20.4	3,588	+15.0	3,987	+11.1
Georgia	3,943	4,588	+16.4	5,464	+19.1	6,295	+15.2	7,002	+11.2
Florida	4,952	6,791	+37.2	9,740	+43.4	12,340	+26.7	14,527	+17.7
East South Central	12,050	12,808	+ 6.3	14,663	+14.5	16,081	+ 9.7	17,216	+ 7.1
Kentucky	3,038	3,221	+ 6.0	3,661	+13.7	4,063	+11.0	4,400	+ 8.3
Tennessee	3,567	3,926	+10.1	4,591	+16.9	5,042	+ 9.8	5,409	+ 7.3
Alabama	3,267	3,444	+ 5.4	3,890	+12.9	4,259	+ 9.5	4,544	+ 6.7
Mississippi	2,178	2,217	+ 1.8	2,521	+13.7	2,717	+ 7.8	2,863	+ 5.4
West South Central	16,951	19,326	+14.0	23,743	+22.9	26,792	+12.8	29,330	+ 9.5
Arkansas	1,786	1,923	+ 7.7	2,286	+18.8	2,541	+11.2	2,752	+ 8.3
Louisiana	3,257	3,645	+11.9	4,204	+15.3	4,527	+ 7.7	4,758	+ 5.1
Oklahoma	2,328	2,559	+ 9.9	3,025	+18.2	3,349	+10.7	3,620	+ 8.1
Texas	9,580	11,199	+16.9	14,228	+27.1	16,375	+15.1	18,200	+11.1
WEST	28,053	34,838	+24.2	43,165	+23.9	48,959	+13.4	53,627	+ 9.5
Mountain	6,855	8,290	+20.9	11,368	+37.1	13,589	+19.5	15,385	+13.2
Montana	675	694	+ 2.9	787	+13.3	890	+13.1	973	+ 9.3
Idaho	667	713	+ 6.9	944	+32.4	1,112	+17.8	1,246	+12.1
Wyoming	330	332	+ 0.7	471	+41.6	537	+14.0	590	+ 9.9
Colorado	1,754	2,210	+26.0	2,889	+30.7	3,475	+20.3	3,958	+13.9
New Mexico	951	1,017	+ 6.9	1,300	+27.8	1,517	+16.7	1,687	+11.2
Arizona	1,302	1,775	+36.3	2,718	+53.1	3,411	+25.5	3,972	+16.5
Utah	891	1,059	+18.9	1,461	+37.9	1,711	+17.1	1,915	+11.9
Nevada	285	489	+71.3	799	+63.5	937	+17.3	1,045	+11.5
Pacific	21,198	26,548	+25.2	31,797	+19.8	35,370	+11.2	38,242	+ 8.1
Washington	2,853	3,413	+19.6	4,130	+21.0	4,410	+ 6.8	4,635	+ 5.1
Oregon	1,769	2,092	+18.3	2,633	+25.9	2,977	+13.1	3,266	+ 9.7
California	15,717	19,971	+27.1	23,669	+18.5	26,394	+11.5	28,592	+ 8.3
Alaska	226	303	+33.8	400	+32.4	479	+19.8	532	+11.1
Hawaii	633	770	+21.7	965	+21.7	1,110	+15.0	1,217	+ 9.6
TOTAL	179,311	203,302	+13.4	226,505	+11.4	247,858	+ 9.4	264,723	+ 6.8

Source: The National Journal, 14 November 1981, p. 2019.

Index